Japanese Science Fiction: A View of a Changing Society
Robert Matthew

The Japanese Numbers Game: The Use and Understanding of Numbers in Modern Japan
Thomas Crump

Ideology and Practice in Modern Japan
Edited by Roger Goodman and Kirsten Refsing

Technology and Industrial Development in Pre-war Japan: Mitsubishi Nagasaki Shipyard, 1884–1934
Yukiko Fukasaku

Japan's Early Parliaments, 1890–1905: Structure, Issues and Trends
Andrew Fraser, R.H.P. Mason and Philip Mitchell

Japan's Foreign Aid Challenge: Policy Reform and Aid Leadership
Alan Rix

Emperor Hirohito and Shôwa Japan: A Political Biography
Stephen S. Large

Japan: Beyond the End of History
David Williams

Ceremony and Ritual in Japan: Religious Practices in an Industrialized Society
Edited by Jan van Bremen and D.P. Martinez

Understanding Japanese Society: Second Edition
Joy Hendry

The Fantastic in Modern Japanese Literature: The Subversion of Modernity
Susan J. Napier

Militarization and Demilitarization in Contemporary Japan
Glenn D. Hook

Growing a Japanese Science City: Communication in Scientific Research
James W. Dearing

Architecture and Authority in Japan
William H. Coaldrake

Women's *Gidayû* and the Japanese Theatre Tradition
A. Kimi Coaldrake

Democracy in Post-war Japan: Maruyama Masao and the Search for Autonomy
Rikki Kersten

Treacherous Women of Imperial Japan: Patriarchal Fictions, Patricidal Fantasies
Hélène Bowen Raddeker

Japanese–German Business Relations: Competition and Rivalry in the Inter-war Period
Akira Kudô

Japan, Race and Equality: The Racial Equality Proposal of 1919
Naoko Shimazu

Japan, Internationalism and the UN
Ronald Dore

Life in a Japanese Women's College: Learning to be Ladylike
Brian J. McVeigh

On the Margins of Japanese Society: Volunteers and the Welfare of the Urban Underclass
Carolyn S. Stevens

The Dynamics of Japan's Relations with Africa: South Africa, Tanzania and Nigeria
Kweku Ampiah

The Right to Life in Japan
Noel Williams

The Nature of the Japanese State: Rationality and Rituality
Brian J. McVeigh

Society and the State in Inter-war Japan
Edited by Elise K. Tipton

Japanese–Soviet/Russian Relations since 1945: A Difficult Peace
Kimie Hara

Interpreting History in Sino-Janapese Relations: A Case Study in Political Decision Making
Caroline Rose

Endô Shûsaku: A Literature of Reconciliation
Mark B. Williams

Green Politics in Japan
Lam Peng-Er

The Japanese High School: Silence and Resistance
Shoko Yoneyama

Engineers in Japan And Britain: Education, Training and Employment
Kevin McCormick

The Politics of Agriculture in Japan
Aurelia Geroge Mulgan

Opposition Politics in Japan: Strategies Under a One-Party Dominant Regime
Stephen Johnson

The Changing Face of Japanese Retail: Working in a Chain Store
Louella Matsunaga

Japan and East Asian Regionalism
Edited by S. Javed Maswood

Globalizing Japan

Ethnography of the Japanese presence in Asia, Europe, and America

**Edited by
Harumi Befu and
Sylvie Guichard-Anguis**

RoutledgeCurzon
Taylor & Francis Group

LONDON AND NEW YORK

First published 2001 by Routledge
11 New Fetter Lane, London EC4P 4EE

Simultaneously published in the USA and Canada
by Routledge
29 West 35th Street, New York, NY 10001

First published in paperback 2003 by RoutledgeCurzon

RoutledgeCurzon is an imprint of the Taylor & Francis Group

Typeset in Baskerville by
Prepress Projects Ltd, Perth, Scotland
Printed and bound in Great Britain by
TJ International Ltd, Padstow, Cornwall

British Library Cataloguing in Publication Data
A catalogue record for this book is available from the British Library

Library of Congress Cataloging in Publication Data
Globalizing Japan : ethnography of the Japanese presence in Asia, Europe,
and America / edited by Harumi Befu and Sylvie Guichard-Auguis.
      p. cm.
   Includes bibliographical references and index.
      1. Japan–Foreign economic relations. 2.Globalization–Economic
aspects–Japan. 3. Globalization–Social aspects–Japan. 4. Corporations,
Japanese. 5. Japanese–Foreign countries. 6. Corporate culture–Japan. I.
   Befu, Harumi. II. Guichard-Anguis, Sylvie, 1951–

HF1601 .G56 2001
337.52–dc21   2001019472

ISBN 0–415–24412–9 (Hb)

ISBN 0–415–28566–6 (Pb)

Contents

List of figures   xii
List of tables   xiii
List of contributors   xiv
Series Editor's preface   xvii
Preface   xix
Acknowledgments   xxii

PART I
Introduction   **1**

1   **The global context of Japan outside Japan**   3
    HARUMI BEFU

    Human dispersal 5
    Nonpermanent sojourners 5
    Permanent sojourners 6
    Exploiting the cultural capital 9
    Organizational transplant 10
    Cultural diffusion 13
    Imagining of Japan 15
    Interrelationships among the four categories 18
    Conclusion: center–periphery 19

PART II
Human dispersal   **23**

2   **Objects, city, and wandering: the invisibility of**
    the Japanese in France   25
    KAZUHIKO YATABE

    A cultural migration 29
    An individual and temporary migration 30

PART III

Organizational transplant

41

3 Positioning "globalization" at overseas subsidiaries
   of Japanese multinational corporations   43
   MITCHELL W. SEDGWICK

   Coping with complexity on a large scale 43
   The political economy of Japan's globalization 44
   The "globalization" of Japanese managers: from the macro to the micro 45
   Positioning globalization 48
   Conclusion 49

4 Japanese businesswomen of Yaohan Hong Kong:
   toward a diversified globalization of a Japanese
   "ethnoscape"   52
   DIXON HEUNG WAH WONG

   The cultural model of Japanese female workers 53
   Differences between supermarkets and
   *   department stores 54*
   Yaohan as a regional supermarket 55
   Yaohan's arrival in Hong Kong 56
   Yaohan's staff recruitment strategy 57
   Yaohan's female employees going overseas 59
   Response of female workers 60
   Conclusion 66

5 Neverland lost: judo cultures in Austria, Japan, and
   elsewhere struggling for cultural hegemony at
   the Vienna Budokan   69
   SABINE FRÜHSTÜCK AND WOLFRAM MANZENREITER

   Territorialization of Japanese judo culture 71
   Self-colonization: seeing the difference 76
   Universalization: the national and the transnational 81
   Conclusion: Japan outside Japan? 86

6 Soka Gakkai in Germany: the story of a qualified
   success   94
   SANDA IONESCU

   Who does the defining? 97
   What is the purpose? 100

Parameters 101
Conclusion 104

PART IV
Cultural diffusion

109

7 Japanese comics coming to Hong Kong

111

CHERRY SZE-LING LAI AND DIXON HEUNG WAH WONG

Comics in Japan 111
Some history of comics in Hong Kong 113
The general images of comics in Hong Kong: the politics of
*   everyday life 115*
Japanese comics coming to Hong Kong 116
The effect of Japanese comics on local comic culture 118
Conclusion 119

8 Japanese popular music in Hong Kong: analysis of global/local cultural relations

121

MASASHI OGAWA

Hong Kong pop music history 121
Globalization in Hong Kong popular music history 126

9 Global culture in question: contemporary Japanese photography in America

131

JULIA ADENEY THOMAS

Hiroshi Sugimoto 133
Toshio Shibata 137
Yasumasa Morimura 141
Conclusion 144

PART V
Images

151

10 A collision of discourses: Japanese and Hong Kong Chinese during the Diaoyu/Senkaku Islands crisis

153

GORDON MATHEWS

The Diaoyu/Senkaku Islands dispute: a brief history 153
Japanese tourists in the midst of the dispute 156
Japanese residents of Hong Kong in the midst of the dispute 158

Hong Kong Chinese activists in the midst of the dispute 160
A complex of motives 162
Positions, interests, cultures, and discourses 165
Capitalism and nationalism as world discourses 168
Conclusion: the shadows of history 170

11 Images of the Japanese welfare state   176
ROGER GOODMAN

The construction of positive views of Japanese welfare 179
Conclusion 185

**12 Consuming the modern: globalization, things
Japanese, and the politics of cultural identity in Korea**   194
SEUNG-MI HAN

Learning from the enviable enemy: the coexistence of desire and
    enmity in Korean perceptions of Japan 195
Globalization and the regulation of Japanese popular culture
    in Korea 197
Transnational public, hybrid identity, and the "unfinished
    project" of modernity in Korea 200
Postscript: the Asian financial crisis, regime change, and
    the logical similarity in the debates on Comfort
    Women and Japanese popular culture 202
Postscript 2: the perspectives of Koreans in Japan 204

**13 Japan through French eyes: "the ephemeral"
as a cultural production**   209
SYLVIE GUICHARD-ANGUIS

Japanese Days, Japanese Weeks, or Year of Japan in France:
    from origami to matsuri 210
Sister cities and international relations 214
Japan and "the ephemeral" as a cultural production 216

**14 The *Yamatodamashi* of the Takasago volunteers of Taiwan:
a reading of the postcolonial situation**   222
CHIH-HUEI HUANG

The last returning imperial soldier 223
Memories recalled and testimonies proffered 225
History, texts, and authors 235

Battlefield trick: reversal and elevation in the hierarchy 240
Postcolonial situation after dual colonialism –
 forms of resistance 242
Conclusion: the reality and illusion of the Yamatodamashi *245*

Index 251

Figures

9.1   Hiroshi Sugimoto, "Ionian Sea, Santa Cesavea I, 1990."   134
9.2   Hiroshi Sugimoto, "Goshen, Indiana, 1980."   136
9.3   Toshio Shibata, "Kashima Town, Fukushima Prefecture, 1990."   139

Tables

2.1	How the French feel about the non-French	31
2.2	What the French think about marriage	32
2.4	How Japanese residents feel about marriage with French people	33
2.3	How Japanese residents perceive the attitude of the French toward them	33
2.5	Discrimination as experienced by Japanese residents	33
2.6	The feeling of otherness	37

Contributors

Harumi Befu is Professor emeritus in the Department of Cultural and Social Anthropology, Stanford University. His current interests include globalization and Japan's cultural nationalism. He recently co-edited *Globalization and Social Change in Contemporary Japan* (2000).

Sabine Frühstück is assistant professor of East Asian languages and Cultural Studies at the University of California, Santa Barbara. Her research interests center on problems of power and knowledge in modern Japanese history and on the relationship between the military and society in contemporary Japan. Recent publications include *The Culture of Japan Seen through Its Leisure*, co-edited with Sepp Linhart (1998).

Roger Goodman is lecturer in the Social Anthropology of Japan at the University of Oxford, specializing in the study of Japanese education and social welfare. He is author of *Children of the Japanese State* (2000).

Sylvie Guichard-Anguis is researcher at the French National Center of Scientific Research (CNRS) and a member of the research group "Space and Culture" in the Department of Geography, University of Paris IV Sorbonne. Her research interests include culture heritage, tea culture, and children's illustrated books in Japan. She is currently co-editing the proceedings of a symposium "Crossed glazes at international cultural heritage" with the collaboration of the United Nations Educational, Scientific, and Cultural Organization (UNESCO).

Seung-Mi Han is Assistant Professor in the Japanese Studies Program of the Graduate School of International Studies, Yonsei University. Her research interests include consumer and corporate culture, culture industry, and transnationalism. She is the author of "Culture and structures of corruption in East Asia: the case of Japan" (*Yonsei Management Review*, 1998).

Chih-huei Huang is an Assistant Researcher at the Institute of Ethnology, Academia Sinica, Taiwan. She has carried out fieldwork in Japan, Okinawa, and Taiwan and is currently conducting research on the Japanese colonial legacy in Taiwan and on the cultural connection between Okinawa and Taiwan.

Sanda Ionescu was, at the time her chapter was written, a Research Fellow on Japanese new religions at the Centre for New Religions at King's College London. She is currently working as a business analyst in London. Her most recent publication is "Adapt or perish: the story of Soka Gakkai in Germany," in Peter B. Clarke (ed.) *Japanese New Religions in Global Perspective* (2000).

Cherry Sze-ling Lai has just completed an M.Phil. thesis on the comparison of Japanese and Hong Kong comics in the Department of Japanese Studies, the University of Hong Kong. She is currently teaching at a secondary school in Hong Kong.

Wolfram Manzenreiter is Assistant Professor at the Institute of East Asian Studies, Vienna University. His recent research interests include socioeconomic aspects of telecommunication in contemporary Japan. He is the author of several books and articles on popular culture, leisure, and sport in Japan, most recently *Die soziale Konstruktion des japanischen Alpinismus: Kultur, Ideologie und Sport im modernen Bergsteigen* (2000).

Gordon Mathews is Associate Professor in the Department of Anthropology at the Chinese University of Hong Kong. He is interested in cultural identity in Hong Kong and Japan. He has written *Global Culture/Individual Identity: Searching for Home in the Cultural Supermarket* (2000).

Masashi Ogawa is a language instructor in the Department of Japanese Studies at the University of Hong Kong. He researches on Japanese popular music in Asia and the Japanese backpacker culture. Included in his publications is "Pop music of Japan in Hong Kong" in C. Y. Chan and H. Murakami (eds) *Prospect and Retrospect of Japanese Language Teaching and Japanese Teaching* (2000).

Mitchell W. Sedgwick is Senior Research Fellow in Cross-Cultural Studies, Oxford Brookes University. He has conducted research on homes for the elderly, Japan's Korean minority, postwar employment, and Japanese multinational corporations. Recent publications include "Do Japanese management practices travel well?" in D. Encarnation (ed.) *Japanese Multinationals in Asia* (1999).

Julia Adeney Thomas is Associate Professor of history at the University of Wisconsin, Madison. She is the author of *Reconfiguring Modernity: Concepts of Nature and Japanese Political Ideology* (2001). Her essay in this volume is part of a book-length project provisionally titled *Trans-Pacific Pictures: Cultural Policy and Fine Art Photography in Postwar Japan.*

Dixon Heung Wah Wong is Assistant Professor in the Department of Japanese Studies, University of Hong Kong. His current research interest is in Japanese companies overseas and the expansion of Japanese popular culture in East Asia. He is the author of *Japanese Bosses, Chinese Workers: Power and Control in a Hong Kong Megastore* (1999).

Kazuhiko Yatabe is Assistant Professor at the University of Paris VII. He is currently conducting research on migration and ethnicity. His recent publications include "Bruno Latour, and the question of the 'in-between' (Bruno Latour, aruiwa 'chukan' no tsuikyu)" (in English and in Japanese), in *Kuku no Chi* (2000).

Series Editor's preface

At the beginning of the new century Japan, widely seen as a 'miracle country' between the late 1950s and early 1990s, was struggling out of its recession, which became particularly acute between 1997 and 1999. The 1990s were a time of turbulence in Japanese politics as in the economy, and pressure for restructuring has been strong. Grave weaknesses in the banking system were revealed in the form of a massive overhang of bad debt inherited from the boom period of the late 1980s and the subsequent collapse. An ambitious programme of reform of the political and economic system was announced by the Hosokawa coalition Government that replaced single-party rule by the Liberal Democratic Party in 1993, but the path towards implementing reform proved far from smooth.

Through the succession of administrations following from that of Hosokawa, the process of reforming the system seemed to take a step back every time there was a step forward. Nevertheless, there seems little doubt that Japan is gradually changing. It is widely recognised that in many areas of life the old methods do not work well any more and need radical surgery. Even so, the view, widely expressed at the beginning of the new millennium, that the only viable course for Japan is to converge towards a North American model of political economy, needs to be treated with a dose of scepticism. For one thing, a major civilisation such as that of Japan does not ditch its embedded traditions overnight, merely because the economy is failing to reach former heights of performance and growth. For another, there is a long history of concern about the 'particularity' of Japan in debates going back many decades. Even though these debates have at times contained elements of absurdity and even gross liberalism, they constitute part of a mind-set that sees the nation called 'Japan' as an entity that needs to find its own way in the world, rather than consuming in an automatic or haphazard fashion influences that press upon Japan from outside.

The Nissan Institute/Routledge Japanese Studies Series was begun in 1986 and recently published its fiftieth volume. It seeks to foster an informed and balanced, but not uncritical, understanding of Japan. One aim of the series is to show the depth and variety of Japanese institutions, practices and ideas. Another is, by using comparisons, to see what lessons, positive or negative, can be drawn for other countries. The tendency in commentary on Japan to resort to out-dated, ill-informed or sensational stereotypes still remains, and needs to be combated.

The literature of external influences upon Japan is quite rich, whether it is the influence of China in medieval times, the influence of Europe between the 1850s and the 1930s or the influence of the United States since 1945. What this book explores, by contrast, is the Japanese presence, and by extension the Japanese influence, in Asia, Europe, and America. Some might consider the timing here a little odd, given that in the past decade some of the lustre appears to have been rubbed off the Japanese model, following economic recession and concerns about future viability in a rapidly ageing society. Nevertheless, if we take Asia, for instance, Japan is a hugely dominant economic influence. The gross national product of Japan is still six or seven times that of the People's Republic of China, even though the economy of the latter is growing fast. Japan's GNP constitutes much more than half of the total GNP of East and South-East Asia, while figures for Japanese trade, overseas development aid and overseas investment are similarly impressive.

In these circumstances it is hardly surprising that Japanese influence has come to extend well beyond economic matters, from cameras to sushi to Pokemon to *anime*. In the words of the editors, "Japan has become part of the daily life of common people in most parts of the world, and just about everyone of all ages is affected by the Japanese presence in one way or another." It is hardly necessary to posit any of the more extreme "globalised" scenarios to suggest that, while Japan is gradually becoming more part of the outside world, the outside world is also gradually becoming more a part of Japan.

J.A.A. Stockwin

Preface

All over the world, Japan has been increasingly penetrating our everyday life, what with its cars, electronic goods, cameras, cuisine, cultural accoutrements, and so on and on. France was even moved to publish a guidebook on the Japanese presence in Paris. This is not just a guide for sightseeing things Japanese in Paris, but also for consumers interested in buying commodified Japan. It lists restaurants, shops for fashion, cosmetics, jewelry, books, antiques, videos of feature films and animation movies, and classes in martial and decorative arts. But such "Japanese presence" is hardly limited to France; it is seen throughout Europe, North and South America, Asia, and (although less extensively) in the Middle East and Africa. This global Japanese presence today is a quantum level more pervasive than a century ago, when things Japanese abroad was by and large limited to art and antique goods of wood cut prints *(ukiyoe)* and porcelain *(Imari* and *Kutani)* varieties. In those bygone days, only a select few enjoyed things Japanese. In a major contrast, nowadays Japan has become part of the daily life of common people in most parts of the world, and just about everyone of all ages is affected by the Japanese presence in one way or another. In the year 2001 few youngsters of the world are unaware of Pokemon. Most of them in fact are captivated by it.

As part of Japan's globalization process, the presence of Japanese nationals abroad in developed and developing countries has grown to the extent that now they are ubiquitous, with upwards of ten million Japanese traveling overseas every year. These Japanese are varied, constituting several categories. Most of them are sightseeing tourists, of course, but businessmen dispatched from Japan, with their families, are stationed throughout the world. These Japanese, with those in the hotel, restaurant, and other types of service industry, have created almost self-contained Japanese communities in Asia, the Americas, and Europe, with members numbering tens of thousands in each of them. Then there are those who have left Japan permanently as immigrants and brides (and, less frequently, grooms) of international marriage.

In addition, Japan is becoming the center of a vast number of unassuming networks all over the world. Aside from the obvious business-related networks, people are coming into contact with Japan and with each other through one or another of Japan's cultural expressions. Japanese schools of tea ceremony or flower arrangement, religious groups such as Zen and Soka Gakkai, and martial arts such as judo have branches all over the world, each school and group creating a global network of contact and communication and, moreover, a global community of like-minded people with Japan as its center.

Ethnographic field works represented in this volume demonstrate the process of "glocalization" or "creolization," whereby globalizing elements modify themselves to adapt to local social and cultural conditions. Ionescu, for example, shows that German followers of Soka Gakkai have shed certain Japanese practices as irrelevant, while agreeing with the universal value of this religion. Presumably Soka Gakkai members in other cultural contexts might drop and eliminate different "nonessential" practices, resulting in an international Soka Gakkai community with many local variations – a veritable process of glocalization, i.e. localization of globalizing culture. The chapter by Frühstück and Manzenreiter illustrates a somewhat different globalization process. Here, judo, with specific Japanese practices and spiritual ethic as a martial art, has lost its spirituality, and it has also adopted new rules as it transformed into an international championship sport. Judo thus became a "universal property."

One of the processes of Japan's globalization, especially in the 1970s and 1980s, was the export of Japanese management style with its emphasis on harmony and production practices, as in the "just in time" system. In those days, the "Japanese model" was much touted and in demand. Since the bursting of the economic bubble in Japan in the early 1990s, however, clamoring for the Japanese business model has declined. But as Goodman shows in this volume, Japan can still supply a model in yet another area, this time in social welfare.

Globalization does not proceed evenly from a center to all peripheries. Geographic distribution of field sites of the contributions in this volume may be regarded as an indication of this fact. They focus on East and Southeast Asia, Europe, and North America. They reflect Japan's strong presence in those regions and sparse presence in other parts of the world, with the notable exception of South America. Chapters on "Japan in Africa" or "Japan in South America" would have offered fruitful insights into the understanding of differing paces of Japan's globalization. In spite of such limitations, the chapters in this volume offer significant insights into how Japan globalizes.

Globalization not only proceeds at different paces, it also manifests differing creolization processes depending on the locale. As Ogawa shows in this volume, Japanese popular songs are appropriated and embraced by Hong Kongese, but a similar process is not likely to take place in Europe or North America. Thus chapters in this volume inform us that different processes of globalization are grounded in the unique local conditions.

These unique conditions may be historical. For example, the three chapters by Mathews, Han, and Huang, respectively, focus on World War II and the

Japanese colonization in Asia. They show the impact of the memory of the experience of the war years and the colonial control of the past upon the present situation. The memory is invoked by the Hong Kongese to fight the Japanese claim of the Diaoyu/Senkaku Islands. It blocks Korean youths from unconditionally enjoying Japanese popular culture. And it makes the Austronesian Takasago people of Taiwan proud of their past as having served in the Japanese Imperial Army.

How are we to conceptualize or identify "the Japanese presence"? This seemingly innocuous question becomes rather complex as we examine empirical situations. Pages in this volume are replete with debate on the definition of Japaneseness. Contestation of Japaneseness is illustrated in Yatabe's assertion that the Japanese identity is now multiple, fragmented, fragile, and constantly renegotiated. Also, Thomas in this volume stresses the difficulties that one encounters in defining what "Japanese" photography is. The problem is further complicated in analyzing Japan's globalization by the fact that what is Japanese to one person may not be Japanese for another. There are many American Toyota drivers who are not aware (nor do they care) that they are driving a Japanese car. Toyota's sales figure would not vary one dollar whether or not the buyer is aware of the Japanese origin of the car. But if one were interested in the perceptual or attitudinal aspects of globalization, awareness of origins of things on the part of the participants in the globalization game is crucial. Globalization maps would be very different in these cases.

One conclusion is abundantly clear: globalization does not simply proceed from one center, namely the West, as is too often assumed. Instead there are many centers. This volume hopes to demonstrate Japan as one undeniable center.

Acknowledgments

This volume puts together papers given in a special section for the Japan Anthropology Workshop on "Japan outside Japan" at the eighth International Conference of the European Association for Japanese Studies, which took place in Budapest, Hungary, in 1997. As not all papers presented at the conference could find room in this volume, we would like to thank the participants who contributed to the success of the section, but whose papers could not be included in this volume. Christoph Brumann, Katarzyna Cwiertka, Helen Diakonoff, Jill Kleinberg, Beverley Lee, Andreas K. Riesland, and Masae Yuasa are not to be forgotten.

Conference papers usually are not in immediately publishable form, but need much editing before they are ready for printing in a book. Papers for this conference were no exception. We are indebted to the Institute for Cultural and Human Research of Kyoto Bunkyo University for financial support for the editing process. For the actual editing, Joanne Sandstrom and Hilary Powers provided impeccable professional services, for which all contributors wish to express their gratitude.

Julia Thomas wishes to thank the Michael Shapiro Gallery, the Laurence Miller Gallery, and the Sonnabend Gallery for their help in researching this project.

The extracts from E. Hayashi's 1998 work *Shogen: Takasago-Giyutai*, reproduced in Chapter 14, are used with the permission of the publisher.

The article 'Consuming the modern: globalization, things Japanese, and the politics of cultural identity on Korea' by Han Seung-Mi was first published in *The Journal of Pacific Asia* and appears here with the permission of the publisher.

Part I
Introduction

1 The global context of Japan outside Japan

Harumi Befu

Since the late 1980s "globalization" has been a buzzword in the Japanese media.[1] Japan is said to be "globalizing" in all respects, but, above all, in its economic sphere. The greatest proponent of this idea is no doubt Kenichi Ohmae (1987, 1995), who has written numerous books on the subject. While Japan's globalization in the economic sense has been widely discussed, Japan's social and cultural globalization has not been a topic of much discussion so far. This volume addresses these much neglected aspects of globalization of Japan.

"Globalization" has displaced "internationalization," which was popular in the 1970s and 1980s. This displacement signals an important shift in the perception of the positioning of Japan's worldwide economic expansion and related overseas developments. Internationalization implies a relationship between two or more nations: a minimum of two nations can engage in "international" relations. Indeed, when the term internationalization became popular in the 1970s and the 1980s, the reference was usually to Japan relating to one or another country. For example, when Osaka established a sister-city relation with San Francisco or when Nepal and Japan engaged in a cultural exchange program, it was a case of internationalization.

"Globalization," on the other hand, implies simultaneous extension and expansion in all directions. At least in intent, the term implies that Japan is extending its interests all over the world in a network (Katzenstein and Shiraishi 1997). If Japan was simply having an association with one or two countries, it would not warrant the term. "Globalization" as a concept, indeed, designates the empirical reality of Japan's common presence throughout most parts of the world. The appellation is an *ex post facto* affirmation of a reality that has existed since at least the 1970s.

What is the theoretical relevance of the endeavor undertaken in this volume? Why do we need to examine Japan's globalization? Let me offer two major reasons. One is the ethnocentrism of the received globalization theories of such well-known scholars as Arjun Appadurai (1996), Peter Beyer (1994), Roland Robertson (1992), Immanuel Wallerstein (1974), and Malcom Waters (1995). Analyzing the theories offered by these scholars, one is left with a strong impression that there is only one center of globalization and that this center is the West. While detailed documentation of this observation will be left to another occasion (Befu 1998a), it is safe to say that these and many other authors of globalization see globalization either as a transformed end product (or consequence) of modernization or simply a continuation thereof. Whatever the position, inasmuch as modernization is and has been a project of Western civilization, globalization as its outcome must emanate from the West. The West's ethnocentrism is made clear when we examine the contents of what it claims to globalize. These theorists argue that globalization involves such palpably Western values and ideologies as humanism, human rights, equality, democracy, and progress.

If only one center of globalization can be recognized, we can hardly speak of a theory of globalization. What we have is merely a series of generalizations. We cannot have a theory of globalization based on a single case any more than we can have a theory of the family based on one family.

The set of essays in this volume shows that in addition to the West there is at least one other center of globalization in this world, namely Japan. If we show that Japan can be, in fact is, a center for globalization, then it is an easy additional step to demonstrate that there are many other centers as well. We thus need to speak of multiple globalizations. Only after analyzing plural cases of globalization can we begin to formulate a theory of globalization through comparison. The task has not even begun. This volume is a modest but important step in this direction.

The second major import of the present volume is that all of the studies in it are ethnographically based. They are grounded on intensive fieldwork of the traditional anthropological kind. A perusal of the existing globalization literature will at once convince the reader that we have virtually no "theory" firmly based on solid ethnographic fieldwork. Without data deriving from such a basis, generalizations tend to be speculative and intuitive. In the absence of solid data, conclusions seem to drive the argument instead of being derived from it.

What we offer in this volume are solid data that no one can dispute. I believe that any theory of globalization has to be based on a solid empirical foundation, just as any other theory. We offer such a foundation in this volume. This is not to say that data presented in this volume are sufficient to start constructing an adequate theory of globalization. We must have a great deal more solid data. We need to postpone theorizing about globalization until we have sufficient data. This volume is an important first step in the right direction.

As a way of analyzing Japan's globalization, not so much its economic aspects as its cultural and social consequences, I offer a fourfold framework consisting of human dispersal, organizational transplantation, cultural diffusion, and imagining of Japan. It is hoped that this framework will help readers to comprehend the data presented in the subsequent chapters as globalization phenomena.

Human dispersal

The dispersal of Japanese resulting from Japan's economic globalization may be classified into long-term (or permanent) and short-term (or non-permanent) categories. The former designates those who leave Japan permanently, or who have no definite plans to return to Japan. The latter includes those who intend to return to Japan or at least leave the foreign country within a definite period, most of them within 5 or 6 years.

Nonpermanent sojourners

The most prominent in the category of nonpermanent sojourners no doubt are business expatriates and their families. Japan's economic expansion abroad has necessarily been accompanied by movement of people. As multinational corporations are established all over the world, corporate soldiers are sent abroad to set up beachheads as the front line of Japan's economic imperial expansions, as illustrated in Sedgwick's and Wong's chapters in this volume. These business expatriates may go alone, as most of them did in the early days of Japan's globalization in the 1960s, but nowadays, with Japan's increasing affluence, they are more likely to be accompanied by their families. In areas with a large concentration of Japanese multinationals, such as Seoul, Hong Kong, Manila, Bangkok, Singapore, Los Angeles, Chicago, New York, London, Paris, and Düsseldorf, resident Japanese business expatriates and their families number in thousands. In Hong Kong, these Japanese multinationals are aided by hundreds of "office ladies" who serve as clerical staff, as reported by Wong in this volume. These women are either sent by the companies that they work for, as in the case of Yaohan described by Wong, or go on their own to a foreign country, where they are hired locally by Japanese multinationals. In these cities of high Japanese concentration, a variety of businesses that in one way or another serve expatriate families (and also each other) are established by Japanese, who may have come to these cities to establish such businesses or who may have arrived for some other purpose and entered the businesses later. Their numbers significantly increase the local Japanese population.

Other nonpermanent sojourners include scholars and students who go abroad for research and study. They are not as likely to be accompanied by their families. Of course, scholars and students have been going abroad since long before Japan's globalization became a well-known phenomenon. But it is unquestionably Japan's economic affluence and the consequent availability of financial resources among the Japanese that have increased the numbers of students and scholars manifold in the last few decades. Many parents send their children to foreign – mostly American – colleges for undergraduate work because it costs nearly as much to send a child to, say, Tokyo for schooling, including room and board, as to send the child abroad.

Scholars, of course, go to the location where the desired research institution or university is situated, and not necessarily where business expatriates concentrate. The same can be said of graduate students with a specialized field of research. Undergraduates, on the other hand, often go to areas of high concentration of Japanese for the familiar living conditions that they find there.

Permanent sojourners

Permanent sojourners include those who are definite about residing in a foreign country permanently as well as those whose plans are quite indefinite. This group includes several subcategories.

Conventional emigrants

The Japanese have been dispersing throughout the world since the sixteenth century, although the early expansion into Southeast Asia was abruptly interrupted by the policy of the Tokugawa Shogunate.[2] Although we do not have a clear picture of the Japanese who were stranded in foreign lands as a result of the Tokugawa seclusion policy, we do know they lived in, and they eventually became absorbed into, the local society.

From the first year of Meiji, Japanese began to move abroad, as the term *gannen-mono*, referring to the migrant laborers who went to Hawaii in year 1 of the Meiji era, demonstrates. This early Japanese "diaspora" began with dispersal to the New World, but it also saw Japanese people migrating to East and Southeast Asia.[3] Early emigrants were usually those of relatively poor economic background who were trying to find opportunities not available in Japan. Emigration, of course, stopped during the Second World War, but resumed after the war and continued into the 1960s, with emigrants going almost exclusively to South America.

The discontented

No modern, industrialized society is able to satisfy all of its members. Japan is no exception. Structurally or culturally, many Japanese feel dissatisfied with the particular situation that they find themselves in. For instance, in my interview sample, a faculty member at a national university (where the "chair system" is in operation) found the senior professor under whom he must work unbearable, and opted to leave for a position in the United States. In another case, a Tokyo University graduate employed by a major national bank found employment conditions – 15 hours per day of work – intolerable. He resigned, and went to the United States for graduate study. In a third case, a woman did not wish to marry the man her parents had betrothed her to. Not finding any way out, she enrolled in an undergraduate program in the United States to escape from parental pressure. A divorcee, who could not stand the social stigma attached to the divorced status, went to England. A woman graduate student, anticipating employment discrimination in Japan, opted to go to the United States for further graduate work.

Such losses of human resources as these are a serious issue with national policy implications: with an effective social policy, Japan could be made a more comfortable place for these Japanese to live and contribute to the society. Conservatism of the Japanese society and Japan's policymakers, however, seems to prevent execution of such social reform.

International marriage

A large number of women in Japan marry foreigners and leave Japan when their husbands return to their country. These women may be included in the category of "the discontented." But their numbers are large enough and their motivation specific enough to warrant a special category. Given the statistical improbability of a Japanese woman finding a foreign, eligible man, compared with the high probability of finding a Japanese male partner, the choice of a foreign man over a Japanese man is clearly a psychological declaration of rejection of Japanese men as marriage candidates.

As women gain higher status and become more educated, many of them are more and more likely to find Japanese men unacceptable as marriage partners. For such women, foreign men offer an attractive alternative. Most of the partners are Caucasian, but Asians – Koreans, Taiwanese, Hong Kongese, Thais, and Singaporeans – are also chosen. Another psychological factor not to be forgotten is the century-old Japanese inferiority complex toward the West and Caucasians. The Japanese look up to Caucasians as superior and more desirable, an attitude that induces many Japanese women to prefer Caucasian men as marital partners.

Opportunities abroad

Besides the obvious fact that multinationals are spreading out globally, independent businessmen and businesswomen, seeing business opportunities abroad or finding business practices too restrictive to their liking in Japan because of government regulations, move abroad to carry on or start business, often in a totally different line. These individuals usually go to a familiar foreign country. They may have lived there as a student, traveled as a tourist, or visited a friend, and the personal experience gave them enough confidence of likely business success there.

In addition to business opportunities, some Japanese seek cultural opportunities unavailable in Japan. Yatabe reports in this volume of an overwhelming number of intellectuals living in the area of Paris – some 90 percent – who went in search of artistic, musical, and other cultural opportunities.

Volunteer spirit

Younger Japanese – in their twenties and thirties – are found in the Third World carrying out volunteer work in a variety of fields, from education to social welfare to medical services. Most of these individuals, like the businessmen and women mentioned earlier, had been to the country they now serve and decided to return to continue the service. They may have gone there as a member of the Japanese "Peace Corps"; or they may have simply traveled as a student and had an experience that moved them enough to send them abroad.

"Un-returnees"

Another category of Japanese living abroad that is increasing in number is the children of business expatriates who grow up abroad and opt for college education outside Japan, usually in North America or in Europe. Although the difficulty of their employment in Japan has been easing in recent years, especially if they opt for a foreign multinational, they still face disadvantages for a variety of reasons compared with those who graduate from Japanese colleges. Some of them, for example, do not have native competence in Japanese; others do not have adequate enculturation as Japanese.

Also, they are at an extreme disadvantage in the practical business of job seeking compared with those in Japanese colleges, who are already in the job market early in their senior year and who usually have their job contract all but signed months before graduation. Those in colleges abroad do not have this luxury. For this reason, most expatriate children are sent back at high school age to receive adequate preparation for the college entrance examination, and most manage to graduate from a college in Japan. Those who miss this opportunity are likely to be excluded from the Japanese job market and eventually work outside Japan (Mori 1992).

It is important to keep in mind that the distinction made above between a "permanent" and a "nonpermanent" sojourn is not clear-cut. Some people first leave Japan intending to live abroad permanently but change their plans later, and some others who leave Japan with the full intention of returning after several years end up abandoning the original intention. This is illustrated in Wong's chapter by Numaguchi, an office lady who left the company that brought her to Hong Kong to avoid being eventually sent back to Japan and instead secured a more or less permanent situation in the local job market. Even some multinational expatriate executives decide that life in the foreign country is more suitable and more comfortable and they resign from their company and establish permanent residence abroad.

The indeterminate

In recent years more and more young Japanese of both sexes are leaving Japan without definite plans either to stay abroad or to return to Japan. Many of the Japanese who go to the United States or Canada and enroll in community colleges and English-for-foreigners classes (where academic requirements are minimal) belong in this category. The women of "yellow cab" fame, made well known through the book of the same title by Shoko Ieda (1991), are also in this category, although much of this account of Japanese women seeking boyfriends, especially Afro-Americans, in New York has been discredited by Toyoda (1994). People in this group have fluid plans, if any, and change them as their situations change. They either are supported by remittances from home or support themselves with odd jobs. In the United States, many work at Japanese restaurants, since little skill is required except to look Japanese and have a Japanese cultural background to help make the establishment look authentically Japanese. Many of these people leave Japan with a tourist visa, overstay the limit, and work without a proper visa.

Exploiting the cultural capital

The Japanese who go abroad more or less permanently for whatever reasons must somehow make a living wherever they settle. In most cases they end up exploiting their cultural capital, their language being one of the most useful resources. If they enroll in a university as graduate students in humanities or social science, they are likely to choose Japan for specialization and, if in a doctoral program, write their dissertations on a topic related to Japan. If they take a teaching job, they are most likely to teach Japan-related courses. If they take nonacademic employment, their work is likely to involve Japan or Japanese companies or clients.

If they take up employment after arriving in a foreign country rather than enrolling in school, such employment, again, tends to relate to Japan in some sense, e.g. by working for a Japanese multinational as a local hire or working for a Japanese travel agency, bookstore, supermarket, restaurant, or the like, where Japanese language, manners, and etiquette are valued. Of course, those with financial resources can start their own business catering to Japanese business expatriates, their families, and others. Some of these businesses, such as travel agencies, cater exclusively to Japanese clients, so much so that these agencies respond to phone calls in Japanese only, thus: "*XYZ toraberu de gozaimasu*" (this is XYZ Travel).

One important implication of this observation is that long-term sojourners by and large engage in activities that directly or indirectly contribute toward Japan's further economic expansion. Those who work as local hires for Japanese multinationals most obviously do so. Those who establish their own business such as a travel agency or bookstore – and those who work for such businesses – also aid Japanese multinationals by providing amenities and services needed by business expatriates and their families. Even scholars who teach at college level contribute to Japan's economic growth to the extent that their teaching on Japan is generally designed to make students appreciate

Japan and induce positive attitudes toward the country, so that they might work for a Japanese multinational or at least frequent a sushi shop.

Organizational transplant

Multinational corporations

Although Japan's globalization may have begun back in the Meiji period with Japanese students going abroad to study and foreign scholars and technical advisers coming to Japan, and with Japanese art objects being exported abroad, the engine that runs Japan's current global presence is multinational corporations, which form the central filter, as Sedgwick states in his contribution in this volume, through which Japan interacts with the world. They are by now emblematic of Japan's globalization. As of 1995, there were 11,441 Japanese firms around the world (Japan, Ministry of International Trade Industry 1996: 116). These firms inevitably go through organizational adaptation to fit into the local culture (Kim 1995). On one hand, Japanese multinationals adapt to the local scene, and, on the other, local corporations emulate "the Japanese management style." The literature in this field is too voluminous to be listed.

Although Japan's multinational corporations have moved into all continents, they are not distributed evenly throughout the world. For a variety of important historical reasons, they have moved most heavily into North America and East Asia, including Southeast Asia. These are the regions of the world with which Japan has long had historical ties. Japan's relationship with the United States since Commodore Perry's visit to Edo Bay in 1853, checkered as it is, is too well known to be reviewed here. Its relationship with East Asia obviously goes even further back. It is not at all a surprise, then, that the Japanese presence is most conspicuous in these regions. In this volume, this situation is illustrated by Yaohan's move into Hong Kong, as discussed by Wong. Although Yaohan's first move abroad was into South America, its most extensive expansion, until its recent demise, was in East Asia (Wong 1999).

One variable in the extent to which organizational change must take place is the ratio of expatriates to local hires. Trading companies generally have a heavy expatriate ratio compared with manufacturers such as automobile assembly plants. Where the expatriate ratio is high, the organization understandably tends to retain much of its Japanese character. For example, according to Wong in this volume, Yaohan as a Japanese multinational corporation in Hong Kong maintained the Japanese organizational style by putting all of its Japanese female workers in a dormitory, true to the concept of *in loco parentis* but also with an almost paranoiac concern for its own reputation lest its employees commit some untoward act if left unsupervised after hours.

Also, expatriates hold top positions and make key decisions in most

Japanese multinationals – in frequent consultation with the head office in Japan. As Sedgwick notes in this volume, a decision-making process of this sort involves the use of the Japanese language, and calls to Tokyo must be made during Japan's working hours, which in the United States and Europe is the evening, after most local hires have gone home. Excluding locals from the decision-making process in this way creates possibilities of conflict between expatriates and locals.

Where hundreds or thousands of locals are hired, adaptations are necessarily made to accommodate local cultural and social needs. Nonetheless, efforts have been made by Japanese multinationals to introduce such procedures as quality control, just-in-time production *(kanban), kaizen* [(continual effort for) improvement], and the concept of corporate culture into their foreign subsidiaries. At any rate, the issue of whether or not – and to what extent – "Japanese-style management" can be introduced in Japanese multinationals abroad is a topic that continues to be debated in numerous studies.

One of the issues in transplanting Japanese multiculturals abroad is the prejudice and discrimination against local hires. This is especially rampant in the developing countries, such as in Southeast Asia, where ethnic prejudice by Japanese against the local population is strong and has contributed to the formation of the image of "ugly Japanese."

But such prejudice and discrimination are also known in Japanese multinationals in the so-called "advanced" countries. Caucasian employees have faced discrimination in pay and promotion. Female local hires have suffered from such discrimination more than male and notably from sexual harassment by Japanese managers, who tend to assume that norms and expectations regarding treatment of female employees that are current in Japan also operate in foreign host countries.

Expatriate community

Where multinationals concentrate, organizations catering to the needs of their expatriate employees and their families also emerge. Prominent among these organizations are Japanese schools, full-time or Saturday, with the principal and some of the teachers being dispatched from the Ministry of Education in Japan. Since these schools are designed to help students return to the Japanese school system with minimal difficulty, necessarily they are modeled after schools in Japan in terms of curriculum, textbooks, and teacher–student relations as well as relationships among students. Other "transplant" organizations include the Japanese Association and the Japanese Chamber of Commerce, which are common in cities of large expatriate populations. These, too, are "transplanted" in the sense that basic organizing principles involving structure and norm are basically Japanese. In addition to these formalized organizations, secondary organizations also emerge to meet the needs of the expatriate community, be they flower arrangement societies, bridge clubs, or golf tournaments (Befu and Stalker 1996).

Japanese expatriate communities may be generally divided into (1) those consisting of business expatriates and their families and (2) those composed of the "permanent sojourners" discussed earlier. The former constitute what may be called "rotational community" in the sense that its members leave within a few years – in a staggered schedule – but are replaced by others. Thus as a community it has permanence, although its members are temporary and impermanent. The latter community, on the other hand, has permanent members, who stay more or less for life, at least in intent. These two Japanese communities have relatively little in common and even have some amount of antipathy toward each other. The two communities differ in their reason for living in a foreign country and their attitude toward Japan. And unlike the expatriates, permanent sojourners tend not to enroll their children in Japanese schools and have little interest or concern about education in Japan, such as the entrance examination.

For the sake of completeness in speaking about Japanese dispersal in a globalizing world, two other communities should be added here. One consists of tourists, such as in Waikiki Beach, Hawaii, and may be called the "revolving door" community, whose members are even more impermanent than those in the rotational community. Most members remain in the revolving door community for no more than a week or two. But as a community consisting of Japanese tourists, Waikiki Beach is as permanent as any. At any one time, several thousand Japanese tourists are found there. Superimposed upon this revolving door community is a rotational Japanese community consisting of those serving in the local tourist industry – owners, managers, and employees of hotels, restaurants, gift shops, travel and tour agencies, as well as business expatriates, Japanese schoolteachers, and the like.

The second type of community to be added here consists of the Japanese who went to the New World before the war or soon after the war – in the 1950s and 1960s – and their descendants, for whom the term "Japanese American" most aptly applies. This is a New World phenomenon. Before the end of the war, such communities thrived throughout East and Southeast Asia as well as in Micronesia. But because of forced repatriation of the Japanese in these areas upon Japan's defeat in the war, virtually all of them returned to Japan. However, a few of them have remained in these parts of the world, and, although their numbers are small, in some areas such as the Philippines they constitute a community (Ohno 1991).

The relationships among these four types of Japanese community in the New World, and among three of them in the rest of the world, are complex. Although they remain more or less distinct and recognizable as separate communities, and subjectively members of these communities recognize themselves as being different from others, they maintain intricate symbiotic relationships with one another, and their borders form complicated interstices.

Cultural diffusion

Industrial consumer products

The most prominent diffusion of Japanese culture in the globalizing age, of course, is manifested in industrial products, especially consumer products such as automobiles, electric and electronic devices, time pieces, and video games. These products have made Japan famous worldwide. The fact that such names as Toyota, Sony, Panasonic, Casio, and Nintendo are household names around the world is a testimony to Japan's global economic expansion.

Popular culture

These products from the 1960s and electronic advancement since then have enabled the spread of popular culture, including manga, animation movies, karaoke (Shirahata 1996; Mitsui and Hosokawa 1998), and certain television programs such as *O-shin* (Shiraishi 1998). Ogawa's chapter in this volume outlines the process through which Japanese music spread to Hong Kong. But the important point is that although this process may seem unique to Hong Kong Japanese popular music was fast diffusing to other parts of Asia as well. This popular culture is most widely spread in East and Southeast Asia – so much so that, in a volume on diffusion of Japanese popular culture into Asian societies, Igarashi (1998) has called the process "Japanization." Aficionados of manga, however, are found in North America and Europe, too (Shirahata 1996). And Nintendo and Sega Enterprises games are regular fare among children in North America; so are Japanese animation films for children in North America and Europe.

As "Japanese management" styles and practices go through hybridization abroad, popular culture, too, is subject to change. Local, distinct styles and lyrics are introduced in Japanese songs and music in adopted locales, according to Ogawa in this volume. The same may be said of manga (Shiraishi 1998) as well as of karaoke (Kelly 1998). The process of the adaptation of Japanese manga in Hong Kong is illustrated in the chapter by Lai and Wong. Here, as in Ogawa's chapter, one appreciates the historical background leading to the adoption of Japanese manga. Hong Kong, with a previous history of its own manga, but not quite the right kind, proved to be a fertile ground for the adoption and adaptation of Japanese manga more suitable for Hong Kong tastes. As for karaoke, in the United Kingdom karaoke singing, usually performed in a public house, ends in a boisterous chorus of all present, drowning the singing of the person with the microphone. In Vietnam, karaoke bars, which in Japan are considered to be places of healthy entertainment for families and friends, are generally associated with the sex industry – places where prostitutes await customers.

Martial arts

The overseas spread of martial arts such as judo, kendo, karate, and aikido began before World War II. However, their popularity and wide acceptance date from the 1960s and 1970s. Incorporation of judo into the Olympics has gone a long way in transforming judo from a quaint and uniquely Japanese martial art to an international sport. In the process, however, the sport has had to make adjustments and revise its rules to make it acceptable to players abroad, so much so that Frühstück and Manzenreiter question in this volume whether judo as an international sport is genuinely Japanese or whether it is "owned" by the world instead.

Religion

Japanese religion, which has also been spreading abroad from before World War II, may be grouped into two categories for present purposes. Historically, as soon as Japanese began emigrating in the nineteenth century, they took their religion with them. Buddhist and Shinto sects of various sorts still thrive today in immigrant communities in North and South America. Thus Jodo Shinshu is by far the largest religious group among Japanese Americans in the United States. Its success in establishing roots in the new setting, in large measure, lies in its adoption of institutional arrangements paralleling the Christian religion. For instance, the Buddhist "temple" became a Buddhist "church" and thus acquired a Western appearance. Having pews in the church building, having Sunday services, singing hymns and having the minister give sermons all help to make Buddhism in the New World an institution paralleling Christianity. Members of Jodo Shinshu thus did not have to feel that they were practicing a strange and exotic religion. In the future, for globalization of religion, Japanese as much as any other, the Internet and other electronic processes will no doubt play an increasing role (Ikoma 1997; Kokugakuin University, Research Center for Japanese Culture 1997).

Entirely apart from the immigrant-sponsored religion, Japanese religion has also spread among non-Japanese. This is particularly true for such "new religions" as Soka Gakkai, Mahikari, Tensho Kotai Jingukyo, and Perfect Liberty. Even Aum Shinrikyo at its height of prosperity in the 1980s had as many as 49,000 members in the then Soviet Union. At the beginning, as these religions spread abroad, Japanese members went as missionaries and contributed the core group and leadership in most cases. But as time went on, the membership became more and more non-Japanese and local, and, now, many such groups have no or very few Japanese members. These religions began their overseas missionary work with the explicit purpose of converting non-Japanese local residents. Although not to be classified as a new religion, Zen, too, has been a religion of and for non-Japanese locals, whether in Northern America or Europe.

In the diffusion of Japanese religion, too, local adaptation has taken place as inevitably as in sports. For example, in the practice of Soka Gakkai in Germany, according to Ionescu in this volume, what is required as essential for its practice had to be disaggregated from nonessential "Japanese" practices.

Imagining Japan

It is as well to remember that the imagining and construction of the Other is a selective process, and ultimately an instrument to rationalize one's existence here and now in relation to the object of what is remembered, imagined, or constructed. Verbalized memory, in addition to being at the mercy of what one can remember, is subject to willful manipulation of the remembered past. What one remembers and forgets is itself a result of a continual selective process. An accumulation of this selective remembering is the image of the object here and now. Imaginings of Japan form just such memory, such an image.

The Japanese abroad

Both Japanese expatriates and locals in foreign countries alike imagine Japan, but their imaginings are quite different from one another (Befu 1998b). Even among the former, depending on a variety of biographical vicissitudes, "Japan" is remembered quite differently: a corporate soldier, for example, proud of being at the frontiers of expanding the Japanese economic empire, holds a different view of the country from that held by a sojourner who left Japan because of dissatisfaction with life there. As Ben-Ari (1997) argues, corporate expatriates often use the rhetoric of *Nihonjinron* – an essentialized and idealized view of Japan – to explain their own and their fellow expatriates' behavior. One sees these managers accepting a certain stereotype of Japan – more laudatory and self-serving than reality warrants. Those who abandoned Japan for want of better opportunities, on the other hand, understandably tend to maintain a more critical view of their homeland.

Most Japanese abroad, whether tourists on a 1-week program or long-term sojourners, have a tendency to idealize Japan. Their attachment to Japan is enhanced in a foreign environment, where language is different and communication difficult, where customs are different and expectations unmet, where anxiety accompanies every move, where cherished values are not honored and alternative values are upheld. In such circumstances, Japanese away from their familiar and accustomed surroundings are likely to become frustrated and nostalgic for their homeland. Japan is thus remembered as a land of beautiful cherry blossoms and fall colors – the beastly heat of summer and the bitter cold of winter being tempered in memory. It is remembered as a society of people who care about one another, and the unreasonable demands that people make on one another or the fact that some take advantage of relationships are less well remembered. Expatriates in this sense are the most ardent patriots. Tourists in Hong Kong during the Diaoyu/Senkaku crisis reported in Mathews's chapter illustrate this situation; they tend to take the Japanese side in the dispute or want to be left alone, claiming no relevance or responsibility for Japan's action.

But not all Japanese abroad idealize Japan. Women who left Japan for lack of career opportunities retain an image of Japan as a sexist country. A businessman who could not bear restrictive government regulations and went to Mexico to start a business remembers Japan as a country with an impossible bureaucracy. These are the individuals who have set up more or less permanent residence abroad. They blame Japan for their inability to return home to live. One often senses a bit of resentment on their part for not being able to make a career at home.

On the other hand, these individuals tend to idealize the land where they now live, enumerating the good things they see there but could not find in Japan. They learned selectively to value certain ingredients of the land they adopted in constructing its image. The vast outback of Australia, individual freedom in England, and large affordable homes in America thus become indispensable values for them. This does not mean that they totally castigate Japan. They do remember good things about Japan, and do not mind returning there from time to time to enjoy what they still value. But they construct a new value system that places Japan in the distance and incorporates their new country as an integral part.

The local community abroad

The image that the local people have of Japan is based on their past experience with and knowledge of Japan. Direct experience includes visits to or residence in Japan, personal relationships with Japanese, and so on. Knowledge of Japan may also be gained through reading about Japan or viewing programs about Japan on television. The locals' views about Japan are also shaped in part by the historical relationship between Japan and their new country, to the extent that this history is part of the collective memory of the nation as well as of the individual's consciousness.

This is most graphically illustrated for Korea, with whom Japan has had a checkered historical relationship. In early history, Korea was Japan's mentor. Chinese civilization was introduced to Japan by Korean intellectuals such as scholars and priests. Japan owes Korea in no small way for the foundation of its civilization, including religious, political, and aesthetic life. But, in the view of Koreans, Japan paid its debt with vengeance by invading Korea in the sixteenth century and plundering the country, massacring people, and forcibly bringing back Koreans to Japan. In modern times, too, Japan continued its exploitation of Korea by colonizing it and subjecting Koreans to forced labor and sexual services. After World War II, it was natural for Korea to invoke these shameful experiences of the past to create a nationalism based on anti-Japanese feelings.

What is problematic, however, is that Korea had to rely on Japan's economic aid and technical assistance for its own economic recovery and development after the Korean War. The adoption of state-guided development strategy and community-oriented business practice, according to Han in this volume, is a result of selective use of the Japanese model. The teaching of Japanese language in schools since the 1970s, too, is to facilitate the process of learning from the Japanese model. Korea's attitude toward Japan is thus "bifurcated"; as Han puts it, hatred toward Japan for all the evils it has wreaked on Korea through history and respect for all of Japan's accomplishments – economic, technical, and otherwise. The Korean use of the Japanese model and the Korean interest in learning Japanese, however, are based purely on practical considerations: Korea harbors no sentimental pro-Japanese feelings. This fact is important in that too often the Japanese, for example, interpret the number of people learning Japanese in a given country as an index of the degree of pro-Japanese sentiment. Han's analysis warns against such a facile interpretation. The same can be said, according to Han, about the popularity of Japanese consumer goods, which are accepted and used for practical reasons without admiration for Japan. But there seems to be a generational difference: younger generations were accepting Japan's popular culture through underground markets long before President Kim Dae-Jung's initiative to legalize importation of Japanese popular culture. Older generations still disapprove of it as illegitimate.

What can be said of Korea could be said of China, Taiwan, and the whole of Southeast Asia, as well, in varying degrees. Their images of Japan, therefore, are necessarily different from those of such countries as India or Turkey, whose history is not trammeled by unfortunate past relationships with Japan. Images of Japan in these Asian countries are complicated by the fact that their governments and businesses need Japan's capital and technological assistance in spite of the memories of their hateful colonial and occupied past and wartime experience of Japan. This need forces these countries to adopt a compromising posture in relation to Japan. In addition to such political–economic compromise on the part of the leaders in these countries, the masses clamor for Japanese products such as automobiles and Walkmans and crave parts of Japanese popular culture such as manga and karate, further complicating the hate–love image of Japan.

Guichard-Anguis's discussion of the Japanese Day/Week/Year in this volume exemplifies a typical way in which Japanese culture and, consequently, Japan's image are disseminated throughout the world. It demonstrates the role of cooperation between local individuals or communities and relevant Japanese counterparts. Often either or both governments are involved in executing the event, as the French Year in Japan, executed in 1998, shows. Material as well as nonmaterial culture is brought to a foreign country to represent Japan. What is important is, as Guichard-Anguis argues, not the material objects themselves, but what meanings are attributed to them by local people and what image or images of Japan they create. Here as elsewhere, on one hand, the Japanese (the French organizers of "Japan events") "present" events that "represent" a "Japan" and, on the other, the receivers formulate an image of Japan based on what is presented.

It is only in an abstract sense that the historical past to be deployed for constructing an image of Japan is there as a constant. In the subjectivities of foreign locals, such a past may or may not be part of their conscious knowledge. Even if it is, it need not necessarily be invoked for an imagining of Japan until it is found convenient or useful. Mathews's discussion of how the Diaoyu/ Senkaku Islands crisis was handled by Hong Kongese illustrates this point. Normally, the World War II experience of Hong Kongese and the memory of the atrocities wrought by the Japanese, not necessarily in Hong Kong but in China at large, are a deeply dormant matter, not to be awakened easily. But the experience and the memory, along with the fact or claim that Japan has not fully apologized for the wartime atrocities, became important ingredients for constructing an image of ugly Japan and to fan the flames of patriotism and nationalism when the Diaoyu/Senkaku Islands incident erupted. Mathews also demonstrates the critical importance of the media in spreading the ugly image of Japan and eliciting jingoistic anti-Japanese nationalism among the Hong Kongese.

Japaneseness thus created is imagined as being mapped on a particular people and a definite place, as Thomas says in her chapter, and this imagined Japaneseness then serves as the basis for interpreting new experiences. This image, stereotyped as it may well be, allows photographic critics to "see" Japaneseness in photographic works when the critic knows the artist to be Japanese. Certain artists may be typecast as quintessentially Japanese because they fulfill a certain cultural type, such as simplicity and love of Nature, as enunciated in *Nihonjinron,* even though the subject matter may portray something totally unrelated to Nature.

The image of Japan as a utopian welfare state is, again, derived from selective and, according to Goodman, biased and perhaps faulty represent-ations of Japan. The bias, as Goodman puts it, was an intentional creation by the British government for a specific purpose. The purpose of the government was to cow the parliament and people into accepting a better welfare program – of the sort Japan supposedly had.

Interrelationships among the four categories

These four categories of human dispersal, organizational transplantation, cultural diffusion, and images of Japan are closely interrelated in a complex manner.

For example, the dispersal of the Japanese throughout the world ushers in a setting for these dispersed Japanese to form their community in a typical Japanese pattern. An organized Japanese community in turn attracts more Japanese, some of whom come to start businesses catering to Japanese, such as travel agencies. Others come simply because a fully fledged Japanese community minimizes the necessity to adapt to the local culture. Thus movement of the Japanese out of Japan (human dispersal) is closely related to the preexistence of a Japanese community abroad, one with familiar organizational patterns into which new members can readily adapt (organizational transplant).

Such a Japanese community is likely to have a full array of Japanese cultural amenities, such as a sushi restaurant, a karaoke bar, and a Japanese bookstore with manga on its racks (cultural diffusion). Transplanted Japanese create images of Japan to suit their taste, one that is most instrumental in rationalizing their current situation abroad. Locals also create their images of Japan based not only on whatever they learned through the media but also on the local Japanese presence in the broadest sense, including Japanese expatriates whom they come into contact with and Japanese culture – cars, cameras, and karaoke – that they encounter, purchase, or participate in (images of Japan).

Space limitation does not allow further elaboration on the inter-relationships. Suffice to say that it is through the dynamic relationship that Japan's globalization proceeds.

Conclusion: center–periphery

A major conclusion that one arrives at in considering Japan's globalization is the undeniable presence of Japan as a center and its peripheries. Photography, which originated in the West, is no longer a monopoly of the West but an activity engaged in throughout the world, as Thomas argues in this volume, with Japan as one of its important centers. Likewise, at one time automobile manufacture was limited to the West, but now it is decentered; automobiles are made in other parts of the world, including Japan, which is a center rivaling the West. Thus the center–periphery concept has to be understood in temporal terms: the center multiplies and moves.

As centers multiply, peripheries of a center might move to become peripheries of a new center, and one center's periphery today may be another center tomorrow, as Japan emerges as a center challenging the West.

Frühstück's and Manzenreiter's chapter illustrates the dynamic process of relativizing the center. Judo was once a sport exclusive to Japan. It began to spread slowly to Europe and the Americas before World War II. At that time, and immediately after World War II as well, Japan was the unquestioned center of the sport. However, once judo was added to the list of Olympic sports, and an international organization was formed, new rules began to be formulated by the international body, such as adoption of weight classes, use of different grades of judgment, use of different-colored belts, and even different-colored uniforms. At the same time, world championships are no longer monopolized by Japanese judo experts. Japan may still be looked upon as the Mecca of the sport, but Japan no longer has hegemony in terms of its governance or prowess. The same sort of deterritorializing and relativizing is happening to Soka Gakkai in Germany, according to Ionescu, although in a somewhat less intense sense. There, what seems peripheral and what is essential for the religion are sorted out and only the latter strictures are accepted and practiced. Local believers abandoned the former as nonessential without abandoning the religion. Here again, one sees the process of the hegemony of the headquarters in Japan being challenged and its position compromised.

Ogawa's discussion of popular music in Hong Kong reiterates the importance of the appreciation of the temporal dimension in globalization. Hong Kong's rise in the popular music scene is directly a function of the demise of Shanghai as a center of Chinese popular music. As Hong Kong began to expand its music horizon, it took in Japanese music to satisfy local demands; now Japanese music is a staple of the Hong Kong popular music scene. A new dimension was added when Japanese singers in Hong Kong began to sing not only in Japanese but also in Cantonese and Mandarin. It is interesting that, according to Ogawa, Japan is accepted as – or assumed to be – one of Hong Kong's musical centers. Ogawa's analysis also emphasizes the interaction between center and periphery, in which the latter is not simply a passive receptacle of what is delivered from the center but reacts to it to assert its own identity. But the very process of asserting identity in this case requires creativity wanting in Hong Kong as a periphery, for which it seeks infusion of more global culture; hence a cyclical dynamic of the relationship between center and periphery is set in motion. This is not to deny other centers and interrelations among them or to say that peripheries cannot be centers.

The image of Japan, in Ogawa's analysis, is influenced by the fact that it is assumed to be a musical center *vis-à-vis* Hong Kong. Thus the Japanese can do no wrong: they are supposed to be better singers, and, even if Japanese singers are lip-synching, the Hong Kongese believe they do not do so, but are singing in real time. This is the "value added" bestowed upon the center. That is to say, once a place takes the position of being a center in a given field, it is assumed to have value as a center that peripheries do not have. Music from Japan, then, acquires this value added, which is attached to Japanese music.

Notes

1 The research on which this paper is based was supported by funds from the Institute for Cultural and Human Research of the Kyoto Bunkyo University, the Ministry of Education (grant nos 10041094, Model of Global Japan and Globalization, and 08041003, A Study on the Asian Pacific Groups in the United States), the International Nikkei Research Project of the Japanese American National Museum, Los Angeles, the Ito Scholarship Foundation, and the Ito Foundation USA, to all of which a grateful acknowledgment is made herewith.
2 One might speculate how the Japanese "ethnoscape" à la Appadurai (1990) might have looked by the middle of the nineteenth century when Japan reopened its

ports for foreign intercourse. It is likely that at least tens of thousands, possibly hundreds of thousands, of Japanese and their descendants would have been living in all parts of East and Southeast Asia, if not farther afield.

3 The term "diaspora" is put in quotation marks in order to indicate divergence in meaning from the original Jewish diaspora, which is characterized by dispersal due to loss of homeland, among other causes.

Bibliography

Appadurai, A. (1996) *Modernity at Large: Cultural Dimensions of Globalization*, Minneapolis: University of Minnesota Press.

Befu, H. (1998a) "Fundamentals of globalization theory," paper presented at the conference on Fundamentalism and Science, September, Bonn, Germany.

Befu, H. (1998b) "Imagining Japan," *Romanian Journal of Japanese Studies*. Online at http://www.opensys.ro/rjjs.

Befu, H. and Stalker, N. (1996) "Globalization of Japan: cosmopolitanization or spread of the Japanese village?" in H. Befu (ed.) *Japan Engaging the World: A Century of International Encounter*, Denver, CO: Center for Japanese Studies, Teikyo Loretto Heights University.

Ben-Ari, E. (1997) "Globalization, 'folk models' of the world order and national identity: Japanese business expatriates in Singapore," in M. Soderberg and I. Reader (eds) *Japanese Influences and Presences in Asia*, London: Curzon.

Beyer, P. (1994) *Religion and Globalization*, London: Sage.

Ieda, S. (1991) *Yero kyabu – Haneda o Tobitatta Ona tachi (Yellow Cab: The Women Who Left Haneda [Airport])*, Tokyo: Koyu Shuppan.

Igarashi, A. (1998) "'Japanaizeeshon' towa nanika" (What is "Japanization"?), in A. Igarashi (ed.) *Hen'yo suru Ajia to Nihon – Ajia Shakai ni Shinto suru Nihon no Popyura karucha (Changing Asia and Japan: The Japanese Popular Culture Seeping into Asian Societies)*, Yokohama: Seori Shobo.

Ikoma, T. (1997) "Intanetto jidai no shukyo" (Religion in the age of the Internet), *Kyoto Shinbun* 11 September.

Japan, Ministry of International Trade Industry (Sangyo-seisakukyoku Kokusai-kigyoka, ed.) (1996) *Dai 25 Kai Wagakuni Kigyo no Kaigai Jigyo Katsudo (Activities of the Japanese Overseas Enterprises – the 25th Report)*, Tokyo: Printing Bureau, Ministry of Finance.

Katzenstein, P. and Shiraishi, T. (eds) (1997) *Network Power: Japan and Asia*, Ithaca, NY: Cornell University Press.

Kelly, W. (1998) "The adaptability of karaoke in the United Kingdom," in T. Mitsui and S. Hosokawa (eds) *Karaoke Around the World: Global Technology, Local Setting*, London: Routledge.

Kim, C.-S. (1995) *Japanese Industry in the American South*, London: Routledge.

Kokugakuin University, Research Center for Japanese Culture (Kokugakuin Daigaku Nihon Bunka Kenkyusho, ed.) (1997) *Gurobaruka to Minzoku-bunka (Globalization and Ethnic Culture)*, Tokyo: Shinshokan.

Mitsui, T. and Hosokawa, S. (eds) (1998) *Karaoke Around the World: Global Technology, Local Setting*, London: Routledge.

Mori, S. (1992) "Nihon Kigyo niyoru Gaikoku Daigaku-sotsu Nihonjin Koyo no Henka: Itsudatsusha kara Kokusaijin e?– Amerika Yonensei Daigaku Sotsugyosha no Baai" (Changing employment of Japanese graduates of foreign colleges by Japanese Enterprises: from drop-outs to internationalists? In the case of U.S. four-year college graduates), in K. Iwauchi *et al.* (eds) *Kaigai Nikkei Kigyo to Jinteki Shigen (Overseas Japanese Enterprises and Human Resources)*, Tokyo: Dobunkan.

Ohmae, K. (1987) *Beyond National Borders: Reflections on Japan and the World*, New York: Kodansha International.

—— (1995) *The End of the Nation State*, New York: Free Press.

Ohno, S. (1991) *Hapon – Firipin Nikkeijin no Nagai Sengo (Hapon: The Long Postwar of the Philipino Japanese)*, Tokyo: Daisan Shokan.

Robertson, R. (1992) *Globalization: Social Theory and Global Culture*. Thousand Oaks, CA: Sage.

Shirahata, Y. (1996) *Karaoke Anime ga Sekai o Meguru (Karaoke and Anime Circulating Around the World)*, Kyoto: PHP Kenkyusho.

Shiraishi, S. (1998) "Manga anime no gurobaraizeshon" (Globalization of manga and anime), in A. Igarashi (ed.) *Hen'yo suru Ajia to Nihon – Ajia Shakai ni Shinto suru Nihon no Popyura karucha (Changing Asia and Japan: The Japanese Popular Culture Seeping into Asian Societies)*, Yokohama: Seori Shobo.

Toyoda, M. (1994) *Kokuhatsu! "Iero Kyabu" (Indictment! "Yellow Cab")*, Tokyo: Sairyusha.

Wallerstein, I. (1974) *The World System: Capitalist Agriculture and the Origins of the European World-Economy in the Sixteenth Century*, New York: Academic Press.

Waters, M. (1995) *Globalization*, London: Routledge.

Wong, H.W. (1999) *Japanese Bosses, Chinese Workers: Power and Control in a Hong Kong Megastore*, Surrey, U.K.: Curzon.

Part II
Human dispersal

2 Objects, city, and wandering

The invisibility of the Japanese in France

Kazuhiko Yatabe

I accepted the invitation of professors Harumi Befu and Sylvie Guichard-Anguis to prepare an essay for this volume on "Japan outside Japan" and – without asking myself too many questions, I confess – proposed a communication centered on the Japanese in France.[1] For things are essentially simple: the Japanese living in France are, by definition, outside Japan, unless they are gifted with ubiquity.

Before any detailed analysis of this population, as an epistemological preamble, I would like to settle for a while on the link between the perspective of the Japanese in France (but they could as well live in Thailand, Brazil, or Turkey; in Los Angeles, London, or Düsseldorf ...) and the perspective of Japan outside Japan. To this aim, I will start with the following question: are we talking in both cases of the *same* Japan? In fact, the ontological status conferred to the geographical and social entity known as "Japan" as well as to its members changes according to the perspective chosen. Let us study them briefly.

What is the perspective of *the Japanese in France?* Generally speaking, a researcher who studies a migrant population amid a global society is interested in the processes of negotiating and interacting established between the two parties, a sociological, economic, psychological process ending – or not – with the assimilation or integration of one by the other. To this end, the researcher will of course observe and list the cultural (norms and values) and social (family, village, and so on) resources that the mother society transmits to the migrating population. But the model frame for this research will most of the time be the host society: on the cognitive level, it constitutes what could be defined, as by Geertz (1988), as the "here" of the researcher – who belongs, as a citizen or scholar, to the global society, be it French, American, or other. The classic use of notions such as the *ethnic group* or *minority* shows clearly that the immigrants embody an "elsewhere" and are studied according to the norms of the host society. Hence, the Japanese are conceived so to speak in a restricted way: the researcher does not want to contribute to a global definition of *nipponity* but to understand the precise way in which the Japanese settle in the host society. There is thus schematically an opposition between the "here" of the researcher and the "elsewhere" embodied by Japan and its migrating population, the Us and Not-Us in the words of Geertz. In this sense, the fundamental attitude adopted is the posture of the sociologist whose task, in its traditional definition, consists of exploring the modern universe in which the researcher is implied. To be more precise, the perspective of *the Japanese in the society X*, frequently endorsed by non-Japanese searchers or by searchers of Japanese origin living in the host society, is inscribed in the paradigm developed by the sociology of migration. It is an inductive approach: the aim is to understand the observed facts. The culture of the mother society, perceived as an independent variable, is referred to as an explanation factor. This perspective, for obvious epistemological and theoretical reasons, is not therefore centered on the understanding of Japanese society and culture, even if the use of the word *Japanese* by the researcher or actors is an implicit reference to Japan as a geographical and social entity.[2]

Let us consider the example of France. As is well known, in the Western world, this country has been, with the United States, the most concerned by the migration phenomenon since the mid-nineteenth century (Noiriel 1988; Horowitz and Noiriel 1992). Speaking *in France* of the Japanese living on French territory is like considering them, for historical and political reasons, as foreigners, even immigrants. To gauge the presence of the other, the unit of measure has long been, politically or academically, the republican values that are the base of the French nation-state. The resulting key concept, still valid although in a more and more controversial way, is that of integration (the use of the concept of ethnicity, which does not exist in the common language, is just beginning to appear in the French academic world) (Schnapper 1991; Brubaker 1993; Martiniello 1995; Streiff-Fenart 1997). The political debate about the Republic and the universalist values born of the philosophy of the Enlightenment is all the more intense as the various institutions – including education and the military – that have allowed France to become a modern, integrated, and integrative society (in the Durkheimian sense) are now confronted with a reality in constant evolution as the globalization of trade and the European construction challenge the borders, in space as well as in the mind, that used to define the limits of what could be called the French identity (Wiewiorka 1996; Derrida 1997). Obviously, speaking of the Japanese in France in such a context leads us to consider them as representatives of the "over there," but taken in their relation to the French "here." If it is admitted that the classic repartition of the themes between anthropology and sociology is achieved along the divide between here and there, then the question of the Japanese in France would be inscribed in a sociological approach. However, one question remains to be answered: is it possible not to consider the double relation, the one that links the migrants to their mother society but also that which links the researcher to the latter?

Conversely, is it possible to consider the perspective of *Japan outside Japan* – a perspective that I would define as anthropological – without any reference to the specific historical, political, cultural context of the country hosting the Japanese immigrants? Traditionally, the study of the Japanese universe expanding outside the archipelago was part of a broader interrogation about the nature of Japanese society and its members; the Japanese outside Japan were invoked as witnesses of a nipponity shared by all Japanese. It was a well-known characteristic approach of the school of thought known as *Nihonjinron* and of its initiator, the author Ruth Benedict. Her work, *The Chrysanthemum and the Sword,* is typical of an approach giving, on the cognitive and methodological level, the same ontological status to the Japanese of the outside as to those of the inside – probably involuntarily, the war having prevented her from going to Japan. Without going into details, it can be postulated that Japanese authors inscribed in the nippological paradigm have subsequently adopted the same approach, characterized by the absence of homology between the oppositions outside Japanese/inside Japanese and Us/Not-Us. Japan outside Japan is not elsewhere, it is a part of Us – a concept on which is based the reflection of Chie Nakane (1972), for instance, who, through a reflection on the overseas Japanese, tries to isolate the anthropological specificities of Japanese culture. On the epistemological level, the second perspective is therefore not a simple inversion of the first, the Us becoming the Not-Us and vice versa: the nippological perspective as a vernacular anthropological theory developed by non-Westerners such as the Japanese ignores the Not-Us. But it has to be admitted that *Japan outside Japan* – when one takes into account the people and not the objects – does not evoke an unreal place free of any alterity: if this Japan outside Japan exists, it is necessarily situated in the world such as we know it today, inside nation-states such as France, Thailand, Brazil, and so on. According to the chosen perspective, the view of Japan and the Japanese will be radically different. While the migration sociology universally underlines the high adaptability of the Japanese migrants (which compromises the survival of Japanese communities in the United States or Brazil), the second perspective insists on the inability of the Japanese to manage what is different because of the specificity of their culture. To judge Japan outside Japan according to Japanese society is a position clearly linked to cultural anthropology. It has but rarely taken into account the concrete situations of interaction between the migrating population and its host societies. Consequently, the analysis of the social–political frames of the host society that determine the margin of action of the immigrant has often been ignored.

We can undoubtedly say that, in the study of the Japanese living outside the archipelago, there was some mutual blindness that was proof of the development of different fields with their own problematics. Should we try to fill in the gap between these two perspectives? If the answer is yes, then how? I do not want to elude these questions, but, in a way, they are obsolete.

The evolution of modern societies has rendered inoperative any shift toward one or the other perspective, for the development of distinctive paradigms is closely related to the state of the world that they want to understand. The foundations of the normal anthropological approach have been shaken by the transformations – decolonization, industrialization, urbanization, and so on – touching the countries that were the traditional territory of the anthropologist as well as by the mutation of scientific description and explanation: according to Geertz (1988: 131), "things are less simple on both sides of the anthropological equation: on the side of the presence there and on the side of the presence here." The distinction between here and there is thus blurred: as Augé writes, none will today contest the fact that, on the Western side, "the death of exotism is the essential characteristics of our actuality" (Augé 1994: 10). This is also true of sociology: do societies still exist that can conceive themselves only in the frame of the nation-state used by the sociologists? It is also usual to say that the concepts built to analyze the industrialized countries cannot account anymore for the complexity of the modern world: the here that interests the sociologist has ceased to be a space whose limits are accurately determined by its traditional, institutional, ideological, or political borders. More than ever, the here is porous. Any deterministic view dominating the social element as envisioned by Durkheim must more and more be completed by an approach considering the meaning that individuals of various origins give to their acts. Because of the growing imbrication of diverse universes, whether in traditional or modern societies, the opposition Us/Not-Us is day after day more problematic – notwithstanding that the Us refers to a sense of belonging of the individuals studied or of the researcher.

It must be added that, on the Japanese side, the myth of the uniqueness of the Japanese people and of the specificity of Japanese culture and social organization is toppled by the social, economic, and political constraints weighing on the modern Japanese society as well as by the advances of the research in social studies.[3] The Japanese identity is now multiple, fragmented, fragile, constantly renegotiated (Yatabe 1996). The society does not offer any global definition anymore of what the typical Japanese should be; it is as if the Japanese of the inside, because of their discrepancy compared with the classic view of nipponity as group oriented, centered on the rural community and consensus minded, were joining those of the outside.[4]

Be it in France or in Japan, elsewhere is not an absolute elsewhere anymore, and here is not this inviolate place where territory, history, culture, language, and institution fit harmoniously together. It is in this context, which is ours today, that one must consider the subject of the Japanese living both inside and outside Japan. The Japanese living in France seem to be ideal–typical, in their approach to the French society, of a population occupying an in-between space where the boundary between here and there becomes problematic – in other words, a population still relatively impervious to the dominant political ideology of the host society but without creating an enclave maintaining and reproducing the cultural orthodoxy of the mother country. In the following sections, I will first briefly recall the characteristics of this Japanese presence in France; based upon this particular case, I will then try to suggest some paths to follow for the articulation between globalization and Japan outside Japan.

A cultural migration

Compared with other types of migration, especially the classic economic migration (the Japanese in Brazil or in the United States; the Poles, Portuguese, or Algerians in France; the Turks in Germany, for instance), the Japanese migration in France is characterized by the following points: it is *cultural, individual, temporary*. One must emphasize that if we view these characteristics as the constitutive elements of a new type of migration typical of the modern era in which we witness the emergence of what Lévy (1996) called the "globalized" class, nonetheless they initially plunge their roots in a particular history, the history of Franco-Japanese relations.

If France has been since the mid-nineteenth century a demographic depression zone toward which converged important migratory flows, first from neighboring countries and then from more distant lands (including China), the Japanese migration has remained outside its sphere of attraction. This might be explained in two ways:

1   Macrosociological conditions have impeded the incoming of Japanese economic immigrants. Unlike immigration to the countries of the New World, immigration in France in the last century was not a settlement migration (it is therefore no surprise that no Japanese are to be found in the rural zones). The issue for France was its industrialization. Japan, unlike China and Indochina, had been spared by colonization and could not serve as a manpower reserve. What is of equal importance is that the Japanese leaders of the Meiji era could not let men whose respectability and civility they doubted leave and settle in a country symbolizing Civilization (see Wakatsuki 1979: 49). Consequently, the Japanese sojourned in the model countries – England, Germany, France – and migrated elsewhere. This opposition was matched on the administrative level by a difference in status (some obtained the privileged status of *hi imin*, "nonmigrants," the others being considered as *imin*, "migrants"). This difference in itself was a reminder of distinctive social origins. A hierarchy was thus set in place: on one side, the people contributing to the modernization of Japan; on the other, the people left aside by the social earthquake of the Meiji Restoration of 1868. And Europe did not host the latter.

2   It must be added that France very soon ceased to be a social model for Japan after 1868. The first decades of the Meiji era corresponded to a period during which Japan detached itself from the French example – which prevailed in the last years of the Tokugawa – to follow the way shown by Bismarck's Prussia. Of the two opposed concepts structuring the social and state vision in nineteenth-century Europe – French universalism and German romanticism – the latter was able to answer the question of the necessary reformulation of the national identity, a prior condition to the construction of the modern state. On the ideological

level, Herder prevailed over the Enlightenment, whereas on the political and economic level the constitution of a military–industrial oligarchy under the aegis of the emperor was seen as a primary necessity. Thus France, which Japan did not want to admit as a promoter of a universalist and Jacobin conception of society, was turned into the country of Culture.

This image of France – and of Paris as its capital – as a vector of the Western culture deeply influenced the nature of the Japanese migration (as it influenced the American migration, for instance). It is true that various statistics dating back to the Roaring Twenties show the presence of professions other than intellectuals and artists, such as workers and servants. Moreover, today, the impact of the French culture is not what it used to be (except, probably, in the field of social studies). But on a heuristic level, it is probably not false to consider this migration to be "cultural," as opposed to the economic or political migration. It embodies a type of migratory movement based on a distance to need, the need to leave the mother country as well as the need to settle in the host society. The other characteristics of this migration find their origin in this almost scholastic distance, in the sense given to it by Bourdieu (1997), from the material constraints of day-to-day life.

An individual and temporary migration

Contrary to the Japanese migration to the United States or Brazil, the act of leaving did not need a strong collective mobilization, be it at the local or the national level. It remained a mostly individual endeavor, and the coming of the migrant to France had a double motivation: the exploration of the individual's own subjective universe, of personal interiority through a confrontation with the Western way of thinking – this has especially been true between the wars, with a massive arrival of Japanese painters and intellectuals in the French capital, and also after the last war, notably in the years of Sartrian existentialism – and the assimilation of Western knowledge and know-how. The migration can also be considered as individual inasmuch as – once in Paris, the one and only destination of the Japanese – they did not organize themselves in communities, as can be observed in San Francisco or Sao Paulo. No physical safety airlock was created to maintain a link between the mother country and the host society. This lack is of course the result, on one side, of the urban organization of the French capital – sustained by republican logic, which prevents ethnic regrouping – and on the other side of the sociological profile of the migrants and their motivations.

The almost general refusal to get involved and participate in the French artistic or intellectual domains must also be noted; the French experience is above all implicitly or explicitly taken as cultural capital that must be converted into social capital once back in Japan – hence the essentially temporary nature of the original migration.

Table 2.1 How the French feel about the non-French (*n* = 350; percentages).

Country or region	Positive feeling	Indifference	Negative feeling	No idea	No answer	Total
Spain	74.0 ·	17.7	4.0	4.0	0.3	100
Italy	72.3	12.6	12.6	2.3	0.3	100
Africa	68.3	10.6	18.0	2.9	0.3	100
China	68.0	11.7	13.7	6.0	0.6	100
United States	58.9	16.6	19.4	4.9	0.3	100
Japan	*58.3*	*18.0*	*16.6*	*6.9*	*0.3*	*100*
United Kingdom	52.6	30.3	12.9	4.0	0.3	100
Vietnam	51.4	18.9	19.7	8.9	1.1	100
Morocco	45.1	19.7	30.9	4.0	0.3	100
Germany	40.6	31.1	24.3	3.7	0.3	100
Russia	40.6	17.7	34.0	7.1	1.1	100
Israel	38.0	18.9	32.9	10.0	0.3	100
Algeria	13.7	8.3	74.0	3.7	0.3	100

It can be said that this model elaborated during 50 years (from the 1870s to the 1930s) has enduringly determined the shape of the Japanese migration in France. The break during World War II has not modified its basic principles. One of the consequences of the cultural, individual, and temporary migration is the weak Japanese presence in terms of numbers.

For a decade or so, the number of the Japanese in France has been estimated at 20,000–30,000 people. According to official statistics, the total number of residents has stabilized and even decreased in Paris. According to data communicated by the Japanese embassy, 20,060 Japanese lived in France in 1996, of whom 9,012 lived in Paris. As a host country for Japanese residents, France was tenth in 1996, far behind the United Kingdom (which has 55,372 Japanese, a total that places the United Kingdom third, after the United States and Brazil) and Germany (eighth, 24,117) and also behind Singapore (25,355) and Thailand (23,292) (Japanese Ministry of Foreign Affairs 1997). Moreover, according to the census of 1990, 3.6 million foreigners (people living in France without French nationality, whether they were born in France or not) live in France (6.4 percent of the overall population). The number of immigrants (people living in France without being born there, with or without French nationality according to the French definition) is 4.13 million, of whom 1.29 million have French nationality.

According to these data, the Japanese population in France is demographically speaking almost negligible. One can talk of an *objective invisibility* amid the host society because of this small number. But its *social invisibility* should also be stressed. Unlike other migrant populations, notably of Maghrebian origins, the Japanese in France do not create an event – as if by some sort of social magic, to quote Marcel Mauss, they had become transparent. And it should probably be added that if the Japanese are transparent for the French then the reverse is also true: the French, for the

Japanese living in France, are so to speak invisible. In other words, the French and Japanese identities are not defined according to one another. They do not constitute poles of attraction or repulsion according to which they must take a position.

Thus, on the French side, the Japanese are perceived neither as foreign bodies mining the French social tissue from the inside nor as individuals especially near them. Being the object neither of love nor of hatred, they seem to take in the French imagination a place similar to that of the Americans on the sympathy scale (behind the Latin peoples, the Africans, and the Chinese but before the British and the Germans), and to that of the Chinese when speaking about outmarriages (after the Europeans and the Americans, but before people from Third World countries and Israel). Table 2.1 outlines French views of other nationalities in general, and Table 2.2 presents French views of outmarriages.[5]

As to the Japanese living in France, 42.5 percent think that the French have a favorable attitude toward them, 31.7 percent think they arouse indifference, and only 25.8 percent speak of hostility (Table 2.3). The idea of outmarriage is accepted by 47.6 percent (Table 2.4). Moreover, Japanese nationals, despite an obviously different phenotype, are rarely victims of discrimination, wherever they are (Table 2.5) – an experience quite different from that of the West Indian, Maghrebian, or African populations living in France (see Yatabe 1992).

Why this relative invisibility, which is notably explained by the absence of any discriminatory behavior of the French toward the Japanese? It might have many interconnected grounds.

1　In my opinion, the first reason is of a *macrosocial* order and is related to the relations between France and Japan as states. As has been previously

Table 2.2 What the French think about marriage (*n* = 350; percentages).

Country or region	For	Indifferent	Against	No idea	No answer	Total
United States	61.8	28.9	8.3	1.1	0.0	100
Italy	61.4	29.1	8.6	0.9	0.0	100
Spain	61.1	31.7	6.3	0.9	0.0	100
Germany	55.7	29.1	13.7	1.1	0.3	100
United Kingdom	55.1	32.6	11.7	0.6	0.0	100
Japan	*42.0*	*29.1*	*24.3*	*4.6*	*0.0*	*100*
China	40.0	31.1	24.6	4.0	0.3	100
Russia	38.9	28.0	28.0	5.1	0.0	100
Africa	38.6	22.3	35.1	4.0	0.0	100
Vietnam	38.0	31.4	26.6	4.0	0.0	100
Israel	34.3	23.4	38.0	4.3	0.0	100
Morocco	31.1	20.3	44.9	3.7	0.0	100
Algeria	25.7	14.9	54.9	4.6	0.0	100

Table 2.3 How Japanese residents perceive the attitude of the French toward them (*n* = 476; percentages).

Benevolent	Malevolent	Indifferent	Total
42.5	25.8	31.7	100

Table 2.4 How Japanese residents feel about marriage with French people (*n* = 476; percentages).

Highly favorable	Rather favorable	Rather unfavorable	Highly unfavorable	Total
22.2	25.4	42.2	10.2	100

Table 2.5 Discrimination as experienced by Japanese residents (*n* = 476; percentages).

Site	Often	From time to time	Rarely	Never	Total
Office, school	4.7	18.7	33.5	43.1	100
Restaurant	2.4	25.5	39.4	32.7	100
Bar, café	2.4	20.0	40.6	37.0	100
Transport	1.0	13.6	42.6	42.8	100
Street	1.7	16.2	43.8	38.3	100
Shop	4.8	28.3	37.9	29.0	100
Media	8.5	35.1	35.6	20.8	100

emphasized, there was never any relation of dependence between the two. The absence of a colonial past and the economic weight of Japan, which from the 1960s onward imposed itself as an industrial power, contribute to the construction of dispassionate representations. The balance between both national entities in the historico-political or even economic fields (both countries are capitalistic and democratic societies) determines the perception schemes. Everything leads us to believe that the Japanese are first considered to be members of a category coming from a common universe – the modern world. We cannot of course deny the cultural differences, but they intervene only later: the Japanese are not sent back, like the people coming from Maghreb, to an unvanquishable otherness seen as menacing to the host society. It might be said that the Japanese, for the French, are on this side of a primary boundary separating the industrialized from the nonindustrialized countries, the societies giving a meaning to (post)modernity from those being submitted to it.

2   Let me here quote the second reason, as a working hypothesis, linked to the *microsocial* dimension. In my view, it is only possible to really understand the way in which the Japanese and the French interact in France if one undertakes an analysis of the objects as products (industrial or not) of the Japanese society: cameras, television sets, Walkmans, cars, mangas, video games, clothes, karaoke bars ... . The way these objects – "warm" objects, as says Latour – are accepted and inscribe themselves in the day-to-day environment of the French and the way the latter appropriate them and give them a meaning are clearly linked to the way the French accept the Japanese themselves (see Latour 1991).

   The relation to the objects appears to be double. When these objects are taken in the economic dimension, the reference and analysis frame is situated at a relatively vast, most often national, level: one questions their effect on the economy of the country. The values that they are given can conjunctionally be either positive or negative. The period of the speculation bubble, during the second half of the 1980s, is interesting in this regard. Those were the years when Japanese objects, perceived as the materialization of Japanese power menacing local industry, were seen as carrying negative values. These very concrete objects were then turned into symbols of an aggressive and hostile economy (which in turn led to symbolic measures on the part of France, such as the withholding of Japanese video recorders by the customs in Poitiers):[6] through them, the Japanese society and the Japanese in general, taken as a whole, were stigmatized. This economic approach toward Japanese objects teaches us two things. First, it is still part of the nation-state context: it reproduces the oppositions based on the traditional borders. Then, it stipulates that these objects must be translated abstractly into numbers, data, statistics; the evaluation of their danger is the responsibility of the elite, able at first to achieve this transformation (political leaders, managers, economists) and, later, to elaborate and pronounce a normative discourse (media).[7]

   One thing remains to be said: the stigmatization process of the Japanese economy has had no influence on the behavior of the French toward the Japanese living on their territory, according to the experience of the latter; there is a manifest disconnection between discourse and practice. This might be explained by the image of Japan in France, i.e. as an industrial power and civilized country. But it is assuredly not the only explanation: the absence of any discriminatory practice could also be a consequence of the presence of Japanese objects in the domestic space. Studying their concrete role in day-to-day life, one can suppose that these objects are mediators giving access to the most contemporaneous, the most actual present of our world. Or, more precisely, they *are* this modernity. In this regard, they would bear a positive meaning because they take part fully in the construction of a meaningful world; they establish a link with the world. It is today commonplace to say that postindustrial Japanese capitalism heralds a culture that ignores state borders. For the first time in its history, the archipelago is imposing a certain way of understanding reality and the relation to the other, a certain mentality, and a new sociability on the rest of the world. We have been witnessing for a dozen years, in France as elsewhere, the adoption of a Japanese way of life that insists on intimateness, immanence, and imagination; concepts that all tend to reject the Western subject as defined by the philosophy of the Enlightenment. One might regret it, but one thing is sure: far from being on the defensive like France, forced to forge the idea of cultural exception, Japan emits with no second thought the norms and values of a globalized culture.[8] A study undertaken in 1998 among 460 French people living in Paris and its outskirts shows that the possession rate of Japanese objects is as follows: household electrical appliances, 17.8 percent; computer equipment, 18.0 percent; cars, 16.3 percent; audio–video equipment, 68.3 percent. Moreover, 80.4 percent of French people participating in the study expressed their trust in the Japanese brands (for Taiwanese, Korean, Chinese, and Vietnamese brands, the figures are 36.3 percent, 35.7 percent, 23.3 percent, and 12.7 percent respectively).[9] It is therefore possible to suggest the following hypothesis: the French, who use Japanese objects to build their familiar environment, their universe of recognition, do not need to libel the Japanese, once again in the sphere of day-to-day life, as foreign beings because they are in the continuity of the world which these objects offer them. This mediatization through the object would then erase the cultural or phenotypic distance. The invisibility of people would correspond to the visibility of the objects.

3   It must be added that this distance is also strongly attenuated by the characteristics of the migration. There is a strong presence of "managerial migrants" – journalists, high officials, members of the academic world (students, teachers, researchers), and professionals (in a total of 17,052 long-term residents, managerial migrants 39.8 percent, journalists 0.8 percent, high officials 6.1 percent, members of the academic world 35.0 percent, and professionals 8.3 percent):[10] nothing has really changed since the 1920s (apart, paradoxically, from the decrease in the number of students in later years, which probably shows the weakening power of attraction of the French culture). University graduates are more than ever overrepresented (73.6 percent); having specific competencies or hoping to acquire them, coming from an urban environment (almost half of them come from Tokyo and its surroundings) (Yatabe 1992), generally mastering the French language, they are able to adapt to the French urban fabric, especially in Paris, which shows an exemplary concentration of globalization.[11] They thus succeed in finding an immediate correspondence with the French (and also with other foreigners) people they mix with at work, in the university, in public spaces: they share with them a common habitus that relegates ethnic

origin to the background. There is social invisibility because there is a sharing of social habits; there is invisibility because the Japanese do not organize themselves as an ethnic group that wants to affirm its presence and its singularity amid the French society.

When referring to the concept of ethnic boundary (Barth 1969), it appears that it does not isolate the social world of the Japanese in France from the rest of French society. As was said before, French society does not mobilize itself to classify the Japanese in a special category; at the same time, the Japanese do not mobilize to claim a Japanese ethnicity. Lacking a socially constituted and hence visible border clearly showing the Us/Not-Us opposition, one may say that statistically speaking, in terms of trends, *the Japanese make good wanderers:* the macrosocial conditions are met so that, as illustrated in Table 2.6, they can happily move through the French public spaces without being reminded that they are inscribed in a society, a history, and a culture that belong to the French without being prisoners of their cultural and ethnic identity. A great majority of them do not consider themselves to be foreigners.

This does not mean, of course, that all of them are inclined to *wander* – in its primary meaning, to walk quietly through the urban space, and in what I shall define as its metaphorical sense, as a presence in the social world without needing to commit fully to it. Depending on their sociological profile, the Japanese can be positioned in a continuum the ends of which can be represented by the Wanderer – who, having "sacrificed his identity," can be totally present while enjoying the multiple dimensions of his individuality, according to Joseph (1984) – and by the Lost – prisoner of the existential tension and embodying in this way the feeling of being a stranger to the world.[12] Without going into further details, I will simply say that the factors intervening in the positioning of the Japanese between these two poles are more of a sociological order (short- or long-term stay, member or not of the socioeconomic system of the mother countries, arrival at an age implying a stable social status, for instance) than of a cultural one (speaking or not the vernacular language, attached or not to Japanese food, and so on).

I would like to conclude with this idea of the possibility of wandering. The space of this wandering, a concept studied by Benjamin and again by Joseph, is not the one of the polis supposing the intervention of state powers identifying the citizen and the noncitizen. As Joseph (1984: 14) says, the public space, where the wandering takes place, "has two limits, each as terrifying as the other: the terror of identification – the public space is where traitors and translators roam – and the terror of invasion – the public space is both reservation and walls." What is important is that in this space characterized by its accessibility and therefore finding itself on the opposite end of the territory as materialization of a specific history, the experience of

Table 2.6 The feeling of otherness (*n* = 476; percentages).

Situation	Response	Total for category
Does not feel foreign	19.1	
Except when applying for or renewing residence permit	42.4	63.6
Except when applying for or renewing residence permit, and during identity checks	2.1	
Does feel foreign at the office, at school	7.1	
At the office, at school, but also when applying for or renewing residence permit	5.7	
At the office, at school, but also during identity checks	0.2	13.2
At the office, at school, when applying for or renewing residence permit, and during identity checks	0.2	
Does feel foreign in public places	9.5	
In public places, but also when applying for or renewing residence permit	6.5	
In public places, but also during identity checks	0.2	16.4
In public places, when applying for or renewing residence permit, and during identity checks	0.2	
Does feel foreign in public places, at the office, at school	1.9	
But also when applying for or renewing residence permit	1.7	4.0
But also during identity checks	0.4	
Does feel foreign in all circumstances	1.5	1.5
Other	1.3	1.3
Total	100	100

the fluidity of the co-presence, the fragility of the world, the moving and superficial quality of anything social – this experience is possible and precisely defines the wandering. In short, the wandering needs both an urban space out of phase compared with the nation-state space as integrated and integrating entity, as said above, and individuals who know how to enjoy the multiple dimensions of their individuality without letting themselves be enclosed in a monodimensional, especially ethnic, identity.

Thus, running the risk of an extreme schematization (after all, many of the Japanese living in France do not live in Paris), the thema of the Japanese in France can be globally summed up as an encounter between a city, Paris, and a population coming from a society that actively contributes to the meaning of our present. With London and New York, Paris is a "world city," in the words of Ulf Hannerz (1996), which, although submitted to the authority of the French state, outflanks it from all sides; it offers niches that, without being ghettos, allow those who wish it to escape physically and mentally the clout of the globalized society; it imposes itself as much as a mobility and circulation space as an integration space; it also offers these asepticized and marked out spaces that Marc Augé (1992) has defined as "non-place": hotels, restaurants, museums, gardens, underground, and so on, all-purpose places typical of (post)modernity. Cities of this type, with multiple configurations, are perfectly adapted to all the categories of Japanese living here: housewives wishing to remain among themselves, young Japanese women fleeing the constraints of their mother society, young artists looking for new experiences, homosexual musicians able to prosper in a milieu where homosexuality can live in the open, etc. (It must be added that the Japanese in France are able to benefit from the spaces that the city offers them because their status, or when they do not have any confirmed social status the dominant position of Japan as an economic power, allows them to go through the pain of the administrative process to obtain the residence permit – the only time when they are reminded of their condition of foreigners by the power of the state – more easily than immigrants from the Third World.)

Japanese objects construct a recognition universe shared between an increased number of individuals beyond local cultural logic; Paris as a world city frees the individual from the weight of a unidimensional identity; the Japanese society engenders a globalized culture related to its economic power – a globalized culture that, against the traditional image of the *Homo japonicus,* socializes even "abnormal" individuals in Japan. The invisibility of the Japanese in France is the result of this triple element. It may be a characteristic inherent in all forms of temporary migration as a way of moving between highly differentiated societies, with strong industrial capacities, modernity producing, consubstantial to the internationalization of the world. In this sense, their invisibility gives us a clue not only about the nature of Japan outside Japan but also about the United States outside the United States, Germany outside Germany, Sweden outside Sweden, etc. One thing is certain: like the Japanese, and unlike the Maghreb people, the Americans, Germans, or Swedes enjoy in France the same invisibility, the same ability to wander. Might it be the essence, both fluid and complex, of all these "countries in foreign countries" that gives globalization to materiality?

Notes

1 I also wish to thank Raymond Clarinard, without whom this English version would not exist.
2 This position has been explicitly exposed by W. I. Thomas and F. Znaniecki (1988): "Naturally, the type represented by Wladek Wiszniewski is determined in its social content by his social milieu: we cannot properly understand it *without some knowledge* of Polish society in general and of the particular layer of Polish society to which this type belongs" (emphasis added). The sociologists try here to understand Wiszniewski as an individual in a migrating situation; Polish society and the mutation of the rural world intervene as an explanatory factor, not as an element to be explained.
3 I especially mean the new Japanese history as postulated by the historian Y. Amino or the studies of the ethnologist N. Akasaka.
4 A telling proof is how the Japanese public welcomed two writers, Murakami Haruki

and Murakami Ryu. Both authors have created worlds set aside from any reference to "nippological Japan," even if they both have been socialized in Japanese society. Not only are they the first writers to put into words the *possibility* of new sensibilities, unheard of relations to the world and the others, but also, by the immediate welcome that their works enjoyed, they are proof of the *true being* of other Japanese identities as the almost official ones defined by cultural anthropology and imposed by various institutions such as school and enterprises. To me, the career of Murakami Haruki, who has long lived outside Japan while mesmerizing an especially vast audience, is a perfect symbol of the new link between inside Japan, outside Japan, and, more simply, outside. It is an immediate, transversal link, enabled by the rejection of culturalism.

5   Data in Tables 2.1 and 2.2 come from an enquiry undertaken in 1994 that was part of a series of unpublished studies undertaken by students of the Université Lyon–2 under my supervision in the Rhône-Alpes region from 1993 to 1997 on the topic of foreigners and the opinions and attitudes that they evoke in the French population.

6   Note that Poitiers is the town where Charles Martel stopped the Muslim invasion in AD 732.

7   We still remember that France, like the United States, was touched by a "Japan bashing" phenomenon, the apex of which was the famous declaration by the then prime minister, Edith Cresson, who claimed at the beginning of the 1990s that the Japanese were "deceptive ants." Before that, the media had also unleashed a violent campaign with such titles as "Japan, the country to fear," "The killing Japanese," and "Is the devil Japanese?" in the magazines *Le Point* (18 December 1989), *Le Nouvel Observateur* (12 January 1990)and *Valeurs Actuelles* (10 November 1989) respectively. It is therefore not surprising that the media are the only space where the Japanese feel discriminated against (Table 2.5). This situation has evolved at a time when Japan is having doubts about its ability to escape its economic dead end; with the financial crisis that overran Asia in 1997, the media and officials shifted their attacks to the countries of Southeast Asia.

8   Alain Finkielkraut's work (1987) analyzes with extreme acuity the distinction between universalism and globalization. The answer to the question asked by Ulf Hannerz (1996) – are there too many or too few cultures? – is unambiguous: the French philosopher denounces, for the sake of (inevitably French) Culture, the proliferation of cultures leading to a capitulation of the universalist thought.

9   The study was carried out under my supervision by students of Université Paris 7 – Denis Diderot in 1998. The research was centered on the image of the Asians in France. Unpublished material.

10   Japanese Ministry of Foreign Affairs (1997). The percentages also take dependent people into account.

11   It might be said that the concept of "asylum cities" developed by Jacques Derrida as the location of a new cosmopolitanism relies on the proof of the emergence of globalization through the megalopolises.

12   It is among those nearer to the Lost pole that one meets the Japanese victims of the "Paris syndrome" described by Ota (1991).

Bibliography

Augé, M. (1992) *Non-Lieux. Introduction à une Anthropologie de la Surmodernité (Non-places: Introduction to an Anthropology of Supermodernity)*, Paris: Seuil.
—— (1994) *Le Sens des Autres (A Sense for the Other: the Timeliness and Relevance of Anthropology)*, Paris: Fayard.

Barth, F. (ed.) (1969) *Ethnic Groups and Boundaries: The Social Organization of Culture Differences*, London and Oslo: Allen & Unwin and Forgalet.

Bourdieu, P. (1997) *Méditations Pascaliennes (Pascalian Meditations)*, Paris: Seuil.

Brubaker, R. (1993) "De l'immigré au citoyen" (From immigrant to citizen), *Actes de la Recherche en Sciences Sociales* 99: 3–25.

Derrida, J. (1997) *Cosmopolites de Tous les Pays, Encore un Effort (Cosmopolites of All Countries, Keep Going)*, Paris: Galilée.

Finkielkraut, A. (1987) *La Défaite de la Pensée (The Defeat of the Mind)*, Paris: Gallimard.

Geertz, C. (1988) *Works and Lives: The Anthropologist as Author*, Stanford, CA: Stanford University Press.

Hannerz, U. (1996) *Transnational Connections: Culture, People, Places*, London: Routledge.

Horowitz, D. L. and Noiriel, G. (eds) (1992) *Immigrants in Two Democracies: French and American Experience*, New York: New York University Press.

Japanese Ministry of Foreign Affairs (1997) *Annual Report of Statistics on Japanese Nationals Overseas*, Tokyo: Ministry of Foreign Affairs.

Joseph, I. (1984) *Le Passant Considérable (The Considerable Passer-by)*, Paris: Librairie des Méridiens.

Latour, B. (1991) *Nous N'avons Jamais Été Modernes. Essai d'Anthropologie Symétrique (We Have Never Been Modern. An Essay of Symmetrical Anthropology)*, Paris: La Découverte & Syros.

Lévy, J. (1996) *Le Monde pour Cité (The World as City)*, Paris: Hachette.

Martiniello, M. (1995) *L'Ethnicité dans les Sciences Sociales Contemporaines (Ethnicity in Modern Social Sciences)*, Paris: P.U.F.

Nakane, C. (1972) *Tekiyo no joken (Requirements for Adaptation)*, Tokyo: Kodansha.

Noiriel, G. (1988) *Le Creuset Français, Histoire de l'Immigration XIXe–XXe Siècle (The French Melting Pot: A History of Immigration in the Nineteenth and Twentieth Centuries)*, Paris: Seuil.

Ota, H. (1991) *Pari shôkôgun (The Paris Syndrome)*, Tokyo: Toraberu janaru.

Schnapper, D. (1991) *La France de l'Intégration (France and Integration)*, Paris: Gallimard.

Streiff-Fenart, J. (1997) "Les recherches interethniques en France: le renouveau?" (Interethnical research in France: the revival?), *Migrants-Formation* 109: 48–65.

Thomas, W. I. and Znaniecki, F. (1998) *The Polish Peasant in Europe and America* (in French), Paris: Nathan.

Wakatsuki, Y. (1979) "Imin seisaku hyakunenshi" (A hundred years of immigration policy), *Rekishi Koron* 15: 15.

Wiewiorka, M. (ed.) (1996) *Une Société Fragmentée? Le Multiculturalisme en Débat (A Fragmented Society? Arguing Multiculturalism)*, Paris: La Découverte.

Yatabe, K. (1992) "Les Japonais en France. Parcours d'adaptation et ethnicité: dialogue ou autarcie?" (The Japanese in France. Process of adaptation and ethnicity: dialogue or self-sufficiency?), unpublished Ph.D. dissertation, Ecole des Hautes Etudes en Sciences Sociales.

—— (1996) "Identité et altérité dans la société japonaise contemporaine" (Identity and alterity in modern Japanese society), *Bulletin du Centre d'Analyse et de Prévisions, Ministère des Affaires Étrangères* 66: 39–73.

Part III

Organizational transplant

3 Positioning "globalization" at overseas subsidiaries of Japanese multinational corporations

Mitchell W. Sedgwick

Coping with complexity on a large scale

Japan's multinational corporations, especially manufacturers, are experiencing the most intensive global interactions of all Japanese organizations. When we think of keywords relating to "Japan and the world" – for example, financial flows, government and private foreign relations, media, the movement of ideas (including technology transfers), labor, law, families abroad, careers, education – it is difficult to find an arena that is not touched by Japan's multinational corporations. And this is the case for Japan more than any other nation. In the language of political science, it would be written this way: Japan's late-twentieth-century global interactions are dominated by the spread of Japanese capital in a mercantilist form driven by a business–state coalition. In other words, Japanese corporations are the central filter through which "Japan" interacts with the world,[1] collectively surpassing the Japanese state as an actor in international affairs.

Having forwarded their relevance, how is one to treat these grandiose subjects? As a consequence of their scale and enormous complexity, large organizations – and especially multinational corporations – are indeed unwieldy subjects for anthropology, which has traditionally favored the analysis of far more discrete social units. We might choose to derive analytical comfort, then, by treating events unfolding at overseas subsidiaries of Japanese multinational corporations as windows onto specific day-to-day concerns in a complex social field. That would allow us to generate insights into, say, individual or group strategies for coping with organizational life, such as localizing or scaling down information that is potentially generated from a vast range of sources to a more familiar and manageable level.

This chapter, however, moves in quite a different analytical direction. It focuses on the meanings implied by the fact of complexity in Japanese multinational corporations. The analysis here applies generally to large Japanese multinational corporations. However, the specific organizations that are the subjects of this study are first-tier, global-scale Japanese manufacturers – indeed "household names" in electronics and motor vehicles. They have for decades been closely watched as gauges of Japan's economy and are viewed as leaders in engendering and innovating "typical" Japanese corporate practices.[2] I conducted fieldwork at the headquarters of some of these corporations in Japan in 1991–2, at subsidiaries in Thailand in 1992–4, and at subsidiaries in France in 1996–7.[3] The context engaged, then, is the globalizing processes within these firms which, in a very short period of time, have required a formal acknowledgment by the firms themselves of increased organizational complexity. The subject matters are the ideas, the experiences, and the conflicts surrounding globalization for Japanese managers in Japanese subsidiaries abroad. The goal is to stimulate thinking about "globalization" as a complex process in general, and one with which the analytical experience of anthropologists remains relatively limited.

Anthropology has, I think, acknowledged that "our" contemporary "villages" are substantively influenced by global phenomena. Typical of an early stage of interest, however, we are caught up in identifying the effects of globalization in the communities that we study; we are naming rather than analyzing. The so-called *macroanthropology*, which takes on board global phenomena, is less proficient, so far, in dealing with the by-now typical social arenas – which are increasingly the sites of field research – "where diversity ... gets organized" (Hannerz 1989: 365).[4] This chapter is an attempt from within a particular social field to explore how "globalization" is used, both by laypersons and academics, to explain such global complexities.

The political economy of Japan's globalization

The spreading in time, space, and quantity of Japanese "economic" exchanges has led to a proliferation in Japan of the term "internationalization," and later "globalization," in domestic economic, political, and social arenas.[5] By the late 1980s, with Japan's global economic work already in full blossom, Japan needed to tell the world and, more important, itself a story about its newly achieved worldwide influence. With significant cash reserves in hand, especially following the 1985 revaluation of the yen, the Japanese government became the world's biggest ODA (official development assistance) donor. Japan spread "butter rather than guns" to the developing world via its own bureaucracy and in highly visible, and arguably disproportionate, economic support of the multilateral institutions, especially the International Monetary Fund, the World Bank, and the Asian Development Bank, which always has a Japanese president. These moves coincided with a relative decline in U.S. government commitments to development, and so in filling a gap Japan could position itself as a major player in the "development game" among its North American and Western European peers in the G-7 nations.

At the corporate level, surplus trade figures *vis-à-vis* most of the G-7 – and, except for some OPEC (Organization of Oil-Producing Countries) members, most of the world – explicitly exhibited Japan's relative wealth. By the early 1980s Japanese manufacturers, fearful of trade barriers into G-7 markets, had moved into production abroad, especially in motor vehicles and electronics. The revaluation of the yen in 1985 generated more international political pressures for more investment into these deficit countries. Here we begin to see highly visible investments of Japanese private capital into real estate, Hollywood, and buy-outs of faltering industrial enterprises (such as automobile firms in the United Kingdom and steel firms in the United States), while the Japanese government assisted the U.S. economy by buying a high volume of U.S. treasury notes. Elsewhere, with government development aid behind them, Japanese corporations positioned themselves to benefit from opportunities in rapidly expanding markets, especially in Southeast Asia and China. Thus by providing investment, employment, and development aid, Japanese entities became in a very short time important domestic economic, political, and social players in a large number of foreign countries.

The material manifestations of globalization for businesses of course depend on the business sector under discussion. In Japan's business media, for example, "internationalization" was for a long time an attention-grabbing subject for pundits; it sold newspapers, magazines, and talk shows. Interest in "internationalization" also drove publishers to place more reporters abroad. For its part, manufacturing has the particular characteristic of direct, high-density, and wide-ranging interactions with local environments. In the foreign context, this has meant that compared with other types of Japanese enterprises, such as banks or trading houses, Japanese manufacturers have caught up large numbers of foreigners and local institutions in their globalizing processes.

It is in this context that in the late 1980s a proliferation of terms such as "internationalization" and "globalization" appeared in the slogans of Japanese corporations as well as in the ministerial cajolings of the government and the quasi-governmental organizations affiliated with it. As in government circles, these terms filtered down into Japanese manufacturers as overarching policies, reflecting "goals" for what had in fact already occurred.

The "globalization" of Japanese managers: from the macro to the micro

A hypothetical Japanese manager in a consumer electronics firm on a 5-year posting in a subsidiary abroad experiences globalization at many levels. As suggested above, with his compatriots at home he has been subjected to the rising profile of globalization in the public media. As a matter of corporate ideology, it appears as private media in both headline synopses of the president's thinking on the corporate future as well as data in articles on the corporation's extensive projects abroad. At corporate ceremonies, it appears in a speech delivered by a visiting top manager (a "biggy") from Japan (delivered in English translation to 300 Thai employees on the day shift and their twelve Japanese colleagues) to commemorate production of the 10,000th automobile from a Thai subsidiary. These, then, are examples of macro-globalization as rhetoric in two separate but, of course, complementary arenas – public and corporate.

Meanwhile, his work, which engages the day-to-day consciousness of this Japanese manager at a subsidiary abroad, is thoroughly involved in the cross-systemic and cross-cultural interchanges that are meant to supply the social contents – the daily social interactions, if you like – of the rhetorical vessels called "globalization" or "internationalization." These activities are seldom explored in macro- or official texts. For example, a Japanese manager might engage in analyzing why an assembly line is working inefficiently. He must communicate his findings in a mélange of English, French, and Japanese, by drawings on available sheets of paper and by the physical handling of machines, in which communication within such environments precariously and creatively floats. For example, he is at first surprised to find the office empty of French colleagues for an hour and a half at midday when he finished his lunch in 15 minutes, but over several months he learns to appreciate the slow midday meal he takes about once a week. For example, when he can pull himself together after a 70-hour working week, he studies French at 8:30 A.M. on Saturdays.

Let me surface some of the subtexts in these descriptions of the effects of globalization at this intimate micro-level. On the one hand, I am describing efforts made toward cross-cultural communication. In spite of hierarchical and other relations of power, compromises are made by all involved in the work of generating understandings across cross-cultural boundaries. Anthropologists are professionally, and perhaps as a matter of temperament, style, and experience, familiar with such processes. Japanese managers, however, would suggest that rather than cross-cultural work it is their long hours and their authority over analysis and actions to be taken on the assembly line that provide the essential theme in these descriptions. Although in the organizational chart of the overseas subsidiary Japanese managers are likely to appear as marginal "advisers," their authority is realized. By this I mean not merely legal 49 percent, 51 percent, or 100 percent Japanese ownership of the firm; I mean *de facto* power over the means of production in the broadest sense.

On the ground in subsidiaries abroad, the medium of this "ownership" is in part the functional reach of technical know-how and financial resources, but it is also the psychologically dense descriptions of their work, themselves, and their organization that Japanese managers require to work well. Remuneration enhances commitment, but the motivations of Japanese managers are deeply rooted in the particular visions that they hold of the corporation and their activities within it. Their "corporate culture" holds organizational value – it generates activity at their organization – because it is made personal; they are, indeed, incorporated into the organization.

A range of icons focus their attentions. These include ideas as broad as "their" firm's "Japaneseness," or even their firm as the "most inter-nationalized among Japanese firms," and as specific as personal identification with, and the fetishizing of, the particular machines and products upon which they have labored in the course of their careers. They are likely to be involved in the development of specific work practices surrounding the manufacture or distribution of these products. The attempt to reproduce these practices abroad is focused through the commitment of Japanese managers and engineers to maintain the "product quality" upon which the very survival of the corporation is claimed to depend. As in Japan itself, the Japanese who manage foreign subsidiaries continuously target local employees in their campaigns of "quality control and improvement" in order to create stable, high-quality output. The means are explicitly articulated manufacturing and accounting techniques (quality control circles, just-in-time production, and so on) in addition to an enormous range of unconscious configurations of a Japanese management model that is deployed as a "natural" consequence of Japanese managers' postings abroad as a part of Japanese investment in foreign manufacturing.[6]

The Japanese manager reproduces himself as he participates in his corporate practices in a powerful cycle of activity. He makes every effort to sustain his corporate practices in his sojourn abroad in ways that substantively differ from the experiences of expatriates at non-Japanese multinational corporations in foreign settings (Sedgwick 1999). And I choose the word "sojourn" with precision to convey the experiential quality of an overseas posting as temporary and peripheral to essentially conservative corporate practices that have been experienced over long duration and with great intensity in Japan itself. From the perspective of the Japanese manager, the large Japanese corporation emerges – in Goffman's (1961) sense of an asylum, or a prison, but without the locked gates – as a total institution.[7]

Although the above paragraphs may seem to suggest otherwise, in subsidiaries abroad Japanese managers cannot and do not reproduce the Japanese corporation as it exists in Japan. To conduct business in foreign settings, the technical, financial, and social boundaries of the firm and the individuals who work in it must be permeable to its exterior, foreign environment. This fact, in turn, alters practices interior to the firm. Daily, then, at the subsidiary abroad Japanese managers cope with discontinuities from and therefore challenges to familiar patterns of social behavior, as they cope with sales markets that are structured differently. They build cross-cultural understandings out of frustrations, they get assembly lines to work "almost as well as in Japan," they do business, and they make friends.

The tensions generated in these technical and cross-cultural forms of work reflect inconsistencies between the rhetorics and facts of globalization and other rhetorics and facts of the firm, such as its "corporate culture." These are stresses characteristic of Japanese corporations' participation in global economic processes, which are perhaps captured in the logical contradictions, or at least logical acrobatics, of another of corporate Japan's contemporary slogans: "global localization." Is this slogan, which is targeted for the consumption of both members of the firm and the public at large, meant to convey global homogenization or global heterogeneity? Or is it meant to pique Japanese managers', and our, sense of ambiguity, mystery, exoticism, even irony, about the processes of globalization?

For Japanese managers abroad, globalization is complicated. It plays both within the tangible experience of day-to-day international corporate life and within the abstract metaphors of corporate rhetoric. Globalization competes, furthermore, with other experiences and metaphors within the corporation itself and within the life view of the Japanese manager in a complex constellation unfolding in large organizations and, indeed, throughout his contemporary, modern life.

Positioning globalization

Because of its presence in a wide range of discourses, in this chapter I have focused on globalization as illustrative of the labeling produced to account for some of our experiences of complexity in our times. I fully doubt that I have exhausted the various positions, or the reach, of globalization as experienced by Japanese managers by making explicit its rhetorical usage by the media, government, and the corporation as a phenomenon connoting action as a matter of corporate policy, and as some "thing" occurring in complex and multidimensional ways in the day-to-day individual and organizational life of the subsidiary abroad. It is precisely my point that we generate terms such as "globalization" with meanings as varied, diffuse, multiple, and vague as the phenomenon itself. Eventually, definitions of "globalization" will be made coherent by usage and habit. (Possibly this term will come to occupy a special status as representational of the current epoch.) So domesticated "globalization" will be superseded by other terms meant to account for blurry observation of a new contemporary.

This purposeful allowing of definitional free play to "globalization" is a difficult analytical position to sustain, and is one that I have attempted through a description that is as personal and as nuanced as possible of the Japanese manager's experience abroad. I have taken the risk made explicit by Hannerz (1986: 365) that "[a]ctor-centeredness ... can become another means of avoiding the intellectual confrontation with problems of scale and complexity." I press this approach because more fully abstracted alternatives to a focus on the processes occurring within and generated by actors seem only to provide boxes into which descriptions of global phenomena are categorized; they are lists of what globalization "is." Anthropology's most widely circulated example here is Appadurai's (1990) five "scapes" of global cultural flow: *ideoscapes, ethnoscapes, financescapes, mediascapes,* and *technoscapes.* Such exercises are helpful at the start for defining an analytical field, but their feel is detached and externalized; they seem flat. We gain no sense of how these "scapes" intersect with each other, as they obviously do, how persons move within and between them, nor a sense of what difference it might make to engage such categories at macro- or micro-scales of analysis. I have implicitly argued that such an engagement requires an analysis of the meanings and usages attached to "globalization" by its users, not a listing of what globalization is or is not. Phenomena at this scale and at this level of complexity are best examined through actors' own engagements in varied organizational contexts between their immediate physical and social environment and the "global" environment.

Methodologically this may, and many would argue should, lead to a personalized investigation of some kind, i.e. a method that positions, or at least acknowledges, the investigator as structurally, and so analytically, entangled with his object of study. Although we have been informed – through the "lit crit" movement, structuration theory, and in-depth debate in anthropology concerning the vicissitudes of fieldwork, its disciplinary core – that avoiding these entanglements is problematic intellectually, and perhaps morally dishonest, nonetheless many analytical risks lurk behind these new analytic opportunities. In particular these exercises require great care to avoid overindulgence, foiled as self-awareness, in which the reader wonders whether the anthropologists ever left, metaphorically, their own campfires. (In this chapter, I have partially deflected these complications through the rhetorical strategy of generating viewpoints on "globalization" from the perspective of another – the Japanese manager.) In making analysis in some form personal, we would seem at least obliged to explore seriously, and to make explicit at the very least to ourselves, the motivations behind the analyses we generate. Personally, I am still waiting to be introduced to someone who is not affected by the complexities generated by processes of globalization. This person would provide a great deal of comparative insight into an analytical problem that I feel is important. However, at most I can only expect to design a project that allows analysis of the conditions under which other persons experience globalization differently from myself.

Japanese managers working in corporate subsidiaries abroad are actors who – like ourselves – may deploy terms such as "globalization" or "internationalization" and "cosmopolitan" or "borderless" to describe the world around them and to explain their lives to themselves. They inject these words with multiple meanings that both overlap with and diverge from our other – academic – usages of such terminologies as abstract categories. With them, the practices of globalization are now inscribed on us to a far more intimate degree than at other times in history. We are all observers of our participation now.

Conclusion

This chapter has focused on the meanings implied by increased structural complexities found in Japanese multinational corporations as a result of their expanding global interactions. I have argued that the term "globalization" is likely to be used by Japanese managers during a posting at a subsidiary abroad to describe macro-experiences (public and pan-corporate) and micro-experiences (day-to-day work and home). For these managers, globalization of the firm competes, meanwhile, with other metaphors, rhetorics, and observed facts of corporate life, such as the firm's "corporate culture." As a result, personal and organizational stresses that I claim as characteristic of participation in global "economic" processes are generated.

The mobilization of the perspective of the actor, in this case the Japanese manager, has been proposed as a valuable means for anthropologists to come to analytical grips with the implications of global processes. The emphasis on the actor has been forwarded as an alternative to current anthropological perspectives, which have for the most part merely provided evidence of global phenomena without analytically accounting for their implications and meanings. In addition I propose that we use reflections on our own global engagements as a resource for exploring the meaning of the global to our subjects of study.

Notes

1 While one does not want to overstate the potential cooperation of the wide range of interests engaged in Japanese business abroad, the argument can be soundly made that these entities represent on a global level a far more unified force than the corporations of any other of its peers in the so-called Group of Seven (G-7) advanced industrial nations.

2 Starting with such "findings" as the use of similar uniforms implying that firm members are unaware of hierarchical divisions, I would be the first to suggest that the conceptual load that the categories "typical Japanese corporate practices," "Japanese manufacturing," and "Japanese techniques" have been asked to carry must be problematized by those who study social relations in industry. This is, indeed, one of the tasks of an ongoing project of which this chapter forms a part.

3 I fully acknowledge the distinctions between these large firms and the diverse set of medium-sized and small Japanese firms that are appropriately forwarded to undermine generalized claims about "Japanese enterprise." For example, it is important to recognize that at its peak fewer than one-third of Japanese employees were beneficiaries of the lifetime employment that is understood to be typical of Japanese firms. As for their forms of internationalization, small- and medium-scale Japanese firms have had related but different and thoroughly interesting histories abroad, none of which will be related here.

   For the classic literature on the organization and management of large-scale private enterprises in modern Japan, see Cole (1971), Dore (1973), Rohlen (1974), Clark (1979), and Abegglen and Stalk (1985).

4 Hannerz's full quote is as follows:

   The macroanthropological project entails a strategic selection of research sites which would take ethnographers to those interfaces where the confrontations, the interpretations and the flowthrough [*sic*] are occurring, between clusters of meaning and ways of managing meaning; in short, the places where diversity gets, in some way and to some degree, organized.

   Hannerz's interests would seem to overlap with Marcus's call for multi-sited ethnography. See Marcus (1995).

5 "Internationalization" is written in Japanese in *katakana* (Japanese's phonetic alphabet for foreign words) and in Chinese characters (as *kokusaika*). "Globalization" (with its derivatives, such as "global" and "globalized") has remained largely a *katakana*-based term when it is not romanized.

6 The model's deployment abroad is a different matter from its "successful" installation. For a treatment of the Japanese model abroad as it relates to shop-floor techniques and managerial communication patterns, see Sedgwick (2000).
7 Large Japanese corporations are, of course, not literally "total institutions" as Goffman defines them; Japanese managers may physically leave them. What I am trying to preserve here is a mental sense of these corporations as all-encompassing. For a Western audience, the image of a "total institution" is the appropriate marker. Our "embodiments" of institutions – how we carry them in or with us – are most successfully described, of course, by Foucault (1963, 1975).

Bibliography

Abegglen, J.C. and Stalk, G., Jr. (1985) *Kaisha: The Japanese Corporation*, Tokyo: Tuttle.

Appadurai, A. (1990) "Disjuncture and difference in the global cultural economy," in M. Featherstone (ed.) *Global Culture: Nationalism, Globalization, and Modernity*, Thousand Oaks, CA: Sage.

Clark, R. (1979) *The Japanese Company*, New Haven, CT: Yale University Press.

Cole, R.E. (1971) *Japanese Blue Collar*, Berkeley: University of California Press.

Dore, R.P. (1973) *British Factory, Japanese Factory*, Berkeley: University of California Press.

Foucault, M. (1963) *Naissance de la Clinique: Une Archeologie du Regard Medical (Birth of the Clinic: An Archaeology from Medical Perspective)*, Paris: Presses Universitaires de France.

—— (1975) *Surveiller et Punir: Naissance de la Prison (Discipline and Punish: The Birth of the Prison)*, Paris: Gallimard.

Goffman, E. (1961) *Asylums: Essays on the Social Situation of Mental Patients and Other Inmates*, New York: Anchor Books.

Hannerz, U. (1986) "Theory in anthropology: small is beautiful? The problem of complex cultures," *Comparative Studies in Society and History* 28: 362–74.

—— (1989) "Culture between center and periphery: toward a macroanthropology," *Ethnos* 54: 200–16.

Marcus, G.E. (1995) "Ethnography in/of the world system: the emergence of multi-sited ethnography," *Annual Review of Anthropology* 24: 95–117.

Rohlen, T.P. (1974) *For Harmony and Strength: Japanese White-Collar Organization in Anthropological Perspective*, Berkeley: University of California Press.

Sedgwick, M.W. (1999) "Do Japanese business practices travel well? Managerial technology transfer to Thailand," in D. J. Encarnation (ed.) *Japanese Multinationals in Asia: Regional Operations in Comparative Perspective*, Oxford: Oxford University Press.

—— (2000) "Japanese manufacturing in Thailand: an anthropology in search of 'efficient, standardized production,'" in I. Reader and M. Soderberg (eds) *Japanese Influences and Presences in Asia*, Richmond, U.K.: Curzon.

4 Japanese businesswomen of Yaohan Hong Kong

Toward a diversified globalization of a Japanese "ethnoscape"

Dixon Heung Wah Wong

In a recent article, Befu and Stalker criticized the current theories of global cultural process on two points.[1] The first is methodological. They complained that these theories are always too general, abstract, and unsupported by solid data (Befu and Stalker 1996: 104). Second, these theories are in fact totalizing the Western experience of globalization without taking into account that the phenomenon of globalization "is not an abstract process, but is deeply embedded in specific context" (Befu and Stalker 1996: 115). They then demonstrated through a detailed, empirical study of the movement and mobility of Japanese businessmen and their families, scholars, tourists, and expatriates into all parts of the world (but mostly the United States) that the globalization of the Japanese ethnoscape did not bring about the homogenization that many theorists of globalization predict. Instead, they conclude:

> The Japanese communities abroad are consistently oriented toward Tokyo, resulting in Japanese "villages" abroad, *whose residents make maintenance of cultural, economic, and political ties with the Tokyo center their foremost concern* … . Thus, the Japanese situation abroad cannot best be understood through the landscape model. At least in the Japanese case, this model does not identify the source and origin of activities within the "scapes." It provides a distribution map that indicates the spread of Sumitomo bank offices or Honda employees, as the case may be, but it fails to indicate *the genesis and heart of the power relationship, Japan, which directs and motivates the activities of daily life in the periphery.*
> (Befu and Stalker 1996: 118, emphasis added)

Following Befu and Stalker, this chapter offers an empirical study of a Japanese ethnoscape of businesswomen: a group of Japanese female employees of a Japanese supermarket chain, Yaohan, who are sent to work in the company's Hong Kong subsidiary. This study suggests that we cannot treat Japanese businessmen or businesswomen as a homogeneous group with the same orientation toward the Tokyo center across industries and across different sizes of companies within the same industry. Such treatment obliterates the specific context in which the motives, intentions, and imaginations of Japanese businesspeople are constructed. Instead, we should pay attention to the position in the corporate world of industries of the company concerned. The position of a company within what Clark (1979: 50) calls the "society of industry" "not only circumscribes the organization and administration of this company but also conditions the way people think of work and the way discipline is imposed upon them." Therefore, in the accounts that follow, I investigate how the marginal position of Yaohan within Japan's retail industry produces the company's recruitment strategies, which – mediated by the domestic trend of internationalization – attract a particular group of Japanese women who take working abroad rather than finding a marriage partner in the workplace as their major personal goal; how the fact that Yaohan as a regional supermarket cannot pay its employees well discourages its female workers from marrying their male counterparts; and how this marginal position drives the company to send some of its female workers overseas to polish their corporate image.

The second part of this chapter focuses on how these female workers react when they come to understand that Yaohan, like other Japanese companies, treats them as transient and auxiliary workers: they adopt one of two orientations – rebellious or defensive toward the company's authority. Which orientation a given Japanese female worker adopts and the concrete strategies she then undertakes are a function of personal interests and other circumstantial factors. However, none of these orientations is directed or motivated by the Tokyo center. Instead, these female workers adopt different strategies to ensure that they will not be sent back to Japan, or they exploit the company's resources to equip themselves to find a better job elsewhere. Moreover, they do not maintain a strong identification with the cultural role of Japanese female workers. Even those who adopt a defensive orientation conform to the cultural role only at a minimal level, and the rebellious female workers do so even less. This study will also point out, however, that the cultural role itself makes both orientations possible. The rebellious orientation that seems to reject the role of a Japanese working woman as a transient and auxiliary worker and the defensive orientation alike serve to reinforce such a role. That is why Befu and Stalker (1996: 118) said, "Traditional cultures are not lost here."

The cultural model of Japanese female workers

Quantitatively sophisticated work on gender stratification in Japan shows that Japanese female workers are not only transient but also auxiliary members of the labor force. First, most of them will begin work in a company upon graduation from school, resign from their company on marriage or childbirth, and then, when the children grow up and no longer need intensive maternal care, rejoin the labor force as part-time workers (Pharr 1990: 63; Hoyt 1991: 139–40; Brinton 1993: 29; Roberts 1994: 23–5).

Second, the majority of female workers are assigned to auxiliary positions. The most prominent example is the "office ladies," young, white-collar female employees who are just helpers in the office, assisting their male colleagues in sharpening pencils, taking messages, photocopying, and distributing memorandums. They, as Smith (1987: 17) points out, are also expected to "provide tea for everyone (in addition to performing other duties) and maintain a demure and pleasant manner toward all."

Ethnographic studies such as Rohlen's (1974) *For Harmony and Strength: Japanese White-Collar Organization in Anthropological Perspective* and McLendon's (1983) "The office: way station or blind alley?" also describe Japanese women in microcircumstances as a unique actualization of the above general image. For example, the new female workers in a general trading company dubbed Yama by McLendon were trained to serve tea at 10 A.M. for the men in their section and at 3 P.M. to serve coffee or tea to guests whenever any visited the section, and to keep the section area clean and neat (McLendon 1983: 166). Yama women were positioned by their female senior strategically around the table so that every man was served by one of them at parties such as *bōnen-kai* and *sōbetsu-kai* (McLendon 1983: 168). Like Yama women, female workers in Rohlen's Ueda Bank were expected to resign when they married; otherwise they had to resist co-workers' pressure. Moreover, getting married was the goal of most of the female workers in both organizations. Some Ueda Bank women openly stated that "for them working is an opportunity to meet young men informally" (Rohlen 1974: 236); Yama women used their company as "a place to find husbands" (McLendon 1983: 159). And the companies hire women with the "right" level of education and beauty for its young company men.

The image of Japanese workers portrayed in these studies, however, is somewhat dated, and also too simple if not downright misleading. Individual female workers are "in exile" in these studies, in which they were described as a unique actualization of the cultural role of transient and auxiliary Japanese female workers. But that would miss the point because individual Japanese women are subject to circumstances and interests that are not included in the cultural roles. In the following sections, I will first situate the Japanese female workers of Yaohan Hong Kong in the interplay among Yaohan's position as a regional supermarket, Yaohan's recruitment strategy, and the domestic trend of internationalization. Then I will show how personal interests together with other circumstantial factors guide the strategies of these female workers within the company.

Differences between supermarkets and department stores

My point of departure is the differences between supermarkets and department stores in Japan. The discussion is needed here because it helps to establish the marginality of Yaohan. Department stores and supermarkets are different in three major ways: the organization of their operations, the number of their outlets, and their social prestige. Supermarkets are self-service operations, with chain-style organization; in other words, they separate merchandising and store operations. Department stores, unlike supermarkets, do not differentiate between these functions (Sato 1978: 232–3). The second characteristic of supermarkets is their large number of outlets. Supermarket chain stores dot residential areas all over Japan. In contrast, major department stores operate far fewer stores. Department stores and supermarkets are also different in social prestige, a status rooted in their histories and in the physical location of their stores (Larke 1994: 169). Department stores, especially those such as Mitsukoshi or Daimaru from the so-called kimono tradition, can boast longer histories than supermarkets, and, in Japanese business generally, a long corporate history tends to be related positively in consumers' minds to quality and prestige. The "goodwill" created and sustained by stores over a long time as a result leads to a good corporate image. According to a 1979 *Nihon Keizai Shinbun* survey on the corporate image of retail companies, of the top twenty companies regarded as the most prestigious retailers, sixteen were department stores (Katayama 1983: 215). Thus, as Larke (1994: 184) notes, supermarket chains "can offer everything that a department store can, except the name and the prestige".

Looking at differences in their business strategies suggests some meaningful connections between the categorical distinctions of prestige and such elements as merchandising policies, prices, locational strategies, clientele, and staff. Department stores in Japan generally locate their stores in the earliest established central business districts and sell expensive luxury merchandise to comparatively wealthy customers; supermarkets build their stores outside the downtown area, close to residential areas, and provide daily necessities for ordinary customers at a low price.

More important, a prestigious department store is more likely than a supermarket to recruit graduates of elite universities. And prestige is an important consideration for the job-hunting university graduate. Moreover, prestigious department stores can offer employees job security, high wages, and a range of benefits. The survey mentioned earlier showed that the ten most popular companies among job-hunting graduates were department stores, while the large supermarkets Daiei and Itō-Yōkadō were ranked seventeenth and eighteenth (Katayama 1983: 225). Although academic ability may not correlate positively with management talents, the differences between the graduates of the best and the worst universities are very marked (Clark 1979: 71–2). In other words, department stores are on average more likely than supermarkets to recruit high-quality employees.

Yaohan as a regional supermarket

Yaohan started as a family business establishment in Atami, a hot-spring resort town 50 miles west of Tokyo, in 1930. At that time, Yaohan was just a village grocery store that delivered groceries to customers in bamboo baskets slung over the ends of a shoulder pole. In 1962, it turned into a modern supermarket and started its chain business. Given the limited capital of the founding family, Yaohan chose to go regional rather than national and established a supermarket chain in the Tōkai region, operating in Shizuoka, Kanagawa, Aichi, and Yamanashi Prefectures and having no stores in Tokyo, Osaka, or Nagoya. Therefore, Yaohan is classified in Japan as a regional rather than as a national supermarket. A national supermarket must, by definition, operate outlets across more than four prefectures and have a network of outlets in two or more of the following cities: Tokyo, Osaka, and Nagoya (*Nikkei Ryūtsū Shinbun* 1993: 2). The Daiei, Seiyu, Itō-Yōkadō, Jusco (Aeon), and Uny groups are several well-known examples of national supermarkets. These companies enjoy a significant share of the market and are invariably on the list of the Big Four in Japan's retail industry. Regional supermarkets are smaller and are less well known.

As a regional supermarket, Yaohan could not compete with national supermarkets. The difference in corporate strength and reputation between the company and national supermarkets has been significant throughout its history. In the 1960s, for example, Daiei recorded sales of ¥100 billion, whereas Yaohan's sales were just ¥3 billion (Wada 1995: 73). Given its tiny market share, Yaohan, not surprisingly, has never been listed among the Top Ten of Japanese retailing. Moreover, although Yaohan had become famous for its success in Southeast Asia in the 1980s, most Japanese living in Tokyo or Osaka were unaware of its existence.

We can see that Yaohan is marginal in two ways. First, it is small in size, has a tiny market share, and operates regionally. More important, just as supermarkets generally are less prestigious than department stores, as a regional supermarket Yaohan has the lowest status within the supermarket category.

Yaohan's arrival in Hong Kong

The marginality of Yaohan is an important background against which the going overseas by the company should be understood. While Yaohan was building its chain stores within the Tōkai region in the 1960s, supermarkets such as Daiei and Seiyu started to go national, establishing stores throughout Japan. This expansion threatened the survival of many regional supermarkets, including Yaohan. However, instead of merging with other regional supermarkets or selling out to a larger firm, the company chose to go overseas. Kazuo Wada, the company chairman, repeatedly stressed that Yaohan should keep its own identity (Ono 1992: 34–6). Most of the employees, including board members, opposed the plan at the time, arguing that the company should concentrate on its domestic market instead of spreading its already limited capital into an unknown market (Itagaki 1990: 105–6). Wada tried to convince his subordinates with Sony's "gap theory." As he recalled:

At that time, the big names in the Japanese distribution circles had developed powerful retail chains yielding a turnover of over ¥100 billion per year. While thinking there would be no other way for Yaohan to survive unless we managed to advance to Tokyo, but faced with the knowledge that we lacked both the capital and staff to do so … . It was at this point that I learnt of the Sony Corporation's "gap theory." … When Messrs Masaru Ibuka and Akio Morita of Sony were repatriated to Japan after World War II and attempted to set up an electrical home appliances company, the leading manufacturers in this field already possessed vast sales networks existing from pre-war times. Sony, perceiving the existence of an "opening gap" in that none of these makers had ever thought of advancing overseas, promptly began to do so, *with the result that the reputation the company acquired in foreign parts was fed back to Japan and enabled them to close the "gap" between them and the existing networks* … . Following this example set by the Sony "gap theory," I then sought to find a way to ensure Yaohan's survival by adopting an overseas advancement strategy.

(Wada 1992: 10–11; emphasis added)

In the end, Wada successfully suppressed the overwhelming opposition from employees and board members and made his first overseas investment in Brazil in the early 1970s (Itagaki 1990: 113–15).

The interesting point here is that, although Yaohan's marginality in Japan's retailing world drove it overseas, Wada's ultimate goal, like Sony's, was to return to Japan with a reputation gained in foreign countries that would enable it to compete with national supermarkets and even department stores. That is to say, Japan was still Wada's reference point, so that, at that time, "going international" was ultimately a means for Yaohan to become more "Japanized." Therefore, although the company was forced to close its Brazil business in the second half of the 1970s, it continued to open stores in other countries.

In 1984, Yaohan established its subsidiary called Yaohan Hong Kong and opened its first store there. This store proved to be so successful that the company decided to expand, and it increased the number of its stores to nine during the next 10 years. In 1990, Wada even moved the company's headquarters to Hong Kong, aiming to use Hong Kong as a base to develop Yaohan from a simple retailer into an international conglomerate by diversifying its business there. A holding company called Yaohan International was established to coordinate the activities of its affiliated companies in twelve countries, develop large-scale projects, and control all domestic and overseas subsidiaries.[2]

Yaohan's staff recruitment strategy

Yaohan's marginality can also account for its recruitment strategy. Yaohan, as a regional supermarket, has a disadvantage in attracting good-quality staff to work for it. The lack of such staff did not constitute a vital problem for the company in the first decade after it had established itself as a modern supermarket, because its operations at that time were moderate in scale. However, as Yaohan internationalized its operations, it needed to recruit good-quality staff who could work in an international business environment. To compete with national supermarkets and department stores, Yaohan offered recruits something that other companies could not provide: opportunities to work abroad.

These opportunities became more desirable in the late 1970s, a period during which *kokusaika* (internationalization), according to Goodman, began to replace *kindaika* (modernization) as a powerful political rhetoric (Goodman 1993: 221). With this change of major political rhetoric in Japanese society, Japanese workers no longer regarded being transferred to an overseas subsidiary as punishment but rather as normal practice and in some companies as a "must" for advancement into senior positions (Ben-Ari 1994: 1). At the same time, a growing number of Japanese women began to leave Japan, seeking job opportunities in the more equal atmosphere of other countries; among them, booming Hong Kong was the biggest draw. Usually, they went to study Cantonese at the Chinese University of Hong Kong or the University of Hong Kong. Having more or less mastered the language, they applied for jobs there. Most of them ended up working in Hong Kong subsidiaries of Japanese companies as "local hires." As local hires, they received no benefits, just a monthly salary, which in 1997 averaged only HK$15,000 for a new hire. Given the expensive housing in Hong Kong and that they have to pay for their medical care and other necessities, the life of local hires is very tough.

For those who are unwilling or who are unable to withstand such a tough life, joining a company that may one day transfer them to work in its overseas subsidiaries as *kaigai shukkōsha* (overseas transferees) constitutes an attractive alternative. An overseas transferee enjoys an extensive range of benefits (Wong 1996: 203–12) and is thus able to have a comfortable life. Therefore, it is not surprising that many young Japanese began to seek work with Yaohan; it is equally unsurprising that Yaohan has become attractive to job hunters from elite universities such as Tokyo University, Waseda University, the University of Hiroshima, and so on.

Yaohan's recruitment strategy had an unexpected outcome: those who wanted to work overseas were self-selected to join the company. According to the company magazine, Yaohan recruited 400 new graduates in 1991. Seventy percent of these new graduates said that they joined the company because they wanted to go overseas. In other words, Yaohan men and women, in contrast to those described by Befu and Stalker, did not consider upward mobility back home as their ultimate goal; working in foreign countries was the most dominant personal goal of Yaohan's younger employees, both men and women. The lack of interest in upward mobility is reinforced by the position of Yaohan in Japan's retailing world. A regional supermarket such as Yaohan cannot offer high salaries to its employees, and senior positions in the company do not necessarily imply high social status in society. Therefore, upward mobility in Yaohan is not desirable, particularly among its female workers who, in any event, were not given an equal chance to develop their careers inside the company. The goal of these Yaohan women then is to ensure that they are not sent back to Japan but that they remain in Hong Kong to enjoy the comfortable life or to exploit the resources of the company so that they can find a better job or open their own shop.

Yaohan's female employees going overseas

Yaohan transferred the first ten female employees to work in its overseas subsidiaries in 1990. Five of them were sent to Hong Kong. Of these five female employees, Numaguchi and Kondo were assigned to work at Yaohan Hong Kong; Miwa, Oda, and Sawada were assigned to Yaohan International.[3]

According to them, they were very happy when they learned that they had been chosen to be sent to work in Hong Kong, inasmuch as working overseas was their major reason for joining the company. For example, Numaguchi told me that she had dreamed about going overseas since she was a child. Her father was a journalist who went overseas very often. Every time her father returned to Japan, Numaguchi, recalled, he told her something interesting about foreign countries. Moreover, her father had many travel books on his shelves, and Numaguchi had read some of them. When she went to university, she chose Chinese language as her major subject, and she traveled around China during the summer vacations. Upon graduation, she started looking for a job. The only criterion, according to Numaguchi, was that the job should offer her a chance to work overseas. She knew from company information books that Yaohan was active in overseas operations. Numaguchi later attended the company's recruitment talk. She told me that at that time she decided to join the company because she was convinced by the recruitment officer that the company did not discriminate against female employees and that she would be given an equal chance to develop her career within the company. More important, she might be sent to work overseas along with her male colleagues.

Numaguchi did not use Yaohan as a place to find a husband. In fact, she did not put marriage as her first priority. This can be partially accounted for by Yaohan's position in the retail industry: getting married to an employee of a regional supermarket such as Yaohan does not necessarily provide a woman with a financially comfortable life. Thus, a female employee will probably place the opportunity to work abroad higher than her search for a husband. Therefore, Numaguchi did not hesitate to accept the transfer even though she and her boyfriend, who was also a Yaohan employee, had to live apart. They broke off their relationship after Numaguchi went to Hong Kong.

These five female employees could not escape their fate as women workers, however. When they had worked in Hong Kong for a while, they discovered that they were used by the company as showpieces to boost its corporate image as a fair employer. As mentioned earlier, Yaohan is marginal in Japan's retail business in scale of operation and in social prestige. Expanding its business scale in overseas markets alone could not enhance the company's social status in Japan's corporate world. To get rid of its image as a regional supermarket, Yaohan also had to do something "social." It capitalized on the domestic trend of internationalization by portraying itself as an international conglomerate. Being "international," the company had to show itself as a liberal and thus "modern" employer that treated female employees fairly. One of the most effective means was to send women to work in its overseas subsidiaries. Numaguchi told me that she was often called upon by the company to be interviewed by reporters from Japanese newspapers and magazines.

The company, however, was not serious about providing the women with chances to develop their careers. These women, like their counterparts in other Japanese companies, were assigned to perform "women's work." Sawada and Miwa were used as office ladies in Yaohan International, while Numaguchi and Kondo were assigned to teach local sales clerks Japanese customer-service manners, such as the Japanese ways of wrapping and bowing – typical "women's work." They were never invited to learn how to manage the company. Moreover, the company expected them to quit on marriage, as their male superiors frequently hinted to them.

Response of female workers

These female workers adopted a variety of strategies in this environment.[4] Kondo and Sawada, for example, adopted defensive strategies designed to avoid "mistakes" that might cost them their jobs in Hong Kong. They understood clearly after coming to work in Yaohan Hong Kong that they had no hope of being promoted to senior positions, and they were not interested in developing their careers inside the company; they were also not eager to capitalize on the company's resources to equip themselves with knowledge for future advance either. They enjoyed living in Hong Kong and wanted to stay as long as possible.

With the monthly housing allowance of HK$15,000 in 1992, Kondo and Sawada could live in very comfortable apartments and, as they were still single and did not have family burdens, could lead lives of luxury. Kondo loved the night life of Hong Kong. With a monthly salary of HK$20,000 she could afford to go to discos or bars in the central district of Hong Kong. On the same monthly salary, Sawada traveled a lot, from Southeast Asia to Europe. She was learning to dance the fandango in Hong Kong and even attended a short course in Spain. Then she took up horseback riding, which is an expensive sport in Hong Kong. Kondo moved in with her boyfriend, who is Hong Kong Chinese, although she had not yet decided to marry him. Still, she was unwilling to be sent back to Japan because she and her boyfriend would have to separate. Sawada continued to search for a marriage partner, preferably non-Japanese. In fact, all her boyfriends in Hong Kong were non-Japanese. Thus, Sawada and Kondo adopted defensive strategies to avoid the risk of losing their jobs in Hong Kong, so that they could maintain their pleasant private lives.

The first rule of this defensive posture was to avoid taking risks. "Safe" responses had to be ascertained before venturing to speak out or act. The precise nature of these "safe" responses derived from the cultural roles of Japanese female workers. For example, female employees working in the office were expected to empty wastepaper baskets and ashtrays, clean the tops of their male superiors' desks, and serve them hot tea when they came to the office in the mornings. Moreover, they were usually assigned only clerical work such as typing or making photocopies. Those who adopted defensive orientations met these expectations at a minimal level. Therefore, Sawada and Kondo did not refuse to serve their male superiors tea every morning and did not complain when they were asked to make copies.

The same calculation applied to after-work *tsukiai* (obligatory socializing). As Sawada put it:

> I do not like after-work *tsukiai*, but my superior is a man. Even though he came to Hong Kong with his family, he still feels lonely in Hong Kong. Therefore, he likes to invite me to have a drink with him before going home. If I completely refuse to spend my after-work hours with him, he will become unhappy. However, if I accept his invitation each time, he will take advantage of my kindness. Recently, I have refused his invitations several times and he has started to complain. It is time for me to accept an invitation.

We can see that female employees who adopt this defensive posture want to avoid the potential hazards of obligations imposed by the cultural gender role and simultaneously maintain the goodwill or at least the neutrality of male superiors. Therefore, when her superior introduced his friend to her in the hope that she would go out with him, Kondo, even though she hated the idea, could not show her anger but carefully crafted her response to avoid offending her superior.

Numaguchi undertook a rebellious strategy. She joined the company in the hope of developing her own career. She gradually discovered, however, that she would not be given a chance to advance into the top management; she was treated as a transient worker and expected to quit when she married. Furthermore, when she came to work in Yaohan Hong Kong, she became worried about the future of the company. On one occasion, she told me that she wanted to quit. I suggested that she stay in the company for 2 more years. She said that she was not sure that the company would be "alive" for 2 more years because it had many problems that could not be solved.

Nevertheless, Numaguchi decided to stay in Yaohan Hong Kong, but for no more than 2 or 3 years.

Having decided that, Numaguchi started to change her strategies within the company. She told me several times that she had to maximize her exploitation of the resources of the company to equip herself with knowledge so that she could find a better job or open her own shop. Numaguchi, funded by the company, was the only Japanese employee of Yaohan Hong Kong who attended a local evening commercial school to study business and a language school to learn Cantonese.

More important, although she knew that she would not have the chance to be promoted to the top or even to middle management, she still tried to go as far as the company would let her and sometimes even went beyond the limit. She used several strategies to attain these goals. First, she refused to perform office lady's work such as pouring tea for her male colleagues. Second, she tried to make the company dependent on her by actively searching out the company's operational problems, then pressing the company to solve them, and finally suggesting her own remedies. Once the company recognized that there really were problems in its operations and accepted her proposed solutions, it had to rely heavily on her to implement them.

This reliance of the company on Numaguchi gave her bargaining power when she fought for her own personal goals. For example, in late 1991 Numaguchi worked in several stores for a month and a half to study the company's cashier control procedures. Since she could understand and speak the local language, Numaguchi was able to discover some serious operational problems in the system through interviewing and observing the cashiers' work on the spot. On her return to headquarters in January 1992, Numaguchi wrote a report on the cashier control system and submitted it to the company's president. The president admitted that management would never have discovered these problems if Numaguchi had not carried out her investigation. He then directed her to launch a project to improve the cashier control procedures, and even asked her to write a proposal on this project for the board, which the directors approved.

Right after the project, Numaguchi bargained with the company to let her move out of the company dormitory. Company housing is always considered not only in Japan but also in other countries as one way for companies to interfere in their employees' private lives. For example, people in the former West Germany use the saying "company housing is a lock made of gold" to describe company housing policies (Sataka 1993: 54). This is particularly true in Japan. According to the Minister of Labor's 1971 survey, 95 percent of companies with more than 5,000 employees had company dormitories (Sataka 1993: 54–5). Having a place in a Japanese company dormitory means living under the authority and social pressure of the company for 24 hours a day (Sataka 1993: 54–8). Life in the women's dormitory, according to Lo (1990), is completely regulated. New residents receive a handbook in which rules are prescribed to regulate every aspect of dormitory life in detail (Lo 1990: 51–71).

Yaohan Hong Kong did not have such a handbook, but used employees themselves to monitor each other. All Japanese employees and their families were given company housing, either in company property or in flats rented for them. The director of the Administrative Division decided the location of the dormitory, and in the case of bachelor employees he assigned who would live with whom. As the only two female employees of Yaohan Hong Kong at the time, Numaguchi and Kondo were assigned to live together in Shatin when they first arrived. However, they were not on good terms. Although they lived together for 2 years, they seldom talked to each other except for essential communication such as deciding who should pay the telephone bill. To avoid talking to each other, they never stayed in the living room when both of them were at home. They stayed in their own rooms, each waiting for the other one to go out. Therefore, it is no surprise that Numaguchi did not even realize that Kondo had changed her hair-style when other Japanese employees knew.

This situation continued until the end of February 1992. One day in that month, Kondo came back to the flat at 3:30 A.M. Her return woke Numaguchi up, and she did not fall asleep again until dawn. Numaguchi was very tired and did not go to work that morning. She telephoned me to say that she would come in that afternoon to tell the director that she wanted to move out. She could not live with Kondo any more.

Numaguchi finally talked to the director of the Administrative Division on 2 March 1992. Their conversation as recalled by Numaguchi is very revealing and deserves complete quotation:

Numaguchi: I want to apologize for disturbing you concerning a matter that has no direct relationship with my job in this company. I want to live alone; I do not get on with her any more. For example, I did not meet her for two or three days, and I later found out that she was on a business trip to Japan. And I had no idea!

Director: However, the company wants the two of you to live together so that you will be safe if something happens.

Numaguchi: We are not on good terms; I don't know where she is or what she is doing and I don't care.

Director: If you move out and live alone, the company won't know whether you are working or not.

Numaguchi: However, the local staff will know.

Director: Local staff will not say anything.

Numaguchi: What do you mean "they won't say anything"?

Director: Local staff will not care whether you are working.

Numaguchi: I am sorry but you are wrong; if I even am 5 minutes late, everybody will be worried about me.

Director: It may be true in your case, but who is to say they will worry about other Japanese employees?

Numaguchi: Doesn't this mean that there are some communication problems? However, if it were me, even if Kondo did not go to the company at all and stayed at home every day, I would not report on her to my superiors. As a Japanese, I do not want to ruin my personal relationship with other Japanese so there is no point in reporting her case to my superior, right?

Director: It is very dangerous for a single employee to live alone.

Numaguchi: If one day your wife phones the company to say you are sick and would like to take a rest at home, would the company believe her?

Director: The company would.

Numaguchi: But what if you are actually out playing golf? This could happen whether one is married or a single employee.

Director (angrily)*:*   I would never do that!

Numaguchi: Therefore, it is not sensible to say that no single employee can live alone. If I stay at home all day and do not contact the company, it would be very strange, and the local staff would worry about me. Therefore, there is no problem.

Director: If you live with Kondo, you can keep an eye on each other. If you live alone, the company will not know whether you bring a man to your home or even live with your boyfriend.

Numaguchi: My personal relations have nothing to do with the company, and the time after office hours belongs to me and not to the company. The company should not control me outside office hours. Furthermore, if the company were to interfere in my personal life, it would actually affect my work. You can present the matter for discussion at the directors' meeting, but, whatever the company says, I will move out. If the company agrees to pay my housing allowance that is fine. If the company does not pay my housing, I still will move out even if I have to spend all my salary on rent.

Director: I see, I see. I will think about it.

Numaguchi was later informed that the company had agreed to let her move out and would pay her housing allowance. She moved to Whampoa Garden and lived there alone. Kondo was also allowed to move out and went to live with her boyfriend. Ultimately, Yaohan's management allowed its Japanese employees to rent their own apartments. Instead of providing housing (and thereby controlling who would live with whom), Yaohan provided a housing allowance (HK$15,000 in 1992).

From this conversation, it is evident that management believed that the company had the right to direct the after-hours activities of its employees and that company housing was one of the institutions whereby the company interfered in the private lives of its employees. It is equally evident that Numaguchi was successful not only in moving out of the company flat but also in transforming the meaning of company housing from being a means of company control to being a place for employees to live. Yaohan's right to interfere in its employees' private lives was thus denied, and the positional relation between them changed accordingly. But how could an individual who was fighting for her own interests bring about such changes in the larger structure?

The calculation involved in Numaguchi's bargaining may provide an answer. I asked Numaguchi why she had risked confronting the director. She confessed that, knowing that the president admired her performance in the cashier project, she knew that the company acknowledged her performance and the value of her existence. She had to capitalize on this opportunity to fight for her own interest because she did not know what would happen to her after the cashier project. She had to propose to move out at a time when the company still needed her. If the director did not agree to let her move out, she would resign. If she resigned, the president would interview her, and she would tell him why she resigned. The president might then blame the director for letting a competent employee resign. Therefore, she was confident that the director would let her move out. Numaguchi admitted that if the cashier project had not been carried out, she would not have fought to move out.

Second, Numaguchi also knew that the vice-chairman of Yaohan International liked her. She told me that, at the New Year party held at Yaohan International, the vice-chairman singled her out to greet her when she was standing among other Japanese employees. In front of many other Japanese employees, he praised her work in the Training Section, which had reduced the local staff turnover rate of Yaohan Hong Kong. Numaguchi calculated that if she was rejected by the company, she could turn to the vice-chairman for help and ask him to use his influence to press the management of Yaohan Hong Kong.

The company never expected her, as a female employee, to stay with the company for long, which meant she was not competing with her male colleagues. This made male employees more patient with such a *wagamama* (stubborn) woman even when she did not conform to the social rules. Numaguchi knew that the director of the Administrative Division was especially weak in dealing with female employees, and she capitalized on this cultural perception of female employees to fight for her own interests.

Using similar strategies, Numaguchi successfully occupied positions vested with managerial power. She headed the company's Training Section from 1992 and persuaded her superiors to upgrade the section to a new independent department in 1993. Numaguchi was the first female Japanese department head in Yaohan Hong Kong. And in 1994, she successfully lobbied to establish a new department, the Store Operation's Management Department, to improve the company's operations, which she was allowed to head.

Conclusion

In this chapter, we have seen at the macrolevel how the marginal position of Yaohan has forced the company to adopt a recruitment strategy that emphasizes to potential employees the possibility of being sent to work in overseas countries. We have also shown that this recruitment strategy attracts a group of women who take working abroad rather than finding a marriage partner within the workplace to be their major personal goal under the domestic trend of internationalization. The low wage offered by Yaohan encourages such a personal goal. The marginal position of Yaohan also forces the company to polish its corporate image by sending its female employees abroad. As a Japanese company, however, Yaohan was not serious about providing the women with opportunities to develop their careers; it treated them just as office ladies. In this environment, the women expatriates of Yaohan Hong Kong responded in various ways. I have described at the microlevel two strategies – rebellious and defensive – adopted by the five female expatriates toward the company authority.

There are broader implications here for the globalization of the Japanese ethnoscape. First, none of these Japanese female workers considered Tokyo as their foremost concern. They wanted either to stay in Hong Kong as long as they could to enjoy the comfortable life there (Kondo and Sawada) or to exploit the resources of the company for their own (Numaguchi). The strategies they adopted in the everyday life of Yaohan Hong Kong did not display the attachment to the cultural role of Japanese female workers, either. Instead, Numaguchi refused to be a transient and auxiliary female worker and adopted a rebellious attitude. Kondo and Sawada did make concessions but only to the extent that they conformed to the cultural role of Japanese female workers at a minimal level. Therefore, it can hardly be said that these Japanese female workers maintained a strong identification with the cultural role of Japanese female workers.

Second, no matter which strategies they adopted, these three women engaged in what Burawoy (1979) calls "strategizing subordination." Kondo and Sawada retained their jobs in Hong Kong by meeting the cultural expectations of their male colleagues (notwithstanding at a minimal level); Numaguchi convinced her superior to let her move out by manipulating the cultural role of Japanese women as transient workers. That is to say, even the rebellious Numaguchi affirmed the cultural role because what enabled her to be rebellious is the role itself. The more successful Numaguchi was in fighting for her own interests, the more the role was reinforced. Her success confirms the perception that the cultural role of Japanese women in the workplace provides a power basis even for activities directed at its erosion. It becomes evident that the reproduction of the cultural role of Japanese women within the Japanese workplace is as much a function of efforts directed at its elimination as it is of activities that accept the role. As long as social practice continues to be pursued within the cultural role of Japanese working women, both the defensive and the rebellious strategies will serve to perpetuate the cultural role of Japanese working women. That is why, at a general level, "what one sees is persistent retention of ethnic culture abroad" (Befu and Stalker 1996: 117).

Notes

1 This chapter is a revised version of part of a chapter of my Ph.D. thesis (Wong 1996) submitted to the University of Oxford, which was turned into a book, *Japanese Bosses, Chinese Workers: Power and Control in a Hong Kong Megastore* (Wong 1999). My graduate study at the University of Oxford was funded by a Swire/Cathay Pacific Scholarship (1989–92), Overseas Research Student Awards (1989–92), and the Sasakawa Foundation (1991). I am very much obliged to them. Part of this chapter was published in Japanese under the title "J Sha no honkon kenjihōjin no nihonjin jōsei jugyōin ni tsuite" (About the Japanese female workers of the Hong Kong subsidiary of J company) (Wong 1997: 239–56).
2 The company closed all its overseas subsidiaries at the end of 1997.
3 Fictitious names are used in this paper to refer to the Japanese female workers to protect their identities.
4 Walder (1986) identified two orientations of workers of state enterprises in mainland China toward company authority, active – competitive and passive – defensive, to show the logic behind their calculation. Following Walder, I do a similar analytical operation here. However, readers should be reminded that this classification is not always clear-cut, because these female workers may adjust their behaviors according first to their own desired outcomes and second to their calculation of the possible consequences of certain behaviors in different situations.

Bibliography

Befu, H. and Stalker, N. (1996) "Globalization of Japan: cosmopolitanization or spread of the Japanese village?" in H. Befu (ed.) *Japan Engaging the World: A Century of International Encounter,* Denver, CO: Center for Japanese Studies, Teikyo Loretto Heights University.

Ben-Ari, E. (1994) "Globalization, 'folk models' of the world order, and national identity: Japanese business expatriates in Singapore," photocopied manuscript.

Brinton, M.C. (1993) *Women and the Economic Miracle: Gender and Work in Postwar Japan,* Berkeley: University of California Press.

Burawoy, M. (1979) *Manufacturing Consent,* Berkeley: University of California Press.

Clark, R. (1979) *The Japanese Company,* New Haven, CT: Yale University Press.

Goodman, R. (1993) *Japan's "International Youth": The Emergence of a New Class of Schoolchildren,* Oxford: Clarendon Press.

Hoyt, E.P. (1991) *The New Japanese: A Complacent People in a Corrupt Society,* London: Robert Hale.

Itagaki, H. (1990) *Yaohan,* Tokyo: Paru.

Katayama, M. (1983) *Isetan 100 nen no shohō (The Isetan Way of Doing Business in One Hundred Years),* Tokyo: Hyogensha.

Larke, R. (1994) *Japanese Retailing,* London: Routledge.

Lo, J. (1990) *Office Ladies/Factory Women: Life and Work at a Japanese Company,* Armonk, NY: Sharpe.

McLendon, J. (1983) "The office: way station or blind alley?" in D. W. Plath (ed.) *Work and Lifecourse in Japan,* New York: State University of New York Press.

Nikkei Ryūtsū Shinbun (1993) "Chōsahōhō" (The Research Method), *Nikkei Ryūtsū Shinbun* (Tokyo) 29 June: 2.

Ono, H. (1992) *Naze Yaohan no kourishōbō dake ga kaigai de seikō suru no ka? (Why Does Only Yaohan's Way of Doing Retailing Business Succeed Overseas?),* Tokyo: Asuka.

Pharr, J.S. (1990) *Losing Face: Status Politics in Japan*, Berkeley: University of California Press.

Roberts, G.S. (1994) *Staying on the Line: Blue-Collar Women in Contemporary Japan*, Honolulu: University of Hawaii Press.

Rohlen, T.P. (1974) *For Harmony and Strength: Japanese White-Collar Organization in Anthropological Perspective*, Berkeley: University of California Press.

Sataka, M. (1993) *Kigyōgenron (A Theory of Corporations)*, Tokyo: Shakai Shiso Sha.

Sato, H. (1978) *Nihon no ryūtsūkiko (Japanese Distributive Machinery)*, Tokyo: Yuhikaku.

Smith, R.J. (1987) "Gender inequality in contemporary Japan," *Journal of Japanese Studies* 13: 1–26.

Wada, K. (1992) *Yaohan's Global Strategy: The Twenty-First Century Is the Era of Asia*, Hong Kong: Capital Communication.

—— (1995) *Yaohan chūgoku te katsu senryaku (Yaohan's Winning Strategy in China)*, Tokyo: TBS Buritanika.

Walder, A.G. (1986) *Communist Neo-traditionalism: Work and Authority in Chinese Industry*, Berkeley: University of California Press.

Wong, H.W. (1996) "An anthropological study of a Japanese supermarket in Hong Kong," unpublished Ph.D. dissertation, University of Oxford.

—— (1997) "J Sha no honkon kenjihōjin no nihonjin jōsei jugyōin ni tsuite" (About the Japanese female workers of the Hong Kong subsidiary of J company), in H. Nakamaki and H. Kōichirō (eds) *Keiei Jinruigaku Koto Hajime (Toward an Anthropology of Administration)*, Osaka: Oriental Publisher.

—— (1999) *Japanese Bosses, Chinese Workers: Power and Control in a Hong Kong Megastore*, Surrey, U.K.: Curzon.

5 Neverland lost

Judo cultures in Austria, Japan, and elsewhere struggling for cultural hegemony

Sabine Frühstück and Wolfram Manzenreiter

In the past, judo,[1] along with other oriental martial arts, has not been thought worthy of investigation by scholars in the field of Japanese studies.[2] When thinking about processes of cross-cultural dissemination and about representations of "Japan outside Japan," however, we need to reevaluate Japanese martial arts for their role as culture brokers. Approximately 15,000 Austrians – or 0.2 percent of tiny Austria's total population – along with 2.5 million other Europeans are regularly exposed to ideological, material, and social aspects of Japanese culture when they dress in Japanese-style *judogi*, practice at the local *dôjô*, take part in training sessions framed by the rituals of *o-rei* and *zazen*, and communicate in a jargon abundant with Japanese terms such as *hantei, soto, maitta, hikiwake, tori, kata, shiai,* and the like. The numbers above indicate only the surface of a much larger phenomenon: these 15,000 *jûdôka* are officially registered members of the Austrian Judo Federation (AJF), whose general secretary estimates that there are another 15,000 practitioners who are less interested in membership and the concomitant rights of taking part in official competitions or obtaining *kyû/dan* grades. Furthermore, other Japanese martial arts, such as karate, *kendô, kyûdô, aikidô,* and jujutsu, have many adherents of their own but draw on similar systems of meanings.

Why judo? We decided to focus our analysis on this particular subculture because of its dimensions in terms of size and time span: compared with other combat systems, judo attracts the largest following in Austria as well as everywhere else in the world. In historical perspective, judo is of major importance because the development of oriental martial arts in Austria began with the introduction of technical systems closely related to the now dominant style of kodokan judo. In addition, Kano Jigoro's kodokan judo, developed during the late 1880s, exerted tremendous influence on the codification and interpretation of other major martial arts during the twentieth century.

The success of kodokan judo validated Kano's system. Of course, Kano's personality and the various offices he held – among others, he acted as director of the First High School and of the Tokyo Teacher Seminar *(Tôkyô kôtô shihan gakkô)*, as a high-ranking official of the Ministry of Education, as a member of the Upper House, and as Japan's first member of the International Olympic Committee (IOC) – furthered the system's prosperous development. In general, Kano was highly successful precisely because he managed to arrange judo along the developmental axis of lifelong improvement and within the structural framework of a modern Western sport. In terms of integration, the new cultural space that Kano had opened found appropriate niches in Japan as well as in the Western world.

The diffusion of judo, which was Kano's life mission, has been and still is a complex of perpetuating processes of varying topicality, locality, and directionality. Cultural flow is thus one of the central topics of this paper, which looks into the conditions of cultural transfer, adaptation, and integration. Such processes have been scrutinized by other scholars in terms of deterritorialization, domestication, globalization, creolization or accustomization, thereby assuming a more or less unidirectional development from one point of departure toward a new point of arrival. However, as Hannerz (1992) has argued, the increasing degree of cultural complexity prepares ground for a multidirectional flow with the peripheries changing back to the center. In the case of Austrian judo, the localization of centers and the identification of agency and agents behind the processes will be indispensable prerequisites for analyzing the triangular relationship among Japanese judo, sports, and the Austrian territory.

A second predominant task of this study is to illustrate the internal organization of the Austrian judo subculture. Culture as a system of meaning offers itself for analysis at three levels where cultural representations become highly visible: ideological, material, and social.[3] The ideological dimension of culture refers to entities and processes of the mind; the material dimension of culture is best explained as the various modes and artifacts in which meaning is accessible to the senses; the social dimension is demarcated by the ways in which the cultural inventory of thoughts and things is distributed throughout a community and its social relationships. The macroscopic perspective that we are using is condemned to fail to take all kinds of interpretations, self-imaginations, deviances, and mainstream conformities into consideration. What we want to explore are the ways in which Austrian judo culture is open to interpretation: in a very narrow sense, is judo, despite all its Japanese characteristics and modes, really a representation of Japanese culture? Or is it a "Japan outside Japan"? Or do we rather have to grasp all these "Japanese" entities as detextualized constructs of a transnational culture?

Our exploration begins at a very suggestive landmark of materialized Japanese judo culture. The Matsumae Budo Center (MBC) in Vienna seems to be a miniature version of its big brother in Tokyo, the Budokan. The similarity of the buildings is not limited to architectonic structures but leads far beyond because the Vienna Budo Center was supposed to fulfill the same function as the Budokan in symbolizing the Mecca of martial arts, each on its respective continent.[4] Despite the ambitious and highly personal initiatives of Matsumae Shigeyoshi, former president of the International Federation of Judo, who had the building erected at private expense in 1984, the Vienna

MBC has never been more than marginally significant: it is even situated at the fringe of the city. The local administration contributed only by providing the MBC with a 4-hectare plot of ground for building. By chance, the ground selected for the application is situated in the tenth district of Vienna, a traditional housing center of the labor class. Thus ironically the center-to-be of Austrian judo returned to its roots, as everything had started with the body culture of the working class.

This chapter is structured into three parts, each of which describes a set of developments, processes, and their implications within the framework of cross-cultural transfer and adaptation of judo subculture. The first part focuses on what we term the territorialization of judo culture in the case of Austria, the second describes self-colonization processes, and the third takes up the main steps toward the universalization of judo culture. Although the structure of the chapter suggests a chronological order of these three phases in the history of judo in Austria, it is important to note that the boundaries of each phase are far from being clear-cut and rigidly set. Even more important, developments described in each section of the chapter overlap, and segments of each phase interact with each other. Hence, judo subculture is contextualized in a threefold manner: in Austrian culture and society as a territorial entity, in Japanese culture, and in international judo culture.

Territorialization of Japanese judo culture

The early history of judo (or jujutsu) outside Japan during roughly the first four decades of the twentieth century is best described by the term *territorialization,* which signifies "the extension of judo culture by adding new territory and its naive integration into territorial culture." Territorialization is described as a twofold, multidimensional process rather than a one-dimensional, linear development. First, when judo was introduced to Austria and other European countries, geographical territorialization took place. As will be explained below, the introduction of judo as geographical extension includes a number of different agents and a whole set of activities that were not directly related to each other and that cannot be described as coherent. These activities ranged from the return of the first Austrians who received their jujutsu training in Japan to the visits by Japanese *jûdôka* who came to Austria for judo demonstrations with the explicit aim of making judo known outside Japan, from the foundation of the first jujutsu clubs to the translation and publication of exercise books in the German language.

Second, territorialization of judo involves a significant social side. In the beginning, only very specific segments of Austrian society came into contact with and were interested in judo. Whereas in Japan jujutsu was reinvented during the late nineteenth century mainly for the physical training of upper-class students,[5] Austrian practitioners included policemen, soldiers, and blue-collar workers – social groups that had typically been engaged in boxing or wrestling. Pierre Bourdieu has described the choice of combat sports as characteristic for the lower classes. In demanding both strenuous effort and insensitivity to pain, such sports represent the "instrumental relationship" that the lower classes have with their bodies (Bourdieu 1984: 212–3). Additionally, all early jujutsu practitioners in and outside Japan were male. Although the Kodokan set up a women's department as early as 1923, Austria did not see a female practitioner until 1958, when Edith Felsinger became the first woman to be awarded a *dan*.

Judo was introduced abroad for the first time in 1887. After the turn of the twentieth century, enthusiasm for judo grew increasingly in Europe and America. Not only did the founder, Kano Jigoro (1860–1938), himself give both expositions of the art and guidance in its practice on the occasions of his several trips abroad, but also some of his distinguished disciples were sent overseas from time to time to initiate foreigners into the intricacies of judo. In 1902, Yamashita Yoshiaki, one of Kano's oldest and ablest disciples, went to the United States at the request of President Theodore Roosevelt, while at about the same time Maeda Mitsuyo, another senior member of the Kodokan, traveled to North and South America to teach judo (Tomiki 1956: 4). Uenishi Sadakazu, who had been educated at the Tenshin Shinyô School together with Kano, taught courses at the London Budokai, one of the most important centers for the dissemination of judo, second only to the Budokai in Paris. It was there that Hans Köck – most probably the first Austrian to learn jujutsu – started his training at the beginning of the twentieth century. Later he translated Uenishi's *Textbook of Ju-jutsu as Practised in Japan* (London: Athletic Club, shortly after 1900) and thus published the first and, for a long time, only authentic exercise book in the German language.[6] It is not known when he returned to Austria; the first jujutsu classes in Austria were not held by him but by Karl Bauer from 1912 onwards and were resumed by Bauer's student the quarter inspector Josef Diwischek at the Athletic Sports Club of Vienna. Another pioneer, Franz Sager (also known as Willy Curly), had received his basic education in jujutsu in Japan. Immediately after his return in 1919, he founded Vienna's first jujutsu school, which became known for its distinctive Japanese flair and equipment imported directly from Japan. Roughly at about the same time, two important developments were initiated. First, Sager's student and brother-in-law, Heinz Kowalsky, founded the Vienna Jiu Club. After breaking with Sager, he rose as a central figure of jujutsu in Austria as a result of his successful attempts to introduce jujutsu as a sport for workers in 1924, a year before the Austrian Workers' Sports Club was founded. He organized regular expositions, and the popularity of jujutsu increased significantly. Only 3 years later, the number of workers engaged in jujutsu training within the framework of the Austrian Workers' Sports Club had risen to 2,000. The second important development concerned the recruitment of practitioners from Vienna's police. Bauer's successor as jujutsu instructor at the Athletic Sports Club of Vienna, Josef Diwischek, began to train Viennese policemen and was head instructor of the jujutsu section in the Police Sports Association, which had been founded in 1922. Like his fellow pioneers, he organized a number of promotional expositions, the most spectacular of which was the Jujutsu Revue in 1927 (Gerstl 1994: 39). The constituent assembly in 1929 of both the board and the technical committee of the Federation of Judo and Jujutsu marked a new era of public exposure among Austria's sports organizations.

The 1930s were a crucial period for the development of jujutsu in Austria in three respects. First, jujutsu's popularity increased significantly. Second, the first championships in Austria were held. Third, Kano Jigoro, the founder of kodokan judo, visited Austria. After 1930, Diwischek's student Franz Rautek[7] – *jûdôka*, examiner, and one of the most important jujutsu instructors in Austria before World War II – further contributed to the popularization of jujutsu by giving courses not only for policemen and judicial officers but also for commoners at "people's universities,"[8] and from 1941 onwards at the Sports Department of the University of Vienna. The people's universities devoted themselves to the popularization of science in particular and the mediation of knowledge in general. They boomed during the first three decades of the twentieth century as a result of a quite diverse program of public lectures and recreational courses. Founded in various districts of Vienna, they were open to the general public and especially well received by the less fortunate classes.[9]

In 1931, the First Jujutsu Championship in Austria took place within the framework of the Workers' Olympic Games. Kano Jigoro's visit in 1933 greatly influenced the pioneers of judo in Austria as well as the development of judo as a mass sport after World War II. He came to Vienna on a goodwill tour of Europe. Two Japanese *jûdôka* who accompanied him demonstrated judo methods in Edmund Gabriel's and Otto Klimek's First Austrian Jujutsu Club. Kano gave three talks, one publicly and the other two in the clubhouse. One of the participants clearly recalls the impressive event as follows:

> I remember the year 1933 when Kano and his assistants Kotani and Takasaki were in Vienna very well. His talks and the demonstrations were so convincing that there was no doubt about what was meant by judo. These findings made clear that the few true advocates of this weaponless art in Europe had to completely relearn their lesson and start from the beginning. They put an end to what they had been doing up to then and followed and propagated the new judo system. Since then the followers of judo have increased in a number of modern nations.
>
> (Gerstl 1994: 44, translation by authors)

During his visit to Vienna, Kano awarded the first *dan* to Klimek, then director of the First Austrian Jujutsu Club; he thus became the first Austrian *dan*-holder. Klimek had taken his first steps in judo under the guidance of members of the Japanese embassy. These contacts had enabled and greatly motivated him to support Kano's visit. During the same year, Klimek followed Kano to Berlin, where he received the second *dan* from him. Because he was the highest-ranking Austrian *jûdôka* for a long time, Klimek gained public attention as an expert on martial arts; he continued his efforts to promote jujutsu as a sport for everyone. On 16 June 1937, the Elite Movie Theater advertised a film titled *Dschiu-Dschitsu-Film* with the following words:

> The director of the first Austrian Dschiu-Dschitsuklub, Otto Klimek, succeeded in obtaining this original film, which has never been shown anywhere in Europe before, from the school of *dschudo* (Kodokwan) in order to show it here in Vienna. In his introductory lecture with slides Mr. Klimek will describe the similarities between the Japanese system and wrestling matches that have been practiced for ages in the provinces of this country.
>
> (Gerstl 1994: 52, translation by authors).

The second founder of the Austrian Federation of Judo and Jujutsu, Edmund Gabriel, received his first *dan* during a judo summer school in Frankfurt (Germany) on 12 August 1939, and the second (1948), third (1950), fourth (1953), and fifth (1955) *dan* during similar summer schools in Switzerland from Japanese or Korean instructors.[10] Although there were quite a few Japanese living in and visiting Austria during that period, the contact between them and those who adapted what they perceived as oriental martial arts techniques was limited to individual visits with a few *jûdôka*. The techniques that they taught as jujutsu, however, were closer to wrestling and boxing than to the Japanese judo that had been invented by Kano. Japanese jujutsu of the old school was a synthetic art of fighting and comprised various techniques. When both contestants were empty-handed, they would stand apart and strike, thrust and kick, or grapple with each other and throw, hold, strangle, or crush. Other techniques were used when one was empty-handed and met an opponent armed with a dagger, a sword, a spear, or a club, and still others when both parties were armed. That Austrians held on to these old techniques rather than adopting contemporary judo can be explained by both the lack of Japanese trainers and the lack of knowledge about the ethical and pedagogical principles of judo. The situation changed a great deal as a result of Kano's visit. Immediate expositions of his conception of judo and guidance in its practice on the occasion of his visit to Austria not only affected Austrian trainers and practitioners but also received considerable coverage in Austrian newspapers. There it was explained to Austrian readers that kodokan judo was based on a new educational point of view. Thus certain techniques had been eliminated and a system of training with throwing and holding as its basis had been established. The aim of judo training now was not only to acquire skill in the art but also to cultivate the mind and build up character. And, as in most of the martial arts of Japan, certain elements were worth being handed down and spread among any people at any time either as cultural assets or as a help to national education.[11]

New rules were implemented according to Kano's methods, which had been taught in the Kodokan under the name of judo in contradistinction to jujutsu, which had been taught by different Japanese masters of feudal times. With the completion of the syllabus of kodokan judo, Kano did not simply add another school of weaponless combat systems to the many hundreds established mainly during the Tokugawa period. What he had in mind was the ultimate combination of the best elements that the various classical martial arts had to offer, not for military purposes but for the good of the body, the mind, and the nation. His determination to break with tradition is most subtly indicated by the name he gave to the new art: whereas the former wording of jû*jutsu* stressed the technical aspect, his concept of jûdô integrated the physical activity into a much larger concept of education and self-refinement.[12] To make judo suitable for youth education, he tamed the martial art by stripping off violent and dangerous techniques; he also incorporated a clear-cut grading system and competition rules. The general principles of judo, expressed by the Kodokan motto *seiryoku zenyô* (maximal effect with minimal effort) and *jita kyôei* (mutual welfare and benefit) were to be exercised during training and applied in all aspects of social life.[13]

Former schools relied heavily on learning by observation, but the Kodokan, literally "the school for studying the way," emphasized verbal explanation and rationally arranged patterns of *kata* (training form), *randori* (free sparring), and theory. "The way" is the concept of life itself as is explained in Kano's introductory book, *Judo (Jujutsu)* (Kano 1937: 11–19), published in 1937 by the Japanese Tourist Board in an attempt "to provide foreign tourists with accurate information regarding the various phases of Japan's culture" (Kano 1937: editorial notes). Judo and jujutsu are each composed of two words: *jû* meaning "gentle" or "to give way," *jutsu* "art" or "practice," and *dô* "way" or "principle." Thus, judo means "the way of gentleness" or of "first giving way in order ultimately to gain victory," whereas jujutsu means "the art and practice of judo." Kano further explained that the same principle can be applied to the improvement of the human (read: male) body, making it strong, healthy, and useful, and so constitutes physical education.[14] In fact, he had introduced a principle broad enough to cover the improvement of intellectual and moral power as well as mental and moral education (Tomiki 1956: 15).

Less than a year after the majority of Austrians gladly welcomed Hitler and the incorporation of Austria into the German Reich/Nazi Germany in 1933, the First Austrian Jujutsu Club was renamed Erster Ostmärkischer Judo-Klub (First "Austrian" Judo Club) and incorporated into the Deutscher Reichsbund für Leibesübungen (German Imperial Federation for Physical Training) as a precondition for the participation in German championships such as the First European Judo Championship in Dresden in the same year and the First German Festival for Gymnastics and Sports in Breslau in 1938. At both occasions, the new judo techniques and rules were applied. Although the increasingly critical political situation made it more and more difficult to participate in international championships, a few Austrian *jûdôka* managed to do so. Edmund Gabriel and Alois Feik had to cycle over bumpy roads from Vienna to Budapest to meet the *jûdôka* of the Hungarian club Nemzeti Torna Egylet, which already had a reputation for producing good *jûdôka*. This meeting led to several visits by Hungarian instructors to Austria and to Austrians being invited to Hungary. The first friendly championship took place in Vienna on 7 June 1935 and ended in a draw, 5 to 5. Many attempts to popularize judo in Vienna followed during the same year. On 6 July, Austrian *jûdôka* performed in the presence of the mayor of Vienna and 320 spectators. On 11 August, similar performances attracted up to 600 spectators. By the late 1930s, there were more than 3,500 judo practitioners, and in 1939 – when the first Gau Meisterschaft (regional championship) was held from 18 to 21 April – as many as forty-four instruction books in the German language were on the market. On the basis of this championship, the German sports magazine *Heavy Athletics* ranked Austria's national team ninth after Germany, England, Switzerland, France, Belgium, Norway, Sweden/Denmark, and Estonia/Latvia. Although in Japan the name *jujutsu* had long been superseded by the new name *judo*, it survived in Austria and other European countries for a much longer time. The transcription of jujutsu variously as *yu-yitsu* (used by Köck), *ju-jitsu* or *jiu-jitsu* (used by Sager and Kowalsky), or *dschiu-dschitsu* (used by the Elite Movie Theater) might well be taken as an indicator of how distanced Japanese culture and language were perceived during the first decades of the twentieth century and how little the accurate naming mattered to practitioners. In 1928, jujutsu was still described as "the art of breaking bones" or "the secret art of the samurai" in a book on body culture (Fischer 1928) and it was considered to be "a practical combative method with deadly techniques" rather than a sport.

Self-colonization: seeing the difference

The visit of Kano Jigoro to Vienna and the foundation of the European Judo Federation in the early 1930s initiated a significant change in the self-conceptualization of Austrian judo. With the increasing spread of knowledge about judo history, terminology, techniques, and ideology, sensitivity to authenticity and difference became more refined. As the *jûdôka* had finally found a common framework endowing their activities with complex sets of meaning, they fostered the ideological and organizational separation from jujutsu, the popularity of which rapidly fell behind after the occupation forces legalized martial arts again in 1946. Territoriality remained a significant factor during the following period of reorganization, but with the Kodokan approaching visibility, a new center gained importance.

From a conventional perspective, the Kodokan – which is the name of the art and of the main building of the school as well as of the organization – is the obvious world center of judo. Everything had started there, and if ever a *dôjô* has been regarded as a sacred space then it must have been the Kodokan. The bulky six-story building in Tokyo still attracts hundreds of thousands of visitors each year. Kano's life work is safeguarded by the statutes of every national and international federation declaring to support the organization and dissemination of Kodokan-style judo. In terms of gravity, the Kodokan has never again been so close to the center of judo as it was during the first two decades after the World War II. It did not take great efforts to secure this position. Quite the contrary, the internationally growing consciousness toward a common system of meanings established the arrangement of a "natural order" with the Kodokan in the center.

The underlying attitude might be most appropriately labeled as *self-colonization*. In this context, self-colonization refers to processes of cultural flow in which submission is accepted and even deliberately sought. Indeed, the period when self-colonization was most influential was comparatively short. We start with the discussion of self-colonization in the historical context of postwar history on the basis of two arguments. On one hand, self-colonization was a major thread throughout the immediate postwar history of Austrian judo. On the other hand, it is still a remarkable cause of power distribution between certain parts of the global judo diaspora.

Despite the official ban by the occupation forces, *jûdôka* started again to practice their sport as early as 1945. Resources were scarce, and the lack of equipment challenged the imagination and creativity of the small community. Old flour sacks were used for the *judogi*; wrestling mats had to replace the *tatami* inside the cold, dimly lit training rooms. In 1946 judo clubs joined the Austrian Federation of Sports Involving Strength, a necessary act for participating in regional or national championships. This act of "border crossing" was obviously motivated by strictly pragmatic considerations, as the emphasis on and the awareness of purity and authenticity was now much stronger than ever before. Only 2 years later, judo was autonomized by the foundation of the Austrian Amateur Judo Federation (AAJF). Contrary to previous patterns of organizational culture, membership in this federation was limited to clubs concerned with judo exclusively and signified an intentional breaking away from the mélange of judo and jujutsu.[15]

At the time of the autonomization, the new federation represented some 500 members, less than 15 percent of the jujutsu adherents counted a decade before (about 3,500). Proportions of size and of importance, however, changed rapidly. Deliberate commitment and socially required loyalty to one master, one school, or one system of meaning are essential patterns of social organization in Japanese culture and as such part of the social relationships within and among the various schools of martial arts (Sanbonmatsu 1994).[16] The growing awareness of difference in styles, traditions, and schools supported the growth of judo but weakened the position of jujutsu, which is a cover term for all kinds of Japanese weaponless combat styles and not a single, elaborated system. With numerous schools, ideologies, and masters striving hard to coexist, jujutsu could never establish the kind of strong following that judo did. The lack of a common focus prevented schools of jujutsu in Austria as elsewhere from unionization until the late 1960s, and even today the national, continental, and world federations of jujutsu are less embracing than their judo counterparts. In the Austria of 1948, however, jujutsu organizations were accepted to join the judo federation because of their common history, and still today the federation represents the interests of the autonomous section of jujutsu. What seems to be an irony of history has been caused by the differing degree of complexity of content on the one side and stringency of organizational aspects on the other; these factors are responsible for the inversion of power relationships between judo and its predecessor and inspiration, jujutsu.[17]

The formation of the national federation was but the first step in assembling the administration of the sport according to democratic principles favoring a federalist, loosely centralized structure. Following the policies of the First Republic (1918–38), regional governments were bestowed with administrative authority over all sport matters. The central institution of the AAJF coordinated the activities of the regional associations and represented the Austrian *jûdôka* in international affairs. Of course, the statutes of the AAJF and its successor, the AJF (Austrian Judo Federation, renamed in 1958), exert prescribing influence on the statutes of the subordinate organizations. The AJF itself had to define its task in accordance with the principles and decisions of the European Judo Federation (EJU), and since 1952 with those of the International Judo Federation (IJF), which was founded in that year.

What is the meaning for the individual judo practitioner of joining any such organization? Merits are manifold, but two are especially significant: grading and competitions. Grading is a substantial parameter of social relationships in any culture. As many commentators on Japanese society have pointed out, hierarchy and status consciousness are major essentials for the "pre-social work" of locating the self and the other in face-to-face interactions. The analyses of the social dynamics at the *dôjô* support such assumptions that stress the importance of status patterning for *iemoto*-like secondary social groups. Kano's principles of "teaching the way" and of mutual benevolence were, to a certain degree, conditioned by traditional arrangements such as the master–pupil relationship, or direct transmission of knowledge from the superior to the subordinate. The elaborated system of kodokan judo differentiates between the *dan*-holder *(yûdansha)* and non-*dan*-holder *(mudansha)*; the groups are internally segmented into ten and five grades respectively. Technical skill and knowledge determines the individual grading, which is in turn symbolized by the colored belt.[18] However, *dan* grades higher than the sixth are awarded only for extraordinary efforts for the spread of judo or for the realization of judo (as a way) in everyday life. Furthermore, belt examinations contain both practical and theoretical parts, with the latter testing the knowledge of judo terms and techniques, judo history, and philosophy. These procedures are highly efficient in securing the correct transmission of authentic or legitimate codes and modes of kodokan judo in Japan, Austria, and everywhere.

This system works only when the grades involved have a universal meaning. It is not pure chance that holders of the eighth *dan* or even above are abundant among *jujutsuka* where bestowal is dependent on the subjective calculation of a master of a certain school. In contrast, judo grades are arranged in a rational, comprehensive fashion following international standards. To a certain degree, variations exist where regional (*kyû*) and national (dan) federations are the authorities controlling belt examinations.[19] The stringency of the judo grading system, however, allows the comparison of skills and knowledge on a worldwide level because of the directives issued by the world federation.

A second advantage to joining the federation is the chance to test one's skills in tournaments. The present system differentiates among at least three major categories of tournaments registered in the judo calendar. International tournaments are conducted in A, B, C, and D categories with decreasing significance; national and regional championships require the supervision of the federations. Thus, federation membership is essential for anyone who wants tournament experience; club championships or club tournaments are of no concern to the federations. As it is well known from sport history, the codification of rules and the formation of administrative organizations have been both causes and results of the growing interest in competition, no matter whether on local (interscholastic football tournaments) or on global scales (soccer world championships). Thus the first national championships in Austria in 1949 afforded the incorporation of the AAJF. In a similar manner, the incorporation of the EJU was necessary for the organization of the European championships.

The first Austrian performance on an international stage occurred during the European championship in Paris in 1952. In the same year the AAJF adopted the Japanese counting system of *ippon* and *waza ari*. This change of rules again symbolized the shifting orientation as the old scale, which followed the conventions of wrestling and boxing bouts, was abandoned for the sake of conformity with Japanese judo. At the initiative of the EJU, the decision was made in 1952 to form a world federation. At the extraordinary meeting in Paris in December 1952 with seventeen nations, all from Europe, attending, it was decided to invite the All Japan Judo Federation to join the IJF. At the same time Kanô Risei, the son of Kano Jigoro and third director of the Kodokan, was offered the directorship of the IJF. At the first world championship in Tokyo in 1956, Kanô in his opening speech addressed the seventeen member nations, ten more with affiliated positions, and three waiting for approval.[20] Although he emphasized the particular role of Japan, "the motherland of Judo," he noted that judo was no longer just the judo "of Japan, but of the people of the world." As president of the Kodokan as well as the president of the IJF, he expressed his sincere hopes that "Japan, which is more advanced in the way of judo, should be able to serve the Judo circles of the world, and to contribute to the development of the judo of the world." Kanô's self-assurance perfectly matched the consciousness of his audience. The Kodokan was the spiritual center of their world, and the results of the world championship, in which Japan's *jûdôka* had won every bout against international guests, had contributed toward their readiness to learn from Japan.

Conflicts were bound to follow. Kanô felt that his first obligation was to the tradition of the Kodokan and the safeguarding of its position. Thus he stressed the ethical and educational part of judo, while the members of the IJF focused on judo as a championship sport. Since 1953, the IJF had requested that judo be accepted as an international Olympic sport. With the growth of the federation and the establishment of national organizations on every continent, this aim was finally achieved in 1960, 4 years before the Tokyo Olympic Games. The dominance of the Kodokan inside the Japanese federation was criticized by those *jûdôka* who favored the tournament system. Criticism also increased when the dominance of the Japanese *jûdôka* waned: in 1956 the unofficial motto in Japan was "Don't hurt the foreigner"; in 1958 "Watch out for the foreigner"; and finally in 1961, "Don't lose to the foreigners" (Saeki 1994: 308). Actually, the Japanese lost that year, when the Dutchman Anton Geesink became the third – and the first non-Japanese – world champion. This was probably the final incentive for the Kodokan to give up its reservations against weight categories. The open category, which was of course rooted in the traditional belief that proficiency of the art should enable the weak one to defeat the strong one, turned out to be a major disadvantage for the average Japanese physique. Japanese judo again attained supremacy after the introduction of weight categories. Japanese *jûdôka* went on to dominate most international tournaments until 1973.

In contrast to the politics of the center, *jûdôka* in Europe had always competed in weight categories because such categories were traditional among wrestlers and boxers. This adherence to European tradition is another indication of the early integration of Japanese martial arts into existing systems of combative sports in Europe. The merger of judo and European-style weight categories is not simply a matter of territorialization but is also bound to the political economy of modern sports. One of the major features of modern sports is the guarantee of an equality of chances, in this particular case supported by distributing the *jûdôka* according to their natural advantages of physical weight.

With *jûdôka* still a rare species outside Japan and with the overwhelming supremacy of Japanese *jûdôka*, the idolization of everything Japanese happened quite naturally. Any living witness of the early postwar period in Austria remembers vividly the awe and respect all felt in front of the rare Japanese visitors. What the semigods had to say, or what was heard from Japan, was considered to be of law-like rigidity. Contacts were still very limited: at the first summer schools, which opened in 1949, the Korean Hanho Rhi, who lived and taught in Switzerland, had to stand in for a Japanese teacher. Franz Nimführ was one of the first Austrian *jûdôka* to visit Japan, but the majority of Austrian *jûdôka* experienced the Japanese judo wizards only at international tournaments or at the summer schools in Obertraun, where London's Gunji Koizumi held classes in 1952 and 1953.

To summarize the major trends of the period from 1945 to 1965, judo in Austria lost many of its previous local characteristics. As a consequence of contemporary developments, international relationships increased, as did knowledge of real judo. The Kodokan in Tokyo was the center of the global judo community; there, the heirs of Kano Jigoro had succeeded in securing their hegemonic position even after the decentralization of the sports bureaucracy induced by the occupation forces. The Japan Judo Federation was tightly controlled by the previous members of the Blackbelt Association of Kodokan (Kôdôkan yûdansha kyôkai), who held federation offices at local, prefecture, and national levels. Japanese judo dominated the world in both ideological and sports terms, even beyond the cathartic experience of the foreign reach for the championship title. While the general level of proficiency was gradually equalized, Japanese supremacy was maintained by the introduction of weight categories. The Austrian *jûdôkas'* vivid feeling of inferiority was probably a major cause for their fascination with things Japanese; their interest in Japanese culture and *budô* philosophy reached its climax during these years.

Universalization: the national and the transnational

The integration of judo into the official program of the Olympic Games was a milestone in the history of judo, and it also signified a turning point. Although Kano Jigoro's dream of disseminating judo to the people of the world had finally been fulfilled, the transition from a Japanese sport to a world sport inevitably transformed major parameters of the art. Kano intended that judo tournaments be pedagogical instruments, places where practitioners could refine the basic principles and merits such as awareness, flexibility of mind, the ability to make quick decisions, readiness, and mental composure in a contest. Kano was convinced of the benefit of these capacities for everyday life. The ongoing "sportification," however, transformed the means into an end. The quest for contest and victory influenced judo organization and judo practice in Austria and in varying degrees in all other regions of the world.

Thus since the late 1960s the center of judo has clearly moved away from Japan and the Tokyo Kodokan. We will discuss the processes that led toward "world judo" with the concept of universalization, because since the late 1960s the center of judo culture has been more difficult to locate than in previous times. In any case, judo finally had reached the stage of deterritorialization; it was no longer the judo of Japan, but rather the judo of the International Federation of Judo, which was practiced worldwide. In this sense, judo is universal property; in addition, some of the internal dynamics of this judo clearly have universal dimensions. To handle specific agendas in an efficient way, judo is, as is any system of meanings, in need of a political economy integrating its ideological, material, and social dimensions into a coherent totality. While the more influential frames of reference of meaning during the first and second periods of Austrian judo were derivations from territorially bound conventions, transformations in the third period were in line with transnational particularities of modern sports. As we have seen before, the narration of Austrian judo history increasingly demands the consideration of the position of the national within the international.

The Japanese domination of international judo was interrupted in 1965 by a revolt of European and American members of the IJF. Although the Kodokan had attempted to maintain its hegemonic position by setting the agendas of the world federation, some strategic misjudgments of the Kodokan had undermined its importance, as the former president of the European Judo Federation Kurt Kucera recollects. Formerly a starter on the Viennese national team, Kucera began his career as an AJF official in 1967. For two decades, he served as president of the AJF; in 1984 he was elected president of the European Judo Federation, a position he held until 1995; because of this office, he served also as vice-president in the IJF. During his terms of office, Austrian judo prospered remarkably, as Kucera was able to spark the interest of business and media in the increasingly popular sport of judo. Seen from the level of sports achievements, both in terms of mass sports and of top class sports, judo was emancipated during his service. During this time, Austrian *jûdôka* were repeatedly successful at international tournaments, winning world championship titles and Olympic gold medals. The gold medals of Peter Seisenbacher in Seoul (1984) and Los Angeles (1988) helped popularize judo. Statistics indicate a significant relationship between achievements at the top level and recruitment at the bottom, especially if compared with the modest success of the Judo Day, a publicity campaign aimed at the public since 1981. In a recent campaign, some schools in Austria began developing plans for integrating judo into their sports curriculum.

It goes without saying that the media, most notably television, serve as a link between top and bottom levels. Precisely because of the extensive television coverage of national achievements, the Austrian public developed a taste for judo. Of course, television coverage is limited to or emphasizes those sports that promise huge audiences. Television revenues are one of the major sources of income for judo, where private sponsorship usually benefits individuals rather than organizations. The European Judo Federation was especially quick to accept this simple logic and to adapt particular aspects of judo to the unwritten rules of the media world. Kucera, when asked for the predominant features contributing to the development of judo, named four innovations: the double repackage system, which replaced the cup system;[21] the electronic scoreboard; the introduction of differently colored *judogi* (although this innovation is still waiting for final approval); and affording women's judo the same opportunities and rights as men's judo. Although he did not explicitly refer to the introduction of weight categories and time limits for fights, both of these innovations were equally crucial for the development of judo and its relationship with the media, and they were caused by European initiatives.

Whatever these innovations might imply for the relative importance of the European federation compared with the other four continental ones, in any case they underline the decreasing importance of a Japanese "copyright" on the definition of judo. Furthermore, they indicate that some nations are less and some are more willing and able to break with the traditional kodokan judo of Kano Jigoro. With reference to the last innovative initiatives of blue and white *judogi*, the minutes of the general congress of the IJF illustrate vividly the varying strategies of argumentation that conservative and progressive parties are employing. During the congress meeting of 1989, the EJU proposed changing the contest rules to allow the colored *judogi* for World Championships and the Olympic Games. The European representative, Besson, hinted at the experiences gained during 2 years of practice at A-level tournaments in Europe and stressed the importance of making the sport more transparent for spectators, i.e. television audiences. However, the proposal was refused by the majority of votes for another four consecutive meetings. Japanese representatives especially referred to the tradition of judo, to the symbolic purity of the white *judogi* and its 100-year-old tradition:

> Mr. Abe said that a lot has been told about the colored judogi. The reasons speaking against the colored judogi are economical ones since the sportsman would now need four judogi instead of two. White is the traditional color. It symbolizes the spirit of judo, and according to Kano it is extremely important to use the energy of spirit and body in the best possible manner. Judo shall also become a philosophy anxious to keep this tradition. Japanese TV and sponsors have provided a lot of money to judo. During the coming years sums amounting to US$550,000 will be paid, since the traditional judo in Japan has become a world sport. The blue judogi is met with refusal in Japan which has also consequences for the sponsors. Judo must remain white.[22]

Some nations supported the traditional argument by referring to the philosophical principle (Brazil) or to the pure spirit of Kano's judo (Sri Lanka, India). Others expressed practical considerations – disturbance of concentration, increase in travel baggage, fading color – for their reluctance to change. Yet more important were the economic considerations of representatives of developing nations. They were concerned that they would not be able to bear the financial burden of two additional *judogi* for each *jûdôka*, although various Europeans emphasized that the change of rules involved only some 400 or 500 top *jûdôka*[23] and expressed their willingness to provide colored *judogi* to nations in need.[24] However, with taekwon-do entering the Olympic Games in 2000 and with the intentions of the only recently founded World Karate Federation to join the 2004 Olympic Games, resistance is weakening, and even Japan has announced its approval of the colored *judogi*.

Although the dispute apparently incorporated various fields of discourse, the dissent was caused by the differing degree to which questions of sponsorship and media presence were considered to be of vital importance to a nation.[25]

The *judogi* issue entered the stage in 1989 when two important personalities left the IJF: Anton Geesink and Matsumae Shigeyoshi. The living celebrity of European judo, Anton Geesink, who had first beaten the Japanese at their own game in 1961, resigned his position as director of the Education and Diffusion Commission because he felt deeply dissatisfied with the policies of the new president who was succeeding Matsumae.[26] Geesink had developed a training system as early as the 1960s. This system was adapted by the AJF in 1972 as the official training system. Having served for more than 10 years as technical director of the AJF, Geesink contributed significantly to both world judo and Austrian judo. Much more important, however, was the role of Matsumae Shigeyoshi, who directed the IJF for 8 years (1979–87) and who because of especially close relations with the Austrian representative Kucera sponsored the building of the Matsumae Budo Center in Vienna (1984).[27]

With Matsumae Shigeyoshi in office, Japanese judo returned to the center. Despite various strategies within this decade of "re-Japanizing" the judo of the world, we are reluctant to deploy the notion of monolithic judo in Japan, and a major incident during the 1980s lends support to this reluctance. In 1982 the Students' Union rebelled against the Kodokan-dominated All Japan Judo Federation (AJJF) and withdrew from the organization; in consequence, the student organization was ostracized from the AJJF.[28] The conflict centered on two issues: the dominance of the Kodokan organization within the Japanese federation and the issuing of *dan* diplomas, which IJF president Matsumae had granted to national federations. Some European federations had protested against the Kodokan policy of awarding *dan* grades to visiting *jûdôka* without taking local regulations into consideration. The Japanese representative at the IJF protested against the new policy, which disregarded the Kano tradition, and requested that, at least, the image of Kano Jigoro be removed from the "letter of recognition."[29] The conflict finally spread over to the agendas of the IJF because Matsumae (with whom Japanese students sympathized) and the IJF spoke clearly in favor of the students, while the AJJF insisted on national sovereignty in solving the matter. The conflict was eased only in 1989 after threats, pressures, and negotiations by parliamentarians, the Monbushô, and the All Japan Amateur Sport Federation resulted in the public incorporation of the AJJF and the disunion of the AJJF and Kodokan into two independent, separate organizations. Although tournament judo and educational judo were at last separated, the situation remained critical because Kodokan president Kanô Yukimitsu was nominated as president of the new AJJF.

Matsumae himself was a strict adherent to the tradition of Kano Jigoro, but he opposed the policy of the Kodokan organization. In addition, he supported the development of judo into a tournament sport, whereas the Kodokan demanded more stress on the educational and moral aspects of judo. Internationally minded, Matsumae proposed during his election campaign to restructure the IJF and to promote activities of the underdeveloped federations; he also launched a number of support programs at private expense.[30] The Budo Center in Vienna was part of his wish to establish a European center of martial arts, and he sponsored the Matsumae Cup to be held there every 2 years. Matsumae was not as successful here, however, as in the IJF reformation. The Matsumae Cup, although privately financed and with top athletes starting at the first round in 1985, was repeated only twice. The tour program in Europe was simply too narrow for adding another top event. In any case, the Matsumae Budo Center was too small to conform to the safety standards for international tournaments. In addition, the finance and accounting program of the MBC needed reconsideration because the *budô*-related income of the MBC did not cover the permanent expenses. A Japanese investment group was formed to develop a leisure and sport complex around the Budo Center that would offer tennis, squash, badminton, physiotherapy, a solarium, massage, and other services. Currently, office buildings, a golf course, and the Bôsei Hotel belong to the properties decorated with the emblem of the MBC. Behind the scenes of a nonprofit organization (Verein des Matsumae Budo Center), the conglomerate supervises. The president of the charitable organization is Matsumae Tatsurô, the son of the late Matsumae Shigeyoshi, and Kurt Kucera is vice-president. Other members of the board are well-known municipal and national figures, government officials, and members high in the hierarchy of the sport.

The charitable organization is headquartered in two modest rooms on the fourth floor of the Starview Hotel. National as well as international honorary awards, documenting the political weight of the office holder, decorate one wall of the inner room; another is plastered with a nearly life-size portrait of Matsumae, wearing a *judogi*; a third one depicts the success story of the Kucera era. Is this the center of Austrian judo, in the shadow of the MBC building, at the headquarters of MBC Leisure and Recreation Inc., where business interests and sports facilities merge? Or is the center rather at the headquarters of the AJF, where office space is much more generous, although the decor is the same? Or is the center somewhere else, at some west Austrian *dôjô* known for its strong *jûdôka*, or at the Austrian television broadcasting company, or at the local branch of Adidas or Coca-Cola? Is there a center at all?

In speaking about the relationship between Austria and Japan in matters of judo, Japan is no longer the primary point of reference. Contacts are well established, but only of limited importance. Japanese and Austrian *jûdôka* are joining mutual exchange programs. Summer schools or tournament preparation camps are conducted either in Japan or under the auspices of Japanese educators. Contacts are a matter of choice, however, not of dependency. The Austrian side is even to some degree reluctant to intensify contacts, as experiences with Japanese trainers repeatedly followed the same pattern: after a certain period, the Japanese experts attempted to influence the politics of the Austrian federation. Furthermore, although some Japanese universities offer excellent training conditions for top *jûdôka* from Austria because they can provide a huge number of strong sparring partners, for reasons of culture shock, some athletes do better to limit their "judo homestay" to a mere couple of weeks. For them it is much easier (and cheaper) to exploit the various relationships with other centers of excellence in Europe.

The shift of power is clearly rooted in a better-developed sports science in Europe. Japanese athletes are said to be overtrained. Presently, the majority of A-level tournaments are staged in Europe, with European *jûdôka* regularly competing for the majority of titles. In addition, the competence of 2.5 million *jûdôka* in Europe contrasts with that of 300,000 in Japan,[31] where two or three decades ago there were 3 million to be counted. The rectified imbalance between European and Japanese achievements induced a new self-awareness and facilitated an adaptation of contest rules and etiquette in accordance with the needs of the time.[32] Judo is no longer only Japan's judo, said Kano's son in 1956, but is judo still Japan's judo at all? Austrian judo is obliged to remain in the realm defined by the statutes of the IJF, with Article 1.2 clearly demarcating its object: "It (IJF) recognizes as judo that which was created by Kano Jigoro, being at the same time a system of physical and mental education, and which now also exists as an Olympic sport."[33] Quarrels continue whether the olympification of judo was for the better or the worse of the judo created by Kano.

Conclusion: Japan outside Japan?

The olympification of judo has certainly contributed to its popularization. Yet who (and what) is profiting from its spread is a justified question. Certainly it is not the Kodokan, whose decline in power goes hand in hand with the decreasing centrality of "Japaneseness" in the center of the system of meaning. The former version of the statutes of the IJF contained nothing about Olympic judo but defined its object in terms of "the judo created by Kano Jigoro and the techniques practiced at the Kodokan in Tokyo" (Kodokan 1961: 50). Mosch (1987) has argued that the evaluation of a regional sports tradition in terms of a national sport, furthermore in terms of an Olympic discipline, implies immense status enhancement for the state and the national culture involved. The successful export of Japanese martial arts, in particular of judo, seems to emphasize the increasing importance of Japan and of Japanese culture for the world. On this premise, judo serves as a culture broker at both levels of sport consumption – as spectator sport and participation sport.

Television and media coverage of international tournaments, most noteworthy that of the Olympic Games, transmits images and associations of "Japaneseness" to many millions of spectators. However, as we have argued, the commodification of judo is an arduous and continuing process of rather modest success. In front of the IJF Directing Committee, IOC president Juan

Antonio Samaranch expressed frankly that "sport is television, and television is sport." Equally frankly, he urged the members to encourage all attempts to make their sport more comprehensive, more transmittable to the public. Without such adaptations – and Samaranch explicitly referred to the issue of the white and blue *judogi* ("sport is [color] television") – judo might be removed from the Olympic program.[34] This argument has been strong enough finally to convert most of the purists, including the Japanese representatives who spearheaded the resistance.

Roughly 10 years earlier, the IJF had won a battle against the IOC, which demanded that the IJF give up the open category. At this time, with Matsumae as president of the IJF, the center of world judo had temporarily returned to Tokyo. During this period, rather by chance than through Matsumae's intention, the Kodokan and other tradition-conscious *budô* organizations of Japan launched initiatives to relocate Japan as the center of judo. These attempts failed, however, because the Kodokan was too weak to effect integrative enfolding. A first and conspicuous setback for the tradition-minded AJJF was the unsuccessful proposal to declare Japanese an official language of the IJF, in addition to English and French. Japanese was already acknowledged as an auxiliary language because of the historical roots and the terminology of the sport. Yet the delegates at the congress in Maastricht in 1981 did not dare to pay tribute to Kano's successors and refused the proposal. The IJF even took sides against the Kodokan during the 6 years of intra-Japanese quarrels and sympathized with the rebellious student organization. No wonder that the Kodokan and the Kodokan-controlled AJJF supported the composition of the *budô* charter, introduced in 1987 by a Japanese consortium representing sports historians, government officials, and representatives of nine martial arts. This document explicitly aimed at the de-sportification of *budô* practice and argued in favor of turning back to the traditional roots of Japanese culture. However, the principles of the charter were and are without practical implications for practitioners, whether in Japan or elsewhere.[35] The final attempt to enter center stage had an unfortunate end: Kanô Yukimitsu, the grandson of Kano Jigoro and present Kodokan director, resigned as director of the Asian Judo Federation in 1984, probably because he felt too sure of winning the election for the IJF presidency in 1985. The congress actually voted in favor of the Korean candidate, Park; thus there is only one Japanese representative to one of the commissions of the IJF.

A similar process occurred at the level of sport participation. Judo practice has been again and again a major incentive for students to enroll in Japanese studies at the University of Vienna. To be fair, encountering judo probably sparks interest in Japanese culture among more *jûdôka* than those who are willing to combine fascination, or curiosity, with college education. The macroperspective of this study tends to overlook the individual opinions of judo practitioners. But according to their trainers, administrators, and representatives, the majority of adherents to Japanese martial arts admit only minor significance to Japanese cultural background, which is a radical shift from the experience of the 1950s or 1960s, when judo was seen much more as a general lifestyle or an entrance to Japanese philosophy. As case studies on the development in other European countries have shown, the situation in Austria was no exception, but rather the norm.[36]

The analysis of the dynamics behind the transformations of judo in Austria, Japan, and elsewhere during the centennial history of the sport offers insight into the nature of the processes of cultural dissemination. We have shown that the spread of judo and its popularization in Austria were mainly guided by forces and tensions within three distinctive fields conceptualized in terms of territorial culture, Japanese culture, and international sports culture. The structure of our analysis in three parts emphasizing the currents among the agents within one of these systems is purely heuristic, as we have also argued that the notion of a complex of overlapping layers is more accurate. Thus each period is signified by flows of meaning and interpretation within each specific cultural logic and between the systems. In many instances, conflicts result from such cross-cultural interactions simply because of mutual misinterpretations of the semiotic relationship between signifier and significant.

The notion of subculture evokes questions concerning the relationship between culture and subculture; in this context, the proper affiliation of Austrian judo. Is it part of Austrian culture, does it represent Japanese culture, or does it belong to the international world of sport? Because of the lack of any strictly hegemonic center, there is no answer along the lines of either–or. Yet in terms of degree, the overall development hints at a relational power imbalance. Considering the influence of the IJF, which issues global directives, the weight of the political economy of world sport exceeds the capabilities of traditional conservationists. Austrian judo, Japanese judo, and even the Kodokan are subject to these politics of "de-Japanizing judo."

Submissive attitudes toward the cultural logic of world sport vary considerably in various national cultures, a situation that indicates the disintegration on the one side and the specific relationships between the three cultural systems in different territorial cultures on the other. That Austria was a forerunner among European countries is probably related to the historical processes behind the formation of modern sports, which originated in eighteenth-century England. The sign system, nowadays property of a global culture, very likely entered into the conceptualization of the Kodokan style when the German medical doctor Erwin Bälz encouraged Kano Jigoro to develop a systematic canon in order to preserve the traditional martial arts. The much more visible sportification of judo occurred during the second half of the twentieth century. In conclusion, the prospect of a completely "de-Japanized" judo is highly unlikely. Inverting the words of Kanô Risei from 1956, 40 years later we know that the judo of today is not only of the world, but also of Japan.

Notes

1 Japanese terms are transcribed according to the modified Hepburn system. However, certain terms that belong to the inventory of most Western languages, such as judo or jujutsu, and recur throughout the paper are neither set in italics nor marked with diacritics. The same convention has been applied for the founder of judo, but not for his descendants; hence Kano Jigoro, but Kanô Risei.

2 Scholars of sport science and pedagogy probably dealt most extensively with topics related to martial arts. Grabert (1996) analyzes the relationship between karate practice and involvement in situations of physical violence. Fredersdorf (1986) compares Japanese *budô* arts with Western concepts of physical education. James and Jones (1982) give a detailed ethnographic account of social processes at and around the karate *dôjô*. Genovese (1980) integrates empirical encounters with karate practice into discourses of Japanese patterns of social organization. Mosch (1987) delineates the processes behind the formation of national sports in Japan and Korea. Saeki (1994) interprets the conflict between the Judo Federation of Japan and its student branch during the 1980s as a struggle between traditionalists and modernists. Much more scholarly work is available in Japanese, focusing on historical, ideological, and organizational aspects of judo in Japan.

3 For a semiotic exploration of the concept of culture, see Posner (1991: 37–74).

4 The background story of the Budokan (built right before and for the Tokyo Olympic Games in 1964) is exhaustively narrated by Saeki (1994). Matsumae was one of the leading proponents of the Budokan at a time when the Kodokan was still hoping to host the judo contests.

5 The medical doctor Erwin Bälz described upper-class university students as malnourished and overworked. After unsuccessful efforts to have a sports hall built for their recreation, he learned about jujutsu and initiated the reinvention of this old Japanese martial arts tradition (Gerstl 1994: 25–6).

6 In 1925, Josef Diwischek's first illustrated book followed: *Jiu-Jitsu die waffenlose Selbstverteidigung* (Diwischek 1925). Among other books on judo were Katsukuma and Hancock (1906), *Das Kano jiu-jitsu* (note the paradoxical term of the book title); Sasaki (1906), *Judo: das japanische Ringkampf;* and Yokoyama Oshima (1911), *Judo: manuel de jiu-jitsu de L'Ecole Kano a Tokio.*

7 Rautek further developed his teacher's techniques, was known for his perfectionism in technique and elegance, and received many honors in and outside Austria. Today he is widely known for his first aid holds, which are applied all over the world (Gerstl 1994: 40).

8 In his historiography of people's universities in Vienna, Klaus Taschwer uses the term "people's university" as the English translation of *Volkshochschule* – mainly to distinguish it from the Danish "folk high school." Whereas the northern European type was much more designed to enhance community among the visitors, the Viennese type was clearly oriented on the model of the university and the school: people met there, but nearly exclusively for the purpose of enhancing knowledge. See Taschwer (1997).

9 According to a contemporary's impressions, the people's universities played a significant role in the lives of Vienna's blue- and white-collar workers:

> Here, one feels truly at home, not only in the inner circle of friends, but also in every new visitor, led here by the same aspiration. Like at halls of the railway-station on all festive days, here meet the excursionists who, removed from the narrowness of the daily-life, want to broaden their horizon and want to search for recreation and refreshment in the mental holiday-destination after monotone and fatiguing professional work.
>
> (Taschwer 1997: 191)

10 Karen Gerstl notes that Gabriel's instructor in Switzerland was Japanese. However, according to other sources the only non-European instructor during the earlier years was the Korean Rhi Hanho.

11 Articles were printed in Viennese newspapers such as *Neue Freie Presse* (21 June 1934) and *Neues Wiener Journal* (22 June 1934). Other articles had described Kano's method as early as 1923 in the sports edition of *Neues Wiener Tagblatt* (15 December) and *Der Abend* (22 September 1927).

12 Actually Kanô did not invent the term but rather paid tribute to the *Kito ryû*, a major source of his kodokan judo, when he deliberately switched from the original *Kanô ryû* to the unusual term of judo that first appeared in documents related to this particular school.

13 In Kano's own words:

> Besides the acquisition of useful knowledge, we must endeavor to improve our intellectual powers, such as memory, attention, observation, judgement, reasoning, imagination, etc. But this we should not do in a haphazard manner, but in accordance with psychological laws, so that the relation of those powers one with the other shall be well harmonized. It is only by faithfully following the principle of maximum efficiency – that is Judo – that we can achieve the object of rationally increasing our knowledge and intellectual power. Can this principle be applied to other fields of human activity? Yes, the same principle can be applied to the improvement of the human body, making it strong, healthy and useful, and so constitutes physical education. It can also be applied to the improvement of intellectual and moral power, and in this way constitutes mental and moral education. It can at the same time be applied to the improvement of diet, clothing, housing, social intercourse, and methods of business, thus constituting the study and training in living. I gave this all-pervading principle the name of Judo. So Judo, in its fuller sense, is a study and method in training of mind and body as in the regulation of life and affairs.
>
> (Kano 1937: 21)

14 Judo for women, however, had as its objects "building up of feminine beauty and the harmonious development of mind and body as well as rhythmical movement and graceful action, through the gentleness which marks the art." See Tomiki (1956: 7).

15 The somewhat surprising appearance of the so-called Judo-do during the early 1950s again caused some disturbance among the public, whose awareness of difference was far less elaborated. Despite extensive media coverage in the early years, in the long run Judo-do only achieved a slightly esoteric status as one among many other small-scale jujutsu schools (Gerstl 1994: 47–8).

16 This article also provides an overview of "classical" studies concerning social relationships in Japanese society and schools of traditional arts.

17 The accusation of one of the leading *jujutsuka* in Europe, Heribert Czerwenka-Wenkstetten, eighth *dan* holder, is interesting but without empirical evidence. He stated that judo intentionally struggled to assimilate or to ignore-to-death its rival jujutsu right from the beginning. See Czerwenka-Wenkstetten (1993: 18).

18 The colored belt was a British invention, spreading to France and the rest of the world. See Brousse (1989a: 11–25).

19 Judo organizations have long quarreled about authoritative questions. As examination fees and license fees are a substantial income source, both national and continental institutions were interested in securing this source of income. The Kodokan in Tôkyô, particularly, enraged national federations when awarding

dan grades without taking the autonomy of national federations into consideration. The climax of the debate is mirrored in the minutes of the Ordinary Congress of the IJF. See the IJF homepage at http://www.ijf.org/cg.html.

20 The following quote is from the IJF homepage at http://www.ijf.org/cg56.html.

> It gives me a great and genuine pleasure that we were enabled to hold today this Congress of the International Judo Federation in Japan, the motherland of Judo. It is a matter to be congratulated that, with the pace of growth so regular as it is now, the prospects for Judo are certainly promising. Judo as it is practiced in Japan today is the Kodokan Judo without exception, although it is also called in Japan today simply Judo. The spread and advance of Judo in the world at the present moment is all but marvelous. Thus, although Judo was unquestionably originated in Japan, Judo today is not only of Japan, but of the people of the whole world.

21 Under the new system, every contestant has two chances to reach the next round. Under the old system, the first defeat was decisive for elimination from the tournament.

22 See the IJF home page at http://www.ijf.org/cg89-11.html.

23 According to Article 12 of the Austrian contest rules, there are no regulations prescribing the color of *judogi* for national tournaments except if the organizing party requests white or blue/white *judogi*. Some clubs in Austria use individually designed *judogi* that obviously enhance possibilities for collective identification of team members and fans. During the interview, the general secretary of the AJF said she hoped for the international acceptance of this custom in the near future.

24 The Education and Diffusion Commission of the IJF has devised various support programs for the developing nations. Among others, *judogi* used at Japanese high schools are distributed. These are available only in small sizes and, of course, only in white.

25 The lobbying of the innovators is remarkable. Currently the campaign is headed by the motto of "The blue judogi, the new tradition!" According to current regulations, 50 percent of the revenue goes to the organizing party and 50 percent to the IJF. Approximately 70 percent of the IJF income is from television rights. Sponsorship, in addition, is probably only for European nations of importance. Interestingly, however, the Coca-Cola emblem decorates the home page of the IJF. For more details on these issues, see the IJF home page http://www.ijf.org/wn-bb-029.html.

26 Geesink's opinion was widely shared, and the new president (from Argentina) was removed from office after some months of service because he wasted federation funds. Apparently the legal aftermath is still unsettled. See IJF home page at http//www.ijf.org/dc.html.

27 Both aspects are interrelated because Kucera had helped to engineer Matsumae's successful campaign for the presidency. The building of the MBC must thus be understood in terms of Matsumae's *ongaeshi* as well.

28 For a detailed analysis of center stage and back stage issues of the conflict, see Saeki (1994).

29 So far for face value, or *tatemae*. In terms of *honne*, with the issuance of a *dan* diploma, substantial sources of financial income and of status ascription were endangered too.

30 Matsumae Shigeyoshi is well known as the founder of Tôkai University. He received a doctorate in natural sciences and devised the deep sea telephone cable. Revenues from his patented invention provided him with money to found the college. Nowadays more than 20,000 students are enrolled at the various campuses

of Tôkai University. Matsumae was repeatedly elected to the Upper House. For his life work, Matsumae was honored with the highest award of Japan in 1982.

31 Depending on the informant, figures differ considerably. Our calculation is based on the statement by Mr. Kucera. Furthermore, the recent edition of the annual Whitebook of Leisure notes 3.1 million *budô* adherents; it seems justified to say that 10 percent are regular practitioners of judo. See Yoka kaihatsu sentâ (1997: 47).

32 For example, as *kyû* examinations are extremely popular among youngsters and their parents, the AJF has devised a number of in-between grades with particularly colored belts. This effective incentive for motivating youngsters is, at the same time, an additional and welcome source of income for the AJF.

33 This is the new wording adopted by the Congress in 1983 in Hamilton, Canada.

34 Compare the comment on the move in an article of the official journal of the Austrian Judo Federation (1997: 13). Obviously the pressure is extending from the IJF to the national federations.

35 Kurt Kucera personally had not heard about the Budo Charter. As the majority of Austrian *jûdôka* are of a younger age (only 3.5 percent are older than 35 years), he welcomed the move because of his conviction of the educative merits of judo for practitioners.

36 On judo in Britain, see Googner (1980: 333–40); for the history of judo in France, see Brousse (1989b: 3–7); for Denmark, see Bonde (1989).

Bibliography

Austrian Judo Federation (1997) "Visionen" (Visions), *Mattenpost* 2: 13.

Bonde, H. (1989) *Judo den Milde Vey (Judo, the Soft Way)*, Copenhagen: Borgen.

Bourdieu, P. (1984) *Distinction: A Social Critique of the Judgment of Taste*, trans. Richard Nice, Cambridge, MA: Harvard University Press.

Brousse, M. (1989a) "Du samurai a l'athlete: l'essor du judo en France" (From samurai to athlete: the rise of judo in France), *Sport Histoire* 3: 11–25.

—— (1989b) "Reflexions sur l'evolution de l'enseignement du judo en France" (Reflections on the development of teaching judo in France), *Bulletin de l'Academie de Judo Michigami* 13: 3–7.

Czerwenka-Wenkstetten, H. (1993) *Kanon des Nippon Jujitsu Bd. 1. Begriffe, Grundlagen, Geschichte, Basistechniken (Nippon Jujutsu Canon: Terms, Basics, History, Basic Techniques)*, Innsbruck: Tyrolia-Verlag.

Diwischek, J. (1925) *Jiu-Jitsu die waffenlose Selbstverteidigung (Jujutsu: the Weaponless Art of Self-defense)*, Vienna: Steyrermuhl.

Fischer, H.W. (1928) *Körper: Schönheit und Körperkultur (The Body: Beauty and Physical Training)*, Berlin: Deutsche Buchgemeinschaft.

Fredersdorf, F. (1986) *Japanische Budo-Disziplinen und abendländische Bewegungskultur: Entstehung, Verbreitung und Verfremdung kulturfremder Sportarten am Beispiel japanischer Kampfkünste (Japanese Martial Arts and Western Body Culture: Origin, Diffusion, and Transformation of Foreign Sports)*, Berlin: Institut für Soziologie der Technischen Universität Berlin.

Genovese, J.W. (1980) *Karate Organization in Japan*. Ann Arbor, MI: University Microfilms International.

Gerstl, K. (1994) "Versuch einer Erklärung des Unterschieds in Bekanntheitsgrad und Verbreitung von Judo und Jujitsu in Österreich anhand der geschichtlichen Entwicklung beider Sportarten" (The historical development of judo and jujutsu in Austria: explaining the overall differences in level of awareness and participation rates), unpublished M.A. thesis, University of Vienna.

Googner, J.M. (1980) "Judo players as a gnostic sect," *Religion* 12: 333–40.

Grabert, K. (1996) *Karate-Do und Gewaltverhalten (Karate-do and Violent Behavior)*, Frankfurt am Main: Peter Lang.

Hannerz, U. (1992) *Cultural Complexity: Studies in the Social Organization of Meaning*, New York: Columbia University Press.

James, A. and Jones, R. (1982) "The social world of karate-do," *Leisure Studies* 1: 337–54.

Kano, J. (1937) *Judo (Jujutsu)*, Tokyo: Board of Tourist Industry, Japanese Government Railways.

Katsukuma, H., and Hancock, H.I. (1906) *Das Kano Jiu-jitsu (The Jujutsu of the Kano School)*, Stuttgart: Julius Hoffmann.

Kodokan (ed.) (1961) *Judo*. Tokyo: Kodokan.

Mosch, N. (1987) "Die politische Funktion des Sports in Japan am Beispiel zweier Nationalsportarten: Judo und Taekwondo – ein Vergleich" (The political function of sport in Japan: examining the national sports of judo and taekwondo), unpublished Ph.D. thesis, University of Vienna.

Posner, R. (1991) "Kultur als Zeichensystem. Zur semiotischen Explikation kulturwissenschaftlicher Grundbegriffe" (Culture as a sign system: on the semiotic explication of basic terms of the humanities), in A. Assmann and D. Harth (eds) *Kultur als Lebenswelt und Monument (Culture as Everyday Life and Culture as Monument)*, Frankfurt am Main: Fischer.

Saeki, T. (1994) "The conflict of tradition and modernization in a sport organization: a sociological study of issues surrounding the organizational reform of the All Japan Judo Federation," *International Review for the Sociology of Sport* 29: 301–15.

Sanbonmatsu, M. (1994) "Waga kuni supôtsu bunka no seishinsei keisei ni kansuru shakaigakuteki kenkyû" (Sociological research on spirit building in Japan's sport culture), *Fukuoka kyôiku daigaku kiyô* 43 (2): 71–82.

Sasaki, K. (1906) *Judo: das japanisches Ringkampf* [sic] (Judo: Japanese wrestling), Berlin: K. Sasaki.

Taschwer, K. (1997) "People's universities in a metropolis: interfaces between the social and spatial organization of adult education in Vienna, 1890–1930," in B. J. Hake and T. Steele (eds) *Intellectuals, Activists, and Reformers*, Leeds, U.K.: University of Leeds Press.

Tomiki, K. (1956) *Judo: Appendix: Aikido*, Tôkyô: Japan Travel Bureau.

Yoka kaihatsu sentâ. (1997) *Rejâ hakusho '97 (Whitebook on Leisure 1997)*, Tôkyô: Yoka kaihatsu sentâ.

Yokoyama, S. and Oshima, E. (1911) *Judo: Manuel de Jiu-jitsu de L'Ecole Kano a Tôkio (Judo: Handbook of Jujutsu of the Kano School from Tôkyo)*, Paris: Berger-Levrault.

6 Soka Gakkai in Germany

The story of a qualified success

Sanda Ionescu

The overseas development of Japanese religions has, until recently, been tightly linked to Japanese emigration policies (Shimazono 1992, 1993; Shimpo 1995).[1] Not surprisingly, it is in regions such as Hawaii, the West Coast of the United States, and South America, where there are well-established Japanese communities, that Japanese movements have been most successful, although different movements appear to have succeeded in different countries and for a variety of reasons. What are we to make, though, of Japanese religions that seek to expand in regions where there is little Japanese immigration and little shared history or cultural background, such as the European countries?

Studying the history and the present-day development of a religion such as Soka Gakkai in Germany raises many questions about the globalization of ideologies and cultures.[2] To what extent can a religion, which has arisen under specific historical and cultural circumstances,[3] become relevant to people belonging to entirely different social, cultural, and temporal contexts? Is it chance or strategy that determines the successful transplantation of a religion beyond its national borders? How much does the religion seeking to enter a foreign culture with proselytizing intentions have to take into account certain core elements of the host culture, and can it do that without losing its specificity and authenticity? Although religion has traditionally been linked with particular cultures, it has always had claims to universality as well. In other words, religious communication has been structured around the immanent/transcendent polarity (Beyer 1994: 101). Religion has been and – in many instances, particularly among the new religions – claims to be still relevant and applicable to almost any situation; yet how are we to reconcile that with the modern world of specialized systems that offer alternatives to the religious solution, thereby displacing, marginalizing, or privatizing these religious approaches (Beyer 1994)?

It is clear that Soka Gakkai acts as a sort of cultural broker, managing a flow of meaning between two very different socioreligious contexts and seeking to articulate its identity as a third culture in both local and global terms. But how does it do that? And to what extent are there tensions, or even downright contradictions, between the globalizing aims of a transnational religious organization and the political and legal systems of individual nation-states? How well can a religion simultaneously satisfy its duties toward the community of members and humanity in general, as stated in its universalistic message (Coleman 1993: 355)?

In this chapter, I examine the proportion of universality to cultural specificity that Soka Gakkai has shown throughout its short history on German soil, a history that has been an eventful process of mutual concessions and adaptations.

Having acquired a solid base of followers in Japan, in the 1960s, under the presidency of Daisaku Ikeda, Soka Gakkai began to expand abroad. While at first the conversion of new members was an informal process (for example, the conversion of American servicemen through Japanese bar hostesses or wives; see Snow 1976: 134), by the mid-1960s the guidelines for a systematic conversion were in place. These were followed largely by long-time Japanese members sent abroad with an explicit proselytizing intention, but even then the long-term perspective was to teach the foreign members to convert their own kind, for "rather than having Japanese convert Americans, we must have Americans converting Americans" (Dator 1969: 24). The movement now claims 1.26 million members in 115 countries (SGI 1993) and the 1991 split with its parent organization, the Nichiren Shoshu priesthood, has not visibly reduced its membership abroad.

The story of Soka Gakkai in Germany, as told to me by German members, contains certain mythologizing aspects, and in what follows I shall use their words.

In 1961, about the time the Wall was built to separate the two Germanys, President Ikeda came to visit Germany and was so touched by this situation that he decided to bring Buddhism to the split country to alleviate the suffering. The first Japanese missionaries – or "pioneers," as the present-day members prefer to call them – arrived soon after, most of them with no more than a backpack on their shoulders; they had little command of the German language and even less knowledge of German culture and society. At that time, a person could get a work permit to stay longer in Germany only by working in certain sectors where there was a shortage of labor, so these pioneers found themselves working in the mines of the Ruhr area (the men) or in hospitals (the women) regardless of their professional qualifications. There was only a handful of these Japanese religious professionals in Germany (no more than fourteen to sixteen of them in all of Europe), but some of them have stayed on in the communities that they helped to build.

The movement grew rather slowly until the mid-1970s, but it now has an estimated 2,000 members and is the largest Japanese new religion in Germany.[4] SGI-D (Soka Gakkai International Deutschland) has taken on wholesale the organizational structure of the parent organization in Japan, in spite of what seems at times to be a cumbersome and excessive system of divisions, branches, and sections. Only a minority of members nowadays are Japanese. That a disproportionately large number of these are in leadership positions is usually explained within the movement by the fact that most Japanese members have been practicing longer than the Germans. The situation is beginning to change now, and more and more Germans are being entrusted with leading roles not just at the local but also at the national and *Bundesland* level. The Germans consider this to be a sign of "indigenization" of the movement and rate it very positively.

This takeover has not always been amicable or unproblematic. The new German local leaders were initially closely watched and occasionally told that they were stepping too far out of line and should do things in a certain way, "as they have always been done in Japan." A furious debate would ensue between the two camps, although there was also a minority of German members always willing to accept uncritically any Japanese suggestion "because they know best." This period was, however, mercifully short, and I was told that German leaders have become more mature and willing to take on responsibility, while the Japanese are more willing to delegate.

Some of the first generation of Japanese missionaries and even more of those who came a few years later, in the late 1960s and early 1970s, have adapted remarkably to German culture, speak German fluently, have often married Germans, and tend to be on the "German side" in disputes about further decentralization or how things should be done. Others are criticized by the German members for still not having learned to speak German properly. One outspoken male informant told me, "I'm sure they would have a lot to tell us, they have such a lot of experience, but they are still unable to communicate well in German, so they churn out the same tired old clichés." These leaders are also the ones who tend to abide fairly strictly by the orders from above (i.e. from the Japanese headquarters), and they have problems accepting the input of the German members.

One of the German women, who has been a *Bundesland* leader for quite a number of years now, described the process:

> We still have a lot to learn from them, but now gradually they are coming to accept that they too can learn from us, that it's an *exchange*. Because at first it was very much a case of "Hush, you don't know anything!" Everything came from above, like a parent with a child. But now we are all parents, from all continents.

The initial strategy of Soka Gakkai expansion in Germany was what I would call "self-selective," i.e. the idea was that Soka Gakkai catered for certain needs and that people from any society who had those needs would find themselves attracted to the movement. These needs were defined as being the same as those that led to the unprecedented success of Soka Gakkai in Japan in the 1950s and 1960s. Not quite integrated, nonintellectual, lower-class individuals, who felt let down by society, who had made a mess of their professional or private lives, or who did not feel central to anything within their society were attracted by the promise of immediate and practical benefits from chanting. The first Soka Gakkai members in the German town where I was based during my fieldwork, for instance, were all recipients of social benefit at the time; they were largely unemployed people, high-school dropouts or relatively poorly educated, and quite often single parents. The proportion of single parents has remained the same, but the membership is now far more mainstream, educated (the initial members in many cases went back to study), and usually employed.

There seems to be a certain amount of overlap between the membership of Soka Gakkai (or indeed of any Buddhist religion) and that of the Green Movement. Although the Green Movement is far more diffuse – Galtung (1990: 237–8) describes it as a federation of movements – it too arose as a reaction to what was perceived as the malfunctioning of industrialized Western societies. Soka Gakkai members frequently cited dissatisfaction with the emptiness of the materialistic mainstream German society as a reason for commencing their spiritual search, which may seem ironic in view of the portrayal of Soka Gakkai as a "chanting for a Porsche" type of religion in some of the mass media. These new religions thus are seen to provide an alternative space to one cultural idiom of sex, kinship and self, of self in society, and of various other vexed concepts such as "politics" and "wealth."

As ecological concerns are becoming more mainstream and socially acceptable, an increasingly affluent middle class is becoming committed to these concerns. Similarly, as Soka Gakkai became more sophisticated and experienced, it engaged in dialogue with its German members and established a new set of needs to which it could then begin to cater. This more recent strategy is what I would call "client-oriented." More intellectual, middle-class, and mainstream sections of society with an interest in the long-term benefits of chanting, especially those of a psychological nature, began to be attracted to Soka Gakkai and contributed to a change of emphasis. In the neighboring town, for example, Soka Gakkai discussion meetings had evolved into highly sophisticated and complex psychological analyses (many of the members there were engaged in professions related to psychology or spiritual healing), an emphasis that other members perhaps found rather far removed from the true meaning of Buddhism.

Any discussion about a common or third culture, Featherstone (1993) postulates, must begin with a thorough examination of who does the defining, to what purpose, and from what parameters. I have tried to view the specific case of Soka Gakkai in Germany through such a lens.

Who does the defining?

Both German and Japanese members believe that they are defining the culture and the community. We therefore start out with two distinct definitions, but I believe that in the course of interaction a new, third definition develops, one made up of the interplay and compromises between the two sides. Nevertheless, it is clear that Soka Gakkai continues to maintain a somewhat asymmetrical core–periphery type of relationship. In spite of some authors' reservations about the actual existence and usefulness of the core–periphery type of model (Hall 1991; Wolff 1991; Massey and Jess 1995), in the case of the establishment of Soka Gakkai in Germany, or indeed of any other foreign religion, it gives us an accurate picture of the forces initially at work. It seems undeniable that at first the Japanese members were reluctant to admit that they could be learning something from those people they had been sent out to teach. This is changing now, although not fast enough for some German palates.

Globalization experts have also been somewhat hasty to assume that external forces or new cultures act in a unified manner upon the host culture (see Wallerstein 1991) without examining how heterogeneous the two cultures are or at what levels the interaction takes place. Most Japanese would deny emphatically that Soka Gakkai is representative of Japanese culture in general; it is no more than a certain lifestyle and ideology, which nevertheless maintains some links to the more general Japanese and Buddhist tradition. Even within Soka Gakkai itself, however, there may be different nuances and interpretations, as between the acclimatized and nonacclimatized Japanese leaders in Germany.

The host community, of course, cannot lay claim to any strong unity of background, shared history, or even geographical proximity. Most members may be German, but some grew up in the Democratic and some in the Federal Republic. There is also considerable variation between towns and countryside, between north and south, and this accounts for the immense diversity of backgrounds, social classes, and professions of members today. Perhaps, in looking at the German Soka Gakkai, we need to redefine the notion of community itself: no longer bounded geographically or characterized by face-to-face interaction (for a critique of the traditional understanding of the authentic community, see Young 1990), but an ideologically homogeneous group, which nevertheless remains open to some extent to unassimilated otherness.

It is striking that, although there were some isolated instances of difficulties in understanding and accepting ideological things, such as karma, it was in fact the sum of small things that almost led to a breakdown of communication between the two sides. The German members were in full agreement with the Japanese members about the aims and meaning of Nichiren Buddhism, stressed the universalistic message and Soka Gakkai's acknowledgment as a nongovernmental organization by the United Nations, and even accepted and found justification for the complicated organizational structure; but problems such as language, clothes worn at meetings, and the sex division of labor proved far more difficult to accept and entailed intense negotiation on both sides. I will just refer to these three examples, which, although trivial, seem typical of the adjustment required from both Japanese and German members.

Most German members consider themselves to be aware of the differences between what is Buddhist and what is merely Japanese tradition in Soka Gakkai, and they scrupulously pointed out that it is the latter they disagree with and not Buddhism itself:

> When I first saw all these niggardly little details, I said to myself: "I don't know – I quite like this type of Buddhism, but do I want to take on board all this Japanese cultural baggage?" We are Buddhists, but we are German nevertheless. And we want to remain German.

Part of the "cultural baggage" was the Japanese language. This did not affect the language of prayer: most members, regardless of nationality, claim to prefer the Japanese version of the Lotus Sutra and seem to consider the difficulties they encountered while trying to learn how to perform *Gongyo* as a sort of initiation process. However, there was less understanding for the Japanese leaders who had been living in Germany for a long time but could not speak the language properly, and also for the lack of sufficient German-language materials. Many of the core works of Nichiren Daishonin or Ikeda are still available only in the English translation, in spite of recent efforts to remedy the matter by running excerpts of Ikeda's commentaries on Nichiren's writings in the monthly *Forum* magazine. Language remains the most significant barrier to any Japanese religion's overseas ambitions, repeatedly pointed out by members of all the movements that I investigated. There is also some concern about the selectivity of translations, as certain volumes are emphasized or not in different countries.

The second example, the issue of clothes, has been satisfactorily resolved. Given the "alternative lifestyle" background of many of the first German members of the movement and that many women were at the height of their punk or hippie experiments at the time, they were at first amused and then exasperated by the impeccably groomed, twin-set clad, and pearl-hung Japanese women and concerned that they might be expected to follow suit. Although the neat Japanese women were, by all accounts, not openly judgmental of the more casual or extreme dress of their fellow members, there must have been some underlying role-model pressure to which the German women reacted strongly, especially the group of lesbian women in Hamburg, who refused to wear skirts to meetings even when advised to do so. They protested that appearance had little to do with the "treasure inside" or with the correct practice of Buddhism, and after some time a truce was declared. The German women began to realize that they were not being forced to take on things they felt strongly against, and the Japanese women began to dress more casually.

Probably the most controversial and ongoing debate concerns the traditional division of labor among the sex- and age-segregated groups. Although few people minded the divisions *per se*, and most agreed that a higher number of activities scheduled for the Youth Divisions made sense, as older members generally had other commitments, there was considerable resentment over the division of labor according to sex. At all larger events, men were responsible for the general organization, the distribution of invitations, and the transportation of guests; the women were relegated to cleaning and catering. Some women deeply resented the cleaning itself: "I don't understand why I have to clean [the *Kaikan*] for my personal development. I do the cleaning at home, don't I?" Others emphasized that it was not the type of activity itself that they resented, but that it was so strictly divided: "If I'm a woman, but I am also a trained stonemason or carpenter or something, why shouldn't I use my skills? And if I were a man with no special skills, why shouldn't I clean?"

Things were beginning to change during my fieldwork, women being allowed to engage in a more varied set of activities after years of protest. One of my informants summed up the situation as follows: "You must do something yourself, not wait for guidance from above. And if at first you don't succeed, you must be stubborn and simply continue hammering at the wall until you wear it out."

What is the purpose?

Kosen rufu[5] is the official purpose that both German and Japanese members will mention in the first breath when asked about the aim of Soka Gakkai or the reason for any of their activities. Underlying this may be hidden or semi-explicit agendas, and these are usually different for the Japanese and German members.

The Japanese members are concerned with building a reliable and efficient power structure of their organization in Germany, one that will continue to function (at least, in broad terms) much as they envisage even after they release the reins of leadership into German hands; gaining new members and keeping those that they have already converted; and creating a financially self-supporting and viable branch of the movement in Germany. This last is a double-sided, potentially damaging goal, because it would give complete freedom of development (perhaps in unexpected directions) and a possible distancing as a result of increased independence from the Japanese headquarters. The German members are concerned with maintaining their national and personal identity, avoiding a personality cult around the figure of the president, Daisaku Ikeda, and gaining access to the higher levels of leadership, while maintaining an effective grassroots approach.

Most German members view the great number of changes that have taken place in the German Soka Gakkai in recent years, especially (I was informed) after the breakaway from the Nichiren Shoshu priesthood, as a promising beginning, but by no means enough. The decentralization that they envisage goes beyond the establishment of predominantly German leaders and adaptation to cultural sensitivities. The following strategy mapped out by a member of the Young Men's Division is typical:

The future belongs to decentralization. That's why we have to build up really strong local groups and encourage local initiative and autonomy. I think that after Ikeda's death there will be no single president, but a sort of confederation of country leaders. Strict hierarchy will disappear. This does not mean a descent into chaos; it's just the natural taking over of power by the new generation. There won't be just one man or one group or one country setting down the law, but a great deal of cooperation and working out what is best for each individual case.

A female leader summed up the German aspirations even more succinctly: "There must be a German way of achieving *kosen rufu*."

Parameters

The limits within which both Japanese and German members are operating are delineated by the German state and its policy toward the new religions; just as important are the prevailing attitudes among Germans toward religious commitment and toward foreign culture. Stark (1987, 1996) and Shimazono (1993) point out certain key elements that they believe may determine the success of a religious movement aiming to expand abroad. One of the most important is the tolerance of the host culture toward other religions in general and how favorable it is toward the culture in which the religion originated. I would venture to widen the concept of "ecology," coined by Stark (1996: 141), to include the whole cultural background to which a new religious movement (NRM) has to adapt upon entering a foreign culture.

Germany is almost equally divided into Catholic (43 percent) and Protestant (40 percent) communities (Harris *et al.* 1992: 415) and was until the mid-twentieth century almost completely dominated by these two churches. From the early 1960s onward, however, with the influx of labor from Turkey and Yugoslavia, Islam became increasingly important and is now the third largest religious community in Germany (Hummel 1994). Less than 5 percent of the population of almost 80 million are involved in the new religious movements, and the two main churches can still levy a 10 percent income tax on all registered church members (Harris *et al.* 1992). However, Kehrer (1980: 102) and Baumann (1993: 330) agree that there is no real religious pluralism in Germany today, merely a "toleration" of the other religions alongside the main churches, i.e. the tolerance shown to a minority by the majority, a toleration of what is seen as "deviation" from the norm rather than an acceptance of the difference (Neumann and Fischer 1987).

The mass media have generally been hostile toward new religions. In Germany the rather inaccurate term *Jugendsekte* (youth sect), propagated by the influential "sect-expert," the evangelical priest Haack, has become established. The protests of the religions thus disparaged have been low key and ineffectual, not very much publicized (Usarski 1988). The ministries for family and youth for each *Bundesland* (state in the federation) publish quite aggressive pamphlets about the threatening sects (for example, one such brochure brought out by the state of Baden-Wurttemberg is titled "How to protect yourselves from dubious guys and bad stuff" and lumps together in comic-book format advice on how to avoid theft, drugs, blackmail, and new religions).

The success of the negative portrayal in the mass media is the result of several factors specific to the German context, including the alliance among parents' initiatives, anti-cult movements, the mass media and some politicians (especially at the local level), and members of the clergy concerning the NRMs; failure by sociologists and historians of religion to provide an alternative image; and the inconsistency between the official rights granted to the NRMs at the level of the national government and the persecution that they often suffer at the local level (for example, government funding for anti-cult campaigners and rehabilitation centers for deprogrammed people).

The proportion of foreign population in unified Germany remains fairly constant at about 5 percent of the total population (4.8 million out of a total of about 80 million; Harris *et al.* 1992). Yet, in spite of this fairly large percentage, the government and major parties "continue to intone: 'The German Federal Republic is not a country of immigration', as if the ritual chant could make the problems go away" (Castles 1987: 6). Much has been made, especially abroad, of the recent racist attacks in Germany, but these reports have been somewhat exaggerated. Although there are a good many tensions, especially as social benefits decrease and unemployment rises, and although the European Values Study places Germany among the least tolerant of countries regarding racial or religious prejudice (Ashford and Timms 1992), racial violence is on the whole confined to extremist groups and there are plenty of counterexamples (for example, poster campaigns proclaiming "Xenophobia? Not here!"). The real problem is the indifference or "grumbling discontent" that the great majority of Germans feel toward foreigners. Few Germans are interested in other cultures (Ardagh 1995: 289–90; Burns 1995: 302), although there is a perceptible growth of interest in alternative medicine and the New Age, with magazines such as *Esotera* dedicated to advertising new publications and seminars in the field. There are a fairly large number of so-called wellness centers, which alongside more conventional methods of relaxation and beautification also offer meditation and yoga classes, Tantric courses, acupuncture, and the like.

It is clear that the Germans do not regard all foreigners with a jaundiced eye: white residents of high occupational status from Western Europe or from North America are positively fawned upon (Castles 1987: 99; Ardagh 1995: 295). The Japanese would tend to fall into this favored category. According to the Japan Zentrum at the University of Marburg, there were about 20,000 Japanese living in Germany in 1996. Most of them are employed by branch offices of Japanese companies and banks. They are especially visible (and wealthy) in Düsseldorf (6,000 Japanese), although most towns in the Ruhr area and Frankfurt are well populated with Japanese. They generally live in luxurious apartments in leafy residential areas or in the suburbs. In Frankfurt and Düsseldorf, the Japanese community has schools for all levels, with Saturday classes for children of mixed parentage, golf and tennis clubs, choirs, and shops, so much so that some Japanese housewives complain that they hardly notice they are living abroad at all (and the incentive for learning German is minimal). The Japanese population in Germany is further made up of Japanese women married to German men (very seldom the other way round), students, and semipermanent residents, usually in the creative professions (personal research at the Japan Zentrum archive, University of Marburg, in 1996).

As recent press coverage of what has been termed "the persecution of Scientologists" in Germany shows, the present prospects are far from cheerful for members of any new religious movement. Soka Gakkai members admitted that they continued to pay church tax,[6] for fear of discrimination in the workplace or for their children at school. If they did choose to declare their beliefs, they would stress the fact that they were Buddhist and belonged to a long line of tradition.[7]

The time frame within which Soka Gakkai is operating is likewise significant, in two ways: diachronically – Soka Gakkai is a comparatively recent entry into German society, it has been around only for 30 years and visible perhaps in the last 10 – and synchronically – the present point in time, with the more traditional 1980s and 1990s having replaced the experimental and rebellious 1960s and 1970s.

Furthermore, there are, as I mentioned earlier, the local variations that Soka Gakkai has learned to live with: the rebellious north, the discouraged east, the diffuse urban community, and the more inbred feuding of the rural community. Other problems perceived as still not fully resolved include sex roles and what, for lack of a better term, I shall call "minority groups." These include unmarried women, single mothers, and homosexuals and lesbians and others whose lives do not quite fit neatly into established patterns. Although there is no open disapproval or discrimination against these groups, some of them (and some who do not belong to these groups but are concerned about what they call the "proper application of Buddhism") would like to see more active support and a greater understanding of their special needs:

> Buddhism has to learn to live with the realities of the German society. There *are* very many broken families here, many single mothers, and you can't present them with little booklets entitled *The Creative Family*, all about women being the sunshine in the home and so on.

One member drew my attention to the fact that local groups tend to form around members who share similar problems or life experiences, such as a town where single mothers predominate among the members, or another with single women, or Hamburg with lesbians, or another with people with nervous disorders. She explained this through karma. It had obviously brought them together to try to solve their problems. The existence of these groups, however, could also be interpreted as an attempt to build "self-help groups" under conditions where they feel insufficiently taken into account by the central organization. Indeed, the member who pointed these groups out to me continued:

> Soka Gakkai still casts a blind eye over these people, still pretends they do not exist. More needs to be done to understand how to apply Buddhism to the lives of people whose lives refuse to follow the prescribed patterns!

Conclusion

I will now return to the questions that I set myself at the beginning of this chapter. The first of these was how a religion such as Soka Gakkai, which arose under specific historical, geographical, and social conditions, could become relevant to people who did not share the same language, history, or cultural assumptions. I think the answer lies in the fact that, although German members agree that a lot about Soka Gakkai is closely linked to 1940s and 1950s Japan, they feel that those are inconsequential details, superfluous baggage that must either be thrown out or tailored to fit present-day requirements, which have changed in Japan as well. The essential part of Soka Gakkai, the Lotus Sutra and the teachings of Nichiren Daishonin as revealed in the *Gosho*, are of lasting and universal value and therefore likely to appeal to "any human being who has ever reflected on the self and its relation to the world" (author's field notes 1996), regardless of historical or social circumstances. In Soka Gakkai they have found an alternative to the cultural idiom that they grew up with and found increasingly unsatisfactory, a way of moving beyond their own "limited" German context.

The second question, strongly related to the first, concerned the proportion of universality and specificity that a religion should have to appeal beyond its national boundaries. The answer seems evident after the examples that I have given. Members were willing to accept wholesale what they perceived as "essential" to Soka Gakkai Buddhism: the teachings, the language of prayer, the organizational structure. It was the details, the things they felt belonged under the label "Japanese custom" rather than "Buddhism" that they objected to: the personality cult of Ikeda Daisaku, the sex segregation of work, clothes, and the like. Minor dissatisfaction with Soka Gakkai is perhaps raised to the status of major problems precisely because members have such high expectations of its universalistic message and believe it to be "above" cultural traditions, historical or social specificity. Nichiren Buddhism, as they see it, is supposed to transcend both Japanese and German customs (or maintain only what is of value from either) and bring about a new world order and understanding. It remains a source of puzzlement to me whether Soka Gakkai's concerns with world peace, environmental issues, fair trade, and the Third World – concerns that are shared by nearly all members that I talked with – actually attract a certain type of clientele who then convert to the movement or whether it is a means of "educating" members and encouraging them to think beyond their immediate surroundings and problems.

Finally, can Soka Gakkai be accused of overadaptation, of having lost its authenticity and specificity in its desire to gain German members? I think not. It is true that Soka Gakkai has changed a good deal in around 30 years of existence in Germany. Long-time members are careful to point out that other religions, including Christianity, have needed much longer to adapt to foreign circumstances. The basis for change is now definitely in place, but German members feel that quite a lot still remains to be done to make it a truly significant religion in their society, although they remain critical of the latter as well.

Identity is at best an ambivalent construct, and in today's world it is more often defined by consumption and lifestyle than by appurtenance to a nation-state, although it should be taken together with those other practices of cultural self-constitution, such as ethnicity, class, and sex (Friedman 1994). Soka Gakkai members in Germany can therefore define themselves simultaneously as Germans, Buddhists, and cosmopolitans, although experiencing an occasional conflict of loyalties. At different stages in their life they may choose to highlight different elements of their multiple allegiances, but they feel that the message they wish to share with everybody, namely the discovery of Buddhahood inside oneself, is of such universal importance and value that they are truly citizens of the world.

Notes

1 An earlier version of this chapter was published as "Adapt or perish: the story of Soka Gakkai in Germany" in *Japanese New Religions in a Global Perspective*, edited by P. B. Clarke. In this revised version, I have tried to incorporate the interesting comments and suggestions following the presentation of this paper at the European Association of Japanese Studies conference in Budapest in 1997. Any remaining inaccuracies are my own.

2 The fieldwork upon which this paper is based was carried out in 1995–6 in Germany. I am especially thankful to Professor Michael Pye of the University of Marburg for his hospitality and help in all matters and to Professor Peter Clarke and the Japanese New Religions Project at King's College London, who made this research possible.

3 Although founded in the 1930s as the lay organization of the Nichiren Shoshu school of Buddhism, Soka Gakkai had its period of spectacular growth in Japan in the 1950s and early 1960s. Various reasons have been suggested for this, including the void felt after Japan's defeat in the Pacific War (see McFarland 1967).

4 There is some cause to suspect that Soka Gakkai underestimates its membership figures in Germany, probably so it does not appear to be a threat to the German authorities. The official figure has stagnated at 2,000 for the past 6 or 7 years, although the movement also claims a net gain in members (offsetting the turnover rate) and that there were hardly any "defections" to the Nichiren Shoshu faction after the split (M. Baumann, personal communication).

5 Literally, "to widely declare and spread," it is usually glossed (on the Internet too, at the Soka Gakkai International home page) as "securing world peace and happiness for all humankind through the propagation of true Buddhism."
6 Income tax in Germany typically includes a small sum to sponsor the two main churches. Theoretically, tax-payers may opt out of the church taxation if they define themselves as belonging to another religion. In practice, many citizens are reluctant to opt out for fear of suffering discrimination, as employers become aware of this choice when they process payrolls.
7 Buddhists, especially those belonging to the Tibetan school, have a positive, if somewhat clichéd, image in Germany as peace-loving, orange-clad vegetarians, in marked contrast to the image of money-hungry brainwashers that the "sects" have.

Bibliography

Ardagh, J. (1995) *Germany and the Germans*, 3rd edn, London: Penguin.
Ashford, S. and Timms, N. (1992) *What Europe Thinks: A Study of Western European Values*, Aldershot, U.K.: Dartmouth.
Baumann, M. (1993) *Deutsche Buddhisten (German Buddhists)*, Marburg: Diagonal Verlag.
Beyer, P. (1994) *Religion and Globalization*, London: Sage.
Burns, R. (ed.) (1995) *German Cultural Studies*, Oxford: Oxford University Press.
Castles, S. (1987) *Here for Good: Western Europe's New Ethnic Minorities*, London: Pluto Press.
Coleman, S. (1993) "Conservative Protestantism and the world order: the faith movement in the United States and Sweden," *Sociology of Religion* 54: 353–73.
Dator, J. (1969) *Soka Gakkai, Builders of the Third Civilization*, Seattle: University of Washington Press.
Featherstone, M. (1993) "Global and local cultures," in J. Bird, B. Curtis, T. Putnam, G. Robertson, and L. Tickner (eds) *Mapping the Futures: Local Cultures, Global Change*, London: Routledge.
Friedman, J. (1994) *Cultural Identity and Global Process*, Thousand Oaks, CA: Sage.
Galtung, J. (1990) "The green movement: a socio-historical exploration," in M. Albrow and E. King (eds) *Globalization, Knowledge and Society*, London: Sage.
Hall, S. (1991) "The local and the global: globalization and ethnicity," in E. King (ed.) *Culture, Globalization, and the World System*, New York: Macmillan.
Harris, I., Mews, S., Morris, P., and Shepherd, J. (eds) (1992) *Contemporary Religions: A World Guide*, London: Longman.
Hummel, R. (1994) *Religiöser Pluralismus oder christliches Abendland? (Religious Pluralism or the Christian West?)*, Darmstadt: Wissenschaftliche Buchgesellschaft.
Kehrer, G. (ed.) (1980) *Zur Religionsgeschichte der Bundesrepublik Deutschland (The History of Religions in the Federal Republic of Germany)*, Munich: Piper.
McFarland, H.N. (1967) *The Rush Hour of the Gods: A Study of the New Religious Movements in Japan*, New York: Macmillan.
Massey, M. and Jess, P. (eds) (1995) *A Place in the World?* Oxford: Open University and Oxford University Press.
Neumann, J. and Fischer, M. (eds) (1987) *Toleranz und Repression: Zur Lage religiöser Minderheiten in modernen Gesellschaften (Tolerance and Repression: the Position of Religious Minorities in Modern Societies)*, Frankfurt: Campus.
SGI (Soka Gakkai International). (1993) *Soka Gakkai International*, Tokyo: Soka Gakkai.

Shimazono, S. (1992) *Gendai kyuzai shukyo ron (Dictionary of Contemporary Religions)*, Tokyo: Iwanami.

—— (1993) "The expansion of Japan's new religions into foreign cultures," in M. R. Mullins, S. Shimazono and P. L. Swanson (eds) *Religion and Society in Modern Japan*, Berkeley, CA: Asian Humanities Press.

Shimpo, M. (1995) "Indentured migrants from Japan," in *The Cambridge Survey of World Migration*, Cambridge: Cambridge University Press.

Snow, D.A. (1976) "The Nichiren Shoshu Buddhist movement in America: a sociological examination of its value orientation, recruitment efforts and spread," unpublished Ph.D. dissertation, University of California, Los Angeles.

Stark, R. (1987) "How new religions succeed: a theoretical model," in D. G. Bromley and P. E. Hammond (eds) *The Future of New Religious Movements*, Macon, GA: Mercer University Press.

—— (1996) "Why religious movements succeed or fail: a revised general model," *Journal of Contemporary Religion* 11 (2).

Usarski, F. (1988) *Die Stigmatisierung Neuer Spiritueller Bewegungen in der BRD (Stigmatizing New Religious Movements in the Federal Republic of Germany)*, Cologne: Böhlau.

Wallerstein, I. (1991) "The national and the universal: can there be such a thing as world culture?" in E. King (ed.) *Culture, Globalization, and the World System*, New York: Macmillan.

Wolff, J. (1991) "The global and the specific: reconciling conflicting theories of culture," in E. King (ed.) *Culture, Globalization and the World System*, New York: Macmillan.

Young, I. (1990) "The ideal of community and the politics of difference," in L. Nicholson (ed.) *Feminism/Postmodernism*, London: Routledge.

Part IV
Cultural diffusion

7 Japanese comics coming to Hong Kong

Cherry Sze-ling Lai and
Dixon Heung Wah Wong

This chapter offers an empirical account of the mediascape of Japan's globalization: the process of Japanese comics coming to Hong Kong and their effect on local comic culture in particular and Hong Kong society in general. We understand this process as a dialectic between human practice and social structure and between Japanese comics and Hong Kong society. Each of these mutually affects the others in such a way that two methodological implications follow. First, Japanese comics coming to Hong Kong should be regarded as a multifaceted historical process that takes into account not only the characteristics of Japanese comics but also the structure of the local comic industry in particular and the sociocultural endowments of Hong Kong in general. Second, as the first point suggests, a comprehensive study of such a process needs to begin in Japan.

Comics in Japan

This section takes us to Japan and examines the characteristics of Japanese comics and the complex structure of Japan's comic industry. It outlines three related characteristics that were to inform the process whereby Japanese comics were introduced to Hong Kong. The first is the emphasis on the individualistic style and originality of comic artists. Although Japanese artists may employ assistants to help them, they themselves do all the creative work (Schodt 1983: 138–9). For example, Osamu Tezuka had his ten assistants do all the noncreative work, but he himself created all the stories, designed the frame layout, and drew and colored the characters and the backgrounds. Artists who rely a lot on assistants are usually criticized as being too businesslike (Schodt 1983: 142–3).

The second is the relative independence of artists from the control of publishers. In Japan, artists are generally not employed by publishers. Usually, the two parties are free to negotiate a deal. If both parties agree on the financial and artistic terms, artists will then create serialized stories for publishers. The extent of independence that artists enjoy is certainly dependent on the sales of their comics. Successful artists may retain the copyright of their comics, change publishers if they are not happy, and work on more than one story at a time. Publishers are unable to maintain control of such artists except that they assign editors to ensure that artists meet deadlines (Schodt 1983: 144). The editor's responsibility is heavy. As Schodt described:

> If the commissioned artist is famous, the editor must be very circumspect in the way pressure is applied. This may take the form of polite phone calls to the artist's manager, coy visits daily to coffee shops or other places the artist frequents in hope of meeting him, and, in short, anything to subtly remind him of his obligation. If all else fails, a more drastic method must be employed: the offending artist is confined to a room, supplied with food, and not let out until he or she finishes the job. Editors, with the full cooperation of the artist's manager, totally control access. At the extreme, phone calls are not allowed, passwords are used to keep out competing editors, and, if in a hotel, visitors may be told at the front desk that the party they seek is not in. The editor must stay by the artist's side night and day until he has the completed work in hand, for to return to the office empty-handed would be a great loss of face. Some artists are so used to this system that they cannot meet their deadlines without it, and they are even known to get angry if the editor dozes while they are still at work in the wee hours of the morning.
>
> (Schodt 1983: 144)

Given the independence of artists in Japan and the emphasis on individualistic style and originality, publishers find it difficult to control or standardize the content of comics. This difficulty results in the third characteristic of Japanese comics: a large variety of choices. According to Schodt, there were comics about samurai for children in prewar Japan; later samurai comics incorporated elements of violence, sex, and philosophy and were aimed at an audience of young men (Schodt 1983: 69–70). *Yakuza* comics and school-gang comics, directly derived from these samurai stories, were popular among student readers (Schodt 1983: 76). Inspired by Japan's successes in the sports world, there were comics featuring baseball, professional wrestling, boxing, volleyball, soccer, judo, rugby, car racing, motorcross, and so on (Schodt 1983: 80–4). Such stories of samurai, adventurers, and sportsmen appeared in almost all comics for boys and men (Schodt 1983: 87).

Comics artists did not ignore girls and women. Like comics for boys and men, those for girls and women were filled with sports stories, comedies, gag strips, mysteries, and science-fiction fantasies. But love was the main theme of all these stories. In addition, artists emphasized the clothes and hair styles of the characters, drew the eyes of the characters "with pencil-thin eyebrows, long, full eyelashes, and [in] the size of window panes that emote gentleness and femininity," and situated their characters in such exotic locales as Europe and the United States (Schodt 1983: 90–2).

Work-related comics constitute a third category. Parallel to the dual economy of Japan, work-related comics are divided into two subcategories. One features young men from disadvantaged backgrounds who have become well-established professionals in pachinko parlors, kitchens, carpentry, and so on (Schodt 1983: 106–11). Another – *sarariiman* comics – depicts the lives of the elite employees of large corporations. Apart from these work-related comics, another genre of comics features gambling at pachinko parlors and other gambling places (Schodt 1983: 111–14).

Finally, marginal comics depict violence, homosexuality, pornography, and cannibalism (Schodt 1983: 120–37). This wide variety of Japanese comics constitutes a sharp contrast with Hong Kong comics.

Some history of comics in Hong Kong

For the past 25 years the development of local comics and the comic industry in Hong Kong has been greatly influenced by the famous artist Wong Yuk Long. Wong came to Hong Kong in 1958 when he was 7 years old (Ling *et al.* 1991: 16). He left school and joined the comic industry when he was 15 years old. At that time, the economy of Hong Kong was underdeveloped, and the general standard of living was low. The major entertainment of Hong Kong people was to go to Chinese herbal tea shops – where radios were installed – to listen to popular broadcast stories, concerts, Cantonese operas, and sometimes live broadcasts of football matches. Young people also went to those Chinese herbal tea shops that had jukeboxes to select their favorite songs (Cheng 1997: 57). Children too young to enjoy Western music and football matches chose comics as their major form of entertainment. At that time, comic books were poorly produced. Only the cover was in color, and the comic book was only one-quarter of the size of a contemporary one. But it was cheap – 20 cents a copy. The profit from producing comics was so little that not many artists could survive. In addition, comics at that time featured sex and violence only. Parents therefore did not want their children to either read or make comics. In short, comics were considered "cheap" entertainment, and comic artists enjoyed a very low social status (Ling *et al.* 1991: 16–17).

Wong raised the social status of comics (Ling *et al.* 1991: 17). First, he started to produce popular comics. In 1971, his *Siu Lau Man (The Little Gangster)*, published by Bo Kwong, was well received in the market (Lai 1997a: 6). It was a story about a group of violent gangsters. Second, Wong built up his comic empire by establishing his own company, Yuk Long Publications Company, through which he published his comics (Lai 1997a: 6). At the same time, Wong integrated the whole production process into his own company. He set up a mass production system to "produce" comics. This system was similar to that of Saitō Productions. As Schodt described:

> Takao Saitō, the creator of *Golgo 13*, works with fifteen full-time staff members of his company, Saitō Productions, and has seven or eight outside

people contracted to supply story scripts. Saitō regards comic story production as comparable to filmmaking, with himself as director. When he receives a job order, he assigns four assistants, according to their particular talents, to work with him as a team, and he stimulates creativity by holding lively discussions with them about the story and artwork. Assistants may specialize in drawing realistic pictures of buildings, machinery, background characters, or landscapes, and for many of them the job is good training and the first step to independence. Saitō at times only pencils in the faces of the main characters.

(Schodt 1983: 142–3)

In Wong's terms, the artist was the *jiu bik* (chief writer) and the assistants *zo li* (assistants). The chief writer created the stories and designed the main characters; the rest was then left to the assistants. Among these assistants, one would be responsible for drawing heads of the characters, the others for drawing the bodies, the background, wind, and clothes.

Apart from this mass-production system, Wong established his own printing factory with advanced printing machines. This factory not only printed comics for Wong but also several magazines for Wong's publishing company. Wong concurrently diversified his publishing business into other fields. In addition to comics, his company published several magazines featuring local celebrities (Lai 1997a: 9). With a mass-production system, a printing factory, and a company with diversified business, Wong built a publishing empire. He himself was the king of this empire; his assistants were his "royal guards."

At the beginning of the 1980s, Wong's empire dominated the industry. In 1986, Wong successfully listed his company on the Hong Kong Stock Exchange and became a millionaire (Wong 1994: 32). People in Hong Kong admired his success and started to reflect on their bias toward the comics industry. However, Wong's domination helped to standardize the content, drawing styles, and production of local comics and thus reinforced the "bad" image of local comics.

In regard to standardization, Wong's mass-production system became the norm. Given Wong's domination of the industry, many artists were forced to join Wong's company as chief writers (Lai 1997a: 10). They had to follow Wong's mass-production system. Moreover, a newcomer who aspired to be a chief writer had to join Wong's company. To control these "outsiders," Wong forced them to sign a 6-year employment contract. Hong Kong artists, in other words, unlike their Japanese counterparts, are employed by publishers. They were transformed from artists to ordinary employees. They had to work in the company's office instead of at home. The company was therefore better able to control them. More important, the copyright of artists' comics belonged to their publishers. Therefore, even if an artist were to leave a company, the company could still continue to publish the artist's comics.

Second, the normative status of Wong's mass-production system also helped to standardize the drawing style of local comics. Newcomers are assigned to be assistants of the chief writer. They then become specialized in drawing parts of the picture such as buildings. They end up producing the same building regardless of the specific context of each comic story. The originality and individualistic style of each artist are thus lost.

Finally, Wong's preeminent position in the industry made him very influential in the content of local comics. Inasmuch as Wong had become famous through his martial art comics, it was difficult for him to encourage his subordinates to diversify the content, difficult to approve any suggestion of change of content. Newcomers who aspired to be future Wong Yuk Longs tended to follow Wong's successful recipe when they made comics. Consequently, martial art comics became the dominant genre of local comics to the extent that martial art comics are *the* comics in Hong Kong.

The general images of comics in Hong Kong: the politics of everyday life

Comics have long been regarded in Hong Kong as harmful to, and thus not suitable for, children and teenagers. In the first place, the graphic nature of comics can never convey a sense of seriousness to the local Chinese people. Second, because of the domination of martial art comics in the local comics market, comics have come to be associated with violence and lower-class children. At the end of 1973 and the beginning of 1974, people from different sectors of Hong Kong society launched a campaign against local comics. They included pressure groups such as the Hong Kong Association of Social Workers, the Education and Professional Association, and some Christian groups. These groups conducted a survey in 1973 on almost 1,000 students from primary and secondary schools in Hong Kong. The result of the survey was later published in *The Report on the Campaign against Violence and Pornography of Comic Books*. The report pointed out that the law at the time was ambiguous: it was difficult for the court to judge objectively whether a comic book was violent or erotic. In addition, the report also complained that the punishment levied on publishers was too light to have any deterrent effect on them. Finally, the report objected to the sale of comics to children and teenagers because, it alleged, violence was described in local comics as the only way to solve problems.

These groups stepped up their pressure on the Hong Kong government to tighten the law by frequently organizing seminars and talks on television and radio and reports in newspapers to discuss how to prohibit all comic books from being sold to teenagers and children. Through these campaigns, comic books were portrayed as addictive, like cocaine or other drugs.

On 30 October 1974, suggestions about controlling comic books were submitted to the Executive Council for discussion. The executive councillors requested that the law be tightened. On 14 November, the attorney general adopted the suggestions and promised to tighten the law. Under social pressure from different social groups and the press, the Hong Kong government proposed a new law and submitted it to the Legislative Council.

Although the new law did not affect the industry very much, comic artists became very self-disciplined. More important, this campaign together with subsequent campaigns throughout the 1980s and the early 1990s successfully linked comics to violence and pornography and reading comics was associated with lower-class activity in people's consciousness. To local Chinese people, *only* manual workers or those who failed in school read comics (Lai 1997a: 7–9).

Japanese comics coming to Hong Kong

The importation of Japanese comics into Hong Kong can be traced to the 1960s, when the local comics market was depressed. Many publishers who could not find good comic stories to publish turned to Japanese comics. They translated Japanese comics into Chinese and sold them in the market. With a good response from the market, some publishers even employed artists to imitate Japanese comics and produce them locally. They usually adapted the famous Japanese comic characters such as Ultraman into their stories and developed new comic series (Lai 1997a: 5–6).

Thanks to the success of Wong Yuk Long, the 1970s was a golden period for local comics. Japanese comics suddenly disappeared from the local market. Not until the beginning of the 1980s did local publishers start to import Japanese comics again. The 1980s can be regarded as the period of the Japanese boom. Everything Japanese soon became popular. Japanese cuisine such as *sushi, sashimi, wasabi, nori,* and so on came to Hong Kong with Japanese supermarkets and department stores; Japanese popular music and pop stars became popular among young people, as a result of the importation of *karaoke* and the promotion of local magazines; Japanese fashion came with *non-no;* and Japanese comics followed the Seal Publishing Company. At the beginning of the 1980s, the Seal Publishing Company played the major role in importing Japanese comics. At that time, the Hong Kong government was very strict about copyright law. The company bought copyrights from Japanese publishers and translated Japanese comics into Chinese and published locally. The publication was always sixty to eighty pages with a color cover, monochrome printed on comparatively rough paper, and with clearly printed information about the authors, original publishers, and original publishing date. The Chinese translation was quite accurate (Lai 1997b: 9–10).

As these translated Japanese comics proved to be very profitable, more and more publishers joined the business. And once the government loosened control of copyright, many publishers translated and published Japanese comics illegally. The quality of translation varied greatly, and the same edition would be printed in different packages by the same company. For instance, Dragon Publishing Company published *City Hunter* in three packages with different prices: the ordinary package, golden package, and Japanese package.

Also, to evade legal responsibility, publishers did not print the information about authors, original publishers, and so on completely or clearly on the cover. To maximize the profit, some publishers even copied directly from the Taiwanese translated edition. This period was by any measure chaotic and uncontrollable. However, although these translated Japanese comics attracted a lot of comic readers, since they were not marketed systematically and the printing quality was low, local comics could still survive (Lai 1997b: 10–11).

This chaotic situation invited the government to tighten control again in 1990. At the same time, the comics industry in Hong Kong underwent a big restructuring because of the collapse of Wong's empire. Many comic artists started to leave Wong's company even before the collapse. Sheung Koon Siu-wei was the first to leave and established his Siu Wei Company. His elder brother followed him and established Kwong's Company. Even Wong's disciple, Ma Wing-shing, who created the best-seller *Chung wah ying hung (Chinese Heroes)*, also wanted to leave. He was later attacked twice, on 14 May 1988 and 1 January 1989. Having recovered from his injuries, Ma established his Jone's Sky Company in 1990 (Lai 1997a: 10–11).

Another who left Wong's company was Lau Ting-kin. Lau had joined Wong's company as a part-time script writer in 1983. In 1986, Wong promoted him to be manager of the Comic Department. Lau, however, was not satisfied with the salary and left Wong's company in 1988. Finally, he decided to establish his own company, Freeman Publishing Company Limited. The first three comics published by Freeman were *Do kim siu (Knife, Sword, and Laugh)*, *Oi sait (Love Kill)*, and *Hing Chu man hwa (Comics of Hing Chu)*. At that time, the artists working for Freeman were Fung Chi-ming, Dik Hak, and Wong Kwok-hing. In 1989, the company changed its name to Freeman Publishing Corporation and opened the first retail shop in a shopping center, Shun Wo Center, to sell the company's publications (Lai 1997a: 11).

Wong Yuk Long suffered great financial loss in the 1987 stock market crisis. In 1989, he lost control of his company and was forced to step down. In 1990 Wong was found guilty of a commercial crime and sent to jail. His company was then taken over by a local media company, Sing Dao Daily, and changed its name to Culture Comics. Although Wong established a new company, Jade Dynasty Publishing Limited, after he was released in 1993, he no longer dominated the industry (Lai 1997a: 11).

The collapse of Wong's empire and the establishment of many new comics publishers intensified the competition among them because the owners of these new companies – who either used to work for Wong or were Wong's disciples – were heavily influenced by Wong's martial art comics and were more or less producing the same genre of comics for the same market. To survive this keen competition, some of them tried to explore new markets by diversifying their products. They turned to Japanese comics to take advantage of the new demand that appeared in the 1980s. As mentioned above, Japanese comics could provide a much wider variety of choices than local comics and were thus able to attract readers from different backgrounds. People who did not read comics before simply because there was no choice except martial art comics now became comics fans when they were introduced to Japanese comics. For example, many office workers, especially women, became fans of Saimon Fumi's comics. More and more university students became fans of comics, because they had been brought up in the 1980s when Japanese comics first became popular. Every year when we ask the first-year students why they are taking classes in our department (Department of Japanese Studies at the University of Hong Kong), 10–20 percent of them say that they want to learn Japanese to understand Japanese comics. In other words, the comics readership is no longer a homogeneous group of manual workers or lower-class students who fail in schools. More and more of the "elite" have joined the group. At the beginning of the 1990s, at the same time that this shift in readership was happening, a new series of campaigns was being launched to attack comics. Therefore, local publishers were very careful in importing Japanese comics. They tended to avoid violent and pornographic Japanese comics and chose *shōjo* (young girl) comics for female white-collar workers, sports comics for secondary and university students, and comics with educational values. For example, Culture Comics bought the copyright of the 300-volume collection of Osamu Tezuka and the forty-five volumes of *Doraemon* from Japan; Jone's Sky bought the copyright of *Slamdunk* and published it in Hong Kong; and Wong's new company published *Candy, Candy* (Lai 1997b: 11). Moreover, these publishers paid more attention to packaging, translation, and publication information. For example, Wong's new company established a new department in its international division to oversee translation work.

At the same time, Japanese publishers were more active in marketing their publications and their related products in Hong Kong. Shows starring characters such as Doraemon and Sailormoon were staged in Hong Kong in 1996, and products from sweets to stationery were sold. In addition, Japanese publishers were very careful in choosing their local partners and maintaining the image of their comics in Hong Kong. For example, it was said that the Japanese publisher stopped the publication of *Slamdunk* by Freeman because the company image was not good and sold the copyright to Jone's Sky in 1996 (Lai 1997b: 12).

The effect of Japanese comics on local comic culture

Inspired by Japanese *shōjo* comics, some local artists started to create Hong Kong *shōjo* comics. The most famous one was *100% feel*, a love story about two young men and one woman. Although *100% feel* was criticized for copying ideas from Japanese comics, it was the first local *shōjo* comic, symbolizing the first step by local comics toward diversification (Lai 1997b: 12).

Apart from the content, publishing and packaging also tended to be more and more like the Japanese. Before the import of Japanese comics, no comic magazine like *Jone's Sky Youngster* was being published in Hong Kong. This format of publishing similar to the Japanese *Shōnen jump* has become popular in recent years. In addition, the packages of all translated Japanese comics are also very similar to those of the originals (Lai 1997b: 13).

Regarding distribution and marketing methods, Hong Kong publishers have learned much from their Japanese counterparts. For example, local publishers, like Japanese publishers, started to manufacture comics-related products, including posters, cups, watches, T-shirts, puzzles, and models. This kind of business has been successful in Hong Kong. In addition, local publishers even set up their own retail shops to sell their publications and comics-related products. For example, Culture Comics, Jone's Sky, and Freeman have their own shops in the most crowded shopping centers (Lai 1997b: 13).

Finally, the import of Japanese comics enhanced the social status of comics. First, with the large number of varieties imported from Japan, comics are no longer an icon of violence and sex. Local people have come to understand that martial art comics form just one genre of comics. Other genres, such as the series of Osamu Tezuke, encourage their readers to reflect upon their lives, reveal social and political darkness, and describe the beauty of love (such as Saimon Fumi's comics). In short, local people started to realize that comics can have educational value (Lai 1997b: 16–17).

Second, the originality and creativity of Japanese artists helped upgrade comics to the level of "art." For example, *Akira* is always used as research material by those studying "postmodernism" and "Japaneseness." As a result, the readership is no longer confined to those "bad" boys who dropped out of school. Moreover, the fact that some Japanese artists such as Osamu Tezuka are university graduates helped to enhance the social status of comics (Lai 1997b: 17).

The final change in social status is related to the change in readership. As mentioned above, many university students read comics. To them, reading Japanese comic books is as usual as reading magazines, and they believe that they can find new ideas in comics. In addition, many universities in Hong Kong, including City University, Hong Kong Polytechnic University, and Shue Yan University, have established Japanese comics clubs, and each has about 250 members. Even at the University of Hong Kong, talks on the comics of Hong Kong have been held frequently. As more and more university students become comics readers, the social status of comics will be enhanced (Lai 1997b: 17–18).

Conclusion

This chapter has described how the characteristics of local comics, the structure of the local comics industry, the general images of comics in Hong Kong, and the legal environment orchestrated the process of importing Japanese comics to Hong Kong. It has also shown, albeit briefly, how the wide variety of Japanese comics influenced the content and packages of local comics as well as the marketing strategies and distribution of local publishers and how Japanese comics changed the local readership of comics and thus enhanced the social status of comics.

The specifics indicate broader implications for globalization theories and for understanding of Hong Kong society. First, globalization processes, at least the mediascape of the Japanese globalization process, are mediated by local societies that "work on some autonomous cultural-logic" (Sahlins 1985: viii) and thus should have different historical processes in different local cultural contexts. Western globalization theories that "are made rampantly, on the basis of anecdotal examples, without solid data to demonstrate the theorizing" (Befu and Stalker 1996: 104) did not notice these diversified local responses. Thus more empirical research should be carried out to demonstrate the diversity of local responses in different "scapes" to global processes, and, in this case, to Japanese globalization processes. Second, given the tremendous effect of Japanese culture on Hong Kong, Hong Kong can on longer be described as a place where "East meets West." This chapter calls for new discourses that are not based on simple contrasts of "East" and "West" to capture the complexity of modern Hong Kong society.

Bibliography

Befu, H. and Stalker, N. (1996) "Globalization of Japan: cosmopolitanization or spread of the Japanese village?" in H. Befu (ed.) *Japan Engaging the World: A Century of International Encounter,* Denver, CO: Center for Japanese Studies, Teikyo Loretto Heights University.

Cheng, S.L. (1997) "Back to the future: herbal tea shops in Hong Kong," in G. Evans and M. S. Tam (eds) *Hong Kong: The Anthropology of a Chinese Metropolis,* London: Curzon Press.

Lai, S.L. (1997a) "Japanese comics in Hong Kong," unpublished paper.

—— (1997b) "History of the Hong Kong comics industry," unpublished paper.

Ling, C.-s., Chou, K.-m., and Chan, C.-c. (1991) "Yao ling hoichi" (Start from zero), in C.-p. Yuen and K.-c. Lo (eds) *Saisou manwa fungwun yunmut (Introducing Famous Comic Writers)*, Hong Kong: Subculture Publications Ltd.

Sahlins, M. (1985) *Islands of History,* Chicago: University of Chicago Press.

Schodt, F. (1983) *Manga! Manga!: The World of Japanese Comics,* Tokyo: Kodansha.

Wong Y.L. (1994) *Sapyik fauwah mong (The One Billion Empty Dream),* Hong Kong: Jade Dynasty.

8 Japanese popular music in Hong Kong

Analysis of global/local cultural relations

Masashi Ogawa

Over the past 40 years in Hong Kong, the influences of Japanese popular culture have become widespread. In particular, Japanese popular music has played a significant role in Hong Kong's popular arts scene since the 1970s. However, the nature of this role has varied over the past decades. To help readers understand the changing development of this influence, this chapter will look first at the history of Hong Kong popular music by focusing on the changing influences of Japanese pop music in the past decades. Second, it will discuss how the image of Japan itself has been working to shape the image of Japanese pop music in the 1990s music scene. Last, it will examine how the globalization process, in the sense of compression of the world, is reflected in the history of Hong Kong popular music by focusing on the relationship between Japanese and Hong Kong popular music.

Hong Kong pop music history

The roots of Hong Kong pop music

Many scholars and music critics agree that the roots or prototype of the Chinese commercial pop song (at least, that of which the composers and lyricist can be identified) is the Shanghai-style pop song known as *Si Doi Kuk* in Cantonese. This style of commercial music, which began to develop between the 1920s and the 1930s, flourished in the 1940s (Wong 1997: 18). The songs were sung in Mandarin and were based mainly on the Chinese traditional minor key combined with some modern musical elements, such as the use of Western instruments (an influence of the "concession culture" of the time in Shanghai). The early establishment of a record industry helped the spread of the Shanghai pop song in China. Baak Doi record company (Hong Kong EMI at present) was established in Shanghai by a British merchant in the 1930s and accounted for about 90 percent of the market share of Mandarin pop song records in China from the late 1930s to the early 1940s (Wong 1997: 21).

The Hong Kong pop music scene (1950s to 1960s)

In response to the political turmoil in China at the end of the 1940s, the main center of production of this type of song moved to Hong Kong. In 1952 Baak Doi moved its operations to Hong Kong. As a result of the influx of large numbers of refugees from mainland China, Shanghai-style popular music became one of the mainstreams of the Hong Kong pop music scene until the mid-1960s. Besides this music, the tunes from Cantonese opera were popular. As a result of British colonial influence and the development of radio broadcasting, Western music was also popular, in particular among the young people born in Hong Kong.

During this period many "cover versions," which would become one of the mainstays of the Hong Kong pop music scene, were produced. This happened with *Si Doi Kuk* in particular. "Cover version" or "cover song" indicates that the song or piece of music is performed by someone other than the original performers. There are several different types of cover versions. In one, the original piece is "covered" by a singer who uses a musical arrangement slightly different from the original. Another type is that where the original is "covered" by a singer and with lyrics translated into a different language. In a final pattern, the original is "covered" by a singer who works with the same melody line but with different lyrics in a different language. This last type is the mainstay of the Hong Kong music scene. Although many of the people involved in the Shanghai pop music industry fled to Hong Kong, many remained in China. This resulted in a lack of composers and producers of Shanghai-style music in Hong Kong. As a consequence, many Western songs were covered using the *Si Doi Kuk* style of musical arrangement.

Some Cantonese pop songs were produced in this period. However, in the 1960s, the production quality of these records was very low and only lower-class local Chinese listened to them. Thus the stigmas of low quality and low social status were associated with Cantonese pop songs in this period (Wong 1997: 23).

In the 1960s the mainland refugees began to think of Hong Kong as their home and to regard urban Hong Kong, rather than Shanghai, as their cultural center, even if they did hold some nostalgic ties to the motherland. With this cultural shift, *Si Doi Kuk* lost much of its attractiveness to its previous audience (Wong 1997: 26–7).

In this period many local bands, such as Roman & the Four Steps and Lotus, became popular. These bands copied Western music, mainly British and American songs, and sang in English. (This trend reached its height in 1964, when the Beatles performed in Hong Kong.) This was the first time that local Hong Kong musicians dominated the Hong Kong hit chart. Although they copied Western songs and sang in English, they prepared the foundations for the acceptance of original Cantonese songs in the next period. It is often said that this band boom ended when the Wynners disbanded in 1978, a year that pop listeners in Hong Kong came to recognize as the end of this kind of band.

In 1967, Hong Kong's first television station, TVB, started broadcasting. From the 1970s to the present, television broadcasting has played a significant role in the developments in the popular music scene of Hong Kong.

The 1970s

During the 1970s Hong Kong pop music emerged into public consciousness. Before this only Mandarin and English cover versions made any impression on the local charts. In 1972, the theme tune to a television drama, "Tai siu yan yun," which was performed by Sindra, was the first Cantonese song to become a smash hit. Samuel Hui's hits "Gwai ma seung sing" and "Seung sing ching go" followed this. Both of these were taken from a movie directed by his brother, Michael Hui. (The former was the theme song, the latter featured in the movie.) The success of Samuel Hui's songs prompted the public to rethink their opinions of their own popular culture. Another significant factor in altering their previously held conceptions of Cantonese songs was that Samuel Hui was a graduate of the Chinese University of Hong Kong, one of the two top universities at that time. His brother, Michael Hui, was a graduate of the other top university, the University of Hong Kong. Furthermore, Samuel Hui had been lead vocalist of Lotus during the band boom in the 1960s. In other words, Samuel Hui, who had been famous for embracing imported Western songs, now topped the local charts with Cantonese songs. These facts helped to elevate Cantonese songs from their previous position as the "poor relation" of Western and Mandarin music. This musical rehabilitation corresponded to wider social movements of the time. For example, in the early 1970s the movement to make Cantonese an official language gained momentum. And in 1974 Cantonese became one of the two official languages in Hong Kong. From this period on, Canto-pop started to enter the mainstream of popular music in Hong Kong.

During this period, many television drama theme songs were smash hits too. This was also the period when many Japanese television dramas, dubbed in Cantonese, were shown. Because of poor production values in Hong Kong's television industry, television companies brought in many higher-quality Japanese-made television dramas. Some of the theme songs to these dramas were covered in Cantonese and went on to become hits. This in turn influenced a Japanese song boom in the 1980s.

The 1980s

In this period Japanese pop, both in its original form and as cover versions, became very prominent, particularly in the early 1980s. A radio program that played only original Japanese pop songs was started, and many Japanese singers became very popular in Hong Kong. Several magazines devoted to gossip about the Japanese entertainment world were published too. At times the Hong Kong readers of these magazines were more aware of the news and scandals in the Japanese entertainment world than the Japanese public was. Even nowadays, I come across people of this generation in Hong Kong talking about the Japanese pop culture of those days with great nostalgia. Many local artists covered Japanese songs. In one notable instance, "Yuyake no Uta," which was originally sung by Masahiko Kondo, was covered by four different singers almost simultaneously in 1989.

Several factors contributed to the abundance of these Japanese cover versions. First, the fact that listeners had become familiar with Japanese songs through Japanese television dramas helped to arouse interest in Japanese pop. Second, listeners had become tired of the formulism of the Canto-pop of the 1970s. Third, the creativity of the industry in Hong Kong lagged behind the advancement of technology and consumer demand. Although technological innovations and consumer demand allowed the industry to produce and sell many more records and CDs than in previous periods, the creative capability within the industry was out of step with the trend. Also in this period, the commercial music industry shifted its marketing strategy from singles to albums. This meant that producers needed much more musical material than before. Originally, Japanese cover versions were brought in as a way of padding albums. But it would appear that listeners preferred the "padding" to the main songs: the Japanese songs became more popular than the "main" Cantonese tracks. Responding to this demand, the industry treated Japanese cover versions as the centerpiece of the albums, and this led the listeners to develop on interest in the original songs and artists.

Music critics have pointed out that the typical Japanese pop song melody line is well suited to Asian listeners, in particular Chinese audiences, in that it is different but not too strange. The typical melody line of Japanese pop music, known as *Yo Na Nuki* in Japanese, dispenses with the fourth note "fa" and the seventh note "ti." An example given of this is the Japanese song "RuJu," which was covered in China, Hong Kong, Taiwan, Indonesia, Burma, Vietnam, Thailand, and even in Turkey.

In the latter part of this period, local bands who played their own, originally produced music became popular. Although this was a very short period, some bands, such as Tai Chi, Grass Hopper, and Beyond, became influential. Part of their appeal was that the words to their music carried a social message. This made quite an impact on a music scene that had previously strongly emphasized love songs and ballads. This movement, then, can be seen as the prelude to a backlash against the previously uninspired diet of cover versions and formulaic love songs.

The 1990s

By the 1990s, this backlash had gained momentum, and original songs became the new trend. In 1995, *Chet Chat 903*, a program on Hong Kong's Commercial Radio 2, announced that it would not broadcast any cover versions of songs.

This move was indirectly triggered by the death in 1993 of Wong Ga Kway, lead singer of the band Beyond. The band had grown weary of the Hong Kong music scene and had started working in Japan. Wong was killed in a television studio accident while shooting a video. Many people in Hong Kong blamed his death on the commercial forces of the Hong Kong music scene. They felt that the Hong Kong pop music industry, by its overreliance on cover versions, did not do enough to nurture an environment where young talent could grow. Following this incident, several broadcasting companies and record companies ran various campaigns to promote young talent in Hong Kong. This resulted in a huge drop in the number of cover versions produced in Hong Kong in 1995 (Hara 1996: 152–7).

Nowadays, the production of cover versions of Japanese pop songs is not as prevalent as before and no longer forms the mainstream of Hong Kong pop music.

Several Japanese singers, however, are popular in Hong Kong. The concerts of Nakajima Miyuki, and Chage and Aska attracted large audiences. The most remarkable part of this recent situation is that these performers' songs became popular more or less simultaneously in Hong Kong and in Japan.

This trend is mirrored in the recent acceptance of Canto-pop in Japan. Although Hong Kong singers are not as popular in Japan as Japanese singers are in Hong Kong, we see the same performers and songs reaching the charts at more or less the same time in both Hong Kong and Japan. In previous times, some Hong Kong singers managed to gain popularity in Japan, although they were relatively few compared with the number of Japanese singers. Most of the Hong Kong artists who did get into the Japanese charts sang in Japanese. These days, however, several Hong Kong performers sing in Cantonese.

Perceptions of Japan among Japanese pop music listeners in Hong Kong in recent years

An interesting finding that arose from my interviews with listeners of Japanese pop songs in Hong Kong in recent years is that they have a very positive image of Japanese pop music. They think of it as being more professional or accomplished than locally produced pop. Many of my interviewees said that they like the original versions of Japanese pop songs because the performers "sing truly." By this they mean that the singers do not merely mime ("lip-synch") along to prerecorded tapes.

For instance, part of an interview with one of my informants went as follows:

Informant: Most of the listeners of Japanese songs in Hong Kong know that Japanese singers sing much better than Hong Kong singers. That is the reason why we like Japanese songs.

Me: But some of the Japanese singers sing very badly, don't they?

Informant: No, no, even if they sing badly, at least they sing the songs themselves. In comparison, many Hong Kong singers, even famous ones, often pretend they are singing, but actually they are just lip-synching to a prerecorded tape. Everyone in Hong Kong knows this.

However, in reality the truth is very different. I have asked several musicians who have worked with both Hong Kong and Japanese singers about this. All said that, unless there is an unavoidable technical problem, most Hong Kong singers, at least those who are well known, sing live. Furthermore, despite the Hong Kong listeners' perception of the perfectionism of Japanese pop, some Japanese singers do sometimes lip-synch to prerecorded tapes in their concerts.

A summary of Hong Kong pop music history

The history of Hong Kong pop music can be summarized as follows: Hong Kong pop music trends have followed one of two models. One of these is whether the song was originally written for a Hong Kong singer or was a cover version of someone else's song. The other is whether the lyrics were sung in Cantonese or not. In the early 1980s, cover versions of Japanese pop songs, sung in Cantonese, were popular. In the 1990s, originally produced Hong Kong Canto-pop with Cantonese lyrics became popular as a backlash against the trends of the preceding period.

The latter framework is directly connected with the listeners' image of Cantonese songs as locally made culture. Until the 1970s, Cantonese songs were deemed to be low-class entertainment, but during the 1970s they entered the mainstream. In the 1980s, as listeners became tired of Canto-pop's mannerisms, they again viewed Canto-pop negatively compared with Japanese pop. Following that, there was another reaction against imported Japanese pop, and originally produced Canto-pop became popular again. In other words, we see in these changing trends a movement back and forth in the public's perception of Cantonese songs.

Globalization in Hong Kong popular music history

The importation of global culture initiated by the industry

Arjun Appadurai (1990) presented a set of concepts to comprehend the processes of globalization. He termed these concepts *ethnoscape, finanscape, technoscape, mediascape,* and *ideoscape. Ethnoscape* refers to the global flow of the people and its mobility. *Technoscape* refers to the global flow of mechanical and informational technology. *Finanscape* refers to the flow of capital. *Mediascape* refers to the flow and spread of the image and idea created by media. *Ideoscape* refers to the flow and spread of political and ideological thought and image. In this context Appadurai uses the term "global" as the antithesis of "international." He suggested that we employ these concepts as frameworks to analyze and comprehend the process of globalization by examining not only these aspects but also the relationships among them. If we define globalization in this way, as Ulf Hannerz (1992) points out, then globalization is not a new phenomenon. Although the present intensification of globalization is greatly different, there have been various globalizations from time to time throughout different parts of the world. In this sense Hong Kong pop music history demonstrates this ongoing process of globalization.

Political turmoil toward the end of the 1940s brought about sudden changes in ethnoscape and technoscape, to a lesser extent in mechanical technology and to a greater extent in the technological skills of people involved in music production in Hong Kong. Many of the people who were involved in the pop music industry in Shanghai, which was the center of Chinese pop music at the time, fled to Hong Kong. This change quickly shifted the Hong Kong pop music industry to the center of Chinese music production from its previous position on the periphery. Since then, the Hong Kong music scene has displayed a peculiar characteristic, which I describe as a "small number of players in a big market."

As the change was sudden, the nascent pop music industry in Hong Kong was lacking in production resources, particularly in creative human resources. Yet the market for Chinese pop music, in Chinese communities all over the world, was huge. Therefore, the industry in Hong Kong had to look constantly to other creative centers to meet this demand. These centers were in Shanghai, China, Britain, and other Western countries in the beginning, and later were in Japan.

The industry quickly resorted to covering the music pieces produced in the centers instead of growing creative talents in their own soil. (This tendency, i.e. looking for other creative centers to solve the shortage of creative human resources in Hong Kong, still exists.)

Another distinctive characteristic of the globalization process in Hong Kong's pop music scene can also be attributed to its small number of players in a big market. It was always the industry, rather than audience demand, that triggered the flow of global culture into Hong Kong. The industry chose different centers at different times to make up for the lack of local creative talent. Of course, this action stimulated an increase in listeners' demands.

Many scholars of globalization argue that a host/local culture responds to the inflow of global culture; it is accommodated through a process of negotiation within the given sociopolitical situation. However, in the context of Hong Kong's pop music industry, the host/local culture initiated the inflow of global culture.

The creation and assertion of local culture engendered by the inflow of global culture

The inflow of global culture often makes local cultures more assertive. In Hong Kong, before the Shanghai music industry fled there, there was no local popular music as such. The inflow of Shanghai pop music made listeners aware of a lack of Cantonese popular songs in their local culture. After two decades of being viewed as low-class entertainment, Canto-pop became the mainstream of Hong Kong pop music. In this sense, Shanghai pop music triggered the creation of Canto-pop in Hong Kong popular culture. Since then, a cyclical pattern of cultural assertion has been recurring. The pattern is as follows:

1   There is an inflow of global culture, initiated by the demands of an industry that lacks creative capability.
2   The inflow triggers an assertion of local culture as a backlash against an overreliance on the inflowing culture.
3   The assertion in turn creates more demand for the production of local culture.
4   To solve the lack of creative capability, the industry initiates another inflow.

Image construction of Japanese pop music through globalization

As we have seen, the perception of Japanese pop music among the local listeners is strongly influenced by this image of Japan. Perfectionism as the image of Japan was molded through globalization in the *technoscape* and *mediascape*. In addition, the inflow of Japanese products and technology helped to shape the image of Japan's perfectionism. And the presentation of this image by local and Japanese media strengthened the image.

Hong Kong pop music: cultural mishmash to hybridized culture

The Hong Kong pop music industry demonstrates another peculiarity in the way that it accommodates inflowing culture. Most accounts of globalization describe a process of negotiation that occurs between the global and local cultures and that results in the creation of a third, hybridized culture. However, this does not seem to be the case in Hong Kong. Here, there has been no hybrid creation, no integration between Japanese-style popular music and local Cantonese music. Rather, the imported music was used as a convenient source to fill a gap in the local music scene. There was little desire or ambition to create something different by employing musical elements from another culture. Rather than incorporating musical elements from foreign styles, the Hong Kong pop music industry simply covered them.

One of my informants, a musician for Canto-pop singers, related his musician friend's experience of recording cover versions of Japanese songs. His friend said that the record producer was present at the recording session to which he had gone to play the bass guitar. The producer played a tape recording of the original Japanese song twice to the session musicians. Then he told the musicians, "Just play it exactly the same as this. No changes, no creativity, just like this." They rehearsed only twice and recorded in one take.

Although the big names of Canto-pop are shown more consideration regarding creative input than this, from my interviews it appears that the attitude of this producer typifies the general attitude of the industry. Judging from this, it is possible to say that, so far, Hong Kong pop music is not hybridized; rather it is a cultural mishmash.

However, in recent times, not only in Hong Kong but also elsewhere in Asia, we can see an increasing possibility of the creation of hybridized culture as a result of intensification of globalization. For instance, until recently, very few Japanese composers wrote Canto-pop tunes. But in 1996, the Japanese musician and composer Rika Arakawa won the top award in Hong Kong City's composition contest. (Interestingly, she won it at the time when Hong Kong was in the middle of a heated debate with Japan over the Daioyu Islands conflict.) Following this success, several Canto-pop stars, such as Cas Pang and Sandy Lam, have asked her to write their songs.

Also, some Japanese music production companies have begun to promote hybridized music in Asia. Hori Production is one of the biggest Japanese music talent management companies. They have started a scouting campaign in Asia. In one case, they held several auditions in China to find talent to promote in China, not in Japan. In 1994, Dai Rao, who won first prize in an audition contest in China, made their debut in China and Japan. The remarkable thing about this is that the producers were targeting China, not Japan, as their market. There were also several attempts, although small in scale, by Japanese companies to find talent in other Asian countries to promote in Japan. This was the first attempt to find talent in Asia to promote in other Asian countries. Companies were set up in Hong Kong and Beijing for this purpose (Hara 1996: 204–6).

The singer and producer Tetsuya Komuro, whose songs dominated the Japanese charts during 1996 and 1997, started a similar campaign in Taiwan to promote Taiwanese singers in Asia. He also held some private auditions in Hong Kong and selected the former semiprofessional model and singer Grace Yip. Ms Yip made her debut at Komuro's Hong Kong concert in December 1997. Komuro has also started up a company to operate his music and promoting activities with media king Rupert Murdoch.

Thus we see that the flow of musical trends between Hong Kong and Japan is no longer one way. And it could be said that Hong Kong pop music now has the potential to become hybridized with global pop music as witnessed elsewhere, and in Japan in particular, through the recent intensification of globalization.

Bibliography

Appadurai, A. (1990) "Disjuncture and difference in the global cultural economy," *Public Culture* 2 (2): 1–24.

Hannerz, U. (1992) "Continuity and change in the global ecumene," paper prepared for University of Chicago Transcultural Conference "The Conditions of Reciprocal Understanding," Chicago.

Hara, T. (1996) *Honkon chudoku (Hong Kong Addiction)*, Tokyo: Japan Times.

South China Morning Post (1997) "Amazing Grace ready to take on music world," *South China Morning Post* 7 December: 4.

Wong, K. (1997) "Sanjunendai Shanhai – Rokujunendai Honkon Chainizu Poppu no Rutsu" *(Shanghai in the 1930s – Hong Kong in the 1960s, roots of Chinese pop)*, in S. Rin (ed.) *Chainizu poppussu no subete Honkon Taiwan Chugoku (All about Chinese Pop, Hong Kong, Taiwan, China)*, Tokyo: Ongakunotomosha.

9 Global culture in question

Contemporary Japanese photography in America

Julia Adeney Thomas

Globalization theory too often takes its cue from business, from the global capital, technology, production, and markets that, as Marx and Engels foretold, chase "the bourgeoisie over the whole surface of the globe" (Harvey 1995). As these forces circle the earth, politics is said to be subsumed by the market,[1] and "culture" refers merely to modes of consumption (Beinart 1997). Even "high culture," once thought to be distinguishable from popular culture partially on the basis of *not* being viable on the open market, can be viewed, so the claim goes, as just another commodity. In other words, it is argued that intellectual and artistic endeavors are subject to the same homogenizing and systematizing forces that are routinizing business practices everywhere. But things are neither so grim nor so simple. Commodity exchange and intellectual and artistic exchange do not function identically because their goals and their means of production are not identical. In fact, it is crucial to our understanding of globalization to recognize the differences between investment and interpretation, between the value of capital and other values.

To support this point, I want to examine a particular band of global exchange – the success of contemporary Japanese fine art photography in American art museums and galleries. I will argue that, although fine art photographs are commodities, they are much more as well. Indeed, several layers of determination must be recognized to understand how Japanese photography is positioned in American museums: (1) "globalization" and what it means for national identities; (2) the broad modes of understanding "Japan" and "the West" organized by the discourses of Orientalism and *Nihonjinron* (Japanese discussions of what distinguishes them as a people); (3) the specifics of America's arch, turbulent art world with its fragile careers, heralded openings, complex institutional structure, and politicized criticism, and the corresponding conditions in Japan; and (4) the individual creativity and vision of the artists. These are different, often contradictory, forces, but together they have created a prominent place in the United States for photographic work called "Japanese."

Following the most optimistic predictions about global markets, Japanese fine art photography has met with resounding success. Even the most casual history reveals sustained and growing support from galleries, museums, collectors, and critics. More than 25 years ago, the Museum of Modern Art (MOMA) in New York mounted an exhibition entitled "New Japanese Photography," the curators of which were jointly John Szarkowski, then head of MOMA's photography department, and the late Shoji Yamagishi, who was Japan's most powerful broker and critic of photography.[2] As Yamagishi indicates in his catalogue essay for this 1974 exhibition, support for Japanese photography in the States surpassed that in Japan, where art museums were without "the experience or the equipment necessary to handle photographic exhibitions" and Japanese photographers had no "opportunity to sell their pictures to public or private collections" (Yamagishi 1974: 11). Indeed, while Japanese photography garnered increasing artistic recognition and financial rewards in the United States between 1974 and 1990, Tokyo's National Museum of Modern Art, to take one example, eschewed all photography shows on the grounds of what its director calls the "inherent limitations" of the medium (Hiroshi 1995: 5). By the 1990s, however, Japanese photography had begun to dispel doubts about its artistic viability at home while reinforcing its triumph in America with new work by younger artists.

Today, private galleries around the United States – from Gallery Luisotti (formerly Gallery RAM) in Santa Monica to the Laurence Miller Gallery in New York – highlight Japanese photography. Major museums in every region have organized exhibitions of Japanese photography either exclusively or as part of multimedia or multinational displays. A brief survey of these exhibitions over the past decade includes the following: in 1986, the Philadelphia Museum of Art's "Black Sun: The Eyes of Four";[3] in 1989, "Against Nature: Japanese Art in the Eighties," originated at New York University (Osaka and Kline 1989);[4] in 1992, the Metropolitan Museum of Art's exhibition of Shomei Tomatsu's photographs, its first one-person show by a contemporary Japanese artist (Goldberg 1992); in 1994, "Inside/Out: Contemporary Japanese Photography" organized in Charlotte, NC (*Inside/ Out Contemporary Japanese Photography* 1994); in 1994–5, "Japanese Art after 1945: Scream against the Sky," a major show that traveled from Yokohama to San Francisco and New York, with work by photographers Yasumasa Morimura and Eikoh Hosoe (Munroe 1994); and in 1997–8, the Chicago Museum of Contemporary Art's exhibition devoted to Toshio Shibata. Public and private collectors have paid corresponding homage in buying prints.

What prevents us from seeing this success in purely commodity terms? On one hand, these photographs are subject to the logic of similarity, which makes them recognizable as commodities in any art market on the globe; on the other hand, by the denotation "Japanese," they function as exotic goods, commanding a premium price from buyers. It might be argued that the tension between capitalism's global logic of similarity and the national logic of difference – mapped for us in various ways by Immanuel Wallerstein and Mike Featherstone – might account fully for the positioning of these photographs. But the predictive hopes of such globalization theories are defied at least in this small sector by the bumptious, unpredictable creativity of artists, curators, and critics and the contingencies of the art world. Ultimately this art refuses to be boxed in by "globalization," by "Japaneseness," or by the tension between the two, despite efforts to contain it within these paradigms. In support of this argument, I want to consider the American careers of four contemporary artists: Hiroshi Sugimoto (b. 1948), Toshio Shibata (b. 1949), Yasumasa Morimura (b. 1951), and Masao Yamamoto (b. 1957). I have chosen these four, all from the generation born after World War II, because, unlike their older mentors and forerunners such as Shomei Tomatsu and Nobuyoshi Araki, their work has arguably been subjected to the forces of globalization from the start and because they are so very different from one another, ranging from Shibata, who can be situated within a conservative genealogy of large-format black-and-white landscape photography, to Morimura, for whom the very designation "photographer" is barely adequate. As we will see, the diffuse, individualistic art world that these photographers inhabit confounds typologies of interaction that govern more corporate global undertakings.

Hiroshi Sugimoto

An examination of the traveling exhibition of Hiroshi Sugimoto's sea-and-sky images, organized at the Museum of Contemporary Art in Los Angeles and exhibited at Chicago's Museum of Contemporary Art from January to March 1995, suggests the complexity of the forces positioning this artwork. From one perspective, Sugimoto's series is the consummate embodiment of global art. He has traveled around the world to create portraits not of people or buildings or even landscapes but of seascapes, portraits of the world's water (Figure 9.1). Seen in conjunction with one another, these deceptively similar 16.5″ × 21.25″ black-and-white prints attune the eye to subtle differences in the texture of waves, the variances created by light and atmosphere. While enlivening the understated presentation of these photographs and engrossing the viewer, these differences, paradoxically, also serve to unify the project. As curator Kerry Brougher writes in a sensitive catalogue essay:

> For Sugimoto, these are not so much scenes of specific seas, but of the Sea, something primordial or from a timeless future, elemental, presented at the child-like moment of discovery, as yet unnamed but at the very moment man must name it.
>
> (Brougher 1993: n.p.)

In this respect, Sugimoto's works are entirely without national identification. Within the frame, their refusal of boundaries or markers is, so to speak, oceanic.

On the other hand, national identity tugs insistently at these images. Sugimoto himself plays on this tension between global and local in the way that he titles the photographs: *Ionian Sea, Santa Cesarea*; *Sea of Galilee, Golan*;

Figure 9.1   Hiroshi Sugimoto, "Ionian Sea, Santa Cesavea I, 1990." Courtesy of the
Sonnabend Gallery.

Sea of Japan, Oki; and so on. But while Sugimoto appears to relish the irony of
attaching the names of precise localities to images of planetary waters, many
American interpreters feel an earnest reluctance to forgo nationality,
particularly Sugimoto's nationality, as a straightforward explanatory
mechanism for his art. If the subject of these photographs is not often "Japan,"
then "Japaneseness" must be found in their style or in their creator. For
instance, a Museum of Contemporary Art volunteer tour guide found in these
images an ineluctable Japaneseness of style, explaining them as "so Japanese
– beautiful but very controlled." This guide went on to describe horizontal
lines as extremely important in Japanese culture and to ascribe the horizons
of Sugimoto's seascapes to this cultural predilection.

For others, Sugimoto's Japaneseness must be biographical as well as
stylistic, although in this respect he bears the taint of a troubling impurity.
Although he was born and educated in Tokyo and graduated from Rikkyo
Daigaku in 1970, Sugimoto chose to study at the Art Center College of Design
in Los Angeles and has lived in New York since 1974. Curator Mark Richard
Leach of the Light Factory Photographic Arts Center in North Carolina toys
with the idea that Sugimoto's long U.S. residence might reduce the value of
"Japaneseness" for understanding these seascapes. With more consternation
than grammatical sense, Leach writes:

Having studied in an American art school and having immediate access to emerging American art developments since moving to the United States, a more believable argument can be made for acculturation and for the artist expressing a more specifically American aesthetic viewpoint. However, there is equally a reason to believe that while he may have refined his vision with American avant-garde principles, we can witness in his seascapes a unique but related vision, one plumbed by other Japanese contemporaries.

(Leach 1994: 9)

In the end, despite these misgivings, Leach includes Sugimoto's work among others, "as prisms, not lenses, through which we can survey the present state of Japanese culture" (Leach 1994: 10). Sugimoto's "Japaneseness" remains, for Leach, inescapable.

Further evidence that "Japaneseness" organizes the reception of Sugimoto's work in the United States can be garnered from the list of group exhibitions in which he has been included. In 1994, for instance, his work appeared in two shows cohering around concepts of Japan: "Space, Time and Memory" and "Japanese Art after 1945: Scream against the Sky." Furthermore, Sugimoto's recent solo exhibition at New York's Sonnabend Gallery in April 1997 evoked responses attuned to his origins, as when *New York Times* critic Holland Cotter saw "Buddhist concepts of permanence in flux" at work in the seascapes (Cotter 1997).

Sugimoto's recent move beyond conventional photography, in a video made from stills of the numerous Buddhist figures filling the main temple hall of Kyoto's Sanjusangendo, shows that he is quite prepared to draw on overtly Japanese imagery for his art. However, Sugimoto's relationship to Japanese tradition in this piece is far from straightforward: as his video runs, the photographs of these meditative faces follow one another more and more rapidly, accelerating until the distinctions among the faces dissolve, "disintegrating ultimately into visual static and then into a blank screen" (Cotter 1997) – a play perhaps between Sugimoto's Japaneseness and its international dissolution. As with the seascapes, Sugimoto's video can be read as sophisticated visual commentary on the difficulty of mapping the world of international art.

In short, the commodification, interpretation, and content of Sugimoto's work oscillates between the national and the global. In some circumstances, such as a 1995 installation at New York's Metropolitan Museum where a photograph from his theater series, "Radio City Music Hall, New York, 1978" (Figure 9.2), hung between photographs by Vito Acconci and William Larson, his work is shown without any national gloss at all. More frequently, "Japaneseness" appears to be necessary for marketing and understanding his images. In this, Sugimoto's position resembles that of many Japanese photographers in the United States. The most obvious theoretical point to draw from this observation is that "the nation" as a cultural category remains

Figure 9.2 Hiroshi Sugimoto, "Goshen, Indiana, 1980." Courtesy of the Sonnabend
Gallery.

potent for many critics and viewers grappling with such work. Belying
arguments by Arjun Appadurai and many others that "we are entering a
postnational world" (Appadurai 1996: 158), the insistence on "Japaneseness"
prevails, guiding the international reception of this photographic art even in
a case such as Sugimoto's, attenuated as it is by his choice of subject matter
and residence and by his own ironic gloss.

The second theoretical point that can be drawn is that "the local" – in the
sense of subnational – appears to have little role in selling or interpreting
Japanese photography in America.[5] While it could be argued that there is
something uncannily local about most straight photography, arising as it tends
to do from a sensuous engagement with place, "Japanese" photographs are
rarely encoded by any smaller geographic or cultural designation. At best,
there may be a faintly recognized divide between the throbbing urban centers
of Japan and the lonely countryside. For instance, David Travis, the Art
Institute of Chicago's curator of photography, responds to Masahisa Fukase's
(b. 1934) dark work *The Solitude of Ravens* by connecting distance from Tokyo
with emotional disengagement. Travis (1991: 128) writes, "When I
inadvertently learned that Hokkaido had served Fukase as a place of escape
after his divorce in 1976, that knowledge gave a certain number of the
photographs a likely explanation, but it did nothing to explain their quality,
their number, or his obsession." Beyond this level of generality, regional
differences within Japan matter little in America.

The third point that must be made is that, where it is used, "Japanese photography" appears to be a cultural (and economic) category mapped rather rigidly upon a particular place and a particular people. As the curator's consternation over Sugimoto's choice of a New York residence suggests, "Japaneseness" in its most desired form compounds style, place, and person together, but the emphasis is most heavily upon a Japaneseness of family, birth, and upbringing. The line cuts exceedingly fine, but runs something like this: the work of Yasuhiro Ishimoto, a Japanese national born in California, trained in Chicago by Harry Callahan and Aaron Siskind, and moving between the two nations, is categorized in many instances as "Japanese photography" even when it depicts African Americans in southside Chicago.[6] At the same time, for many curators and historians, this work is also "Chicago photography." On the other hand, James Osamu Nakagawa, a second-generation Japanese American, may draw some of his imagery from Japan, but his work is not "Japanese photography." Less "Japanese" still are the Tokyo photographs of Nan Goldin, even when she shoots pictures of Japanese boys standing amid swirling cherry blossoms. In other words, "Japanese art photography" does not appear to be among the "clustering of cultural practices," described by Akhil Gupta and James Ferguson, "that do not 'belong' to a particular 'people' or to a definite place" (Gupta and Ferguson 1992: 19). It is clearly imagined as mapped on a particular "people" and a definite place. And this belonging has consequences for both interpretation and sales.

Toshio Shibata

Even if we are suspicious of the isomorphism among race, place, and culture suggested by the phrase "Japanese photography," its potency is undeniable. Paired with the concepts of the "global" or "international," it helps to organize the reception of this body of art work in the United States. But what exactly do these terms mean and why are they deployed? With these questions in mind, let me now turn to the work first of Toshio Shibata, whose photography is heavily encoded as Japanese, and then to the work of Yasumasa Morimura, usually glossed as more international.

Shibata's résumé attests to his enormous popularity with American museums and galleries. His work has been exhibited and purchased by public, university, and corporate collections in Cambridge, MA, Tucson, AZ, Rochester, NY, Santa Fe, NM, Charlottesville, VA, Houston, TX, and Charlotte, NC, as well as by the major museums of New York, Chicago, San Francisco, and Los Angeles. Shibata is not an artist who knocks on closed doors. The question is how his warmly embraced work has been interpreted and marketed, and overwhelmingly the answer is as "Japanese." The reason for this particular denotation, I would argue, is not only that he was born and educated in Japan and continues to reside there but also that he can so easily be made to fulfill the cultural tropes created by Orientalism and *Nihonjinron* in both Japan and the United States, primarily the stereotypic Japanese love of nature and design. Through a recital of these markers of Japan's essential difference, Shibata's work receives a special niche in America.

Given that the primary modes of interpreting Shibata's images are Japan's purported "love of nature" and "elegant sense of design," it may come as a surprise that his subject matter is erosion-control projects. Shibata has indeed made these enormous, earth-shaping engineering marvels into monuments of startling beauty and abstract form (Figure 9.3). In coming to terms with these images at Shibata's 1993 solo exhibit at the Art Institute of Chicago, curator David Travis relies on the continuing power of ancient aesthetic conventions:

> One of Toshio Shibata's photographs shows two tree branches caught in the edge of a man-made dam. They mar the water's perfect calm and streak the consistency of its flow as it passes through them. One could think of them as nature's revenge on a draftsman's calculated precision, but the photographer has a deeper understanding. His photograph shows that imperfection and irregularity can find a harmony with their surroundings. This appeals to an aesthetic sense that the Japanese call *wabi*.
>
> Not all of Shibata's photographs display this duality ... . But even in these cases, Shibata has contained the intrusions within a composition mindful of nature as a patient, surrounding force. The *wabi* sense makes them somehow fit together.

Travis goes on to say that *wabi* has "a new contemporary role, a role that is essential to the ideas not only of tea masters, artists, and philosophers, but to the working attitudes of engineers, industrialists, and politicians."[7] James Enyeart, then director of the International Museum of Photography at George Eastman House in Rochester, NY, concurs with Travis's judgment that Shibata's images epitomize eternal Japanese cultural values. In Japan, Enyeart writes, "a sense of aesthetics pervades every human task, from wrapping a simple package to building great dams and roads" (Enyeart 1992: n.p.). And so it might seem from Shibata's photographs of sculpted hillsides.

Traveling to the actual sites, however, is likely to provide a different experience, as was the case with Anne W. Tucker, curator of the Museum of Fine Arts in Houston, who confesses in an essay on Shibata entitled "Not what I expected" that "having seen some of these sites, I was surprised by how much he had transformed the subject." For Tucker, then, Shibata's work cannot provide a transparent window on Japaneseness, but she still finds the category compelling: "Shibata is photographing the encounter between nature and encroaching civilization, but with a Japanese sensibility. Western critics have written about these structures as ravaging nature for man's convenience, but nature has a planned role in the life of the structures. This is less a tug-of-war than a collaborative and evolving venture" (Tucker 1996: n.p.). Travis, Enyeart, and Tucker, in their use of the category of Japaneseness to interpret

Figure 9.3 Toshio Shibata, "Kashima Town, Fukushima Prefecture, 1990." ©Toshio Shibata. Courtesy of the Laurence Miller Gallery, New York.

Shibata's work, attempt to sensitize American viewers to seeing national difference in the aesthetic style and content of these photographs as well as in the photographer himself.

What aligns these comments with the discourses of both Orientalism and *Nihonjinron* is their insistence on differentiating Japan absolutely from "the West," their treatment of Japan as a realm of internal consensus and homogeneity, and their implication that Japanese values remain constant over centuries. Putting aside the issue of whether or not this interpretation of Japanese culture is accurate, this logic of difference, as it might be termed, is highly utilitarian. In America, under this rubric of Japaneseness, Shibata represents something unavailable from domestic artists, something embraced uncontroversially by all Japanese citizens (thus protecting American consumers from awkwardly "taking sides" in a controversy not their own), and something that has the weight of ancient cultural sanction behind it. In other words, categorizing some photography as "Japanese" augments its marketability and offers an explanation of its artistry. Such a strategy compels conscientious museums to include examples in their collections. Individual collectors can claim interest in a specialized "brand" of art, paying a premium because their dollars chase "Japanese photography" rather than the wider supply of photography in general. Interpreters too gain a certain premium by asserting the esoteric nature of the knowledge necessary for proper understanding.

This approach obviates complexity and locks interpretations of Shibata into a narrow range. For instance, in insisting that Shibata represents Japanese consensus in general and Japanese approaches to land use in particular, it becomes impossible to read the photographs as ironic transformations of ugliness into beauty or as an elegant exercise in finger pointing at the corrupt collusion between government and contractors to build unnecessary, environmentally hazardous projects at gross public expense. (See, for instance, Gavan McCormack's stunning critique, 1996.) There is no room in this version of "Japanese photography" for exploring multiple Japanese points of view – of which Shibata might represent only one or an ambiguous amalgam – or for suggesting that Japanese culture may be a changeable process rather than an eternal, discoverable essence. Nor, of course, does this category leave much space for the possible singularity of Shibata's vision.

Even with Shibata, however, not all commentators rely on the *Nihonjinron* version of Japaneseness as their explanatory matrix. Rather than position Shibata as an exemplar of Japanese tradition, Yoshio Nakamura of the Tokyo Institute of Technology sees Shibata as working within the *sumi-e* (India ink painting) tradition, but only to "discover and create a new type of scenic beauty" (Nakamura 1995: 76), a beauty not of traditional harmony but of tension, eschewing horizons and story lines. The director of Tokyo's Zeit-Foto Salon, Etsuro Ishihara, also questions Japaneseness as the ground of interpretation, arguing that "it is impossible to see the essence of his works within Shibata himself" and thus, presumably, within his Japaneseness. Instead, Shibata's cool abstraction and emotional detachment produce "high precision pure art" (Ishihara 1996: 11).

It appears to be more difficult for American curators and critics to forgo timeworn versions of Japaneseness. No doubt initially garnered from American popular culture's version of the exquisite, Zen-imbued "East," these views are often reinforced through contacts with an older Japanese art establishment purveying similar stylized versions of Japan's cultural essence.[8] In an odd convergence, "Orientalism" and *"Nihonjinron"* work in the same way to imply that serious engagement with an individual artwork is a form of impolite, boorish trespass on the essential difference of culture. Individual works, so the implication goes, must be interpreted as mere samples from an already fully articulated culture: Japanese essence precedes an artist's existence. It is the rare American critic who succeeds in breaking out of this view, as when Donald Kuspit (1993), writing in *Artforum*, complicates the notion of Japaneseness in an account of Shibata's photographs as "peculiarly critical of the Japanese character – in all its insularity and hermeticism – even as they admire and articulate it." Like Nakamura, Kuspit leans on a concept of "Japaneseness," but he does so critically and with an eye to the way cultural tradition is challenged and transformed.

In short, more than one type of "Japaneseness" is attached to Shibata's photography in America, and even these different types do not quite account for all the complications surrounding his work: his postgraduate fellowship at the Royal Academy of Ghent in Belgium, his move away from painting and printmaking under the influence of Edward Weston's photographs,[9] or his exhibits at home, which have ranged from the 1989 "Quintessence of Japan" show to a collaborative project on the theme of Orientalism, for which Shibata took photographs in the Middle East. Nevertheless, "Japaneseness" in some form helps locate his work in relation to other photographers and to his preferred subject matter. Shibata himself in his interviews with Western curators speaks in versions of Japaneseness both narrow, accepting, for instance, the idea of *shakkei* or "borrowed scenic views" to explain his work (Stearns 1995: 64), and broad, accepting a commission from the Museum of Contemporary Art in Chicago to photograph American water-control projects from his particular Japanese perspective (Boris 1997). National culture, then, with its opportunities as well as its constraints, persists as a mode of production and interpretation for Shibata. Under this rubric, he becomes a Japanese photographer and an international artist at one and the same time.

Yasumasa Morimura

If an examination of Shibata's reception in the United States demonstrates that "Japaneseness" can produce different modes of understanding photographic images while providing a profitable marketing category, a glance at Yasumasa Morimura's photography suggests that the concept of "global art" is equally complex. Certainly if there is such a phenomenon as global art, photography must be considered to be one of its principal media. Although invented in France and England in 1839, photographic technology was so quickly dispersed throughout the world and so closely associated with travel, commerce, and colonization that the camera could soon claim no particular national provenance. Even Japan – despite the *bakufu*'s suspicion of foreign things – was introduced to photography almost as soon as it was invented, although the precise date is disputed. The most intriguing version of photography's Japanese arrival is that a wealthy Nagasaki merchant, Shinnojo

Ueno, cognizant of the Satsuma daimyo's interest in Western technology, sought to please him by obtaining a camera from the Dutch traders at Dejima. Although this precious instrument arrived on board a ship in 1841, a mere 2 years after the daguerreotype was perfected, photography historian Takeshi Ozawa contends that it was never unloaded, returning to Holland when the vessel steamed homeward. Only in 1848 did Ueno finally obtain his camera, but that remains, in retrospect, a quick transfer of technology given the time and conditions (Ozawa 1994).

Today, the training of fine art photographers and of museum curators, the development and marketing of cameras and imaging technology, the standards for exhibition in art museums and galleries (white walls, framed prints, wall labels, exhibition catalogues, and so on), the market for prints, the venues for critical writing, and even the aesthetics of the photograph have been internationalized. In both economic and cultural terms, then, national boundaries and cultural genealogies seem at times to have been effaced in the great swirling circulation of photographic art around the globe. As with cars or computer chips, the production, use, and consumption of fine art photography may appear to be governed by the homogenizing system of global capitalism. On the face of it, Morimura is utterly presentable and utterly consumable on this world stage. In his large, performative self-portraits, Morimura inserts his own face and body into the work of the world's artists. National origin seems just another guise he slips into or out of at will. He is Natsume Soseki on the ¥1,000 bill and Jesus on the cross; he is male and female; he is black and white; he is silly and serious; he is the history of art – and he is everywhere. Every year for the past 10 years, Morimura's work has appeared in not just one but several international shows; he is a one-man carnival of postmodern eclecticism.

In the art world to which Morimura belongs, lines distinguishing painting, photography, sculpture, and other forms of visual representation are as seemingly fragile as national barriers. The 1996 Hugo Boss awards, one of which went to Morimura, celebrated an international group of artists whose materials included a loom (Janine Antoni), bloated sheep guts and a Honda engine (Cai Guo Qiang), and a talking plastic parrot (Laurie Anderson). At the Soho branch of the Guggenheim Museum in New York, where the six finalists' work was displayed, a digitized Morimura showed up in his "Actress Series" as Marilyn Monroe, pink skirts flying high to reveal an erect artificial penis. In using paint, costume, digital manipulation, and found objects to make his color photographs, Morimura is fracturing and reworking the distinct genealogies of these various media, globalizing photography, as it were, within the arts.

In 1974 when John Szarkowski considered the possibility of a "distinctively Japanese photography," he suggested that "most of the meanings of any picture reside in its relationships to countless other and earlier pictures – to tradition" (Szarkowski 1974: 9). That being the case, "exceptional local circumstances" might produce distinctive "Japanese photography," or so

Szarkowski argued. But artists working in Morimura's mode of highly theatrical, painstakingly constructed, postmodern tableaux (his peers in this respect include international art world stars Cindy Sherman, Sandy Skoglund, William Wegman, and Jeff Wall) draw directly or indirectly on a vast repository of images from all possible media, transgressing national and generic borders alike. In this sense, Morimura sets himself completely outside the traditional line of postwar Japanese photographers descending from Yasuhiro Ishimoto to Ken Domon to Nobuyoshi Araki. The meaning of his work cannot be located in Japan through this form of cultural genealogy.

The cross-dressing, gender-bending, media-mixing, taboo-breaking spirit of Morimura's work ensures instant recognition by the American, indeed the international, art world. But what exactly do they recognize in Morimura? What is the nature of his globalness, the nature of art world globalization in general? Is Morimura participating in a homogenizing postmodernism spreading from the West across the globe? Or does this eclectic mode of creativity form a "third culture," a hybrid international culture divorced from nation-states?

In trying to answer these questions, it is essential to recognize the ways in which Morimura is still located within Japan despite all that dislocates him. In fact, I would argue along with Mike Featherstone (1996: 47) that "the processes of globalization and localization are inextricably bound together in the current phase," so that Morimura's very globalism entails his national identity. Featherstone, reading postmodernism and the continued importance of the nation-state as "reactions which seek to rediscover particularity, localism, and difference" in the face of globalism, suggests "that globalization produces postmodernism" (Featherstone 1996: 60). By these lights, Morimura's postmodernism is neither an example of a totalizing process whereby a Western logic of similarity erases the particular nor an example of a hybrid, transcendent culture escaping the nation-state.

Morimura's globalness and nationality are inextricably bound together in at least three ways. First, unlike Sugimoto and Shibata, Morimura's biography makes no reference to international training or residence. Educated at the Kyoto City University of Art, he has benefited from Japan's commitment to produce a class of cultural specialists and intermediaries essential to its national identity, an identity that Morimura enacts as the Japanese representative at international art festivals such as the Venice Biennale.

Second, in making his own face and body the focus of his art, Morimura deliberately puts his bodily Japaneseness into play. The electric charge of Morimura's work depends on the viewer recognizing Morimura's Japanese ethnicity, the witty insinuation of his features into unexpected contexts, and the sense of cultural hybridity that is its payoff. One only has to imagine, say, the face of Cindy Sherman rather than that of Morimura as the "Six Brides, 1991" to realize how a face read differently in terms of sex and ethnicity would shift the currents of tension.

Third, and perhaps most important, Morimura's work specifically engages

Japanese circumstances. As curator Robert Stearns (1995: 95) observes, "Morimura's work derives from images of many cultures, yet they offer the most pointed and poignant comments on his own culture." Writing for the exhibition "Japanese Art after 1945: Scream against the Sky," curator Alexandra Munroe concurs. She places Morimura among "several contemporary Japanese artists [who] address Japan's unique brand of late capitalism in their 1990s work, which satirizes Japan's avidity to appropriate status and 'culture' through the sheer power of money" (Munroe 1994: 340). Understood in these terms, Morimura's "Japaneseness" is not a tradition that he exemplifies and reproduces (the claim made about Shibata's work), but a relationship to a particular yet malleable culture that he engages, critiques, and helps to mold through his art.

In all these ways, then, Morimura does not leave Japan when he joins global culture; "Japan" instead gives him a place from which to see, a vantage point on a world not yet, despite predictions, truly hybrid or transnational. Like migrating birds, global culture and its participants need to touch down, to nourish themselves on the particularities of local, daily life. Their art flourishes in the relationship between flight and feeding. I would suggest that what the postmodern international art world recognizes in Morimura is this process of negotiation itself, a negotiation between the particular artist, the national, and the global where none of these entities have been eclipsed.

Conclusion

The photographic art world and its players in Japan and in America present a very particular and perhaps peculiar perspective on globalization. They are but one thin stratum in much larger cultural and economic formations, yet examining them closely allows useful conclusions to be drawn. First, and at a minimum, I hope I have shown how unpersuasive is Samuel Huntington's view of clashing world civilizations. The American embrace of Japanese fine art photography – the respect, criticism, enthusiasm, and commercial value accorded this art form and these artists, and above all the mutual understanding between these art worlds – does not suggest that Japanese and "Western" civilizations are opaque to one another, signaling futilely and menacingly across the wide gulf of the Pacific (Huntington 1993).[10]

Second, my research suggests that, when it comes to Japan, postcolonial theorists who see the demise of the nation have overstated their case. The continuing strength of Japanese national identity may be explained as a result of the extraordinarily vigorous and intelligent campaign begun in the Meiji period to control and particularize the national experience of modernity, preventing "modernity" from unfolding in some predictable, universal, homogeneous way. The national institutions formed in this process mediate the effects of commodity capitalism on contemporary Japanese art as well as other goods. Indeed, the world of fine art photography provides evidence to support Featherstone's contention that globalized systems and nation-states augment one another, a point made as well by Immanuel Wallerstein when he argues that pressures of the world economy, particularly in the advantaged areas, spur national elites "to create cultural–national identities" to protect their interests in the global economy (Wallerstein 1976: 231).[11] According to Wallerstein, this very tension between the global and the national fuels the capitalist world system. Thus, the work of Sugimoto, Shibata, and Morimura arrives in America through this joining of the national and the global where neither "Japaneseness" nor "global culture" can stand alone.

Third, the equity of the relationship between Japanese photographers and American galleries and the routine inclusion of Japanese criticism beside American commentary in exhibition catalogues suggest that too many of our models of global exchange dwell exclusively on unequal relationships.[12] Wallerstein's world systems analysis, for instance, focuses on the hierarchical division of labor between "core-states" with their "higher levels of skills and greater capitalization" and the "peripheral areas" of cheaply exploited labor and resources (Wallerstein 1976: 232). Likewise, the rubric of "Orientalism" foregrounds disparities in the power of the gaze between East and West, rather than tendencies of mutuality and exchange of the kind that prompt, say, American Lee Friedlander to photograph Kyoto's cherry blossoms while Shibata scans water-control projects in the United States. Furthermore, our models of global exchange need to be modified to accommodate cases of intellectual and artistic transfer such as this, where the producer is accorded no less respect and power (and perhaps more) than marketers and consumers.

Finally, we need to be suspicious of our desire to simplify the current state of globalization with overly predictive theorizing before a sufficient range of cultural production has been examined. At least within the world of art photography, the global is neither as systemic nor as homogenized as studies of other commodities might lead us to believe. The categories that I have deployed in this analysis – the national logic of difference in contrast to the global logic of similarity – are themselves somewhat reductive. These two interlocking modes of commodification and interpretation are insufficient to demarcate anything like a precise band of permissible activity in the art world, a world after all counts it as its business to welcome the impermissible. What our current theories do not account for is the inexplicable creativity of artists, the excitement and imagination of curators and critics, and the wild economic contingency of a world whose players sip wine with millionaires one day and worry about rent the next. Little of this random exuberance can be captured in systematic analysis. The individuals in these art worlds still act creatively as "individuals" rather than as "subjects" of "nation-states" or of "discursive formations" or even of "global capitalism." We need a theory of culture's globalization that recognizes and resonates with this same creativity.

To underscore this point, I want to end with an account of photographer Masao Yamamoto's peregrinations in the world of American fine art photography from 1995 to 1996. In the summer of 1995, at the Tokyo

Metropolitan Museum of Photography, Yamamoto presented a work seemingly nostalgic for Europe's colonization of Asia and Africa.[13] On a large, old-fashioned wooden desk accompanied by an antique chair, he placed a handsome, prewar leather suitcase. The label on the suitcase listed the colonies supplied by the English company which manufactured it: names still in use such as "India" and "Kenya" as well as old names such as "Ceylon." The effect recalled Somerset Maugham; the desk, chair, and valise were so evocative that you could almost see the fevered British civil servant longing for his gin and bitters under an ineffectual ceiling fan. In keeping with the theme of old memories, 145 artificially yellowed and stained photographs of nondescript objects and unplaceable places were stashed inside the suitcase. Yamamoto invited us to take them out and finger their rough corners. Their order, whether in the suitcase or spread out on the old desk, was as unimportant as chronology usually is to the play of memory. The images served as templates for any remembrance that we happened to cast upon them. Yamamoto calls this "Kū no Hako," or "A Box of Emptiness."

In Chicago, when "Kū no Hako" appeared at the Catherine Edleman gallery in October and November 1995, the box had filled up in name, becoming "A Box of Memories," but disappeared in substance. Gone was the leather suitcase, the old wooden table, the imaginary tableau of the colonial bureaucrat. Instead, each deliberately scarred image was carefully selected out and framed in thick black metal. No longer were hands or memories invited to tarry over textured surfaces. At first, this transformation appears grist for an analysis of neat cultural dichotomies: East versus West, empty versus full, fingered versus framed, loose and scattered versus controlled and hanging on the walls. Yet things are not so simple.

A few months before the Chicago show, the Michael Shapiro Gallery in San Francisco exhibited these images in yet another way – hung on walls, yes, but also loosely spread out in a Plexiglas display case. Yet even this more casual method of display goes against Yamamoto's desire to have these photographs touchable by gallery-goers. Was this a case of American curatorial obtuseness to the express wishes of a sensitive non-English-speaking artist? On the contrary. It might never occur to the Japanese gallery patron to pocket a Yamamoto image (selling for about $1,000 these days), but the Michael Shapiro Gallery worried that among its visitors some will not resist the temptation to steal unsecured prints. The difference, then, in presentation of "Kū no Hako" has less to do with cultural verities than sociological ones; we must shift the grounds of our analysis, or must we?

In New York, a city not known for its aversion to crime, Yamamoto appeared again in the fall of 1996, at the Yancey Richardson Gallery, with a leather suitcase and the pictures loose inside it. The images were jumbled no differently from the way that they were in Tokyo, but each was enclosed in a transparent preservation envelope. Viewers were invited to slip the pictures out of their envelopes every day except Saturdays, when crowds made shoplifting detection difficult. This old leather suitcase was almost identical in design to the one used in Tokyo, but there were no British names, no evocation of the Raj on its label, which showed it to be of Japanese manufacture. Placed in this receptacle, do the worn images now evoke memories of Japan's colonial adventures? How can we fix the meaning of Yamamoto's piece if we cannot fix its form? How do we frame questions of globalization in ways adequate to art's shape-shifting migration from one locale to the next?

Notes

1 For instance, on 20 March 1997, *New York Times* columnist Thomas Friedman argued that we have entered a "new world of globalization – a world in which the integration of financial networks, information and trade is binding the globe together and shifting power from governments to markets."

2 Five years later, in 1979, Yamagishi teamed up with Cornell Capa to create another exhibition called "Japan: A Self-Portrait" for the International Center for Photography. Please note: all Japanese names are given in non-Japanese order (family name last) since this is the way that they appear in most exhibition catalogues and reviews in the United States.

3 The exhibition "Black Sun: The Eyes of Four" was organized jointly by the Alfred Stieglitz Center of the Philadelphia Museum of Art, the Museum of Modern Art, Oxford, and the Arts Council of Great Britain, and exhibited in both the United States and Great Britain. The catalog was published as a special issue of *Aperture*.

4 The "Against Nature" exhibition traveled to San Francisco, Akron, Boston, Seattle, Cincinnati, New York, and Houston.

5 For a discussion on the continuing importance of regionalism within Japan, contrasted with "the strongly unified national image that Japan projects abroad," see Wigen (1996).

6 For instance, an Ishimoto photograph of a southside Chicago scene was included in the "Tokyo kokuritsu kindai bijutsukan to shashin 1953–1995" (Photography and the National Museum of Art, Tokyo 1953–1995) exhibition at the Tokyo Kokuritsu Kindai Bijutsukan in 1995.

7 This phrase was on a wall label at the Toshio Shibata exhibition, Art Institute of Chicago, 1993.

8 The difficulties of nonspecialist American art curators finding fresh perspectives in the Japanese art world and the particular strength of the trope of Japan's close relation with nature is discussed in Osaka and Kline (1989).

9 This point is from a press release titled "The Museum of Modern Art Expands *New Photography* Series" issued by the museum in September 1992.

10 Huntington lists "Japanese" and "Confucian" separately among the world's "seven or eight major civilizations".

11 For a different form of the argument that global culture does not necessitate the end of nation-states, see Featherstone (1990).

12 For instance, both John Szarkowski and Shoji Yamagishi wrote for the 1974 catalogue *New Japanese Photography*, and both Anne Tucker and Etsuro Ishihara wrote for Toshio Shibata's *Landscape* volume.

13 The show was titled "-ism '95: The 1st Tokyo International Photo-Biennale." A catalogue by the same name was published by the Tokyo Metropolitan Museum of Photography, 1995.

Bibliography

Appadurai, A. (1996) *Modernity at Large: Cultural Dimensions of Globalization*, Minneapolis: University of Minnesota Press.

Beinart, P. (1997) "An illusion for our time," *New Republic* 20 October: 20.

"Black Sun: The Eyes of Four" (1986, Spring) (Catalog), *Aperture* 102: special issue.

Boris, S. (1997) *Toshio Shibata*, Chicago: Museum of Contemporary Art.

Brougher, K. (1993) "Hiroshi Sugimoto: memories in black and white," in *Sugimoto*, Los Angeles: Museum of Contemporary Art.

Cotter, H. (1997) "Hiroshi Sugimoto," *New York Times* 18 April.

Enyeart, J. (1992) "Terraces of splendor and destiny," in K. Yamagishi (ed.) *Photographs by Toshio Shibata*, Tokyo: Asahi Shinbun.

Featherstone, M. (1990) "Global culture: an introduction," *Theory, Culture & Society* 7 (2–3): 1–14.

—— (1996) "Localism, globalism, and cultural identity," in R. Wilson and W. Dissanayake (eds) *Global/Local: Cultural Production and the Transnational Imaginary*, Durham, NC: Duke University Press.

Goldberg, V. (1992) "Cherry blossoms, plastics, morality plays," *New York Times* 20 December, section 2: 35.

Gupta, A. and Ferguson, J. (1992) "Beyond 'culture': space, identity, and the politics of difference," *Cultural Anthropology* 7: 19.

Harvey, D. (1995) "Globalization in question," *Rethinking Marxism* 8 (4): 2.

Hiroshi, U. (1995) "Aisatsu" (Greetings), in *Tokyo kokuritsu kindai bijutsukan to shashin 1953–1995 (Photography and the National Museum of Art, Tokyo, 1953–1995)*, Tokyo: Tokyo Kokuritsu Kindai Bijutsukan.

Huntington, S.P. (1993) "The clash of civilizations?" *Foreign Affairs* Summer: 22–49.

Inside/Out: Contemporary Japanese Photography (1994) *Inside/Out: Contemporary Japanese Photography*, Charlotte, NC: Light Factory Photographic Arts Center.

Ishihara, E. (1996) "Toshio Shibata – the pure art of a craftsman," in *Toshio Shibata: Landscape*, Tucson, AZ: Nazraeli Press.

Kuspit, D. (1993) "Toshio Shibata" (exhibition review), *Artforum International* April.

Leach, M.R. (1994) "Origins? Questions? Translations? A Westerner's meditations on contemporary Japanese photography," in *Inside/Out: Contemporary Japanese Photography*, Charlotte, NC: Light Factory Photographic Arts Center.

McCormack, G. (1996) *The Emptiness of Japanese Affluence*, Armonk, NY: Sharpe.

Munroe, A. (1994) *Japanese Art After 1945: Scream Against the Sky*, New York: Abrams.

Nakamura, Y. (1995) "Landscape today," in T. Shibata (ed.), *Terra: In Pursuit of New Landscape*, Tokyo: Toshi shuppan.

Osaka, E., and Kline, K. (eds) (1989) *Against Nature: Japanese Art in the Eighties*, New York: Grey Art Gallery and Study Center at New York University, MIT List Visual Arts Center, and Japan Foundation.

Ozawa, T. (1994) *Bakumatsu: Shashin no jidai (The Closing Years of the Tokugawa Period: The age of Photography)*, Tokyo: Chikuma shobō, p. 7.

Stearns, R. (1995) "Space, time, and memory," in *Photography and Beyond in Japan*, Tokyo: Hara Museum of Contemporary Art.

Szarkowski, J. (1974) "Introduction," in *New Japanese Photography*, New York: Museum of Modern Art.

Travis, D. (1991) "Fukase's face and photographs," in *The Solitude of Ravens: Masahisa Fukase*, San Francisco: Bedford Arts.

Tucker, A.W. (1996) "Not What I Expected," in *Toshio Shibata: Landscape*, Tucson, AZ: Nazraeli Press.

Wallerstein, I. (1976) *The Modern World System: Capitalist Agriculture and the Origins of the European World-Economy in the Sixteenth Century*, New York: Harcourt Brace Jovanovich.

Wigen, K. (1996) "Politics and piety in Japanese native-place studies: the rhetoric of solidarity in Shinano," *Positions* 4 (3): 491–517.

Yamagishi, S. (1974) "Introduction," in J. Szarkowski and S. Yamagishi, *New Japanese Photography*, New York: Museum of Modern Art.

Part V

Images

10 A collision of discourses

Japanese and Hong Kong Chinese during the Diaoyu/Senkaku Islands crisis

Gordon Mathews[1]

In September 1996, Hong Kong was roiled by a wave of angry demonstrations over a Japanese right-wing group's assertions of Japanese sovereignty over the disputed Diaoyu/Senkaku Islands.[2] Hong Kong mass media decried what they called "a resurgence of Japanese militarism"; anti-Japanese banners and petition drives sprang up throughout Hong Kong; and a number of large and boisterous anti-Japanese demonstrations took place. At the same time, however, the Japanese presence in Hong Kong remained ubiquitous: not only merchandise, but also tourists and other sojourners, most of whom were shocked by the frenzy of anti-Japanese sentiment suddenly before them. How, in the midst of this tension, did Japanese sojourners in Hong Kong perceive Hong Kong and the Hong Kong people's views of them as Japanese? What sense did they make of the Hong Kong people's anger at Japan? How, in turn, did Hong Kong activists perceive the Japanese sojourners in their midst – as innocent tourists and students or as ongoing incarnations of Japanese aggression? And how can we comprehend the very different comprehensions of these two groups?

This chapter seeks to use a very small series of particular events and viewpoints – the Diaoyu Islands protests in Hong Kong in fall 1996 – to arrive, eventually, at an understanding of capitalism versus nationalism, a collision of discourses in today's world. I first set forth the history of the Diaoyu/Senkaku Islands dispute. I then examine the dispute from alternative points of view: those of Japanese tourists and exchange students and of Hong Kong Chinese student activists, correlating these views with mass media reports. I then explore the complex of motivations behind all sides of the dispute. Finally I examine the dispute as a conflict of social positions, cultural shapings, and, most of all, of opposing frames of global discourse, filtered through Japan's worldwide economic reach and Hong Kong's resurgent sense of Chineseness: the discourses of capitalism in its myth of a pastless present and nationalism in its myth of past as present.

The Diaoyu/Senkaku Islands dispute: a brief history

The Diaoyu/Senkaku Islands are a group of small, uninhabited islands some 200 kilometers northeast of Taiwan and 300 kilometers southwest of Okinawa.

China and Japan – and of late, the two Chinas and Japan – all have laid claim to the islands, based on geography and history. The first Chinese mention of the islands was around 1430, in a manuscript by the Chinese navigator Zheng (Wills 1996); this historical claim is used to argue that the islands indeed belong to China. Japan incorporated the islands into its territory in 1895 (Wain 1996), following the Sino-Japanese War; the islands fell under American jurisdiction after World War II. China seemed to accept non-Chinese sovereignty over the islands during the 1950s and 1960s: "Outsiders take the view that Beijing and Taipei's 'sudden' interest in the islands was caused by a United Nations agency report in 1968 revealing the presence of oil in the area" (Lau 1996). In 1971, the first major protest over the Diaoyu/Senkaku Islands took place in Hong Kong, "turning Victoria Park and the streets of Causeway Bay [a central Hong Kong shopping district] into a battleground, with passing cars being stoned and vehicles burnt" (Wan and Kwong 1996); but this did not prevent the islands from reverting to Japanese control in 1972, along with the island of Okinawa.

The current round of unrest began in July 1996, when members of the Japan Youth Federation, a Japanese right-wing group, constructed a lighthouse on one of the Diaoyu/Senkaku Islands, sparking off the demonstrations. In Hong Kong, demonstrations began in earnest in September. On 11 September, Chinese University students held an all-night protest in front of the Japanese consulate (*Ming Pao* 1996a); by 15 September, 12,000 people "took to the streets ... in a growing wave of anti-Japanese sentiment ... . A Japanese military flag was burned to mark the end of the five-hour protest" (Won 1996). On 18 September, the anniversary of the Manchurian incident of 1931, marking the start of Japan's war with China, 6,000 more braved a driving rain to demonstrate (*Ming Pao* 1996b); on the same day, activists scuffled with security guards at Sogo, a Japanese department store in Hong Kong, demanding a boycott in Hong Kong of Japanese goods and ostentatiously buying non-Japanese goods (Lee and Wong 1996). On 19 September, a Hong Kong legislator urged China to set a deadline for Japan's return of the islands, and to go to war if the deadline passed; Japan must understand, he held, that "the Chinese people are not a weak nation" (*South China Morning Post* 1996a). Several days later, the head of the Professional Teachers' Union in Hong Kong said, "We should make use of the [Diaoyu Islands protest] movement to educate our younger generation, alert them to the growing Japanese militarism and let them understand more about China and its history" (Ku 1996).

Demonstrations spread across the Chinese world, at least in Hong Kong newspaper headlines – "Thousands take to the streets in Taipei" (Chan 1996); "Hunger strike planned in U.S." (Li 1996) – but China itself was leery. Chinese activists began a petition drive in mainland China, urging the government to take stronger action against Japan; Beijing responded by sending them on work assignments far from the capital (Chan and Lee 1996). Members of a pro-China Hong Kong political party, traveling to Beijing for a meeting with a Chinese government official, found themselves under surveillance by plainclothes policemen fearful that they might stir up Chinese people to engage in Diaoyu Islands protests; but surreptitious protest groups formed anyway on Chinese campuses (Chan and Yuen 1996).

On 22 September, a flotilla of demonstrators set out from Hong Kong and another from Taiwan, vowing to tear down the Japanese lighthouse and plant the Chinese flag in its place. The first flotilla was turned back by the Japanese Coast Guard, which was present *en masse* to guard the islands. The second ended in tragedy on 26 September when the Hong Kong protest leader David Chan dove into the ocean from his vessel, a freighter, to "swim in what he insisted were the Diaoyu's 'Chinese waters' " (Lee 1996); he was sucked under the vessel and drowned. He was thereafter proclaimed a martyr by many although by no means all of Hong Kong's people, giving up his life in the fight against Japanese militarism (ironically, it was a Japanese medical team that attempted to save his life and did save the life of a drowning fellow protester, airlifting him to Japan for medical treatment). After David Chan's death, the Japanese consulate asked for police protection for its citizens in Hong Kong, so worried were they about a backlash (*South China Morning Post* 1996b). A candlelight vigil mourning David Chan drew 40,000 people (Choy and Won 1996).[3]

On 7 October, another flotilla of 140 protesters on thirty-one boats arrived at the islands, and this time a boat evaded the Japanese Coast Guard and landed several protesters. They hoisted Chinese and Taiwanese flags side by side before quickly departing, and before, just as quickly, the Japanese Coast Guard took the flags down. "MISSION ACCOMPLISHED," the *South China Morning Post* proclaimed, in a capital-lettered headline of a type size usually reserved for the ending of world wars. Its lead story began as follows: "It was ironic that, as the sun rose over the Diaoyu Islands, the forces of the Land of the Rising Sun were at last to be overcome" (Ng, K.-c. 1996). Chinese-language newspapers in Hong Kong outdid one another in expressing patriotic fervor: "The Chinese noble spirit lives on in the Diaoyu Islands forever" (*Ming Pao* 1996d), "Diaoyu heroes write new episode in defending the nation" (*Ming Pao* 1996e), "Long live the Chinese nation!" (*Oriental Daily News* 1996a).[4]

And then, suddenly, the tide turned. Hong Kong protesters had for weeks been demonstrating outside the Japanese consulate and presenting petitions to consular officials; but on 9 October, a dozen Hong Kong protesters, led by two Hong Kong legislators, broke through a police cordon and occupied the consulate. This, many acknowledged, was going too far: "Protest is one thing, lawlessness another," the *South China Morning Post*, suddenly sanctimonious, proclaimed in an editorial (1996c).[5] After this, the Diaoyu/Senkaku Islands suddenly vanished as a topic from television and newspapers in Hong Kong. Small-scale protests continued, but as a topic convulsing Hong Kong, the affair was over.

In retrospect, the Diaoyu/Senkaku Islands crisis may appear, aside from David Chan's tragic (or, from a different view, pathetic) death, as something of a tempest in a teapot: much ado about very little. However, it is clear that the dispute was not simply over a few obscure uninhabited islands and the fish their waters contain and the oil that possibly underlies them. The storm of emotions swirling through the dispute arises, from the Hong Kong Chinese point of view, from the unhealed war wounds that China suffered at the hands of Japan and Japan's failure to apologize fully for its actions in World War II; they arise from "Chineseness" and Chinese cultural pride sensed as having been insulted, belittled, besmirched by the Japanese; and they arise from a history that Japanese may endeavor to forget but that Chinese insist upon remembering. From the Japanese point of view, however, this seems bewildering: why should the poisons of past historical resentments be allowed to infect the benign interchanges of the present? These different points of view become clear from interviewing different parties in the dispute. Let us now examine, in turn, the views of Japanese tourists in Hong Kong, then Japanese exchange students more committed to interchange with Hong Kong's people, and finally Hong Kong anti-Japanese student activists.

Japanese tourists in the midst of the dispute

A survey of Japanese tourist guidebooks shows that virtually none deals with the history of the Japanese incursion into Hong Kong in World War II. Of twenty guidebooks that I examined, only four spend a page or two on Hong Kong history, of which all but one only briefly mention the Japanese invasion of Hong Kong.[6] A typical entry is, in its entirety, as follows: "Japan took Hong Kong under control on 25 Dec. 1941, and thus began its 3-year-and-8-month military administration of Hong Kong" (Oba 1995). Most guidebooks deal only with the present: food and shopping and interesting sights to see.

In late September, before the height of the crisis but after the news of a Japanese flag burned in a Hong Kong protest had reached Japan, my wife (who is Japanese) and I interviewed Japanese tourists of various ages at sites in Tsim Sha Tsui, the leading tourist area of Hong Kong. We heard comments such as these: "We understand the feelings of Hong Kong people, but burning the Japanese flag is too extreme. The dispute should be solved by the two governments." "We saw from the tour bus anti-Japanese banners. There isn't militarism in Japan now – we don't even have nationalism like Chinese people – but because of the war people still think Japan is militaristic. But we don't feel upset, because Hong Kong people are angry at the Japanese government, not at us." "Japan isn't militaristic today, but probably people think there is militarism in Japan because of the war. But this has no relation to us." For these tourists, the shadow of World War II remained an awkward legacy, but one that has vanished in Japan and should vanish in Hong Kong, they seemed to say; and in any case that legacy has nothing to do with them personally, they felt.

In ensuing weeks, however, this insouciance became more difficult to hold. On Saturday 5 October there was a demonstration at the Star Ferry Terminal at Tsim Sha Tsui, featuring exhibits about the islands and who they truly belonged to and showing photographs of Chinese slaughtered by the Japanese in World War II; hundreds of people were jammed into the tiny area, as speaker after speaker decried what they saw as the return of Japanese militarism. The Star Ferry Terminal is all but unavoidable for tourists, and the Japanese tourists we tried to interview in Tsim Sha Tsui on that day were clearly spooked. Asking Japanese tourists about the Diaoyu/Senkaku Islands was, we found, like yelling "fire" in a crowded theater: not only would the person questioned dash away – mumbling, "I'm sorry, I'm busy" or "it has no relation to me" (*watashi to kankei ga arimasen*) – but also all Japanese within earshot would scatter. In malls normally crowded with Japanese tourists, we found ourselves with large spaces around us, as everyone Japanese sought to avoid having to interact with us.

By the end of the first week of October, the Diaoyu Islands protests were having a definite effect on tourism. The Hong Kong television station ATV reported on 9 October that 10,000 Japanese tourists had canceled their planned visits to Hong Kong, often forfeiting deposits; some stores in Hong Kong dealing with Japanese tourists were recording a 40 percent drop in sales. "Tour operators say Japanese tourism has dropped 20 percent since the Diaoyu Islands dispute started," reported the *South China Morning Post* on 11 October:

> Japan Travel Bureau managing director Akira Moriyama said one of his groups was mobbed by activists ... Protesters waving anti-Japanese pamphlets and shouting in Japanese stopped tourists and held banners to tour bus windows ... Legislative Councillor Howard Young said he would hate to see the waste of "the millions" used to promote the territory in Japan. He urged activists to leave Japanese tourists alone.
>
> (Delfino 1996)

As discussed earlier, the occupation of the Japanese consulate and the sense that this was "going too far" led to a cessation of large-scale protest in Hong Kong. My wife and I took a Japanese tour in mid-October and were told by the guide that "the anti-Japanese movement hasn't affected our business at all." Indeed, during the tour we saw no sign of the anti-Japanese movement in Hong Kong, except for one banner proclaiming "Protect Diaoyu Islands"; but since "Diaoyu" is for Japanese an unfamiliar name for the islands, few Japanese tourists would have noticed it. Everywhere the Japanese tourists went on our tour they were greeted with smiles; as tourists, bringers of money, they were shielded from any anti-Japanese sentiment that Hong Kong people might feel.

The Japanese tourists we interviewed came to Hong Kong solely to eat, to see a few sights, and to shop. For them, Japan as a nation, just as China as a nation, has no relation to their tourism. These tourists are in a commercial bubble; many speak no more than a bit of English and no Cantonese, and so they can't have any relation to Hong Kong beyond their hotels and the shops catering to tourists. As Befu and Stalker (1996: 115) write, commenting on Japanese tourism throughout the world, "getting to know the local people is the last thing on … [most Japanese] tourists' minds"; as Bauman (1996: 30) notes, commenting on tourism at large in today's world, "what the tourist buys, what he pays for, what he demands to be delivered … is precisely the right not to be bothered." The Diaoyu Islands protests were precisely such a bother, breaking the implicit touristic contract. It is no coincidence that, when Japanese tourism – and all the money that that tourism brings – was threatened by protesters, voices for restraint were raised in Hong Kong, and the protest movement shortly thereafter abruptly collapsed.

Japanese residents of Hong Kong in the midst of the dispute

Those Japanese who live in Hong Kong have a more extended relation to Hong Kong than do tourists, but they too have tended to live in a bubble. Research on Japanese companies (Wong, W.-h. 1999) and housewives (Nakano 1995) in Hong Kong shows that Japanese tend to associate among themselves, Japan remaining more real than the Hong Kong world they temporarily happen to live in. Japanese tourist magazines sometimes banter about how to become "Hongkongese" – "speak a few words of Cantonese, watch a Hong Kong movie, get some clothing tailor-made, buy some products in a Chinese department store" (*Honkon/Macau* 1996) – and thereby impress one's friends back in Japan with one's international expertise. On the other hand, periodicals for Japanese residents in Hong Kong focus on how to lead a Japanese life in Hong Kong, advertising restaurants serving "sashimi airlifted from Japan," and *juku* (after-school cram schools) for one's children so that they will not forget their "Japaneseness" (Shitakubo n.d.). Japanese tourists in Hong Kong, this implies, want to be seen as cosmopolitan global citizens by their fellow Japanese because they are securely nestled in Japaneseness in their non-touristic lives. Long-term Japanese residents of Hong Kong, on the other hand, seem concerned less with being global citizens than with wanting to preserve their "Japaneseness," a Japaneseness threatened by the fact that they are in some sense global citizens, at least in living outside Japan's shores.

A major source of information for Hong Kong's Japanese residents is the *Hong Kong Post*, a weekly newspaper in Japanese. For the 6 weeks during which Hong Kong was engrossed with the anti-Japanese movement, its reports emphasized the Japanese as the harassed victims of Hong Kong extremists. To take just one example, the newspaper reported on a protest aimed at the students of a Japanese school: activists drew a Japanese military flag on the pavement in front of the school entrance, intending to force students to step on it. It quoted a young Japanese mother as saying, "I feel scared to go out alone with my child. I have this feeling that I might be surrounded by angry demonstrators and shouted at" (Noda 1996a). The newspaper's reports did not, however, indicate surprise or anger at the appearance of such anti-Japanese sentiment in Hong Kong. Indeed, it noted that Japanese businessmen in Hong Kong felt "hesitant to criticize the anti-Japanese protest movement because it has been carried out under the banner of 'protesting against the revival of Japanese militarism'" (*Hong Kong Post* 1996c). No article in the *Hong Kong Post* in this period makes any effort to deny Japan's past, but all make the implicit claim that the past is irrelevant to the present; the newspaper expressed concern that years of effort by the Japanese to contribute to the Hong Kong community might have evaporated (Noda 1996b). A survey of its readers showed that more than half held that the largest factor behind the Diaoyu/Senkaku Islands dispute was not the actions of Japan but the sensationalism of Hong Kong media and the anxiety of Hong Kong people over Hong Kong's handover to China (*Hong Kong Post* 1996b).

The Japanese residents in Hong Kong with whom I have had the most extended relations are exchange students at the Chinese University of Hong Kong. These students have a more personal relation to Hong Kong people than many Japanese in Hong Kong, but they, like most of their compatriots, remain acutely conscious of being Japanese and uniformly bewildered by the protests. One said:

> I was shocked – those people still feel so strongly about Japanese militarism. If you go to Japan, the people there will tell you, "We will never fight a war against China." When I saw a banner saying that "the issue of the island is equal to Japanese militarism. It will lead to the third world war," I was amazed.

In another's words:

> When I saw the demonstrations in Hong Kong, I felt as if I were thrown back to wartime Japan: it seemed so nationalistic ... When I see the news, the anti-Japan banners, the demonstrations, I feel scared. I talk to students, and tell them I'm an exchange student from Japan, and they're friendly. But I live at the university hostel; people are watching TV every night about the issue. I get scared then, because they know I'm Japanese ... When I talk about the issue, I always say, "I understand your feeling. I feel guilty about what the Japanese government did during wartime." As long as I say I feel guilty, they're not going to be too aggressive toward me.

Still another spoke of how, at a meeting of students, she was afraid to speak to her Japanese friends: "I thought that if I said anything in Japanese, I might become the object of their resentment ... I have only a few Hong Kong friends. I don't know how they really feel about the dispute and about the Japanese people." In one of my classes, consisting of both Japanese and

Hong Kong students, a discussion of the Diaoyu/Senkaku Islands prompted one Hong Kong student to say, "Sometimes I feel that we can't believe anything you say, because you're Japanese."

The role of exchange student is generally thought of as involving the bridging of cultural and national differences; in one Japanese student's words, "I came to Hong Kong so that I could understand Hong Kong people. I want to get outside Japan and communicate with people in the world." But the global bridges that students such as this one sought to build were spurned by some Hong Kong students, who saw the Japanese in their midst not as fellow pursuers of international understanding but as untrustworthy strangers, trailed by the ineradicable shadows of history.

These Japanese students seemed well aware of history's shadows. The student quoted earlier may use expressions of guilt as a means of easing her social interactions with Hong Kong students, but she also feels a real sense of guilt over the war: "Many people in Hong Kong and at this university, their ancestors might have been killed by Japanese. I can understand why they feel as they do." But these Japanese students did not feel that they should have to labor under such shadows; the war was not their responsibility, they felt. One said, "I think that the Japanese government and the Japanese people are different, but people in Hong Kong seem to think they are the same." Yet it was not just a government that killed Chinese people in World War II, but hundreds of thousands of Japanese soldiers. "Japan is completely unmilitaristic today. There's no nationalism in Japan," these students say; but there was not so very long ago. Because of that, these students' protestations of contemporary Japanese innocence may be suspect in many Hong Kong eyes. Let us now turn to Hong Kong views of the dispute.

Hong Kong Chinese activists in the midst of the dispute

Hong Kong Chinese newspapers were often remarkably jingoistic in their commentary. To give just one example, a column in *Ming Pao* – the most trusted newspaper in Hong Kong, according to a recent survey – stated that

> Chinese all over the world must think deeply about the fact that … Japan is giving a signal that it is preparing to invade China … . Every awake person, everyone with a Chinese face or identity, must devote himself to preparing for a coming inevitable holy war to protect the Diaoyu Islands. We experienced the eight-year war with Japan. What is now coming is a new and unending war.
>
> (Ng, H.-m. 1996)

However, Hong Kong people quoted in the media by no means shared such patriotic frenzy; one person interviewed by *Ming Pao* about David Chan's death stated, "I don't think there's any reason for Hong Kong people to sail to the Diaoyu Islands"; another said, "I think it means nothing to die as he did" (*Ming Pao* 1996c). A meeting of student activists from different Hong Kong universities yielded no consensus: one student leader argued that "questioning whether or not the islands are really Chinese territory is exactly an expression of how students don't admit themselves as Chinese, and of how weak their national feelings are"; but another said that "shouting about protecting the Diaoyu Islands only intensifies national hatred between China and Japan, making China move onto the path of militarism"; still another said, "I won't protect the Diaoyu Islands for the sake of national feelings!" (*U-Beat* 1996).

I interviewed a number of Hong Kong Chinese student activists at the Chinese University, who, while not as inflammatory in their rhetoric as some Hong Kong Chinese mass media, maintained that, in one student's words, "the Diaoyu Islands are a symbol that Japan might invade China, just as it did before." "My mother told me about the terrible thing that the Japanese did in World War II," said another. "In Hong Kong, after the Japanese invasion, the population dropped sixty percent!" However, their animosity does not extend to all Japanese, they claimed; as one person said:

> It may seem that we hate Japanese, but we don't … Some soldiers admit that they killed Chinese, but the government won't apologize. We don't need any compensation, but only for them to apologize and admit that they did it … Not all Japanese are bad. Some of them are very nice, but they don't even know where the Diaoyu Islands are; and they don't know anything about what Japan did in World War II to China. The Japanese government controls the mass media about this: in Hong Kong we know everything, but in Japan the students don't know anything!

As opposed to this sense of Japan – or at least the Japanese government and Japanese mass media – as the source of evil in Asia, these students strongly expressed their dream of a greater China. "It's time for us to show that we love our country. Yes, China and Taiwan have different political structures, but we are all Chinese, one race and one culture." "We love our country and we want our entire country to be united: Hong Kong, China, Taiwan, and the Diaoyu Islands. As Chinese, we are one."

These students had to admit, however, that their sense of the oneness of China was belied by the fact that the protests were, after all, taking place only in Hong Kong, not in China proper; they reluctantly had to agree with a *Ming Pao* column that appeared early in the crisis: "Every Chinese worries about the Japanese invasion of the Diaoyu Islands. But only in Hong Kong can we see demonstrations in the streets. Where are the mainlanders? … Aren't they Chinese? … Hong Kong people are left lonely in this crisis" (Wong, M.-f. 1996).

Beyond this, there is the mutual antipathy felt by the different governments claiming to be "China." Some Diaoyu Islands protesters carried mainland Chinese flags and others the flag of Taiwan; if the Japanese had simply packed up and left, Taiwan and China would have immediately fallen into conflict over which of them owned the islands. When I discussed this with one student, he said, "The argument between China and Taiwan is like an argument within the family. We can argue within the family very seriously, but no outsider can come in and join that argument." In other words, Japan can serve as the threatening stranger at the door of the home, unifying the bickering family members at each other's throats by giving them a common enemy.

But the irony of this metaphor is that Japan is already in the family home: every one of the family's appliances, not to mention their television sets, radios, and automobiles, will likely be Japanese; many comics, pop music hits, and television programs are also of Japanese origin. As one Hong Kong student said:

> We know there was World War II; we know that the Japanese killed many Chinese in the war. But since I was born, there have been Japanese products all around me – comics, TV, music. Yesterday I listened to the radio and there were many telephone calls from people expressing their anger at Japan; but immediately after that, the radio played a song copied from Japanese musicians. In our culture we have so many Japanese things! You can't avoid Japan. It's part of Hong Kong now.

This student personally knows not Japan's attempted military globalization half a century past but rather Japan's far more benign economic and cultural globalization, making Japan an ineradicable part of Hong Kong. This point was brought home ironically by an activist who raided Sogo department store at Causeway Bay demanding a boycott of Japanese goods: almost everything he wore, from his watch to his shoes, had been made in Japan (*Hong Kong Post* 1996a). I observed another such irony at the Star Ferry Diaoyu Islands demonstration on 5 October. Above the surging crowd, a video played, decrying Japanese imperialism; but the television was National, a Japanese brand. At one point, the video malfunctioned and, bizarrely, the word "National" repeatedly floated across the screen, as if an advertisement: a cool beacon of Japanese global commerce, as against all the heat of anti-Japanese passion on the ground below.

A complex of motives

As these depictions indicate, there was more going on in the Diaoyu Islands protests than readily meets the eye: there is, indeed, a complex of motives on both the Chinese and the Japanese sides.

On the Japanese side, for all the Japanese students' protestations about the lack of militarism in their society, in fact, members of an extreme nationalist group did construct a lighthouse on one of the islands; the Japanese government never repudiated the acts of the group, which were blatantly provocative. One survey (Shapiro 1992: 43) showed that only 6 percent of the

Japanese population say that they would be willing to fight in a war for their country (as opposed to 77 percent of Americans; Hong Kong and China were not represented). On the other hand, as the Hong Kong Chinese student activists I interviewed never tired of pointing out, Japan has never fully apologized for the brutalities it committed in China during World War II. If the Japanese people are not militaristic, the behavior of its government can certainly convey the impression of militarism, with its recent history of cabinet ministers denying the brutalities of the Nanking Massacre and of the colonization of Korea.

Japanese press coverage of the Diaoyu/Senkaku Islands dispute was minuscule compared with press coverage in Hong Kong; only David Chan's death made the front page of most Japanese newspapers. Japanese newspapers criticized Hong Kong newspapers' jingoistic coverage of the dispute. For example, *Asahi Shinbun* argued that "fierce competition among Hong Kong newspapers accelerated Hong Kong people's criticism of Japan" with their sensationalistic reporting of the dispute; it quoted a Hong Kong journalist as saying that "if we write about the Diaoyu Islands dispute, papers sell; if we don't, papers don't sell" (Sakajiri 1996) – but on the other hand, Japan's own newspapers may be criticized for their comparative silence. This contrasts not only with Hong Kong's blaring press, but also with Japanese press coverage of the northern islands, the Kuriles, in recent decades; Japan holds these islands to have been unjustly appropriated by the Russians, and the Japanese press has never been shy about hammering this point. It is far easier being a victim than an aggressor; as Japanese sometimes say, "Those who hit others forget what they did, but those who get hit never forget" (*Tataita hō wa wasuretemo tatakareta hō wa wasurenai*). It was natural that the Japanese tourists and students should have been shocked by Hong Kong Chinese outrage as little in Japan had given them any idea of such massive resentment of Japan. "Internationalization" (*kokusaika*) may be a buzzword in Japan today, but this is an "internationalization" based in present interchanges, remaining, for the most part, blissfully oblivious to the recent past.

On the Chinese side, one aspect of this complex of motivations was alluded to earlier – the fact that anti-Japanese demonstrations took place in Hong Kong and Taiwan but not in China. "President Jiang ... and his colleagues are worried that once public protests begin, they won't stop at the issue of the Diaoyu Islands or Japanese war crimes, but will inevitably turn against the communist leadership itself" (Spaeth 1996). The fact that demonstrations took place in Hong Kong but not in China represents in itself an implicit criticism of China; and, indeed, the political groups most responsible for Hong Kong's demonstrations were those shunned by Beijing. "In Hong Kong, mass rallies have been initiated primarily by pro-democracy groups anxious to demonstrate their patriotism in the face of Beijing's assumption that those who do not back its plans for the territory are 'unpatriotic'" (Bowring 1996). By organizing demonstrations, pro-democracy groups could assert that they were more patriotic than the Chinese government in that they were willing to stand up for China against Japan, as the Chinese government, worried about preserving its economic links with Japan, was not. This was clearly an underlying motive for the protests, although one vociferously denied by the Hong Kong student activists with whom I discussed this.

To some, a mystery of the Diaoyu Islands protests is why so many Hong Kong Chinese seemed to see as their enemy not their totalitarian neighbor and soon-to-be ruler to the north but rather a society across the ocean. A letter to the *South China Morning Post* states this plainly:

> I find recent calls which have been made to boycott Japanese goods most irrational. If taking over an uninhabited island is a crime, is the massacre of thousands of unarmed protesters [at Tiananmen Square] not at least equally criminal? Then why should a people boycott goods from a country that committed the former crime but not from the country that committed the latter?
>
> (Tam 1996)

One Japanese writer in Hong Kong explains the matter simply (Arai 1996). Japan, she argues, is but a scapegoat: "The current fury over the Diaoyu Islands has more to do with Hong Kong people's frustration toward Beijing than anything else." For such assertions, she was apparently forced to resign from the Hong Kong newspaper that she worked for and was roundly criticized in Hong Kong for forgetting history (see Wong, F. 1996): the history of Japanese aggression against China. As a Hong Kong Chinese commentator wrote, "It is said that Japanese are amazed [that Hong Kong people are so involved in the Diaoyu Islands protest] ... but Hong Kong suffered the pain of Japanese occupation. Please do not think that we have amnesia" (Shek 1996).

As noted earlier, anger at Japan serves as a unifying force for diverse political Chinas, normally at one another's throats. This was apparent at the height of the Diaoyu Islands protests; after Taiwanese and Hong Kong activists had succeeded in planting flags on the Diaoyu Islands, returning in triumph to Taiwan, "Taiwan separatists threw eggs and burned China's flag outside an inn where Hong Kong activists were lodged. The protesters were incensed the Hong Kong group had dared to raise the mainland flag on what they insist is Taiwanese soil. Predictably, Beijing also took offense that the banners of Taiwan and China flapped side by side" (Ajello 1996).

Given these political differences, what is the common "Chineseness" that the Diaoyu Islands protesters proclaim? What is the "Chinese family" the aforementioned student proclaimed? These seem to be referring to an ethnic and cultural Chineseness that transcends political difference; but what exactly this larger Chineseness consists of seems problematic (Mathews 1996). If "Chineseness" is held to be "race," then the Hong Kong Chinese I spoke with must account for the fact that the Japanese they so assail are physically all but indistinguishable from Chinese. If "Chineseness" is held to consist of language, then these Hong Kong Chinese must account for the fact that Cantonese and Mandarin are as spoken languages mutually unintelligible. If "Chineseness" is held to be a common cultural tradition, then these Hong Kong Chinese must account for the fact that such tradition has been systematically obliterated in mainland China by communism, just as it has been eroded in Hong Kong by colonialism. The common "Chineseness" proclaimed by the Diaoyu Islands protesters seems an illusion, proclaimed by various political groups for their own power-seeking ends.

We thus can see that both the Japanese and the Chinese arguments are shaped by the underlying complexes of motivations of each side; the tourists and students that I interviewed are shaped and perhaps manipulated by these different motivations. This alone, however, is not enough to explain the two different sides' mutual incomprehension.

Positions, interests, cultures, and discourses

How can we most fully understand the mutual incomprehension of the Japanese and Chinese whose voices we have heard in this chapter? Most simply, there are the social positions from which these voices emanate. In the broadest sense, tourists, expatriates, and exchange students seek, in their own various ways, to transcend cultural bounds, while those at home may seek to reinforce cultural bounds. International tourists tend to seek to experience the foreign in an enjoyable, domesticated package; exchange students tend to seek to transcend the foreign through the interpersonal bridges they build with those of another society. The Diaoyu Islands protests represented a denial of the validity of these social positions by emphasizing not commonality and commerce between Japanese and Hongkongese but difference, not bridges but walls. The Hong Kong student activists acted as defenders of what they saw as their cultural home – becoming a national cultural home after 1 July 1997 – as against the claims to friendship of those they saw as outsiders and former transgressors.

The conflict between these different social positions – the conflict between insider and outsider, between "family" and "stranger" – is universal; but the particular cultural shaping of Japanese and Hong Kong Chinese clearly exacerbates this conflict. The people I interviewed have been shaped, through their societies' educational systems and mass media, to see the dispute within the frame of their societies' self-interests, self-interests obviously at odds. The islands are potentially valuable: the Chinese sides can best stake their claim by decrying past Japanese militarism and its resurgence, whereas the Japanese side can best hold its claim by downplaying its past. In a larger sense, it is in the Japanese interest to minimize World War II, and in other Asian nations' interests to trumpet World War II. "Just as the Japanese deny or play down their aggressive war, the Chinese have been willing to mercilessly and cynically exploit Japanese guilt over what happened" for their own economic and political ends (McGregor 1996). The people I interviewed are not wholly pawns of such shaping – among both the Hongkongese and Japanese I interviewed, there was a range of opinion, and at least a limited degree of skepticism toward one's government and its proclamations, one's education and its blinders. And yet the fact that the two sides could so little comprehend one another indicates the ultimate power of such shaping in fixing the bounds of what one is able to think.

Such shaping, by definition, is cultural, if we see "culture" in terms of the underlying and to a degree enduring values transmitted to each generation within a given society. It seems clear that, to a degree anyway, the two sides have different culturally shaped views of history. The Japanese emphasis on *un*, "fate" (Lebra 1976: 175–6), leads to a view of history not as a matter of rights and wrongs but as the given course of things, with no one to be blamed for what transpired.[7] The Chinese view of a Sinocentric world, impinged upon by colonialism, may lead to a very different sense of history: of the historical wrongs done to China, and particularly to Hong Kong, that must be righted (Wang 1995: 17–24). Perhaps not too much should be inferred from these different views of history. After all, the powers that be in Japan are perfectly capable of inventing history when circumstances suit them – the 2,600-year reign of the Japanese emperor promulgated and believed until the end of World War II – just as the powers that be in China are perfectly capable of obliterating history, as in the more recent case of the Tiananmen Square incident. But in any case these different cultural attitudes do seem to be used at present to serve the interests of their societies: the young in Japan are culturally shaped to forget recent history, while the young in Hong Kong are at present being culturally shaped to remember.

These different cultural shapings come into conflict because of Japan's globalization: the transformation of Japan, in just five decades, from a society devastated by defeat in war and on the brink of starvation to the world's second-largest economy, whose products, corporations, and citizens reach across the world, including, as we have seen, Hong Kong. Largely because Japan's affluence and global reach have occurred so rapidly in history, the cosmopolitanism of many of its citizens may still lag behind the cosmopolitan reach of its products. In Befu and Stalker's words (1996: 115):

> The disposition of the Japanese abroad is not … toward cosmopolitan-ization … Their identification and their pride as Japanese do not diminish during their foreign sojourn. Instead, if anything, these feelings are intensified as the Japanese become conscious of the cultural contrasts between Japan and the culture in which they find themselves.

Indeed, even the Japanese students quoted earlier, eagerly pursuing international understanding, may find that their national–cultural molding as citizens of Japan serves to undermine that pursuit. However, this may be true not only for the Japanese but also for their Hong Kong hosts, and for all of us in today's world. Our national–cultural education within our particular societies may make "cross-cultural misunderstanding" all but inevitable.

But this cultural explanation is not yet sufficient for fully comprehending the miscomprehension of the Diaoyu/Senkaku Islands disputants. Globalization, writes Roland Robertson, "refers both to the compression of the world and the intensification of consciousness of the world as a whole" (Robertson 1992: 8); it is by definition not only national, involving states, but also transnational, involving movement that transcends states. Given the fact of globalization, the idea of discrete cultures exclusively shaping their citizens is increasingly called into question. As Ulf Hannerz has written, it is now "more difficult than ever ... to see the world ... as a cultural mosaic, of separate pieces with hard well-defined edges. Cultural interconnections reach across the world. More than ever, there is a global ecumene" (Hannerz 1992: 218). As Arjun Appadurai (1990, 1996), most notably, has explored, today we live in a world of massive global flows of people, capital, and ideas (Appadurai 1990); as Hannerz (1996: 111) proclaims, "there is now one world culture."

Within such a world, we are all not only culturally separated but also culturally linked; the key for understanding this chapter's disputants is to see them not only as members of separate cultures but also as members of one world culture, a common metaculture [to use, in a somewhat different context, Robertson's term (1992: 41)]. Many theorists have considered global culture and globalization in macrocosmic terms, but what of microcosmic terms: how do people actually use this global culture to make sense of their worlds? To understand most fully the Diaoyu/Senkaku Islands disputants, we must focus not only on their different cultural shapings but also on their common global shaping: their adoption of different contemporary global discourses to formulate and legitimate their opposing views.

Discourse is a slippery term, but I define it as "a linguistically shaped model that determines the preconditions of what may be thought within a given social position and cultural context." Discourse differs from culture in, among other things, its flexibility. Whereas a member of a culture, at least in the more traditional uses of that term, seems all but enveloped in its values and worldviews, its "way of life," discourse is more motile and adaptable. One may situationally use a number of different discourses, despite the fact that these discourses may in some senses be mutually antagonistic and even unintelligible, in that their underlying premises fundamentally differ. I argue that there are a small number of common discourses at play throughout the media-connected globalized world today, with each taking on an interest-specific and culturally specific form within different cultural and personal contexts, but nonetheless remaining still universally recognizable: these discourses include those of science, technology and progress, religious belief, and rule of law. Two of the most dominant of these discourses, as I will now discuss, are those of nationalism and capitalism.

Capitalism and nationalism as world discourses

Simply speaking, the discourse of nationalism specifies who one's group is apart from the world as a whole ("We are Chinese/Japanese/American, unlike you"), while the discourse of capitalism specifies who one is as a part of the world as a whole in its commodification, the global parade of production and consumption. Most people, at least in more affluent parts of the world, situationally use these two discourses in constructing, maintaining, and legitimating their senses of cultural identity.

Japanese tourists, businessmen, and students in Hong Kong seem to have different purposes, but there is a commonality in these groups. The businessman is engaged in making money, the tourist in spending money – eating, shopping, buying souvenirs – and the student in greasing the wheels of commerce through the pursuit of international understanding. Members of all three of these groups may see themselves through the discourse of capitalism. Capitalism, as Marx declared, entails the obliteration of the past by the present and future – "All fixed, fast-frozen relations ... are swept away ... All that is solid melts into air" – and the diminution of nation by trade across the globe – "In place of the old local and national seclusion and self-sufficiency, we have intercourse in every direction, universal inter-dependence of nations ... National one-sidedness and narrow-mindedness become more and more impossible" (Marx 1978: 476, 477). Today's writers on capitalism, from Kenichi Ohmae (1990) to Robert Reich (1991), repeat endlessly the mantra that, in today's "borderless world," the era of the nation and of nationalism is over.

This discourse fits the interests of contemporary Japan in its pursuit of legitimacy and respect in the world. "Nationalism," for many Japanese, refers to the bad old days of the Japanese attempt to dominate the world militarily. When Japanese tourists and students expressed their shock at Hong Kong people's avowals of nationalism, they were giving this word its negative Japanese connotation (a connotation held by all but right-wing groups such as that which built the lighthouse on the Diaoyu/Senkaku Islands, and some troglodyte politicians of the Liberal Democrat Party). As opposed to this dark past connotation, it is commerce with the world's nations that refers, for them, to the bright Japanese present. That such commerce is often seen by outsiders as being less than benign and, indeed, nationalistic (an occasional comment by outsiders in recent decades being that "Japan is trying to do commercially what it couldn't do militarily: take over the world") is beside the point. The point, rather, is that this discourse, of the goodness of international commerce and the badness of nationalism, is self-evident and taken for granted for the Japanese people whose views appear in this chapter.

If for many Japanese nationalism represents an ugly past best forgotten and commerce its glittering present, for many Hong Kong Chinese commerce is the past and present status quo, nationalism a colonially repressed past but soon-to-come proud future. During its recent decades of economic growth,

Hong Kong was often spoken of as a territory of pure capitalism, with minimal government interference; but the other side of this coin was that the colonial government did all it could to blunt the emergence of any nationalist consciousness. As a Hong Kong university teacher that I interviewed said:

> Hong Kong people are pragmatic and rootless ... because we don't have any sense of belonging; we don't learn in school about national identity, citizenship, civics ... My schooling involved ... a total neglect of the Chinese part of my education. I still have no understanding of Chinese literature and history.

Nationalism, for such people, may involve the awakening of a sense of "Chineseness" long repressed by the colonial government – the awakening of Hong Kong people to who they truly are, but have not been allowed to realize that they are.

"The idea of a man without a nation seems to impose a strain on the modern imagination," writes Ernest Gellner. "A man must have a nationality as he must have a nose and two ears" (Gellner 1983: 6). As one young Hong Kong resident told me in 1996, "Every time I travel to another country, I have to fill out the forms and write down my nationality ... I ask the stewardess, 'What should I write for nationality: British, Hong Kong, or Chinese?' " Those in Hong Kong who welcome the coming of Chinese control over Hong Kong do so in part because they will finally then have a national identity: the "nose and two ears" that they feel has long been denied them. They will be Chinese.

Many Hong Kong people have misgivings about reverting to a political China that they see as totalitarian: one survey conducted shortly before the handover indicated that 40 percent of young people in Hong Kong would emigrate if they could, and 30 percent of Hong Kong people were worried about human rights (Yeung 1997; see also Mathews 1997). This is why the Hong Kong students earlier referred to speak of a China that transcends the political: a China that is neither mainland China nor Taiwan nor Hong Kong, but rather the cultural background of them all. This cultural China provides the only basis that these Hong Kong students feel they have for claiming "Chineseness." Just as the Japanese students expressed amazement at Hong Kong people's expressions of nationalism, so too the Hong Kong students expressed shock at the Japanese students' distaste for nationalism, as if to say, "You have your nation, despite the terrible things it did. Why won't you let us have pride in our nation?" These two discourses, forming the taken-for-granted underpinnings of the Japanese and Hong Kong Chinese views that we have recounted, seem to all but preclude understanding between the two groups.[8]

It is important to emphasize that these discourses of capitalism and nationalism are not equivalent to capitalism and nationalism as objective phenomena. Clearly in the world at large, capitalism and nationalism are not simply opposites, but are complexly interlinked. It is on the level of discourse – involving the simplification and streamlining of the objective world, so as to provide contemporary human minds with structures of thought through which to comprehend the world – that nationalism and capitalism may come to function as encompassing opposites. Some discursive structurings are more sophisticated than others – leading some people to be able to view capitalism and nationalism more in shades of gray than in simple black and white – but all discursive structures involve simplification to make the world's empirical chaos comprehensible. Capitalism and nationalism are the labels that I have given to two such discourses, discourses that in their more fundamental, less subtle forms are incommensurate.

It is also important to emphasize that these discourses are situationally emergent, rather than being culturally intrinsic. The Japanese that I interviewed concerning the Diaoyu/Senkaku Islands used the discourse of capitalism, Hong Kong Chinese the discourse of nationalism. But one can imagine a situation – for example, if a Hong Kong trading company were seeking to export China-grown rice to Japan and found its efforts resisted by Japanese farmers and the Japanese public – where the frames of discourse would be opposite: Hong Kong Chinese speaking from the frame of international capitalism, saying "let commerce transcend national borders," and Japanese speaking from the frame of protective nationalism: "Japan only needs Japanese rice!" (Such cries could be heard in Japan a few years ago, when farmers sought to block the importation of American and Thai rice.) There is, again, nothing intrinsically "Japanese" or "Hong Kong Chinese" about the respective frames of discourse held by the two sides in the Diaoyu/Senkaku Islands dispute. Rather, given the nature of the dispute (over land that Japan was viewed to have "usurped," evoking historical remembrance and forgetfulness) and the timing of the dispute (shortly before Hong Kong's return to China and "Chineseness"), these global discourses of capitalism and nationalism were adhered to by Japanese and Hong Kong Chinese as the frames and justifications for their senses of cultural identity.

Conclusion: the shadows of history

The foregoing analysis does not mean that these frames of discourse were adhered to consciously and calculatedly by the people that I interviewed. The sheer "taken-for-grantedness" with which these discourses were adhered to, the clear inability of the two sides fully to comprehend one another, is an indication of how little these discourses were chosen and how much they were seen as a natural, self-evident given by their adherents. Today's Japanese sojourners and Hong Kong Chinese protesters are, to a degree, trapped within their different discourses, pawns of the culturally conditioned patterns of forgetfulness and remembrance within their different societies – patterns that use global discourses for less-than-global ends.

If they are thus in a sense pawns of their conditioned views of history, all the more so were their parents and grandparents: the Japanese soldiers and their Chinese victims in Hong Kong, and in Nanking too, among other places – propelled by global political forces into hundreds of thousands of acts of individual violence. Underlying the all-but-mutually-incomprehensible discourses that we have examined is an existential question, the question of guilt and innocence. Are today's Japanese guilty of what their fathers and grandfathers did? What responsibility do they bear? Japanese brutalities may have been worse than those of some other nation's conquering armies; but finally this issue transcends Japan, to address us all. Why, when our governments call upon us to do so, do we – Japanese, Americans, Chinese, Europeans – slaughter one another in war? All of us are both guilty and innocent: we are such nice people, and yet kill one another so readily when ordered to by our governments.

The discourse of capitalism has its own "false consciousness," breeding its own gross inequities and exploitations, but not the savagery that the discourse of nationalism may breed; and the latter – whether leading to the barbarisms of World War II or the far paler threats of a few protests 60 years later – ever threatens to swamp the glittering forgetfulness of the former. Capitalism forgets, nationalism remembers; and the Diaoyu/Senkaku Islands dispute represented at its broadest the collision of these two discourses. It was a minor collision in this instance, but one with implications far transcending a few specks of island that are home to no one.

Notes

1　Tsang Ching-yi and Miyakawa Yoko were of great help in gathering materials from Chinese- and Japanese-language newspapers and other mass media. An earlier version of this paper was presented at the Workshop on Travelling Cultures in Asia, Hong Kong, 9–11 April 1997, and at the European Association for Japanese Studies Conference, Budapest, 27–30 August 1997. It was then published as Occasional Paper No. 94, Hong Kong Institute of Asia-Pacific Studies, The Chinese University of Hong Kong. I thank Habibul Haque Khondker and Eyal Ben-Ari, as well as this book's editors, Harumi Befu and Sylvie Guichard-Anguis, for their suggestions as to this chapter's revision.

2　When I refer in this chapter to these islands, I label them "the Diaoyu/Senkaku Islands" – by both their Chinese and Japanese names. When referring to the protests in Hong Kong, however, I refer to "the Diaoyu Islands protests" as this is the name by which the islands are recognized in Hong Kong.

3　This made it arguably the largest demonstration in Hong Kong in 1996, rivaling the total reported for the demonstrations marking the Tiananmen Square incident.

4　As I will later discuss, this "Chinese nation" does not refer to any existing Chinese state but rather to the unity of all Chinese states, in an imagined "greater Chineseness."

5　Some Hong Kong Chinese newspapers, however, defended and glorified the action. The *Oriental Daily News* (1996b) proclaimed that "the twenty-four warriors of the Diaoyu movement protest the Japanese occupation of the island with 'an eye for an eye, a tooth for a tooth,' by themselves occupying the Japanese Consulate."

6　The only exception among guidebooks to this omission of history is in the Hong

Kong guide of the *Chikyūno arukikata* series, roughly equivalent to the *Lonely Planet* guides in English. It carries an article entitled "What Japan did in Hong Kong in the past," which urges Japanese tourists to remember that "many people in Hong Kong had their blood relatives killed by Japanese military forces ... . In the minds of Hong Kong people, there is always an anti-Japanese sentiment which can easily be ignited by the least provocation" (Suzuki 1996: 429). It is not surprising that this guide for the independent traveler, presumably dealing to a greater degree with Hong Kong people, should be the lone Japanese guide to address the issue of Japan's past atrocities in Hong Kong. As for the actual extent of such atrocities, in their recent histories of Hong Kong, Welsh (1993) is somewhat less critical of the Japanese occupation than Morris (1997), but both seem to concur with Morris's assessment that "by and large the conduct of the Japanese in Hong Kong [in World War II] was despicable" (Morris 1997: 249).

7 During the 7 years in all that I, as an American, have lived in Japan, I cannot recall even once being in any discussion in which the United States was blamed for its atomic bombings of Hiroshima and Nagasaki (bombings that, arguably, were entirely unnecessary). Partly this was a matter of tact, but, more, I believe it to be the result of the cultural influence of *un*, "fate." As older Japanese have said to me, "That was a bad time back then; many bad things happened. But there's no need for blame. Let us simply be thankful that those bad old days are gone."

8 A number of letters written by Hong Kong Chinese to the *South China Morning Post* during the crisis sought to rebut the views of non-Chinese letter writers in words such as the following: "as a foreigner, [Mr. X] cannot understand the strong patriotic feelings that Chinese people throughout the world feel on this issue" (Chin 1996) – they cannot comprehend the language of Chinese nationalism, a language that, according to the letter, only Chinese can comprehend.

Bibliography

The romanization of books and articles in Chinese published in Hong Kong are given in Cantonese, using the Yale system. For personal names of Hong Kong writers writing in Chinese, I use the more casual Hong Kong style of romanization, since this probably reflects their own romanized spellings of their names. Chinese-language newspapers in Hong Kong are designated by the romanized names they give themselves. The romanization of books and articles in Japanese follow the Hepburn system.

Ajello, R. (1996) "The flames of nationalism: will Diaoyu activists hit the lighthouse next?" *Asiaweek* 18 October.

Appadurai, A. (1990) "Disjuncture and difference in the global cultural economy," in M. Featherstone (ed.) *Global Culture: Nationalism, Globalization, and Modernity*, Thousand Oaks, CA: Sage.

—— (1996) *Modernity at Large: Cultural Dimensions of Globalization*, Minneapolis: University of Minnesota Press.

Arai, H. (1996) "Angry at China? Slam Japan," *Far Eastern Economic Review* 3 October.

Bauman, Z. (1996) "From pilgrim to tourist," in S. Hall and P. du Gay (eds) *Questions of Cultural Identity*, London: Sage.

Befu, H. and Stalker, N. (1996) "Globalization of Japan: cosmopolitanization or spread of the Japanese village?" in H. Befu (ed.) *Japan Engaging the World: A Century of International Encounter*, Denver, CO: Center for Japanese Studies, Teikyo Loretto Heights University.

Bowring, P. (1996) "'Patriotic' outbursts don't serve the interests of Hong Kong," *International Herald Tribune* 1 October.

Chan, Q. (1996) "Thousands take to streets in Taipei," *South China Morning Post* 23 September.

Chan, V.P.-k. and Lee, R. (1996) "Journalists in signature campaign ordered out of Beijing," *South China Morning Post* 17 September.

Chan, V.P.-k. and Yuen, A. (1996) "Protests spread to campus," *South China Morning Post* 14 September.

Chin, K.-f. (1996) "Foreigners cannot understand patriotic feelings," letter to the editor, *South China Morning Post* 12 October.

Choy, L. and Won, L. (1996) "40,000 candlelight mourners pledge to continue struggle," *South China Morning Post* 30 September.

Delfino, B. (1996) "Tourism fears as Japanese hounded," *South China Morning Post* 11 October.

Gellner, E. (1983) *Nations and Nationalism*, Oxford: Basil Blackwell.

Hannerz, U. (1992) *Cultural Complexity: Studies in the Social Organization of Meaning*, New York: Columbia University Press.

—— (1996) *Transnational Connections: Culture, People, Places*, London: Routledge.

Hong Kong Post (1996a) "18 nichi nomi kyakuashi heru" (Only on the 18th did the number of customers decline), *Hong Kong Post* 27 September.

—— (1996b) "Watashi wa kō miru" (This is how I see it), *Hong Kong Post* 11 October.

—— (1996c) "Muhō wa Honkon o sokonau" (Lawlessness damages Hong Kong), *Hong Kong Post* 18 October.

Honkon/Makao (Hong Kong/Macau) (1996) *Honkonjin ni naritai (I Want to Become Hongkongese)*, Tokyo: Rurubusha/Japan Travel Bureau.

Ku, G. (1996) "Teachers call for change to syllabus," *South China Morning Post* 22 September.

Lau, C.K. (1996) "The price of a protest that went too far," *South China Morning Post* 11 October.

Lebra, T. (1976) *Japanese Patterns of Behavior*, Honolulu: University of Hawaii Press.

Lee, C. and Wong, B.W.-y. (1996) "Guards, activists in clash at Sogo," *South China Morning Post* 19 September.

Lee, D. (1996) "Diaoyu crusader drowns as patriotic act backfires," *South China Morning Post* 27 September.

Li, A. (1996) "Hunger strike planned in U.S.," *South China Morning Post* 23 September.

McGregor, R. (1996) "A conflict of history," *South China Morning Post* 8 October.

Marx, K. (1978) "Manifesto of the Communist Party," in R. Tucker (ed.) *The Marx-Engels Reader*, New York: Norton.

Mathews, G. (1996) "Names and identities in the Hong Kong cultural supermarket," *Dialectical Anthropology* 21: 399–419.

—— (1997) "*Hèunggóngyàhn*: On the past, present, and future of Hong Kong identity," *Bulletin of Concerned Asian Scholars* 29 (3): 3–13.

Ming Pao (1996a) "Jùngdaaih hohksàang tùngsìu jihngjoh kongyíh" (Chinese University students hold all-night protest), *Ming Pao* 12 September.

—— (1996b) "Luhkchìn yàhn mouhyúh géinihm gáuyātbaat" (Six thousand people commemorate September 18 anniversary in rain), *Ming Pao* 19 September.

—— (1996c) "Mìhngbou màhnyi tìuhchàh" (*Ming Pao* survey), *Ming Pao* 27 September.

—— (1996d) "Jùngwàh houhhei chèuhnglàuh Diudóu" (The Chinese noble spirit lives on in the Diaoyu Islands forever), *Ming Pao* 8 October.

——— (1996e) "Bóudiu jongsih séhah waihgwok sànjèung" (Diaoyu heroes write new episode in defending the nation), *Ming Pao* 8 October.

Morris, J. (1997) *Hong Kong: Epilogue to an Empire,* 2nd rev. edn, London: Penguin.

Nakano, Y. (1995) "The experience of Japanese expatriate wives in Hong Kong: the reproduction of conservative social patterns," Paper delivered at the Second International Symposium on Japanese Language and Education, University of Hong Kong, 11 November.

Ng, H.-m. (1996) "Bóuwaih Diuyùhtòih yiu chèungkèih kongjin" (Protecting the Diaoyu Islands requires a long war of resistance), *Ming Pao* 19 September.

Ng, K.-c. (1996) "Mission accomplished," *South China Morning Post* 8 October.

Noda, K. (1996a) "Nihonjin gakko ga hyōteki ni" (Japanese school targeted). *Hong Kong Post* 27 September.

——— (1996b) "Senkaku mondai wa doko e?" (Whither the Senkaku dispute?), *Hong Kong Post* 25 October.

Oba, T. (ed.) (1995) *Honkon* (Hong Kong). Vol. 8. *Burūgaido Pashifika* (Blue Guide Pacifica), Tokyo: Jitsugyō no Nihon Sha.

Ohmae, K. (1990) *The Borderless World,* New York: HarperBusiness.

Oriental Daily News (1996a) "Jùngwàh màhnjuhk maahnseui" (Long live the Chinese nation!), *Oriental Daily News* 8 October.

——— (1996b) "Bóudiu yihsahpsei gàmgòng kongyih Yahtbún chàmjim Diuyùhtòih; yíh ngàh wàahn ngah kèuhngngaahg jeunyahp yaht líhngsihgún" (The twenty-four warriors of the Diaoyu movement protest the Japanese occupation of the island with "an eye for an eye, a tooth for a tooth" by themselves occupying the Japanese consulate), *Oriental Daily News* 10 October.

Reich, R. (1991) *The Work of Nations,* New York: Knopf.

Robertson, R. (1992) *Globalization: Social Theory and Global Culture,* London: Sage.

Sakajiri, N. (1996) "Hageshii kyōsō tainichi hihan kasoku mo" (Severe competition between newspapers also increases criticism of Japan), *Asahi Shinbun* 2 October.

Shapiro, A.L. (1992) *We're Number One: Where America Stands – and Falls – in the New World Order,* New York: Vintage.

Shek, K. (1996) "Waihsahmmō kèungliht kongyíh" (Why we protest so strongly), *Ming Pao* 2 October.

Shitakubo, M. (n.d.) "Japanese identity through the description of Hong Kong in Japanese magazines," undergraduate student paper, Department of Anthropology, Chinese University of Hong Kong.

South China Morning Post (1996a) "Go to war if talks fail," *South China Morning Post* 20 September

——— (1996b) "Local Japanese warned of backlash," *South China Morning Post* 27 September

——— (1996c) "Militancy hurts cause," editorial, *South China Morning Post* 11 October.

Spaeth, A. (1996) "Nationalism gone awry: death in the Diaoyus," *Time* 7 October.

Suzuki, Y. (ed.) (1996) *Honkon* (Hong Kong). Vol. 35. *Chikyūno arukikata (Walking the Globe),* Tokyo: Daiyamondo-Biggu Sha.

Tam, J. (1996) "Not convinced," letter to the editor, *South China Morning Post* 26 September.

U-Beat (1996) "Bóudiu sìngjùng, fànlihtdīk daaihhohksāang" (The split in the voice of university students over protecting the Diaoyu Islands), *U-beat* October.

Wain, B. (1996) "Who really owns the Diaoyus?" *Asia Wall Street Journal* 4–5 October.

Wan, M., and Kwong, K. (1996) "David Chan: a driven man," *South China Morning Post* 27 September.

Wang, E. (1995) *Hong Kong 1997: The Politics of Transition,* Boulder, CO: Lynne Rienner.

Welsh, F. (1993) *A History of Hong Kong,* London: HarperCollins.

Wills, D. (1996) "Charting the Diaoyus' troubled history," *South China Morning Post* 12 October.

Won, L. (1996) "12,000 March, as anger over Diaoyu grows," *South China Morning Post* 16 September.

Wong, F. (1996) "Chinese concerns perfectly justified," *South China Morning Post* 2 October.

Wong, H.W. (1999) *Japanese Bosses, Chinese Workers: Power and Control in a Hong Kong Megastore,* Surrey, U.K.: Curzon.

Wong, M.-f. (1996) "Wàihhòh yeuhng Hèunggóngyàhn gùduhk" (Why do Hong Kong people remain alone?), *Ming Pao* 12 September.

Yeung, C. (1997) "Seeing past the hysteria," *South China Morning Post* 5 January.

11 Images of the Japanese welfare state[1]

Roger Goodman

As 1995 turned into 1996, political debate in the United Kingdom was suddenly dominated by discussion of the welfare state in East Asia. Tony Blair, leader of the Labour opposition, made a major speech in Singapore extolling the virtues of its system of private compulsory saving for old age, a system that helped to keep public taxation rates low. The right-wing chairman of the Commons Select Committee on Foreign Affairs, David Howell, commented on the absence in East Asian societies of anything resembling a welfare state – an absence that, he suggested, explained their economic prosperity. Chris Patten, then the governor of Hong Kong, announced that, on returning Hong Kong to China, he intended to write a book on how the British economy would benefit from an Asian-style minimal welfare state. Two other senior Conservatives, John Redwood and David Willetts, saw Britain as the "Hong Kong of Europe," whereas a Blair aide, Geoff Mulgan, went so far as to suggest that "even Thailand will have overtaken the United Kingdom" by the end of the century.[2]

In all these comments, East Asian welfare regimes were perceived to share a number of common elements: comparatively low public spending on the "welfare state"; a system in which extended families and local communities took on much of the burden of welfare that was carried by the state in the United Kingdom and companies retained workers who were not necessarily profitable; a historical emphasis on providing welfare for those who could increase national wealth, i.e. spending on education and public health, rather than those who could not contribute, i.e. spending on those who were socially and physically handicapped;[3] and a system in which welfare spending, as a gift of the state, was used to maintain social cohesion rather than representing the "rights" of certain interest groups. Although Japan was sometimes not mentioned in these debates at all, it was clear that, as the most advanced of the East Asian economies, its welfare state was widely perceived to be the prime example of a system that the politicians and commentators felt the United Kingdom should examine and possibly emulate and that was sometimes called the "East Asian welfare model."

In these debates, politicians and commentators naturally tended to focus on those elements of this perceived East Asian welfare model that fitted most closely with their own political agendas.[4] Conservatives concentrated on the low levels of government expenditure and the small size of the welfare bureaucracy, and lauded the spirit of individual and group responsibility and the crucial role of the family and the community in providing social welfare; Socialists and Social Democrats argued that East Asian governments not only acted in general to promote social cohesion and reduce social inequality but had also taken decisive steps to provide certain key items of social welfare across all sections of society, such as public health and education systems in Japan.

This sudden interest in the United Kingdom in the so-called East Asian welfare model was at first glance rather surprising for a number of reasons.

First, most East Asian societies, and particularly Japan, had always previously been attacked as "welfare laggards," particularly by European and North American politicians who sometimes put down Japan's trade surpluses to its lack of investment in its social infrastructure. Although the idea that these were welfare regimes worth copying had occasionally been espoused by right-wing politicians, it was certainly a new rhetoric for those in the center and on the left of the political spectrum.

Second, the timing of these pronouncements was hard to understand. Although in the 1970s and 1980s many had rushed to learn the secrets of Japan's booming economy and found it in a variety of social practices – law and order (Bayley 1976; Ames 1981), industrial and business management (Ouchi 1981; Pascale and Athos 1981), and education (White 1987; Lynn 1988) – Japan's system of social welfare, in the sense of care for the most vulnerable sections of society, had rarely, if ever, been invoked in these debates. So it was paradoxical that such interest should emerge in 1995 when Britain, for the first time since the late 1950s, had enjoyed a straight 4 years of greater economic growth than that achieved in Japan. Indeed, East Asia as a whole was about to plunge into the Asian economic crisis of late 1997, although this was as yet largely unforeseen.

Third, as Yoneyama (1997) points out, one of the most interesting elements of these debates was that none of them incorporated the views of Japanese, or indeed other East Asians, living overseas in the United Kingdom.[5] Not once in all the media coverage that I saw of East Asian welfare systems during 1995 and 1996 was someone from East Asia itself asked for a view of how their systems operated. Nor indeed were the views of academics who specialized in the area sought.

Fourth, just as interest was being shown in an East Asian welfare model, Japan, the supposed exemplar of such a model, was itself in the midst of its most dramatic welfare reforms of the past 30 years, a system of reform designed to bring it much closer to Europe in terms of welfare expenditure, provision, and rhetoric.

These reforms were sought because Japan is the fastest-aging society in the world. Although in the late 1990s its population was about the same age as that of other advanced industrial societies, government statistics (which are widely disseminated to raise awareness among the general population about the issue) suggest that the percentage of those in the population over the age of sixty-four will reach 25.5 percent by 2020, almost double that of 1990 and higher than that in all the major industrialized nations in the West. Those over the age of eighty will increase to more than three times their proportion in the current population. To help deal with the "problem" (as it is perceived) of the aged in society, the government introduced a wide range of measures throughout the 1980s and 1990s, most prominently the so-called Gold Plan in 1990, which dramatically expanded personal social services for the elderly through programs of home help, day care, and short-stay community centers and nursing homes. The demand for these services, once the supply began, was such that an enlarged New Gold Plan was introduced in 1994.

Not only did the Gold Plan mean an enormous increase in government welfare expenditure – at both the national and local levels – but it also involved the destigmatization of the elderly receiving "welfare" (*fukushi*) by renaming such services as "care" (*kaigo*). The success of the program also suggested that, when such forms of care were available, Japanese families were only too happy to allow the state to have a role in caring for their aged members.

At the same time as the so-called "health miracle"[6] in Japan means that people are living longer, fewer children are being born. This phenomenon in Japan is sometimes referred to as the "1.53 shock" following the 1991 "discovery" (more accurately the decision by government to make an issue) that women were on average having only 1.53 children during their child-bearing years, well below the general 2.1 level indicated by demographers for a population to remain static. With the number of children in the population in the 1990s continuing to shrink year by year,[7] the government has introduced a series of reforms under the name of the Angel Plan to encourage women to have more children by making it easier to have a family while continuing to work. This has led to major increases in day nurseries, drop-in care for nonworking mothers, centers to care for sick children, after-school care centers and counseling for parents with childcare problems (Boling 1998: 177). At the same time, it has sought to remove the stigma from a mother who works and replace it with the idea that the state should support such women to ensure that they can have a full career and bring up their families.

The final point of interest, which largely follows from the previous one, is that, at the same time as politicians in the United Kingdom were expressing interest in Japanese systems of welfare provision, ironically Japanese politicians and bureaucrats were actively taking an interest in elements of British social policy. As Japan struggled to pull itself out of the longest recession it has known in the postwar period, it turned (again) to models from the West, particularly from the United Kingdom, in areas such as the deregulation and privatization of services, which characterized reforms within British social welfare during the 1980s and early 1990s (Katayama 1998: 8).

These apparent paradoxes raise a number of questions of interest to an anthropologist. In particular, why was there such interest in East Asian welfare in the United Kingdom at the end of 1995 and what does it tell us about the United Kingdom, about East Asia, and about the mutual images that they hold of each other? In the context of this volume, a close examination of this question allows us a good opportunity to examine how images of Japan and Japanese social systems are constructed – both inside and outside Japan – and how these constructed images affect efforts to reform social systems in each context.

The construction of positive views of Japanese welfare

Until the mid-1970s, there was virtually no divergence, either inside or outside Japan, from the perception of Japanese society as a "welfare laggard." Japan was heavily criticized for putting economic growth before everything else, including support for the most vulnerable members of society; although, as Watanuki (1986: 261) points out, in fact the low level of welfare expenditure in the 1950s at least could reasonably be put down to a still relatively low economic base, a smaller ratio of aged in the population, and the persistence of the extended family system.[8]

The Japanese government's attempt, which was started in the late 1960s, to "catch up and converge with" the welfare states of the West and the designation of the year 1973 as the first year of welfare (*fukushi gannen*) were thwarted by the "oil shock" of the same year and there emerged, instead, the well-documented development of the so-called Japanese-style welfare society (*Nihongata shakai fukushi shakai*).[9] As Watanuki (1986: 265) says, "The idea of a Japanese-style welfare society is rather confused." But, essentially, instead of the move toward the state taking on the major burden of social welfare, the government expected this role to be played by the three social institutions of the family, community, and company and that government expenditure on social security would be maintained at a lower level than in the Western "welfare state."

The promotion of the Japanese-style welfare state took two distinct forms. On one hand, it was presented in a positive sense as a "natural" outgrowth of Japanese traditional practices, which were very difficult for Western nations to emulate. In the case of the company, a large literature both inside and outside Japan suggested that the modern Japanese company was a natural evolution of the traditional Japanese household (*ie*)[10] (see, for example, Abegglen 1959; Nakane 1973; Murakami 1984). As with the traditional *ie*, the argument went, it was only "natural" that companies should look after the welfare of their members. Indeed, according to this argument, the development of company welfare could be explained by the fact that many of Japan's large companies, such as Mitsui, had developed out of family businesses set up in the feudal Tokugawa period.

The idea of mutual community support was also seen to be a tradition dating from the feudal period when the Tokugawa shogunate divided communities into groups of five families, which were mutually responsible for each other (*go-nin gumi seido*) – a system that was carried into the modern era under the guise of organizations such as neighborhood associations (*tonari-gumi*) (see Bestor 1989).

Finally, in the case of women providing welfare support, it was argued that there was a long tradition of a "natural" division of labor along gender lines in Japan and that women willingly accepted the responsibility for the private and domestic sphere while men worked in the public, extradomestic arena.

The view that Japan's welfare system should be built on these traditional cultural practices was espoused by a large number of the country's leading thinkers during the 1970s, such as Murakami Yususuke, Rôyama Shôichi, and Sakamoto Jirô (Takahashi 1997: 144).[11] At the same time, there developed a powerful rhetoric against the Western-style welfare state, which, only 5 or 10 years earlier, had been held up as a model to emulate. This critique focused in particular on the British welfare system, both because Britain was accepted in Japan to be the birthplace of the first fully developed welfare state and because Britain in the early 1970s was going through a phase of economic stagnation, severe strife in the arena of industrial relations, and a variety of apparently intractable social problems. In much of the literature in Japan, a connection was made between these social and economic problems and a highly developed welfare state that created a "dependency culture," and the phenomenon was labeled the "British disease" *(Eikoku-byô)* (see Shinkawa and Pempel 1996: 305–12; Takahashi 1997: 136–9, 151). During the late 1970s, similar expressions were used about other European countries *(Itaria-byô; Furansu-byô)*, as their economies stagnated and Japan's continued to grow. The Nordic, particularly Scandinavian, model of cradle-to-grave welfare was particularly sharply attacked (*Hokuô Fukushi Kokka-byô*), and it became common in Japanese social welfare debates to refer to it simply in the context of *hanmen kyôshi* (a model to avoid).[12]

As the 1970s progressed, therefore, despite some of the ambiguities in its meaning, indeed perhaps in part because of these ambiguities, senior politicians such as Prime Ministers Ohira and Miki increasingly used the term *Nihongata shakai fukushi* (Japanese-style welfare) to describe the form of social welfare that they wanted to institute in Japan. The term rapidly gained such common currency that the reversal (known in Japanese as *fukushi minaoshi*) of the previous build-up of the welfare state met with very little public resistance – in part because (unlike in other countries where state welfare benefits were reduced or abolished in the 1970s and early 1980s) there was no organized resistance from unions in Japan. Unions, being company based and not national, were essentially interested in maintaining the benefits that they had already secured for the full-time, permanent employees in the companies that they represented, and these benefits were not under threat and indeed continued to grow as the economy expanded in the 1980s (Tabata 1990; Hiwatari 1993). The role of the media also should not be underestimated. Through a content analysis of magazine articles, Takegawa (1988: 242) discovered that, although up to 1975 all articles on welfare took either a positive or a neutral stance, from 1976 onward the vast majority (about 95 percent in his sample) took a negative position. But the main reason for the general acceptance of the rhetoric of the idea of Japanese-style welfare was its use of symbols of Japanese national identity that chimed in particular with the growth of national confidence in Japan in the 1970s and 1980s.

This positive view of Japanese welfare reached its zenith in English with the publication of Ezra Vogel's (1980) provocative *Japan as Number One: Lessons for Industrial America*. Vogel talked about the Japanese model as providing lessons in offering a welfare system in terms of "security without entitlement." Entitlements had been kept low; minimal sense of rights had developed; and the government – or rather the bureaucracy – had been left with the responsibility of effecting the most equitable distribution of the nation's wealth. By the late 1970s, Vogel asserted, its measures of success could already be seen in terms of longevity; good health and education indicators; low costs through reliance on the family, firm, and a large voluntary sector; little inner-city degradation and violence; an active and energetic older generation; high rates of employment; and little or virtually no welfare dependency. Japanese welfare necessitated a minimal bureaucracy (about 10 percent of its American equivalent), thus keeping taxation low and preventing the development of what Ivan Illich and colleagues (1977) had recently described as "welfare professionalism" – professionals and bureaucrats who created systems to serve their own rather than their clients' needs. Instead, Japan preferred to rely on a large number of voluntary, unpaid workers supervised by a small number of professionals – especially in areas such as social work and probation work. These high-status volunteers, generally known as *minseiiin*, in many ways still represent the key figures in the provision of Japanese-style welfare and gain their legitimacy from the idea of welfare being provided by the community rather than the state (see Goodman 1998a).

Japan as Number One sold even better in Japan than in the United States. Throughout the book, Vogel was clearly addressing an American audience about the problems he felt the United States faced, and in doing so he consciously highlighted the strengths of the Japanese social system and downplayed its weaknesses. In Japanese eyes, however, his account not only explained to the outside world how Japanese society worked but was also a means of giving it legitimization (inasmuch as Vogel was a Harvard professor). Since there was still considerable debate at this time in Japan about the nature of the welfare state, it is probable, indeed, that Vogel's work may even have helped to construct the system that he claimed to be describing.

Throughout the 1980s, interest in Japanese social systems grew along with the Japanese economy. This interest tended to be concentrated on the educational and industrial systems, which to a large degree were the two main ways through which Japan invested in its population and were claimed by commentators, both inside and outside Japan, to be the "secrets" of Japan's "economic miracle." Studies of both industry and the education system concentrated on the positive elements and ignored the negative. As Kawanishi (1992: 7–8) says, "To some extent it could be said that the image of Japan's industrial relations has changed with the times and at any particular time has reflected the intellectual climate of the times more than it has the actual realities of Japan's industrial relations."

In education, the Japanese system, which was still viewed in the West in the 1970s as "hellish," had by the 1980s become the main port of call for Western politicians looking for a model for reforming their own systems.[13] In the realm of law and order, the image of a Japanese police-state had been replaced by one of community policing (Ames 1981).

The underlying trope – or theme – of these changes in perception is Confucianism. This explains why the perception of other societies in East Asia (South Korea, Taiwan, Singapore, and Hong Kong), which were held in Western eyes to be part of a common Confucian culture, also changed and why ultimately Japan was seen as the exemplar of some homogeneous East Asian welfare model.[14]

In the immediate postwar period, Confucianism was perceived as a common feudal legacy that all East Asian societies would need to overthrow if they hoped to develop their economies. Confucianism was seen to overemphasize the status quo and hold back the dynamic qualities of younger, more able, creative, individualistic, nonconformist entrepreneurs. All East Asian economies at the same time were weak, and they were all Confucian societies; a connection between the two was accepted.

As the economic strength of the region began to overshadow that of Europe in the 1980s and it looked set to become the center of world economic power, together with the West Coast of the United States, by the turn of the century, so the commonly held perceptions and interpretations of the relationship between Confucianism and economic growth were reevaluated (see Morishima 1982; Berger 1988). Those values that had been perceived to be a negative common heritage of a homogenized East Asia were suddenly given a positive value, and those values that had been so positively espoused in a monolithic West were viewed more negatively.

The process began both within and about Japan, being the first non-Western nation to develop an unquestionably advanced form of capitalism. As the Japanese economy began to take off in the early 1970s, what is generally known as the *Nihonjinron* literature – a genre of writing detailing the essential qualities of what it means to be Japanese – also began to grow, providing for many in Japan a cultural explanation about why Japan was so successful.[15] The process of Occidentalism – the homogenization of all Western societies and the ascription to them of some common, immanent characteristics – resulted in a move from a positive to a less positive evaluation of Western values and attitudes. As we have seen in the case of the Western welfare state, as the economies of the West began to go into decline in the late 1970s and early 1980s, many of those same values – individualism, independence, rationality, universalism, logicality, insistence on rights, heterogeneity, equality, and contractual relations – that had been seen as responsible for the great strength of the West began to be seen in East Asia as responsible for its decline. Positive Occidentalism became negative Occidentalism.

As Arthur Gould (1993) points out in his account of what he calls the "Japanisation" of the British welfare system in the 1980s, the strength of the Japanese economy in the 1980s forced British industrialists to question whether the nation could continue to support an expensive Beveridge-style welfare state rather than specific Japanese welfare programs. To some extent, remnants of this debate can be seen in the discussions mentioned at the beginning of this chapter that took place in 1995 in the United Kingdom.

To use the language of the anthropologist Arjun Appadurai (1990), the images of Japanese welfare that developed in the United Kingdom constituted "mediascapes" and not "ethnoscapes" (with their transfer of people) or "technoscapes" (with their transfer of materials). Indeed, one of the most noticeable aspects of these images is the singular lack of interest in detailed analysis of the systems being examined. Unlike almost all East Asian societies, which continue to fund and send students to follow social work and social welfare courses in universities in Europe as a means of understanding and examining those systems,[16] there are no mechanisms for British students to go to East Asian societies to do likewise. As Gould (1998: 285) in a recent review writes:

> The emergence of Japan as a major economic power in the last few decades has resulted in an explosion of interest in all things Japanese – in all, that is, except social policy. Look on any … library shelf and you will find books on the Japanese economy, the Japanese political system … but next to nothing on Japanese welfare …. Any non-Japanese speaker who wishes to develop an interest in the Japanese welfare system has an uphill task trying to find a decent array of references.

This is important because a sociologically and historically contextualized examination of the basis of the Japanese welfare state leads to a very different picture from that presented by those who describe it as emanating naturally from Japanese tradition and history.

Let us start with the Japanese company. First, the welfare provisions of the Japanese employment system are not enjoyed by all its workers. A clear distinction is made between those who work in the major companies and those who work in subcontracting companies that serve the major companies. Put simply, the bigger the company the better able it is to provide welfare. Moreover, a core–periphery distinction exists within the big companies where many workers – seasonal, temporary, part-time – are also excluded from the benefits of company welfare. As a result of these factors, those who receive –

or can expect to receive – the benefits of lifetime company welfare benefits constitute only about 25–30 percent of the total workforce, and the vast majority of them are men.[17]

Serious questions also need to be asked about the idea that there is a direct historical link between the structure of preindustrial family and occupational relations and the contemporary Japanese company. Early factory management in Japan was far from benevolent (see Hane 1982), and, as Rodney Clark's (1979) description of the development of the Japanese company perhaps most clearly shows, the idea of the company-as-family developed out of the early industrial form of labor relations in the 1890s. These efforts by employers in the 1890s to have the Japanese company seen in terms of a family have been repeated many times over the past 100 years: Dean Kinzley (1991) outlines the details of the Kyôchôkai (Harmonization Society), which in 1919, with government sponsorship, did much to "re-invent" the rhetoric of "natural" management–employee cooperation in Japan; Sydney Crawcour (1978) describes the work of the Zensanren (the All-Japan Producers Union) in responding to increasing union strength in the late 1920s and early 1930s; in the immediate postwar period, faced by increasingly left-wing union agitation, the Japanese government together with the U.S. occupation authorities (facing the Cold War) acted to encourage the growth of company unions in order to serve the interests of the company as a whole, not only its workers. In each case, the discourse called on the structure of the traditional Japanese household as the model for industrial relations in the Japanese company, and in each case it was what Kinzley (drawing on Hobsbawm and Ranger 1983) has termed the "re-invention of a tradition."[18]

This reinvented tradition, however, became by the 1980s the cornerstone of the ideal-type model of the Japanese employment system and figured in any description of how industry worked in Japan. Those lucky enough to have full-time, permanent jobs in companies committed everything to the company in the knowledge that they would be looked after even in times of severe economic recession. As Befu (1980) pointed out at the beginning of that decade, individuals were aware that the practice of lifetime employment applied only to a section (mostly male) of workers who met certain conditions (such as being less than 55 years old), but even in the recession of the 1990s major companies in Japan did everything they could to avoid laying off their permanent staff so as to retain the ideology that there is a category of lifetime employees to which new entrants can aspire. This does not mean that the Japanese labor force has not changed during the 1990s. As Befu and Cernosia (1990) point out, the number of those hired on permanent employment contracts was already on the wane at the start of the 1990s and has continued to decrease as companies have introduced increasingly flexible employment practices. Even so, the practice of hiring a core of lifetime employees has continued, although increasingly with assistants who work under them coming from temporary agencies, a situation that is very different from that anticipated when the economic bubble burst and companies were expected only to hire on Western-style contracts. The real issue for Japanese companies, however, has been with their existing permanently employed workforce. As the recession continued into the second half of the 1990s, Japanese industrialists found themselves unable to respond to calls from foreign governments to increase competitiveness and restimulate their economy by laying off excess white-collar workers, in part because they found themselves trapped in the discourses that they developed and that have been legitimated by external observers who uncritically accepted them as founded in Japanese history and culture.[19]

A similar problem lies in the context of the Japanese family as providers of welfare. The family in this context means essentially the wife or the daughter-in-law, and underlying this has been a powerful and, since the Meiji period, constantly reinforced rhetoric of a gender division of labor.[20] Yet more and more women in Japan have been reluctant to take on the role of being sole caretaker for their children (and for their parents and their parents-in-law), and this is seen as one major reason for the 1.53 shock in the early 1990s.

As Boling (1998: 183–4) points out, the Japanese authorities are caught sending contradictory and mixed messages: "[f]ormal policies that help working parents deal with work–family conflicts … are often offset by 'family policies' found in the interstices of gender socialisation and in institutions and practices that assume and reinforce traditional gender roles."

Once again, the image of the "natural," what Boling calls "traditional," form of welfare may actually prevent Japan from dealing with its biggest social problem of all – the fall in the birth rate and the effect that this has on the issue of the aging society (*kôreika shakai*) in Japan. As with the ideology of the "natural" lifetime employment system, that of the "natural" division of labor on gender lines that has been so successfully nurtured over the past century may come to haunt Japan as it moves into the next millennium.

Conclusion

With the benefit of hindsight, the causes of the sudden outburst of interest within the United Kingdom in late 1995 and early 1996 in East Asian welfare regimes are somewhat clearer. It marked the beginning of 18 months of preelection debate and an election that put the United Kingdom Labour Party in power for the first time in 18 years on 1 May 1997. The future of the welfare state in the United Kingdom was a crucial element in the election platforms of all parties, as indeed it was for all parties in all elections in the 1990s across Europe. As their populations age and as economies bottom out and high rates of economic growth disappear seemingly forever, the postwar promises of minimum levels of quality of life to be supported by the state look increasingly difficult for European governments to meet. Politicians from all sides have to face this economic reality, and East Asia in 1995 still appeared to offer a useful "model" on which to focus in seeking to convince the electorate of this new situation. The intellectual argument seemed to run thus: East Asia has the most dynamic economies in the world and has managed to combine this dynamism with social cohesion, an apparent "health miracle," and very low crime rates while keeping its welfare expenditure low; what can other societies learn from it to restimulate their own economies while preventing the fragmentation of their societies?

The messages that the East Asian welfare model allowed British politicians to use were that the family could provide support for its members, companies could take responsibility for their workers, investment in productive members of society should be placed ahead of support for those who were a drain on resources, and welfare is an individual responsibility and not a right to be demanded from the state. Many of these ideas flew in the face of the ideology on which the British welfare state was based and on which attacks had been seen as politically suicidal. But pointing out that these elements existed in East Asia and that East Asian societies were "successful" societies gave politicians an empirical "reality" behind which they could shelter.[21]

However, it was clearly an idealized view of the Japanese system that British politicians used to attack entrenched and accepted views of current systems as a means of getting their electorates to accept the politically unacceptable. These accounts, just as with those of Japanese industrial relations and Japanese education in the 1980s, ignored the downside of the East Asian welfare model; a downside that became only too apparent in some East Asian countries during the economic crisis of the late 1990s, when the lack of a welfare safety net meant destitution for the poorest sections of society.

That Japanese politicians and leaders themselves by the 1990s were increasingly ambivalent about the Japanese-style welfare model was ignored by the politicians in the United Kingdom.[22] These debates, therefore, tell us as much about the countries and the individuals from which they emanate as they do about the "Japan" that they purport to describe;[23] and this situation suggests that, following Edward Said (1985), what we can call "Orientalist" images are still very active in contemporary political debate but that the development, manipulation, and ultimately the effect of the process of Orientalism is far more complex than suggested in Said's seminal work.[24]

An important point to make is that images of societies reflect economic and political power. As we have seen, negative images of Japanese social systems were replaced by positive ones as the Japanese economy grew exponentially from the late 1960s onward.

Second, economically strong countries such as Japan are able to construct their own countervailing or positive Orientalist images, as can be seen in the *Nihonjinron* literature generally or more specifically in the context of the Japanese welfare system in the work of people such as Baba (1980) and Nakagawa (1979). This process is part of the Orientalist mode in that it involves inverting the evaluation given to the perceived characteristics of some monolithic Occidental Other and clothing them in essentialist language.

The successful development of the concept of Japanese-style welfare is an excellent example of this process.

Third, these Orientalist and Occidentalist images – both positive and negative – can have an effect on the Other that is being described, and it is this process that has perhaps become more important in the 1990s and that needs further exploration. In a world that is becoming rapidly smaller in terms of the speed with which images can be exchanged between societies, such images of other societies can play as important a role in helping to legitimate, even construct, the social systems of societies as they do in explaining them. It has not escaped the notice of politicians and policymakers in East Asia that their social welfare systems, not long ago decried as backward, have recently won the endorsement of politicians across the political spectrum in Britain, the society that developed one of the first truly national welfare systems; in some ways this endorsement makes it more difficult to dismantle those systems at a time when many argue such change is demanded by the Japanese economic recession.[25] As we have also seen, the fact that Japan has been so successful in developing the rhetoric of lifetime employment and family care for the elderly is making it difficult to change to a system that would provide a safety net for workers laid off by their companies and for women who want to continue to work. Japanese leaders have in some ways become victims of their own successful rhetoric, compounded by the legitimization given to the existing systems by those outside the country.

Work has begun on exactly how, historically, ideas of Japaneseness have been used to construct Japanese social systems such as Japanese-style management and Japanese-style welfare. A lot of work still remains to be done, however, on how images of these systems outside Japan have been constructed and used. In particular, the process of what Gordon White and I (Goodman *et al.* 1998: 13) have elsewhere called "an instrumental version" of "welfare Orientalism" (the use of images of other societies to make political capital in one's own) needs to be considered carefully by academics as these images also need to be placed in their appropriate historical and sociological contexts.

Notes

1 This chapter arises from a much larger project, for which see *The East Asian Welfare Model: Welfare Orientalism and the State* (Routledge, 1998), edited by Roger Goodman (a social anthropologist), Gordon White (a political scientist), and Huck-ju Kwon (a social policy specialist). Gordon White died suddenly and unexpectedly of a stroke on 1 April 1998 while copyediting the final proofs of that volume, and I would like to acknowledge here how much this chapter owes to his inspiration and encouragement.

2 For the outlines of some of the arguments by politicians, see Blair (1995), MacShane (1995), Patten (1995, 1997), Smith (1996). For summaries of the

188 *Roger Goodman*

different points of view expressed by these and other politicians, see Cohen (1998), Hutton (1995), MacWhirter (1995), Timmins (1996), Whitaker (1996).

3 Garon (1997) shows that in the early 1920s the Campaign to Foster National Strength promoted diligence and thrift and that poverty was perceived to be a moral problem that could be overcome by instilling in the poor a proper work ethic at as little cost to the state as possible.

4 The debate on *Newsnight* (BBC2) on 4 January 1996 between Robin Cook (Labour) and David Willetts (Conservative), two of the most intellectually respected politicians in the United Kingdom, was a neat example of this divergence of views over what lessons can best be learned from the East Asian welfare experience.

5 Japanese investment in the United Kingdom constitutes about 40 percent of Japanese investment in the whole of the European Community and is far larger than in any other single European country.

6 For more on the "health miracle" in Japan, see Steslicke (1996: 79), who points out: "in 1986 the life expectancy at birth for a Japanese male was 75.2 and for a female it was 80.9 years while in England and Wales it was 71.0 and 77.7 years respectively. In 1955, however, the male and female life expectancies at birth were 65.7 years and 73.0 years in England and Wales and 63.6 and 67.8 respectively in Japan."

7 In 1998, there were for the first time fewer children in Japan than when the country's first census was taken in 1920. Children make up only 15.2 percent of the population – the lowest figure recorded in Japan and lower than all leading industrial countries apart from Italy (14.9 percent) (*Yomiuri Shinbun*, 7 May 1998).

8 Many of the very old in Japan who retired before the reforms of the early 1970s receive tiny pensions, although those who retire today receive pensions that are up to international standards. The pension system, however, is once again undergoing massive reform because of the rapidly aging society, with benefits starting later and premiums being increased (see *Yomiuri Shinbun*, 11 May 1998).

9 See Baba (1980) for the most cited account of what constitute the main features of the Japanese-style welfare system.

10 The two institutions share a sense of their past (and respect for their founders) and an obligation to their future; in both the individual is expected to subsume personal interests to those of the household or the company and to show unwavering loyalty and respect to seniors, especially the head; the head in return is expected to act benevolently toward his (occasionally her) juniors and to take responsibility for all their actions; sharp distinctions are made between those inside the household or company and those outside, both in language use and in behavior.

11 For an extreme version of this argument in English, see Nakagawa Yatsuhiro's (1979) oft cited article on "Japan, the welfare super-power" (originally published in the highly respectable *Chûô Kôron* in 1978 as Nihon koso sekai-ichi no fukushi chôdaikoku da).

12 Kirsten Refsing, personal communication, describing a conference she attended in Hokkaido in 1978 or 1979.

13 See Goodman (1992, 1998b: 3–19) for detailed accounts of how this process took place.

14 See Wei-Ming (1996) for an overview of Confucianism in East Asia that shows how in fact it has very different meanings and significance in different countries within the region.

15 For a good overview of some of the common themes of the *Nihonjinron* literature and some of the problems with its methodology and theoretical assumptions, see Befu (1983), Dale (1986), Mouer and Sugimoto (1986).

16 The tradition for central government to send able junior ministers overseas to

learn about other models of administration – and for local as well as central government to reserve a substantial annual budget for overseas "study tours" – is still very much alive in Japan today. To give just one example, even during the current recession and despite the anti-Scandinavian welfare model rhetoric of the 1970s, as many as 20,000 representatives from Japanese prefectures still visit Sweden each year to learn how to deal with a large elderly population (Sasamoto 1998).

17 For a good overview of the core–periphery distinction in the Japanese workforce, see Chalmers (1989).

18 For an excellent account in English of how this process was repeated over the past 100 years, see Gordon (1985).

19 As Littlewood (1996) points out, the problem is exacerbated in the case of Japan by the long-held tendency of foreign observers to see Japanese society as unique – a view that encourages them to ignore the correct historical and sociological context.

20 Such gendered division of labor can, of course, be traced back to the Tokugawa period among samurai families, who constituted the elite 6 percent or so of the Japanese population but only became widely spread throughout society as a result of what Befu (1981: 50) has termed the "samuraisation" process in the early Meiji period (see Hendry 1981: 28–30; Ueno 1996).

21 There are of course interesting parallels here with what happened during the Enlightenment period in Europe, when those who dared to attack the divine "truths" of their leaders did so by drawing on examples from long-distant pasts and faraway places, including Japan (Roberts 1989).

22 Perhaps the best example of this ambivalence can be seen in the work of Yamanouchi Toyohiro, who was a high-ranking official at the Environment Agency before he committed suicide in December 1989 following criticism that, as head of the agency's Planning and Coordination Bureau, he had failed to comply with the court recommendation that the government settle with the victims of the Minamata mercury-poisoning suit (see Koreeda 1992). Writing under the pseudonym Alice Johannson and pretending to be a Scandinavian journalist who had come to Japan on a scholarship to undertake research on Japanese welfare, Yamonouchi (1992) published a series of articles in the early 1980s that were severely critical of the whole welfare system in the *Fukushi Shinbun (Welfare Newspaper)* and which were reissued in a collected version under the title *Fukushi no Kuni no Alice (Alice in Welfare Land)* soon after his death.

23 Elsewhere we have argued that there is very little about the development of Japanese welfare that cannot be explained through the same models as the development of social welfare in other societies. Put simply, social welfare systems in East Asia, as elsewhere, are rooted in the political, social, and economic conditions of the societies in which they develop. Hence, despite images to the contrary, social welfare systems have in fact developed along quite different trajectories in each East Asian society (see Goodman and Peng 1996; Goodman *et al.* 1998).

24 Said (1985) traces historically how the "West" constructed a perception of the "Orient" onto which it projected all its most negative values: lasciviousness, irrationality, corruption. Drawing largely on sources from the Victorian period – when Western societies, living in a world where the evolutionist paradigm predominated, took it for granted that their "culture" represented the highest pinnacle of civilization – Said presents Orientalism as always being a negative part of the colonial process. Even where, according to Said, Westerners have shown genuine interest in Oriental models, this has only been with a view to incorporating them in their own social systems as part of the colonialist enterprise. The critiques of Said, of course, are already legion (see MacKenzie 1995; Sivan

1985; Lewis 1996; Clarke 1997), and some of these are drawn on in this chapter: Orientalism long predated colonialism; noncolonial powers also engaged in it, and noncolonized societies such as Japan were projected upon; it was never a one-way process and needs to be considered alongside a parallel concept of Occidentalism (see Carrier 1995; Japan is the classic example here with its pragmatic pattern of adopting and adapting from outside). For the argument in this chapter, however, perhaps the two most important criticisms of Said's thesis may be that, even during colonial periods, there were those who looked at Oriental cultures with genuine ideals of constructing universalist cultures – and religions – and not simply from negative viewpoints [what Clarke (1997) calls "Oriental Enlightenment"] and that, if the process of Orientalism is actually a function of the relative power – economic, political, and social – of those projecting and those being projected upon, as the balance of power changes, so do the images and, perhaps more important, the evaluation given those images.

25   For an earlier example of this process, see Campbell (1992: 222) who, writing about the welfare policies – in particular the reduced role for the state – that were proposed in Japan by the second *ad hoc* commission set up in the late 1970s to look at administrative reform, comments that "these ideas were partly derived from, *or at least legitimated by,* similar campaigns waged by President Reagan, Prime Minister Thatcher, and other leaders overseas" (emphasis added).

Bibliography

Abegglen, J. (1959) *The Japanese Factory: Aspects of Its Social Organisation*, Bombay, India: Asia Publishing House.

Ames, W.L. (1981) *Police and Community in Japan*, Berkeley: University of California Press.

Appadurai, A. (1990) "Disjuncture and difference in the global cultural economy," *Public Culture* 2 (2): 1–24.

Baba, K. (1980) *Fukushi Shakai no Nihonteki Keitai (The Japanese-Style Welfare Society),* Tokyo: Tôyô Keizai Shinpôsha.

Bayley, D.H. (1976) *Forces of Order: Police Behavior in Japan and the United States*, Berkeley: University of California Press.

Befu, H. (1980) "Not so permanent 'permanent employment' in Japan," *Reviews in Anthropology* 7: 97–105.

—— (1981) *Japan: an Anthropological Introduction*, Tokyo: Tuttle.

—— (1983) "Internationalization of Japan and Nihon Bunkaron," in H. Mannari and H. Befu (eds) *The Challenge of Japan's Internationalization: Organization and Culture*, Tokyo: Kwansei Gakuin University and Kodansha International.

Befu, H. and Cernosia, C. (1990) "Demise of 'permanent employment' in Japan," *Human Resource Management* 29: 231–50.

Berger, P.L. (1988) "An East Asian development model?" in P. L. Berger and H.-H. M. Hsiao (eds) *In Search of an East Asian Development Model*, New Brunswick, NJ: Transaction Books.

Bestor, T.C. (1989) *Tokyo Neighborhood*, Stanford, CA: Stanford University Press.

Blair, T. (1995) "Patten is misled by the smile on the tiger," *Sunday Times* 29 October.

Boling, P. (1998) "Family policy in Japan," *Journal of Social Policy* 27: 173–190.

Campbell, J.C. (1992) *How Policies Change: The Japanese Government and the Changing Society*, Princeton, NJ: Princeton University Press.

Carrier, J.G. (ed.) (1995) *Occidentalism: Images of the West*, Oxford: Clarendon Press.

Chalmers, N. (1989) *Industrial Relations in Japan: The Peripheral Workforce*, London: Nissan Institute/Routledge Japanese Studies Series.

Clark, R. (1979) *The Japanese Company*, New Haven, CT: Yale University Press.

Clarke, J.J. (1997) *Oriental Enlightenment: The Encounter between Asian and Western Thought*, London: Routledge.

Cohen, N. (1998) "Asia crisis fails to cure Blair's Fukuyama fever," *Observer* 18 January.

Crawcour, E.S. (1978) "The Japanese employment system," *Journal of Japanese Studies* 4: 225–45.

Dale, P.N. (1986) *The Myth of Japanese Uniqueness*, London: Croom Helm and the Nissan Institute.

Garon, S. (1997) *Molding Japanese Minds: The State in Everyday Life*, Princeton, NJ: Princeton University Press.

Goodman, R. (1992) "Japan: pupil turned teacher?" in D. Phillips (ed.) *Oxford Studies in Comparative Education*. Vol. 1. *Lessons of Cross-National Comparison in Education*, Oxford: Triangle Books.

—— (1998a) "The delivery of personal social services and the 'Japanese-style welfare state,'" in R. Goodman, G. White, and H.-j. Kwon (eds) *The East Asian Welfare Model: Welfare Orientalism and the State*, London: Routledge.

—— (1998b) "A model for all seasons? East Asian education and the problem of drawing lessons from other societies," in Y. Yafeh, E. Harari, and E. Ben-Ari (eds) *Lessons from East Asia for the Development of the Middle East in the Era of Peace*, Jerusalem: Harry S. Truman Research Institute for the Advancement of Peace.

Goodman, R. and Peng, I. (1996) "The East Asian welfare states: peripatetic learning, adaptive changes, and nation building," in G. Esping-Anderson (ed.) *Welfare States in Transition: National Adaptations in Global Economies*, London: Sage/UNRISD.

Goodman, R., White, G., and Kwon, H.-j. (eds) (1998) *The East Asian Welfare Model: Welfare Orientalism and the State*, London and New York: Routledge.

Gordon, A. (1985) *The Evolution of Labor Relations in Japan*, Harvard East Asian monographs, no. 117, Cambridge: Council on East Asian Studies, Harvard University.

Gould, A. (1993) *Capitalist Welfare Systems: A Comparison of Japan, Britain and Sweden*, London: Longman.

—— (1998) "Review of Mutsuko Takahashi, the emergence of welfare society in Japan," *Journal of Social Policy* 27: 285–6.

Hane, M. (1982) *Peasants, Rebels, and Outcastes: The Underside of Modern Japan*, New York: Pantheon Books.

Hendry, J. (1981) *Marriage in Changing Japan: Community and Society*, London: Croom Helm.

Hiwatari, N. (1993) "Sustaining the welfare state and international competitiveness in Japan: the welfare reforms of the 1980s and the political economy," discussion paper, Institute of Social Science, Tokyo.

Hobsbawm, E. and Ranger, T. (eds) (1983) *The Invention of Tradition*, Cambridge: Cambridge University Press.

Hutton, W. (1995) "Tory fantasy of Far Eastern promise," *Guardian* 28 October.

Illich, I., Caplan, J., and Shaiken, H. (1977) *Disabling Professions*, London: Marion Boyars.

Katayama, O. (1998) "A taste of Europe: British, French and German influence in Japan," *Look Japan* 44 (507): 4–11.

Kawanishi, H. (1992) *Enterprise Unionism in Japan* (R. E. Mouer, trans.), London: Kegan Paul International.

Kinzley, W. D. (1991) *Industrial Harmony in Modern Japan: The Invention of a Tradition,* London: Routledge.

Koreeda, H. (1992) *Shikashi: Aru Fukushi Kôkyû Kanryô Shinu e no Kiseki (And Yet: The Path that Led to the Death of a Certain High-ranking Welfare Bureaucrat),* Tokyo: Akebi Shobô.

Lewis, R. (1996) *Gendering Orientalism: Race, Femininity and Representation,* London: Routledge.

Littlewood, I. (1996) *The Idea of Japan: Western Images, Western Myths,* London: Secker and Warburg.

Lynn, R. (1988) *Educational Achievement in Japan: Lessons for the West,* London: Macmillan/ Social Affairs Unit.

MacKenzie, J.M. (1995) *Orientalism: History, Theory and the Arts,* Manchester: Manchester University Press.

MacShane, D. (1995) "Why Tony Blair is looking East," *Times* (London) 19 December.

MacWhirter, I. (1995) "Tory lions deluded by the Asian tigers," *Observer Review* 29 October.

Morishima, M. (1982) *Why Has Japan "Succeeded"? Western Technology and Japanese Ethos,* Cambridge: Cambridge University Press.

Mouer, R. and Sugimoto, Y. (1986) *Images of Japanese Society: A Study in the Structure of Social Reality,* London: Kegan Paul International.

Murakami, Y. (1984) "*Ie* society as a pattern of civilization," *Journal of Japanese Studies* 10: 281–363.

Nakagawa, Y. (1979) "Japan, the welfare super-power?" *Journal of Japanese Studies* 5: 5–51.

Nakane, C. (1973) *Japanese Society,* Harmondsworth, U.K.: Penguin.

Ouchi, W. (1981) *Theory Z: How American Business Can Meet the Japanese Challenge,* Reading, MA: Addison-Wesley.

Pascale, R.T. and Athos, A.G. (1981) *The Art of Japanese Management,* Harmondsworth, U.K.: Penguin.

Patten, C. (1995) "Britain, Asia and Europe: a Conservative view," Speech delivered at the Conservative Political Centre, London.

—— (1997) "Patten's Asia: beyond the myths," *Economist* 4 January: 19–21.

Roberts, J.A.G. (1989) "Not the least deserving: the Philosophes and the religions of Japan," *Monumenta Nipponica* 44: 151–69.

Said, E. (1985) *Orientalism,* Harmondsworth, U.K.: Penguin.

Sasamoto, H. (1998) "Swedish social model shines on despite pressure," *Daily Yomiuri* 15 May.

Shinkawa, T. and Pempel, T.J. (1996) "Occupational welfare and the Japanese experience," in M. Shalev (ed.) *The Privatization of Social Policy? Occupational Welfare and the Welfare State in America, Scandinavia and Japan,* Basingstoke, U.K.: Macmillan.

Sivan, E. (1985) "Edward Said and his Arab reviewers," in E. Sivan *Interpretations of Islam: Past and Present,* Princeton, NJ: Darwin Press.

Smith, C. (1996) "Rethinking welfare: tiger feats," *New Statesman and Society* 26 January.

Steslicke, W.E. (1996) "Health care protection and the Japanese way of life," *Journal of Policy Studies* 1: 77–94.

Tabata, H. (1990) "The Japanese welfare state: its structure and transformation," *Annals of the Institute of Social Science* (University of Tokyo) 32: 1–29.

Takahashi, M. (1997) *The Emergence of Welfare Society in Japan*, Aldershot, U.K.: Avebury.

Takegawa, S. (1988) "'Fukushi kokka no kiki' sono ato" (After "The crisis of the welfare state"), in Shakai Hoshô Kenkyûjo (Social Insurance Research Center) (ed.) *Shakai Seisaku no Shakaigaku (The Sociology of Social Policy)*, Tokyo: Tokyo University Press.

Timmins, N. (1996) "The challenge of the Asian tigers: why Britain is looking East for ideas. Both Labour and Tories believe we could learn from Asian welfare," *The Independent* 5 January.

Ueno, C. (1996) "Modern patriarchy and the formation of the Japanese nation state," in D. Denoon, M. Hudson, G. McCormack, and T. Morris-Suzuki (eds) *Multicultural Japan: Palaeolithic to Postmodern*, Cambridge: Cambridge University Press.

Vogel, E.F. (1980) *Japan as Number One: Lessons for America*, Tokyo: Tuttle.

Watanuki, J. (1986) "Is there a 'Japanese-type welfare society'?" *International Sociology* 1: 259–69.

Wei-Ming, T. (1996) "Introduction," in T. Wei-Ming (ed.) *Confucian Traditions in East Asian Modernity: Moral Education and Economic Culture in Japan and the Four Mini-Dragons*, Cambridge, MA: Harvard University Press.

Whitaker, R. (1996) "Sceptics believe the booming economies of the Pacific Rim may turn out to be paper tigers after all," *The Independent on Sunday* 14 April.

White, M. (1987) *The Japanese Educational Challenge: A Commitment to Children*, New York: Free Press.

Yamanouchi, T. (1992) *Fukushi no Kuni no Alice (Alice in Welfare Land)*, Tokyo: Yaegaku Shobô.

Yoneyama, T. (1997) "'Nihon Fukushi Shakai' Hitori Aruku" (The "Japanese Social Welfare Model" stands on its own), *Asahi Shinbun* 5 December.

12 Consuming the modern

Globalization, things Japanese, and the politics of cultural identity in Korea

Seung-Mi Han[1]

On 31 January 1994, the former Korean ambassador to Japan and incumbent minister of foreign affairs in Korea mentioned, in an interview with journalists in Seoul, that "it was time for Korea to examine the possibility of 'opening up' (*kaebang*) to Japanese popular culture." His comment instantly provoked nationwide pros and cons on the issue, not only because it touched on Korea's sensitive relationship with Japan arising from its colonial past but also because it was uttered not by a Japanese but by a renowned Korean diplomat. The issue became all the more sensational because, at the following sessions of the National Assembly in February the same year, assemblymen railed against the government for "secretly" promoting the official importation of Japanese popular culture without "proper" measures. One assemblyman even warned the Minister of Culture and Sports against "becoming the second Lee Wan Yong."[2] To make matters more complicated, President Kim Young Sam commented, at an interview broadcast by NHK (the Japanese national station) in March 1994, that this question would probably find a "solution" during his term of office, insinuating a possible imminent deregulation before the beginning of 1998.

What is the nature of Korean government control with regard to Japanese culture and commodities, and how is it perceived by various segments of the Korean population? What are the criteria that make a thing "Japanese" enough to be subject to government regulation in Korea, and what are the cultural meanings of consuming things Japanese within this particular ideological field?

In this chapter, I note the fuzzy boundaries of what counts as "Japanese" in contemporary Korea and argue that the Korean state's policing of national borders is part of the continuous negotiation of meanings over the colonial and postcolonial relationship between Japan and Korea, rather than an intention to obstruct the transnational flows of culture and cultural commodities. Globalization poses a particular challenge as well as an opportunity at this juncture because the occasion for both countries to recast the hitherto intense bilateral relationships from a wider perspective is at once dangerous and liberating.

Learning from the enviable enemy: the coexistence of desire and enmity in Korean perceptions of Japan

Ever since the independence of Korea from Japanese colonial rule, South Korea has been undergoing long-term, tumultuous processes of decolonization. And to the degree that Japan's colonial policy was assimilationistic rather than separatistic, decolonization meant not only the recovery of political sovereignty but also the recuperation of cultural difference hitherto denied. "Lost" names were returned along with the "lost" language, and the government regulation of Japanese culture began in celebration of independence. Japanese language education was banned,[3] and restrictions were placed on the public performance or broadcasting of Japanese popular songs and movies. But this denial and eradication of colonial heritage did not mean an absolute blockade on overall Japanese influence.

In fact, Korean perceptions of Japan have been multilayered. Unlike the case of China, whose past atrocities and current territorial disputes Koreans somehow choose not to remember,[4] Japan has historically been an object of contempt and hatred largely because of the cultural superiority arising to a great extent from Sinocentric Confucian worldviews. Travelogues and diaries written by Korean officials during the Chosun period are filled with phrases looking down on the Japanese for their "not being Confucian enough" or "not being properly mannered" (Koh 1996), and war crimes and abominations committed by Japanese are recounted and remembered vividly.[5]

It was not until the late nineteenth century that a monumental change in Korean perceptions of Japan occurred among the neotraditional reform-oriented intellectuals, who regarded Japan as a model for modernization because for them Japan seemed to have successfully maintained its cultural identity in the face of foreign challenges (Chung 1995). The hitherto one-way cultural tide that used to flow from China through Korea to Japan began to turn, and as the broadly defined West emerged as a significant other so did Japan as a "transmitter of Western civilization" (Koh 1996). The bifurcated perceptions of Japan – i.e. Japan as an object of hatred or contempt and Japan as a model to emulate – were, from then on, juxtaposed and intensified throughout the bitter experiences of the colonial period, so that to many Korean resistants the prevailing image of Japan was that of a morally discredited "betrayer" rather than an unsophisticated "barbarian," a neighbor that did not keep its word on "the Greater East Asian Co-prosperity Sphere" in the literal sense of the term. The fact that many members of the Korean elite went to Japan for higher education during colonial times and therefore had acquired familiarity with as well as access to mainstream Japanese society reinforced the tendency to learn the outcomes of Western modernity as it was tamed and accommodated by Japan, shorthand and in a convenient way.[6]

One interesting consequence of this bifurcated attitude toward Japan was that the selective adoption of the "Japanese model" and the pervasive use of Japanese machinery, plant equipment, parts, and commodities in postcolonial

Korea took place not with an acute sense of contradiction but with a very practical motivation for modernization, development, and enhancement of the convenience of life. That is to say, because those two seemingly conflicting perceptions of Japan were predicated on the same assumption that a distinct Korean cultural identity exists separate from the Japanese one, the conscious efforts to learn from the Japanese model of "state-guided" economic development and "community-oriented" business practices in the late 1960s, 1970s, and 1980s symbolized not so much a mass conversion into Japanophiles as a legitimate effort to achieve "the modern" that had originated not in Japan but in the West. Likewise, the reintroduction of Japanese language education at high schools in 1973 and the mushrooming of the Japanese Language Education Center since the 1980s came about more out of practical consideration than out of any remarkable growth in "pro-Japanese" sentiments *per se* in post-1945 Korea.

More subtle is the popular consumption of Japanese industrial commodities on a private level, as, unlike the case where the state actively promotes the "Japanese model" in various spheres of public life, such popular consumption occurs in spite of the explicit state policy (1980) to the contrary. The so-called imports source diversification policy (*sooipseon tabyunwha jeongchaek*) regulates the amount and kinds of imports from a specific country to keep the adverse balance of trade under control.[7] This policy's main target is Japan, yet it is not difficult to find various kinds of Japanese consumer goods in Korea. Tourists and peddlers who travel abroad often bring back portable Japanese goods, and people who have lived overseas and consequently are allowed to carry a limited amount of foreign goods for personal consumption bring in Japanese commodities of various sorts, used or unused. Indeed, as the popular distinction between *ilje* (modern Japanese goods) with positive, fashionable connotations and *waesaek* ("Japanese color," or aspects that are "distinctively Japanese" in material, spiritual, or customary ways) with negative, disagreeable nuances indicates, the element of the modern dilutes the possible "poisonous" side of the Japanese industrial commodities and resituates them as "safe" or "harmless" things within the moral geography of Koreans. As a result, Japanese goods such as television sets, radios, cameras, camcorders, compact disc players, watches, cosmetics, kitchen utilities, and Walkmans, to name a few, are received and consumed as part of the broader efforts to relish the modern rather than resisted as "paradigmatically Japanese," in spite of the fact that "electronic Japan" does indeed capture the characteristic images of contemporary Japan more than anything else.

In addition, with globalization of production, what counts as Japanese is getting blurred, as Japaneseness is increasingly becoming a deterritorialized notion (Reich 1995). Because state regulations on industrial commodities define each commodity's national identity according to the place where it is finally produced, the Korean government's commitment to the country-of-origin principle has many loopholes, making the imports source diversification policy almost ineffectual and meaningless. Many "Japanese brand" goods that are not made in Japan – such as Toyotas and Hondas made in the U.S. – are imported to Korea without arousing strong feelings of rejection, guilt, or treason, although Toyotas and Hondas made in Japan have never been allowed to cross the national borders of Korea lawfully.

One conservative Korean who was a youth during the colonial period and was explicit about his "anti-Japanese" stance explained the delicate balance between nationalism and practicality, whereas a fortyish government official at the Ministry of Culture and Sports emphasized how "colorless" industrial and trade policies are compared with the cultural ones:[8]

> People use Japanese products because they are high quality, neatly shaped, and, other things being equal, cheaper than commodities produced in other foreign countries.
>
> (Interview, June 1997)

> Cultural policy is different from trade policy, because the latter is not concerned with the issue of "color" (*saekgal*). "Color" in this case means something that provokes abhorrence or repulsion (*keobugam*) to the Koreans. If anyone wants to annihilate the Korean government's administrative guidance on Japanese popular culture, that person would have to do it without arousing social turmoil (*choyonghi haneungussi choayo*).
>
> (Interview, May 1997)

Globalization and the regulation of Japanese popular culture in Korea

If the mediation of Western modernity felicitously detoxified the "dangerous" consumption of Japanese commodities, the rendering of Japan as a "mere" conduit to modernity was not quite enough to assure Koreans a way to negotiate their identity as modern, Asian, and yet not Japanese. More of the positive measures to guard and police the boundaries of national culture were instituted at the state level to ensure the cultural autonomy of the nation.

Decolonization in the pursuit of an authentic Korean self has always been the official policy of successive Korean governments, although what decolonization exactly meant differed for each regime. Sometimes it meant ruthless galloping into economic development in an effort to catch up and "compete" with Japan; at other times, it meant the undoing of middle and high school uniforms and hairdos that still followed styles of the colonial days (1978). After the death in 1979 of President Park Chung Hee, who heartily followed the Restorationist model of 1930s Japan, and with the end of the Cold War, which had contained many inflammable controversies between Korea and Japan for security's sake, in the 1980s and 1990s issues such as history textbooks, Comfort Women (*ianfu* in Japanese, *cheongshin-dae* in Korean), and Tok Island (*Takeshima*) were politicized one after another in a more forthright manner; at the same time, the need to reformulate a closer

Korea–Japan partnership befitting the wider, global world was officially professed and continuously reconfirmed (1991, 1992).

As the first nonmilitary regime after 30 years of military rule and as the administration that would see the fiftieth anniversary of Korea's independence, the Kim Young Sam government (1993–8), too, paid special attention to making a clean sweep of the colonial legacies in the spiritual realm in the name of the "rectification of history" (*yoksa parosseugi*). The National Museum building, which had housed the colonial government-general of Korea, was torn down, five patriotic souls who had served at the Shanghai Provisional Government of Korea in resistance were brought back from China, and there arose a nationwide movement to get rid of the steel posts at various corners of mountains all over the country, which had allegedly been set up by the colonial government to cut the "life veins" of the Korean peninsula believed to exist according to the folk cosmology (*pungsu chiri*). However, as much as these state policies were aimed at reclaiming past glories and bringing into relief cultural contours of the nation under the commanding leadership of the current regime, they also put the government at bay because any official efforts to compromise this oppositional politics in line with the general trends to globalization seemed to contradict and soil the decolonizing efforts.

Indeed, as globalization emerged both as an international trend and as a governing ideology (*segaewha*) of the Korean government in the early 1990s, state regulation of Japanese popular culture[9] became a point of contention in Korea as, at that time, the forces of collective memory and the flows of global cultural economy clashed head on.[10] For example, the 1994 Japan Cultural Festivals in Korea[11] held at such "strategic places" as the Royal Palace and the National Theater under the auspices of the Ministry of Culture and Sports were met with demonstrations by Comfort Women and the Bereaved Families of the Pacific War, whereas many youngsters without direct war experiences, as well as people at television stations and in the art world, advocated the lifting of the ban, arguing for "the development of Korean popular culture through healthy market competition."[12] In the end, the government (Ministry of Culture and Sports) resorted to repeated public debates (*kongcheongwhoe*) and public opinion polls, which ultimately brought about the slowdown of the government timetable for deregulation for reasons of "national sentiments" (*kukmin cheongseo*) because it was made clear that more than half (average 60 percent; Ministry of Culture and Sports 1995) of adult Koreans were against imminent deregulation of Japanese popular culture. In one citizen's words, "I think it is too early to deregulate Japanese popular culture when in fact there already exist ways for enjoying all kinds of Japanese popular culture without any difficulty in Korea. Only 50 years have passed since our independence" (*Naunuri* Discussion Group, 31 March 1996).

If the Korean state's attempt is under siege domestically for moralistic reasons, its prolonged project of boundary maintenance is also getting problematic technically as the process of globalization tends to undermine the alleged integrity and unity of nationality, Japanese or otherwise (Featherstone 1995). The nationality of actors, singers, composers, and other staff involved, the nationality of languages used, the nationality of capital mobilized, and the place of production as well as the nationality of the production company all played into different combinations in a worldwide cultural and economic process of hybridization, circumventing the state's attempt to anchor the national identity of a commodity as a fixed entity. Which one can be regarded as "more Japanese," and therefore subject to control: a public performance by a Korean–Japanese soprano who sings a Japanese popular song in Korean (allowed) or a jazz record of a Japanese composer whose songs are sung by a Taiwanese singer in English (banned)? Which one is "less repulsive": a movie featuring a Japanese actor with American citizenship acting out an essentialistic ideal of a feudal samurai (*Shogun Maeda*; allowed) or a movie on Comfort Women directed by a Korean producer who nevertheless relies on Japanese actors, actresses, capital, and a production company in Japan (*Ulmittesun Bongsunwha ya*; banned)?

Similar questions that destabilize the tacit isomorphism of culture, place, and people (Ferguson and Gupta 1988) and challenge the assumptions of organically integrated, discrete cultures (Featherstone 1995; Hannerz 1996) abounded in Korea. Indeed, Korean state censorship on so-called Japanese color (*ilbon saek*, or in a more widely used pejorative term, *waesaek*) ironically obscured the very distinction between the two countries that it purported to maintain because the heightened attempt to explore and pinpoint those concrete elements that constituted absolutely distinguishable "Japanese color" only sharpened the realization that the search for immutable icons of national identity may never be successful. In addition, the arbitrary domestication of Japanese cultural commodities that accompanied state censorship – for example, the cutting off of scenes with kimonos, *getas*, and school uniforms or the Koreanization of personal names, school names, and place names in Japanese television cartoons – only helped to pave the way for the unintended further homogenization between the two countries instead of repatriating any sense of cultural difference between them. One Korean television station staff member described the contradictory forces at work in the business of the contemporary Korean state as well as in his own job as an arbiter of globalization and localization.

> Although it is the Korean state that officially discourages importing television cartoons with strong Japanese color, it is also the National Broadcasting Station that buys out every Japanese television cartoon available in the market with its incomparably larger budget. The real problem is that there is nothing you can *not* do in Korea. Everything is possible if you really mean it, even against the state regulations. Because the standard for judging "Japanese color" (*waesaek*) is so ambiguous, the best strategy for people like us in media is "buy first and then push it

through." For instance, in the case of the animation *Sailor Moon*, I had not even tried to buy it because I never thought that it could possibly pass state censorship with its main characters wearing such sailor style Japanese school uniforms. But look what happened! Now *Sailor Moon* is on the air by the National Broadcasting Station without causing any problem and is gathering enormous popularity in Korea. In a situation like this, only a fool would try to abide by state regulations faithfully next time.

However, I am not a "bad" person. In fact, I am doing half good thing and half bad thing; that is, although I am the very person who promotes the import of Japanese *manga* to Korean televisions, on the other hand, I also am the very producer who tries best to make successful Korean television and movie cartoons be exported worldwide. It really is a job that needs lots of "fighting"; it requires a lot of energy to persuade top executives at the TV station, secure financial resources, and gather talented people around me who would consistently work on the actual production of good cartoons.

(Interview with a TV station producer, May 1997)

Transnational public, hybrid identity, and the "unfinished project" of modernity in Korea

The idea of the "modern" that many Koreans believe sanitizes and domesticates things Japanese for safe consumption in everyday life has been keeping Koreans from recognizing Japan as a cultural other in its own right; at the same time, it has brought Japan ever closer to Korea as a political and economic entity. The prevalence of Japanese cultural commodities in Korea – which quite often are distributed through illegal channels – tends to reinforce the negative images of Japanese culture as "obscene," "violent," and of a "low quality," providing many Koreans with one of the main causes for objecting to the deregulation of Japanese popular culture by reinforcing their conviction of "Korean cultural superiority." Indeed, unlike the case of industrial commodities, narratives of the consumers of Japanese cultural commodities remain young and subaltern in Korea, lurking at the interstices of satellite broadcasting, the animation lovers' club (*anidon*), and the transnational cyberspaces of Internet chatting.[13] Notably, in those young and subaltern commentaries emanating from clandestine castles of their own, "cultural diversity" – rather than "the principle of reciprocity" or "the principle of universality" (terms for interstate trade disputes involving "unfair" policies) – emerges as an important rhetoric in support of the consumption of Japanese popular culture, consumption of which would guarantee an alternative to the Western, or more specifically American, hegemony in culture industry. Indeed, the acknowledgment of Japanese cultural commodities, however secretive it might be, reinforces the growing sense of multipolarity and the emergence of competing centers in an increasingly integrated world. In that sense, what Featherstone (1995: 6–9) termed "global moderni*ties*" with reference to Japan and the cases of differential reactions to modernity has a specific resonance in Korea:

> One cannot deter the inflow of Japanese animations any more. Japanese animations are more warm-hearted, have more interesting stories and meaningful social messages than the Disney animation films which simply reinforce boring moral fables in a pedagogical way. For animation lovers like us, Japanese animations are essential to ensure alternatives and cultural diversity.
>
> (*Chollian* Discussion Group, 26 October 1996)

How, then, can we make sense of those college students in Korea who create Japanese pop culture Web sites of their own, remember genealogies of Japanese movie stars and directors, and yet write passionate nationalistic papers on Tok Islands (*Takeshima*) for their final examinations? What Appadurai (1990: 296–301) has termed the "disjuncture" in the global cultural economy – especially the disjuncture between mediascape, technoscape, and finanscape on the one hand and ideascape on the other – aptly describes the situation in Korea because there is a conscious attempt to set apart the ideological realm of official nationalistic identity from the technological, financial realm of modern production. The fact that Korea as a divided country has been keeping a heightened self-awareness of the "unfinished modern project" of nation-building (McCormack 1993; *Kyekan Sasang* 1994, 1995) further legitimatizes this tendency, for the attempt to reinterpret the relationship with Japan through playful postmodern construction of hybrid identity via the creolizing and creolized consumption of "global culture" only gets curbed and marked as of secondary importance in the grandiose nationalistic vision of citizen production.[14]

Indeed, things "Japanese" have been given both positive and negative evaluations within Korean society depending on how they have been classified; those perceived as belonging to the "modern" realm have been welcomed and consumed without resistance, whereas those indexed as "essentially Japanese" have been rejected, erased, and loathed.[15] The issue of "popular culture" (or, more appropriately, cultural commodities with a mass market), situated as it is on the borderline of the "modern" and the "Japanese," poses a particular challenge for the Korean government as both the Korean and the Japanese states try to avoid a head-on confrontation in this period of "globalization," which requires multilateral partnership rather than an intensely complicated bilateral entanglement.

Postscript: the Asian financial crisis, regime change, and the logical similarity in the debates on Comfort Women and Japanese popular culture

The question of the Korean government's official stance toward Japanese popular culture is sensitively linked to political as well as economic issues between Korea and Japan, past and present. Three months after the Budapest Conference in August 1997, for which this chapter was originally written, the Korean economy (along with the economies of other Asian countries such as Thailand and Indonesia) ran into a financial crisis. Korea has since been undergoing painful structural reform as designed and guided by the International Monetary Fund, but, ironically, the crisis forced many Koreans to realize the necessity of strengthening ties to countries other than the United States, especially within the Asian region. Indeed, whereas many people blamed Japan for exporting the bubble economy to Korea, Japan's value as an alternative source of foreign capital and technology loomed larger than ever before.

In November 1997, along with issues of structural reform and economic transformation, the question of the official government posture toward Japanese popular culture was one of the major topics on the television debate among the presidential candidates because it stood out symbolically as one of the most important reference points for examining whether or not Korea and the Korean people are "ready to be globalized" or are "globalized enough" to overcome the current difficulties besieging Korea. Again, there was no disagreement among the presidential candidates regarding the necessity of "opening up" (*kaebang*) the market for Japanese pop culture, and every candidate emphasized, as before the crisis, that it was only a matter of when to deregulate and lift the ban. However, after the election, which brought about the first regime shift between the party in power and the opposition party in modern Korean history, the economic stringency with which the Korean government was confronted softened its official position toward Japan even more; it was promised and reconfirmed by the Korean government that imports of small (under 1,000 cc) "Japanese" cars would be licensed in early 1998,[16] and articles in the major daily newspapers predicted the approaching deregulation of Japanese popular culture at least by the end of 1998 (*Chosun Ilbo*, 8 January 1998).

Unfortunately, the Japanese breach of the Fishery Agreement at this time changed the situation drastically, rekindling the so-called national sentiments debates in Korea, leaving little room for negotiation on the part of the Korean government.[17] The incumbent Minister of Foreign Affairs, Ryu Jong Ha, even mentioned that the Korean government would reexamine the issue of Comfort Women and other delicate colonial issues "more" strictly to the letter, although the subsequent and continuing appeasement policies on both sides led to the new Korean president-elect Kim Dae Jung's official statement in April 1998 that he would actively and decidedly support the deregulation of Japanese popular culture because "Koreans as mature citizens have enough power to digest Japanese culture."

And he did. In his visit to Japan in October 1998, he repeatedly emphasized his determination to keep his promises of lifting the ban on Japanese popular culture, and the mass media in Korea, for the first time since 1945, used the term "Emperor" (*cheon whang*) instead of "Japanese King"(*il wang*) to refer to the living national symbol of Japan. In November 1998, the head of the Ministry of Culture and Tourism in Korea – previously called the Ministry of Culture and Sports – announced that gradual imports of "distinguished" pieces of Japanese popular culture would be allowed before the end of the year.[18]

In retrospect, what is rather surprising is not that the "deregulation" of Japanese popular culture has finally come about – it had to happen anyway – but that it took only the "strong will" of the new president-elect against the background of dire economic necessity to bend and tame the moralistic and nationalistic claims based on the lingering memories of the past.[19] In addition, it is particularly interesting to observe that there is an unexpected, surprisingly marked similarity in the way that the issue of Comfort Women is handled in Japan and the way that the issue of Japanese popular culture is handled in Korea; both questions betray (or cannot sustain) absolute negation because just as it is impossible to ignore the transnational flows of culture and cultural commodities and deny the existence of Japanese popular culture in Korea in the latter case then it is not possible to repudiate the existence of Comfort Women survivors and nullify their narratives in the former case. Both issues are, in fact, not a matter of "proving" a certain intangible fact but a matter of "getting an official recognition of the nation-state," which the governments in question would not "yield" easily in the name of the nation, national history, or "national sentiments."

As Featherstone (1995: 12) argues, postmodernism and postcolonialism pointed to the problem of cultural complexity and the increasing salience of culture in social life through "the greater production, mixing and syncretism of cultures which were formerly held separate and firmly attached to social relationships." However, whereas globalization releases culture from the assumptions of tightly bound nation-state societies and disrupts the isomorphism of culture, place, and people,[20] at the same time globalization, ironically, seems to highlight further the politico-economic value of maintaining the symbolic boundaries of the community as a tool of international negotiation of all sorts. The relationship between Korea and Japan eloquently shows the case in point.[21] Although any discussion linking the two seemingly unrelated issues has never been made in the official arena at this particular historical juncture, it would be interesting to watch what will become of the other structurally similar issue – the Comfort Women – in both countries in the years to come within the dynamics of "partnership" in a globalized world economy. It is not because one is critical of "Japanese" cultural influence in Asia *per se*, but because, even when one acknowledges that technoculture produced within capitalist commodification and accumulation is "always already potentially transnational" (Ching 1996: 191), it cannot be denied that some resistant social forces in Korea – however "residual" they might be – question the argument that the global spread of "Japanese" culture signifies nothing "dangerous" but is simply a concrete manifestation of the emerging multiple centers in postmodern era.

Postscript 2: the perspectives of Koreans in Japan

In January 1999, I had the chance to hear a sermon given by a Korean Christian priest at a Korean Church in Japan. Unlike the muffled controversies in the Korean peninsula, the "opening-up" (*kaebang*) of the Korean market toward Japanese popular culture was hailed by the Korean community in the city, but the main point of the sermon was that Japanese society now must "reversely open up" (*gyaku kaikin*) and accept the Korean culture and people in Japan as one of its legitimate constituents; the examples quoted were Matsuzaka Keiko, Wada Akiko, Izuki Hiroshi, and other famous pop singers who "pass" as Japanese nationals without publicizing their Korean origins officially. The case of a son of the church member who made his first debut as Kurada Shoichi but decided to return to his original name, Lee Chong Ho,[22] was also quoted to emphasize the importance of paying attention to the issues of diversity and identity in Japan.

Notes

1 This research was funded by the 1997 Yonsei University faculty fellowship.
2 Lee Wan Yong was the person who actively promoted the processes whereby Korea first became Japan's protectorate (1905) and finally was annexed to Japan in 1910, and who is therefore remembered in Korean historiography as the betrayer of the country.
3 Contemporary Korean high school textbooks on world history, which is divided into eastern and western parts, include a small chapter on Japan, but Japan is never included in lectures or examinations.
4 The late-seventeenth-century invasion by China (the *keum*) is not as vividly remembered as the late-sixteenth-century invasion by Japan. Korean perceptions of China deserve separate research, but unlike Japan, which established a colonial rule, China has always recognized Korea's autonomy and independence.
5 For example, the invasion by Toyotomi Hideyoshi. Note that Koh's commentary was originally published in 1970 as "Images of foreigners held by the Chosun Dynasty Koreans" in *Baeksan Hakbo*, volume 8.
6 This tendency still persists among many spheres of Korean society, and Japan is regarded as an easy avenue for advanced technology.
7 With the establishment of the World Trade Organization (WTO) in 1995 and with Korea becoming a member of the Organization for Economic Cooperation and Development (OECD) in 1996, the imports source diversification policy was terminated by the end of 1999. The Korean government is currently in the process of deregulation and pronounces a list of newly deregulated items twice a year. As of July 1997, 113 items were still under regulation. (Author's note, October 2000: the deregulation process was completed on schedule.)

8   Interestingly, all the government officials at the Ministry of Culture and Sports that I interviewed were very cautious on the issue of Japanese popular culture and wanted to find out my opinion about it before they answered my question. One told me before he started to say anything about the cultural policies, as if he wanted to ensure that he was not antinationalistic, "Have you been to the front gate of the Embassy of Japan on Wednesday afternoon? There are demonstrations by Comfort Women on every Wednesday." It was clear from the interviews that the government officials knew that the deregulation of Japanese popular culture was necessary and impending, but that nobody wanted to be at the forefront of the movement.

9   The audiovisual sector in general is the scope of administrative guidance. That is to say, the production or distribution of Japanese dramatic movies, video films, comics, CDs, and records as well as the public performance of Japanese popular songs are not allowed, whereas "pure arts" – such as literature, theater, the performance of (Western) classics – and television cartoons for children and youths "without Japanese color" are allowed. It is also very interesting to observe that, although food often symbolizes national identity, Japanese cuisine has never emerged as an object of government scrutiny or popular animosity in Korea and has always been a "safe" item for consumption. A public survey by Keukdong Research Institute in 1994 revealed that Koreans cited food most frequently (56.8 percent) as a way to experience Japanese popular culture (*Segae Ilbo*, 19 March 1994), but never has Japanese cuisine been subject to government control in Korea nor do Koreans seem to think that having a Japanese meal is a step toward losing Korean identity. On the contrary, irrespective of what happens in the international political or economic realms, each country's representative dishes have enjoyed popularity in the other's land for being "tasty" and "healthful" – Japanese sushi, sashimi, and *udong* for their lightness and Korean *kimchi, bulgogi,* and *bibimbap* for their use of healthful garlic.

10   The deregulation of Japanese popular culture has been requested by the Japanese government ever since it was first proposed by the Nakasone government in 1983 at the Working-level Talks for the Formation of Korea–Japan Cultural Exchange. With the controversial comments by the aforementioned Korean diplomat, the Ministry of Culture and Sports has clarified its position of "gradual deregulation" headed by areas of "pure arts" (*susnu yesul*) at international cultural events in February 1994 and March 1995 (Ministry of Culture and Sports 1997).

11   A Japanese musical performance of *Jesus Christ Superstar* and exhibitions of Modern Japanese Design and Traditional Crafts of Modern Japan were included. The events were in return for the 1992 Korea Festival in Tokyo, which was created to further cultural exchanges between the two countries. The Korean government sent "cultural correspondents" (*munwha tongshinsa*), a term used in the Chosun dynasty to describe personnel who had been dispatched to Japan.

12   See, for example, the Gallup survey (Ministry of Culture and Sports 1995) conducted in March 1995 at the request of the Ministry of Culture and Sports, which shows that more than half (60.2 percent) of the adult Korean population objected to the imminent deregulation of Japanese popular culture. A sharp contrast to this official survey is the discussions going on among Korean youngsters; out of 112 responses on the Internet, only seven people (as of July 1997; *Chollian* Discussion Group) opposed deregulation of Japanese popular culture.

13   The messages from Japan sometimes include information on the contents of the newest edition or series of animations, commentaries on the main characters, and upcoming events related to their "shared" interests.

14   Globalization (*segaewha*) did pave the way for openly discussing the place of things Japanese in Korea, but discourses of globalization also animated the possibility

of forming the "national economic community" based upon cultural similarity between North and South Korea with much more eloquence.

15 At the 1997 Budapest Conference, where this chapter was first presented as a paper, a Jewish scholar from the audience commented, "We never use Volkswagen or German audio equipment in Israel, however good they may be!"

16 The partial deregulation of the car market in Korea was an issue discussed even before the deregulation of Japanese popular culture, but it was reconfirmed and reinforced. In fact, many Japanese companies chose to use Korean marketing channels that they already had for the supply of "Japanese" parts for the production of Korean automobiles rather than establishing independent distribution channels (*Maeil Kyungje*, 27 July 1998).

17 The incident was interpreted by some Koreans as a retaliatory measure by the Japanese government against President Kim Young Sam when he became a lame duck toward the end of his rule. His rather careless and crude remark that he would fix the bad habits of the Japanese (*beorut ul kocheo noketta*, referring to the official Japanese stance on the colonial past) in a public reception held for the Chinese leader Zhang Zemin infuriated the Japanese mass media in Korea and in Japan as well, and many Japanese newspapers made an issue out of the incident.

18 "Distinguished" was defined as having received international prizes, and those pieces with international recognition were first allowed to be shown in theaters in Seoul in December 1998. Interestingly, *Hana-Bi* and *Kagemusha*, the films chosen for the first public showings in Korea, did not last more than 3 weeks in theaters in Seoul and did not attract large audiences. One Korean government official is said to have commented that it was in fact a fortunate thing because a wild success of Japanese films in Korea from the beginning would probably have ignited "national sentiments" in Korea, and as a result must have hindered or at least slowed down the process of opening up (*Asahi Shinbun*, 5 January 1999). This view was partly shared by some Japanese in Korea, who nevertheless added their own interpretation of the phenomenon: "It seems that Koreans like *simple* stories and that is why those movies did not reach the audience" (Interview, December 1998).

19 Right after the presidential visit to Japan, there was a small meeting of young scholars and politicians from Japan and Korea in their thirties and forties in Seoul. In contrast to the enthusiastic responses and evaluations of the visit from the Japanese side, the Korean side made quite critical comments on the "easy" deal made by the president.

20 As globalization entails a process of social integration that runs on various levels, the emergent notion of "global society" (Giddens 1994) is far from the conventional sociological notion of society, which is grounded in the nation-state.

21 This can be seen in the cases between France and the United States, or between Canada and the United States, although the postcolonial repercussions are absent in these cases.

22 This was also quoted in *Asahi Shinbun*, 13 January 1999.

Bibliography

Appadurai, A. (1990) "Disjuncture and difference in the global cultural economy," in M. Featherstone (ed.) *Global Culture: Nationalism, Globalization, and Modernity*, Thousand Oaks, CA: Sage.

Asahi Shinbun (1997, 1999) *Asahi Shinbun*, daily.

Baeksan Hakbo (1970) "Images of foreigners held by the Chosun Dynasty Koreans," *Baeksan Hakbo* 8.

Buell, F. (1994) *National Culture and the New Global System*, Baltimore, MD: Johns Hopkins University Press.

Chambers, I. and Curti, L. (eds) (1996) *The Post-Colonial Question: Common Skies, Divided Horizons*, London: Routledge.

Ching, L. (1996) "Imaginings in the Empires of the Sun: Japanese mass culture in Asia," in J. W. Treat (ed.) *Contemporary Japan and Popular Culture*, Honolulu: University of Hawaii Press.

Chollian Discussion Group. Online Internet discussion sites, http://www.chollian.net.

Chosun Ilbo (1995, 1996, 1997) *Chosun Ilbo*, Daily.

Chung, C.-s. (1995) *Neo-Confucian Korean Studies*. Vol. 19. *Changing Korean Perceptions of Japan on the Eve of Modern Transformation: The Case of Yangban Intellectuals*, Honolulu: University of Hawaii Press.

Featherstone, M. (ed.) (1990) *Global Culture: Nationalism, Globalization, and Modernity*, Thousand Oaks, CA: Sage.

—— (1995) *Undoing Culture: Globalization, Postmodernism, and Identity*, Thousand Oaks, CA: Sage.

Featherstone, M., Lash, S., and Robertson, R. (eds) (1995) *Global Modernities*, Newbury Park, CA: Sage.

Ferguson, J. and Gupta, A. (1988) "Beyond 'culture': space, identity, and the politics of difference," *Cultural Anthropology* 7: 6–23.

Friedman, J. (1994) *Cultural Identity and Global Process*, Newbury Park, CA: Sage.

Giddens, A. (1994) "Living in a post-traditional society," in U. Beck, A. Giddens, and S. Lash (eds) *Reflexive Modernization*, Cambridge: Polity.

Hannerz, U. (1996) *Transnational Connections: Culture, People, Places*, London: Routledge.

Hitel Discussion Group. Online Internet discussion sites, http://wwwI.hitel.net.

Kato, S. and Baek, N.-C. (1994) "A conversation: experiences of the modern in Korea and Japan and the search for partnership," *Changjak kwa Bipyung* 22: 4.

Kim, K.W. and Lim, H.J. (eds) (1995) *The Challenges of Globalization and the Korean Responses*, Seoul: Nanam Publications.

Koh, B.I. (1996) *Tradition and Transformation in East Asian History*, Seoul: Munhak Kwa Jiseong Sa.

Kuper, A. (1992) *Conceptualizing Society*, London: Routledge.

Kyekan Sasang (1994) *Kyekan Sasang*, quarterly journal (in Korean), Fall. Seoul: Academy of Social Sciences.

Kyekan Sasang (1995) *Kyekan Sasang*, quarterly journal (in Korean), Spring. Seoul: Academy of Social Sciences.

McCormack, G. (1993) "Kokusaika: impediments in Japan's deep structure," translated in *Changjak kwa Bipyung (Creations and Critics)*, Summer 1994, 22: 2.

Maeil Kyungje (1996, 1997, 1998) *Maeil Kyungje*, daily.

Miller, D. (1995) *Worlds Apart: Modernity Through the Prism of the Local*, London: Routledge.

Ministry of Culture and Sports (1995) *National Survey Results on the Deregulation of Japanese Popular Culture*, Seoul: Gallup Korea.

—— (1997) *Index of Cultural Exchange Policies*. Seoul: Ministry of Culture and Sports.

Moore, H.L. (ed.) (1996) *The Future of Anthropological Knowledge*, London: Routledge.

Naunuri Discussion Group. Online Internet discussion sites, http://www.nownuri.net.

Pred, A. and Watts, M.J. (eds) (1992) *Reworking Modernity: Capitalism and Symbolic Discontent*, New Brunswick, NJ: Rutgers University Press.

Reich, R.B. (1995) *The Work of Nations: Preparing Ourselves for 21st Century Capitalization,* New York: Vintage Books.

Robertson, R. (1992) *Globalization: Social Theory and Global Culture,* London: Sage.

Segae Ilbo (1994) *Segae Ilbo,* daily.

Shirahata, Y. (1996) *Karaoke Anime ga Sekai o Meguru (Karaoke and Anime Run Around the World),* Kyoto: PHP Kenkyusho.

Tomlinson, J. (1991) *Cultural Imperialism,* Baltimore, MD: Johns Hopkins University Press.

13 Japan through French eyes

"The ephemeral" as a cultural production

Sylvie Guichard-Anguis

On 20 September 1998, a flower market and an exhibition of work by amateur artists, which had been organized by the municipality, was held in the marketplace of a French city suburb a few kilometers from Paris. In between the plants and flowers exhibited were several tents. In one of them, rows of bonsai produced by local people were exhibited. In another, origami lessons were being given. The audience was so large that half of them could not see the teacher, who was folding the colored papers rather quickly. The same was true of the tent in which demonstrations of ikebana were taking place. The French master and his assistant, who both belonged to one of the three biggest schools of ikebana, as it was written on their *happi* (workman's livery), used scissors with such dexterity that in a few minutes branches of autumnal plants were displayed in bamboo or ceramic containers.

This small local event included three components of Japanese culture, without any emphasis on this particular link. In other words, they were not associated with some cultural exchange between the two countries. Bonsai, origami, and ikebana were introduced as mere ways of entertaining oneself; the exhibition of home crafts was simply a part of this small event, and French masters (not Japanese masters coming from Japan) were introducing them to this local audience. Such an event shows how deeply some living aspects of Japanese culture have taken root in France.

Despite its small scale, this event shares common features with those organized through international concerns. Japanese cultural events sponsored by the Japanese embassy, other governmental agencies, and many private organizations are increasing all over the world every year. These cultural events happen on so-called Japanese Days, Japanese Weeks, or even a Japanese Year. However long, they bear common features associated with their content. Knowledge of traditional handicrafts, from origami to the making of dolls, and traditional practices, which often include *chanoyu*[1] and flower arrangement, seem to be the main representatives of this conception of Japanese culture in foreign countries.

We may ask why the official culture, i.e. the one sponsored by municipalities in Japan that act as sister cities of cities elsewhere in the world and by the Japanese embassy in foreign countries, is so dedicated to these forms of artistic expression. Why are other means of artistic expression not included in these events but need to be supported by foreign initiatives? This process involves the creation of the ephemeral as a cultural production. Here I will examine the internationalization of flower arrangement (*kadô*), the art of tea (*sadô* or *chadô*), and the way of appreciating incense (*kôdô*) as illustrations of this phenomenon. I will focus mainly on France, laying an emphasis on 1997, declared the Year of Japan in France.

Japanese Days, Japanese Weeks, or Year of Japan in France: from origami to *matsuri*

The field of study being mainly Paris, i.e. a European capital and its surroundings, we have to be aware that some of the events described here are closely linked to this centrality and could not happen elsewhere in France. One of the main sources of information is the regular issues of the cultural calendar from the cultural and information service of the Japanese embassy. There may be some errors, but most of the information available in France regarding Japanese cultural events is included. Before going into detail, let us look at the general picture. In 1997 the 23 April list included fifty-seven events; the 16 May list, seventy-one; the 25 June list, fifty-three; the 1 September list, sixty-three; the 29 September list, eighty-nine; the 4 November list, eighty-seven; and the 16 December list, forty-one. If we compare the figures of 1997 with those of the following year (5 May list, thirty-six events; 8 June list, thirty-eight; and 31 August list, thirty-one), we can see the emphasis is on Autumn 1997. These unusually large numbers are the result of various initiatives stemming from the special circumstances of 1997. The 23 April list includes fifty-seven events that are supposed to take place between March and June 1997. Among them, thirty-two, more than half, occur in Paris and the surroundings cities. The 16 May calendar includes seventy-one events from March to December 1997, with twenty-seven happening outside Paris. So the French capital plays the major part in the definition of this "Japanese culture outside Japan."

These events have little or no connection with academic life: the universities, schools, and so on where Japanese language and civilization are taught. They belong to very different categories: conferences, festivals, exhibitions, concerts, training classes (for instance, calligraphy in an abbey), demonstrations (archery), fashion shows, and so on. Their scale seems to vary according to the length of the general event. They can appear isolated or grouped, apparently with no rules of association. "Japanese Days" or "Japanese Weeks" can take place in private institutions or public ones, be opened to a limited public or to everyone. Schools, museums, public libraries, cultural centers, public buildings such as town halls, private or public gardens, auction halls and so on can be the venue of such events. They can stem from private initiatives as well as more official ones such as those initiated by municipalities having sister-city ties with a Japanese counterpart. In the latter case, some of those affiliations can act in a very dynamic way and produce events regularly. According to my informants, the organization of the events stemming from private initiatives or municipalities without sister-city relations seems to rely first on individual connections in France and sometimes in Japan, and ultimately on the Japanese embassy.

On 12 November 1996, a "Japan Day" took place in a private bilingual school in the center of Paris. The program for the day started with traditional expressions of Japanese culture (demonstration of tea ceremony; training in calligraphy) and ended with contemporaneous and popular ones (karaoke and manga). In Ormesson (in the prefecture of Val de Marne, close to Paris), a French–Japanese cultural week lasted from 24 May to 5 June 1997. The exhibitions included origami, a doll collection, antiques, a teahouse supposed to evoke a *chashitsu* (a room for *chanoyu*), a Japanese garden, crafts, and books for sale. The events included concerts of classical music by Japanese musicians living in France; conferences; storytelling from the *mukashi banashi;*[2] demonstrations of ikebana, origami, and *sumi-e* (black ink drawing) by French masters; martial arts; and traditional dances. For Saintes Savines, a small commune in the Champagne region near Troyes, the program gave the following information: from 18 April to 4 May 1997, three associations (ikebana, bonsai, and martial arts) organized a week around Japanese theater and movies, and exhibitions and demonstrations of bonsai, ikebana, Japanese cooking, a tea ceremony, calligraphy, Raku ware,[3] and origami. The presence of French editors of Japanese literature, conferences by Japanologists, a dojo for martial arts, and a shop selling Japanese products added weight to the week.

Such events, organized by individuals familiar with a specific aspect of Japan but not experts in Japanese culture and based on participants living in France, whether French or Japanese, disclose what is perceived of Japanese culture outside the archipelago. They help to build a "Japanese culture outside Japan." As far as I have analyzed them, their main characteristic does not seem to be a search for authenticity but an attempt to fulfill a curiosity for cultural expression coming from a rather unknown country, which nevertheless seems omnipresent in France through a lot of products (see Chapter 2 of this volume).

Some of this "Japanese culture outside Japan" has taken root in France already, even in the most remote parts of the countryside. Looking for data, I was amazed by the countless initiatives taken by individuals whose lives are involved with Japan in one way or another. This curiosity can turn into a passion, which can lead to visiting the Japanese archipelago. When these people return to France, an association based on some aspects of Japanese culture is created. Martial arts, ikebana, and origami are well represented in these associations and seem to act as bridges between the two countries. In these respects, the French situation seems representative of what is happening elsewhere. As one of my informants said, Japanese culture, by giving birth to countless associations everywhere, plays a unique part in the world nowadays.

Two perceptions are coming into focus: one from local initiatives, the other from official organizations or institutions. By backing individual initiatives, official organizations can give a kind of certificate of authenticity from the inside to the outside, inviting the "inside Japan culture" – in other words, participants from Japan – to participate. For example, from 19 March to 29 September 1997, the film club at the Georges Pompidou cultural center in Paris, part of the Cinémathèque (French museum of cinema), organized a Japanese film festival, which was in two parts (the great classics of the Japanese cinema and the rare and unknown films of the golden age of Japanese cinema from the 1930s to the 1960s) and included all together 200 films. This initiative corresponds to a French perception of culture generally speaking, which considers film culture to be a fundamental part of cultural life. In contrast, Japanese events organized by official Japanese institutions very seldom include films, as they are not identified as a key expression of Japanese culture.

The events based on individual initiatives and on representatives of the "Japanese culture outside Japan" are intended to get local people closer to "real" Japanese traditions. People are not only asked to watch cultural products but to be part of the process as producers themselves of this culture. Learning ikebana or martial arts, for example, compels the amateurs to delve into a particular aspect of Japanese culture as far as they can. When such activities are introduced to the visitors by representatives of "Japanese culture outside Japan" – let us say, for example, by French masters of ikebana – they can lack genuineness, occurring as they are in a completely different environment. But they tend only to be the first steps toward the "inside Japan culture." In other words, practitioners begin their learning in foreign countries and after a few years deepen their experience inside Japan.

Let us explore now some other types of events on a much bigger scale. On 5 June 1996, there was a procession from the Ecole Militaire to the Eiffel Tower: *Haru-hime dôchû*. The pamphlet reads in English, "Symbol of peace – Princess Haru-hime's wedding procession recreated in Paris a colourful event in the tradition of Aichi, the heartland of Japan."[4] Elsewhere it reads, "Aichi is an eager candidate for the hosting of Expo 2005 Japan. Princess Haru-hime's wedding procession is an opportunate occasion for demonstrating Aichi's tradition and culture."

Later on, from 20 to 23 June 1996, a "Festival of the Four Seasons" took place in several parts of Paris. On 20 June, 250 "artists and representatives of the great traditions of Japan" took part in a great parade on the Champs Elysées. The parade included Edo fire brigades called *hikeshi*, Shinto priests from the Tomioka Hachimangu (a Shinto shrine in Tokyo), a palanquin of a Shinto god (*mikoshi*) accompanied by 150 men, folkloric dance troupes, and a concert with drums as the finale. The next evening (21 June, which has been a Festival of Music Day throughout France for the past few years) on the River Seine, another great parade gathered, "a Shinto ritual of purification to make this night unforgettable" (I am quoting the program); there were folkloric dances [*shishi-tô* (lion-mask dance), *shichi fukujin* (seven gods of happiness), *obon odori* (dance of the festival of the dead)], concerts of *shamisen* (three stringed-guitar) and *koto* (long horizontal Japanese harp), and again the Edo fire brigades and Japanese drums. Over the next 2 days, there were exhibitions with demonstrations: *temari* (handball), *tabi* (Japanese socks), *hagoita* (battledore), *kumihimo* (braiding), *sumi-e*, *chanoyu*, ikebana, *kôdô*, and calligraphy. On the last day, a Shinto ritual followed by a fashion show of kimono, and by dances, spectacular calligraphy, and so on was given on the stage of one of the most popular theaters in Paris.

The Year of Japan in France was inaugurated on 11 May 1997, and was followed by the Year of France in Japan in 1998. It was initiated by an official opening party in the newly built Japanese Cultural Center in Paris, the Maison de la Culture du Japon à Paris, by far the largest cultural center of this type in Europe. On the night of 11 May on both sides of the River Seine near the Eiffel Tower a *matsuri* (Japanese festival) composed of elements coming mainly from the north-east of Japan took place. From 6 P.M., there were Japanese drums (*daiko*) from a Shinto shrine, Yushima Tenjin Shiaraume, from Date in Fukushima prefecture and from Haguro, followed by popular dances (*kappore*, associated with the planting out of rice; *shanshan odori*, a dance with an umbrella as a ritual to ask for rain). From Hachinoe came Wakayagi Chikuei's modern-style folkloric dances. A Tanabata festival from Sendai followed a parade with participants dressed in the Heian court style (794–1185), bringing offerings and so on. Akita *kantô* illustrated the Akita version of this same *matsuri*, with its dramatic and famous lanterns. The samurai of the Date clan participated in this parade, followed by Edo fire brigades, mountain priests (*yamabushi*) from Dewa *sanzan jinja* (Shrines of the Three mountains) and again *mikoshi*. At 10 P.M., there was a big fireworks display on the Seine; this was provided by representatives of Aichi, who were still looking for support for their hope of bringing Expo 2005 into their prefecture.[5] Such big events followed one after the other. Jidai *matsuri* (Festival of the Ages) was performed in Paris by its sister city Kyoto in July 1998.[6]

It goes without saying that such amalgams tell a lot about the perception of culture inside Japan. Those medleys composed of "genuine"[7] parts coming from inside Japan but offered out of their time and space can be perceived as a new kind of *matsuri*, belonging to outside of Japan. They are conceived as parades and focus on being spectacular, a trend that is also favored in Japan itself. The periods of antiquity (represented by the Heian court) and the Edo period (represented by the samurai) are the most fascinating of the Japanese past, according to Japanese general opinion. Religions and creeds are invoked because they form the core of Japanese festivals. In Japan different kinds of rituals vary according to the seasons and the *nenjû gyôji* (ritual calendar). These rituals are shown in Paris without any apparent connection to the time of year. The same observation could be made of space inasmuch as rural and urban traditions are shown side by side. So we may say that these *matsuri* tend to be a kind of synthesis of all the *matsuri* happening in modern Japan. A closer look at the ways in which festivals evolve nowadays in Japan could show how much this medley trend is already at work in the archipelago. For instance, a comparison between the *matsuri* in Paris and the Hyaku-man-goku *matsuri* happening in Kanazawa every year in mid-June will give evidence of this phenomenon.[8]

Matsuri of "the outside" share other common features with the ones of "the inside," namely their economic function. As the case of Aichi prefecture shows, a famous local event is used to create an image, to give a cultural identity to a place rather unknown in foreign countries. The perception of local identity acts exactly in the same way inside Japan. The parade of lord Maeda Toshie in Kanazawa belongs to the same trend. Behind those amalgams that make up the parades lies a strong will to assert oneself.

Origami, ikebana, and *matsuri* (not to mention the other components of those events) belong to traditions of know-how, artistic practices, or religions. One of the most striking features of these traditions is that they focus on the creation of the ephemeral as a cultural production. Folded papers, arranged flowers, and parades are not long-lasting things. We may wonder why these aspects of Japanese culture are chosen to be ambassadors of Japan abroad. Why, for instance, does a Japanese city think it necessary to ask a famous *chanoyu* school to perform a tea ceremony demonstration to foreign guests living in its sister city. The answer may lie in the notion of cultural heritage in Japan. But before analyzing that notion, we should take a quick glance at the evolution of the socioeconomic and political context underlying these processes at work.

Sister cities and international relations

A general rule should be stressed before going further into these international relations. A Japanese city, prefecture, or the like organizing a cultural event abroad will look for collaboration with the local cultural associations or groups involved in those traditions associated with the production of the ephemeral. For instance, if a Japanese prefecture organizes an exhibition of ceramic ware in a foreign country, one of the local schools of *chanoyu* will go abroad to perform tea ceremony demonstrations, using some of those ceramics. That the same happens inside Japan gives clear evidence that the perception of these cultural events does not differ much whether inside or outside Japan. In spite of the fact that they belong to traditions that became widespread inside the archipelago, these demonstrations help to foster local identity because they are performed by local representatives of these traditions, making use of local products. For instance, tea practitioners in Kanazawa are somehow bound to use ceramic wares from the local kilns, that is to say Kutani-yaki or Ohi-yaki. These international relations help to spread this aspect of Japanese culture, at least in the case of small events.

As far as international sister-city relations are concerned, the *Japan Local Government Data Book* by the Council of Local Authorities for International

Relations (CLAIR 1996) gives the following figures: as of 1 April 1994, 352 Japanese cities, sixteen special wards, 235 towns, and forty-six villages were affiliated with 924 local government bodies in fifty-two countries. As of the same date 3 years later, sister-city links numbered 1224, including 105 prefectures, 749 cities, and 370 towns or villages in foreign countries (CLAIR 1997). The first sister-city link, between Nagasaki and Saint Paul (Minnesota), dates back to 1955. Seven countries represent 70 percent of these links: the United States, with the largest number (376), China (229), Australia (eighty-two), South Korea (sixty-six), Canada (fifty-seven), and France (thirty-seven).

CLAIR was created in 1988 by the Ministry of Autonomy to foster international relations among local government bodies. It has offices in New York, London, Paris, Singapore, Seoul, and Sydney. One of its main purposes is to gather information on foreign systems of local administration and finance and to introduce Japanese administrative organization to foreign audiences. It helps Japanese local civil servants to be trained in foreign local government bodies, thereby fostering sister-city relations and promoting some aspects of Japanese culture. In addition, such relations help to promote international-ization of local government bodies and economic development.

Among the seven countries that favor these kinds of relations, France has the biggest number of affiliations with Japan in Europe: twenty-eight with cities, three with towns and villages, and six with prefectures in 1994. Germany ranks second (with, respectively, twenty-two, eight, and two) and Italy ranks third (with, respectively, fourteen, four, and one). The first sister-city type of relationship dates back to 1958, when Paris and Kyoto signed a pact of friendship (each city being considered unique and therefore unable to become real sister cities). Some of those affiliations can involve very small local government bodies, as in the case of the villages of Sellières (Jura prefecture in France) and Narusawa (Yamanashi prefecture in Japan) or Cussac-Fort-Médoc (Gironde prefecture in France) and Mitsuse (Saga prefecture in Japan), meaning that Japanese culture is spreading to the remotest parts of France.

A French–Japanese symposium held in Paris in 1997 testified to the differences of approach between the cities of the two countries.[9] In a context of fierce competition, Japanese cities are reassessing their potential, looking for new tools to develop their own special fields. French cities are facing the same reality, but they also favor international cooperation for development in Third World countries. The cities of both countries agree that cultural exchanges should pave the way to economic ones. They should involve individuals and not only technicians from municipalities.

Nancy (in eastern France) chose Kanazawa as a sister city in 1973, and the development of their international relations shows how culture, prestige, and economy are interrelated.[10] A French individual initiative from judo amateurs gave birth to this relationship, which stresses exchanges on several matters – academic, cultural, economic – without forgetting the general population itself. A change in French attitude occurred around the beginning of the 1990s, according to which sister-city relations should foster the local economy by providing foreign investment (*Maires de France* 1997). During the 25 years of relations, the city of Nancy stressed that of all the exchanges that took place the most important event was the 1987 promotional month in Japan, during which local industry was involved.

In 1989, Orléans signed a sister-city agreement with Utsunomiya (Tochigi prefecture). Most of the relations between the two cities seem to rely on academic exchanges between students, on the exchange visits of local government officers and technicians, and on the visits of individual groups looking for information on a specific topic (aging society being one of the most favored during the 1990s). Every year on 7 or 8 May there is a feast commemorating Joan of Arc.[11] Utsunomiya inhabitants have participated several times in the historical parade that precedes this feast. A few major Japanese firms have chosen Orléans prefecture to invest in, and the city emphasizes its international image and its curiosity about Japanese culture. In this context, a Japanese art festival was held on 6–7 July 1996. The program for these 2 days corresponded to the usual lists given above – ikebana, *chanoyu*, Japanese ceramic ware, embroidery, music with *biwa* (a kind of lute) and *koto*, drums, folkloric dances – with a few additions (for example, knitting). The recently created yearly festival of Japanese cinema has become a well-publicized cultural event.

Japan and "the ephemeral" as a cultural production

In their relations with their sister cities, Japanese local government bodies seem to be eager to introduce some aspects of Japanese culture that are bound not to last, i.e. that are ephemeral. The internationalization of ikebana, *chanoyu*, and of the art of incense could be analyzed in this light. The three of them revolve around artistic practices with ritual aspects, transmitted from one generation to the next without interruption for centuries. Introduced from China, they became part of the core of Japanese cultural identity through processes of evolution that took several hundred years and are still going on. During the twentieth century, they came to be favored as Japanese cultural ambassadors. Their constant adaptation through the centuries, and nowadays their introduction to foreign countries, not to mention their origin, tell a lot about the concept of cultural heritage in Japan.

Ikebana is by far the easiest cultural practice to be introduced into foreign countries, as it emphasizes a nearly universal habit, displaying flowers. In contrast, although tea is the most popular drink in the world, *chanoyu* relies on the habit of drinking a special kind of tea, green powdered tea (*matcha*), that is now only found in the Japanese archipelago. The art of incense requires very expensive basic ingredients and, from the start, a great familiarity with some aspects of Japanese culture.

Some schools of ikebana – at least the three biggest ones: Ikenobo, Ohara, and Sogetsu – can boast of having branches in nearly all the developed countries and in some developing nations, particularly in Southeast Asia.

Mapping them would give a general idea of their internationalization. The spread of a worldwide organization such as Ikebana International, founded in 1956, gives clear evidence of the adaptability of this practice. Based on the idea that the everyday culture of the *tokonoma* does not exist any more, it allows those works to be taken into any kind of cultural environment.[12] The only limitation is that they have to retain the spirit of ikebana. Containers as well as materials (branches and flowers) should keep to the originals according to the teachings of the several schools of flower arrangement in Japan. The lines between inspiration and adaptation are not clear-cut, and there lie the problems faced by the internationalization of these artistic practices abroad. The appreciation of these lines varies from one school to the other. Between the ikebana arrangements made only with materials and containers brought at great expense from Japan, the foreign amateurs who grow Japanese materials in their own gardens, and the grand master of a school of ikebana who takes advantage of local elements to produce unique works lies a wide gap. Such different artistic expressions express the dynamism of ikebana culture and the diversity of responses to internationalization. Some very intimate aspects of Japanese culture are brought through the introduction of ikebana abroad: a deep concern for ritual, a sensitivity to the passing of seasons, and a cultural attitude toward beauty (*bi*); these aspects are not obvious to a lot of practitioners, to whom the motto of Ikebana International (Friendship through Flowers) seems familiar.

The introduction of *chanoyu* in foreign countries may be analyzed from the same perspective, as it stresses peace, harmony, tranquility, and love of nature through the drinking of a bowl of tea. This artistic practice brings not only a kind of ritual in making and drinking tea to foreign countries but also a cultural attitude toward cultural properties. It underlines that in Japanese culture some works of art are given a meaning through their use. Instead of being exhibited in museums, these works of art come out of their different layers of protection (wooden boxes, pieces of material, papers, and so on) and come alive through the tea ritual.

To perform tea procedures, a lot of utensils made by craftsmen are essential. They give evidence of the dynamism of the Japanese artistic creation, which focuses on their production and also stresses that another artistic logic is following international trends. For instance, the world of ceramics is given a place in Japanese culture that can hardly be compared to its place in other parts of the world, even those endowed with rich and long traditions, such as Europe. Through potters such as the Raku family, the number of exhibitions in museums, the increasing popularity of big events around sales fairs in towns or cities famous for their ceramics, the classes for making one's own works, the individual's love for these handmade products, the great percentage of papers on ceramics in women's magazines, and so on, this world builds intimate relations with other segments of Japanese life. Tea ceremony rooms (*chashitsu*) were donated and built in several countries, allowing this practice to be performed in an authentic environment.

The art of incense is seldom part of relations between sister cities, in part, perhaps, because of its more subdued presence in Japan itself. For instance, it does not play a significant part in Japanese contemporary *matsuri*, whereas ikebana exhibitions and large tea meetings often are included among the events associated with big festivals. Nevertheless the art of incense is closely associated with Japanese cultural heritage. In 1996 there was an exhibition in Le Grand Palais in Paris of the treasures of the Kokufukuji (Nara prefecture). It was inaugurated by a ceremony of the offering of incense, which was performed by a school that came especially for the event.[13] This exhibition gave a rare opportunity not only to French visitors but also to others to discover treasures that are opened to the public in Japan just a few days a year. Thirteen National Treasures and twenty-one Important Cultural Properties were exhibited. This great privilege granted to the French people was repeated the following year, when in 1997 Kudara Kannon from the Hôryûji in Nara prefecture was exhibited in the Louvre.[14] In front of the statue, rituals were performed, as offerings of incense and of tea were made by grand masters of incense and tea schools. It was the first and last time that this statue was lent to foreign countries before being housed in a special new building constructed in the precinct of the temple the following year. The importance given by the Japanese to rituals attached to cultural properties of religious origin corresponds to the French historical fascination for Japanese Buddhist art.

There are few schools of the art of incense in foreign countries as they rely on Japanese incense being available abroad. In the world of *chanoyu* this problem was solved by the regular shipping of *matcha* to the branches, but in the case of the art of incense, at least in France, it seems to rely on the marketing of the necessary products. Demonstrations of *kôdô* used to occur with demonstrations of ikebana and *chanoyu*. This was the case on 4–5 October 1998, in Paris, when groups of practitioners of *chabana* (flower arrangement for *chanoyu*), *chanoyu*, and the art of incense from Saga prefecture tried to recreate the atmosphere of the fifteenth and sixteenth centuries, when these ways began to take form and were practiced by amateurs.

Ogino (1995) argues that the cultural policy of Japan lies in the relations between the market and the making of a cultural heritage through designations. In other words, the designation of living national treasures helps to boost the local economy by recognizing some of the local producers as exceptionally gifted artists, especially in the world of ceramics. According to him, "the logic of actualization" has been instrumental in keeping apart historical properties. The past as part of the present belongs mainly to remote places, as shown in the conception of the Meiji village (*Meiji mura*) in Gifu prefecture in the Japanese Alps in which are gathered buildings of the Meiji period (1868–1912). In contrast, in France there is a linear conception of time, with a past enclosed in museums. This other logic questions "cultural heritage" as defined by international organizations. It is opposed to the notion of cultural heritage centered on historical monuments (as was the case in

France until a few years ago), embodied in cathedrals and castles that symbolize glorious periods perhaps, but bygone ones. Instead it stresses that cultural heritage can also be nonmaterial, even ephemeral, alive, and evolving. It emphasizes the problem of authenticity of the cultural properties (Larsen 1994).

Among Japanese White Books (which are published by the Government), the one on tourism analyzes the several policies for protection of cultural assets in Japan. It is significant that among those White Books published by the several government agencies not a single one is dedicated to cultural policy *per se*. The association between tourism and protection plays a key role in the making of these policies and stresses their aims. Designations help the revival of local places and products and associate them with leisure activity. More than being cultural references belonging to a remote past and enclosed in museums, they are part of the present through their designation and marketing.

The present frame of protection comes from the merger in 1950 of several laws dating from the end of the nineteenth century and the first half of the twentieth century.[15] The new body of laws centers on the notion of *bunka zai* (cultural property), and categories of cultural properties can be expanded and new ones added. Among them (tangible cultural properties, nontangible cultural properties, folk–cultural properties, memorial cultural properties, protected areas or groups of traditional constructions), several acknowledge nonmaterial cultural properties and the importance of the process of making and producing. A quick glance at the figures gives the following in 1998: works of arts, crafts, and historical documents amount to 1,048 national treasures and 12,028 important cultural properties. In those same two categories, fine arts number 839 and 9,877. As these figures show, national cultural references linked to the present definition of Japan's specific identity are represented by objects rather than by constructions, as is the case in French cultural heritage (Sire 1996). Among the important intangible cultural properties, craft techniques (ceramics, textile making, lacquerwork, metalwork, wood and bamboo work, doll making, stained ivory engraving, and paper making) correspond to thirty-five specific skills, forty-six individuals, and thirteen group recognitions. The makers of some of those objects are even included among those references, showing the existence of cultural properties identified as human beings who practice traditional techniques, known familiarly as *ningen kokuhô* (living national treasures). Last but not least, a great many of those objects are linked to artistic or religious rituals.[16] Folk–cultural properties belong to two categories: nonmaterial (habits linked to food, clothing, dwellings, traditional occupations, religious creeds, festivals, folkloric entertainments) and material (clothing, tools, and dwellings associated with the previous); these characterize everyday life and express the evolution of the ways of life. *Matsuri*, which belong to this last category, are not conceived as artistic expressions but as illustrations of the way of life. Among the 456 designated *matsuri* in 1995, 122 were numbered among the important intangible folk–cultural properties (Agency for Cultural Affairs, 1995).

Designation among Japanese cultural properties helps Japanese cultural heritage to stay alive. The events during Japanese Days or Japanese Weeks in foreign countries give opportunities to introduce another conception of the protection of cultural assets. They give a clear indication that, in the Japanese conception, a great part of the past should belong to the present. The making of objects, the demonstrations of artistic practices, the festivals give evidence of this other logic at work. They belong to long-standing traditions that are still evolving and adapting to present-day conditions. The production of "the ephemeral" is not devoid of marketing concern, but this process is fundamental as it helps these fields of knowledge to stay dynamic. For instance, the demand for utensils needed to perform tea procedures in *chanoyu* helps to keep a lot of handicrafts alive. And not only in Japan. The blown-glass bowl found in some Murano shops in Venice in 1997, which I identified immediately as a summer tea bowl for *chanoyu*, sprovides the best evidence of this ongoing process.

Notes

1 I will more often refer to the tea ceremony by the Japanese word *chanoyu* (hot water for tea) as the concept of tea ceremony does not exist in the Japanese language.

2 Japanese folklorists assign the term *mukashi banashi* (tales of yore) to denote folktales as against *densetsu* (legends).

3 Raku ware was first created by Chôjirô (?–1589), who produced only tea bowls for *chanoyu*; it is now made by Kichizaemon XV (the fifteenth generation of Kichizaemon). Raku ware is a hand-formed, soft, low-fired type of pottery. The potter's family name, Raku, became used for the name of the ware. Nowadays a lot of potters in Japan and abroad not belonging to the Raku family enjoy making this type of ware. See the catalogue La Maison de la Culture du Japon à Paris (1997).

4 Haru-hime came from the Asano family in Wakayama, which sided with the Toyotomi clan in the battle of Sekigahara in 1600. In 1618 she married Yoshinau, a son of Tokugawa Ieyasu, ending long feudal bloodshed. The procession, said to be seven-tenths of a mile long, transported a fabulous dowry.

5 On 12 June 1997, in Monaco, the prefecture of Aichi was selected as the site for the 2005 World Expo.

6 Held annually on October 22, *Jidai matsuri* is the festival of the Heian shrine in Kyoto. The shrine was built to commemorate the 1,100th anniversary of the founding of the ancient capital Heiankyô, now Kyoto. The parade with people dressed in costumes of different periods makes this festival one of the most popular tourist attractions of the ancient capital.

7 I use the term *genuine* to characterize the way that events happen inside Japan nowadays. It is obvious that, even if they represent a tradition, they include a long evolution since their origins. Their authenticity should be perceived through this phenomenon.

8 Hyaku-man-goku *matsuri*, the festival of one million *koku* (180 liters) refers to the revenue from rice in the Kaga fief, which was greatest under the Tokugawa. On 14 June 1583, coming from Nanao on the Noto peninsula, the daimyo Maeda

Toshie entered Oyama castle. The Maeda resided in Kanazawa (later the name of the city) until the Meiji period (1868–1912) and had a great influence on most of its cultural identity. The parade recreated this historical date.

This statement does not prevent questions from arising. The absence of a shrine inside Paris and the real meanings of the Shinto rituals taking place in such an environment need a thorough analysis.

9 A "Symposium for the Promotion of French–Japanese Decentralized Cooperation" was held in the Sénat (Senate) in Paris on 6–7 November 1997. This was the only event planned by CLAIR during the Year of Japan in France.

10 This research was carried out with the help of two town councilors in charge of international relations in Nancy and Orléans, to whom I am greatly indebted.

11 In May 1429 Joan of Arc delivered Orléans, which had been besieged by troops from England and Burgundy allied in the war against France.

12 For centuries, the *tokonoma* (decorative alcove) was the only place where ikebana could stand. Flower arrangements had to be adapted to this space. Until the twentieth century, all the favored historic styles were adapted to this space.

13 The Kokufukuji, founded in 669 in Yamashina near the present Kyoto, was moved to the new imperial capital of Heijô-kyô (present-day Nara). Constructed during 714–17, it was one of the two head temples of the Hossô sect of Buddhism. Destroyed several times, it houses a very important collection of Buddhist sculptures.

14 Founded in 609 in the present-day Nara prefecture, the Hôryûji owns the oldest temple compound extant in Japan and some of the oldest wooden structures in the world. It houses numerous works of Buddhist art, among which Kudara Kannon, a bodhisattva carved from camphor wood, is one of the most famous. Two meters tall, it dates back to the seventh century; its name links it to Kudara (Paechke), a Korean kingdom of that period. The Hôryûji was the first Japanese site to be inscribed in the UNESCO's World Heritage List.

15 The Imperial Cabinet proclaimed the protection of antiquities in 1871.

16 In France, works of sacred art make up the core of those objects (Sire 1996).

Bibliography

Agency for Cultural Affairs (1995) *General Survey of Japan Policy for the Protection of Cultural Assets 1995*, Tokyo: Agency for Cultural Affairs.

CLAIR (1996) *Japan Local Government Data Book 1995*, Tokyo: CLAIR.

—— (1997) *La Lettre du CLAIR (The Letter of CLAIR)*, 25.

La Maison de la Culture du Japon à Paris (ed.) (1997) *Raku: A Dynasty of Japanese Ceramists*, Turin: Umberto Allemandi.

Larsen, K.E. (ed.) (1994) *Architectural Preservation in Japan*, Trondheim: ICOMOS International Committee, Tapir Publishers.

Maires de France (1997) "Quand Nancy mise sur ses jumelles (When Nancy counts on its sister cities)," *Maires de France* 30: 62–3.

Ogino, M. (1995) "La logique d'actualisation: le patrimoine et le Japon" (The logic of actualization: the cultural heritage and Japan), *Ethnologie Française* 1: 57–64.

Sire, M.-A. (1996) *La France du Patrimoine (The France of Cultural Heritage)*, Paris: Gallimard.

14 The *Yamatodamashi* of the Takasago volunteers of Taiwan

A reading of the postcolonial situation

Chih-huei Huang

Through their extensive colonization, which began in the late nineteenth century, the Japanese acquired considerable experience in interacting with the peoples of Asia and Oceania. What did these encounters mean for the Japanese colonials? And what has this contact meant for those who lived under Japanese colonial rule?

With the exception of Hokkaido and Okinawa, Taiwan was the first colonial territory acquired by Japan as a result of war with another nation. Among the territories colonized by Japan, Taiwan's colonial period (1895–1945) lasted the longest. Unlike most postcolonial situations, however, the Taiwanese people have retained a relatively amiable attitude toward Japan after the end of colonial rule. This attitude is frequently mentioned in travel accounts and guidebooks written by the Japanese who visited Taiwan after the war (for example, Shiba 1994; Daiyamondo Sha 1997). In the few scholarly writings dealing with Japanese colonial rule, this attitude has often been held in contrast with postcolonial Korean sentiments toward the Japanese (Tsurumi 1984; Peattie 1996). These comparisons tend to search for an explanation of this difference in the dissimilar ruling methods used in the colonies. This chapter will address the issue from a different direction: through the use of testimonies and confessions made in the postcolonial era, I intend to delineate the complicated struggle for humanity under colonialism and the cultural multiplicity in its aftermath.

The ethnic composition of postwar Taiwan is rather complicated, with Han and Austronesians constituting the two major ethnic categories.[1] This chapter will limit its scope to the non-Han peoples, namely the Austronesians, who have been praised by some Japanese as "the most friendly of peoples toward Japan in the whole world." (Ishibashi 1992).[2] It is especially noteworthy that Austronesian veterans of World War II whom I have interviewed often proudly emphasized their *Yamatodamashi* (literally, "soul of the Yamato people") or *Nipponseishin* ("Japanese spirit"). Such terms are still currently used in their discourses, even as they have grown obsolete in postwar Japanese society.

The subject of this chapter is a group of these Taiwan Austronesians known as the "Takasago-Giyutai," who volunteered for service in the Japanese military during World War II. In the 1990s, five books giving accounts of the

Takasago-Giyutai were published. All of these were written by Japanese authors, one of whom is a nonfiction writer and the rest amateurs. Working without knowledge of one another's investigation, these writers conducted research on an identical topic and gathered quite similar data. I myself have interviewed some members of the Takasago-Giyutai while doing fieldwork; as the results of my investigation are in agreement with those recorded in the above-mentioned books, I will use only texts from the later sources for my analysis.

Although the establishment of the Takasago-Giyutai was a clandestine event during the war and an investigation into its historical details is an extremely urgent task, this chapter's use of contemporary oral testimonies does not have historical reconstruction as its major concern. Rather, it examines how the complex messages contained in these materials can be appropriately appreciated in the present day, some 50 years after the end of the war. Some materials offer reminiscences of war experiences, others present claims and dilemmas concerning personal identity, yet others depict the "mutual gazing" encounters between colonizer and colonized in a postcolonial situation. Most significantly, the discourses and conceptual-izations regarding *Yamatodamashi* are a linkage running through the prewar, wartime, and postwar periods, and will offer some insights into forms of resistance in the wake of two successive colonialisms. By analyzing the experiences of colonial encounter and interaction in terms of Japanese culture *vis-à-vis* the culture of Others, this chapter will attempt to answer the questions posed earlier.

The last returning imperial soldier

A piece of unusual news at the end of 1974 captured the world's attention: a Japanese soldier was discovered on the Island of Morotai, where he had survived alone for 30 years (Sato 1987). According to the Indonesian soldier who found him, the Japanese soldier lived in a small hut built in the mountains and began each day with exercise and worship of the Japanese Emperor.

After being discovered, however, this last imperial soldier chose to return not to Japan but to his home in Hualian, Taiwan. Born a member of the Ami tribe, he had been drafted by the Japanese government in 1943 at the age of 25. In the army, his name was changed to Nakamura Akio. Upon his return, the 57-year-old soldier discovered that Taiwan had been liberated from Japanese colonial rule and had been taken over by the Nationalist Chinese government from the mainland, which had been defeated in China's civil war and had retreated to its remaining island stronghold. In the recompilation of Taiwan's household registration data after the war, Nakamura's name was arbitrarily changed by government officials to the Chinese Lee Kuang-huei. Hence, in the Japanese press the incident was referred to as the "Nakamura Ittohei event," while in Taiwan it was called the "Lee Kuang-huei event." In both news accounts, the old soldier's original Ami name, Suniyon, was largely ignored. Suniyon died of lung cancer 4 years after his return – the result of alcoholism and a three-pack-a-day smoking habit – and thus his personal testimony was lost to history. It has been reported that he was totally unwilling to divulge anything to journalists (Sato 1987).

Suniyon belonged to an Austronesian people once referred to as "raw barbarians" in Chinese. Japanese colonizers used the term *Takasago* to refer to these Austronesian tribes, Taiwan's earliest inhabitants. Over the span of 400 years, successive inroads into the western plains of Taiwan were made by the Dutch, the Spanish, and the Han Chinese, leading to the assimilation or disappearance of ethnic groups in those regions. The Austronesian tribes in the mountains and on the eastern coast were able to retain their autonomous ways of life and they continued to hold on to their respective tribal territories. They frequently engaged in small-scale intertribal conflicts in order to safeguard their hunting grounds and ward off invasions, and some practiced headhunting.

Once Taiwan became a colony in 1895, however, the Japanese education and assimilation policies began to coerce the Austronesians into abandoning their nonliterate, subsistence lifestyle. Japanese anthropological research in Taiwan also started soon after colonization, and the Austronesians were divided according to language and social customs into nine ethnic groups. Significantly, the onset of colonial rule also prompted the nine tribes to adopt a common language – Japanese.

The pervasiveness and success of Japanese-language education was a major feature of Japan's colonial policy in Taiwan (Tsurumi 1984). Compulsory education for the Takasago peoples consisted of only 4 years of primary school, but even this limited schooling afforded more than 80 percent of children the chance to read and write.[3] The curricula were devoted to such practical subjects as horticulture, forestry, and mathematics, but the greatest emphasis was placed on the learning and recitation of the *Chokugo* (the Emperor's edict) as part of Emperor worship. Especially after the declaration of war with China in 1937 and with the proclamation of the National Mobilization Act in 1938, exaltation of military virtues and allegiance to the nation and the Emperor were given the highest priority in schools.

The *Kominka* ("transforming colonials into royal subjects") movement, initiated in Taiwan in the late 1930s, worked speedily to assimilate the native population by having locals adopt Japanese names, speak Japanese, and worship the Emperor. The colonial government instilled in the Austronesians the notion that the highest spiritual achievement was to be attained by serving the Emperor and the nation, even if that meant sacrificing one's own life.

Following the escalation of war, the Takasago were mobilized for labor and warfare in the South Pacific. In 1942 the military chief of Taiwan, who also served as the supreme commander of the Philippines, began calling up Takasago youths to serve in the South Seas (Kondo 1996). In all, eight corps of Takasago-Giyutai were dispatched; also, there were other "special volunteers" units enlisted by the Army, Navy, and Air Force. All told, the number of Takasago youths who volunteered was at least 8,000,[4] a significant percentage of a total Takasago population numbering less than 200,000.

The Takasago-Giyutai fought in battles in the Philippines, New Guinea, the Solomon Islands, Rabaul, Moratai, and other parts of the South Pacific theater. At first they were assigned to transportation and supply divisions. With drastic changes of condition as the war progressed, they were then deployed as riflemen for front-line combat. In the final stages of the war, fifteen officers and forty-five Takasago-Giyutai crew members of the "Kaoru Air Force Attack Corps" (organized in Taiwan before the famous "Kamikaze Attack Corps") "fuselage-landed" their planes on Leyte Island in the Philippines in a suicidal attack on advancing Allied troops.

In Japan's historical documentation of the war, the Takasago-Giyutai are rarely mentioned. Their exact number, battle sites, and military activities remain unclear. One reason for this lack of documentation was the widespread destruction and misrepresentation of records due to fear of impending war crimes trials. The commanding officers of the Takasago-Giyutai were mostly graduates of Nakano Academy, which was founded in 1940 for the express purpose of training guerrilla troops. They had received special instructions (which included the use of poison gas), and were obliged not to divulge any information about their missions. Hence, all things related to this school and its activities are shrouded in mystery. Furthermore, members of the Takasago-Giyutai used Japanese names during the war, making it difficult to separate them from genuine Japanese soldiers. Before its demise at the end of 1943, *Riban no Tomo (Friends of Aborigine Administration)*, the Japanese government publication most concerned with aboriginal affairs, carried just one item related to the enlistment of Takasago volunteers. That report refers to the battle in the Bataan Peninsula, the only victory of the Takasago corps during its existence. Finally, those who survived and returned to Taiwan were dispersed among various tribes and their Japanese names were replaced by Chinese ones in the reregistration of households. Their "collaboration" with the Japanese also made them subject to indiscriminate arrest and prosecution as "Han traitors,"[5] so that the surviving Takasago-Giyutai members were unwilling and afraid to speak for themselves. In 1987, the lifting of the 40-year-old "Emergency Act" removed many constraints on the freedom of speech and thought in Taiwan, and accounts of the Takasago-Giyutai began to appear.[6] The history of the Takasago-Giyutai, long buried and forgotten, is beginning to be disinterred.

Memories recalled and testimonies proffered

The following analysis deals with texts published after 1992: Takashi Ishibashi's *Illegitimate Sons of the Old Colony: Soldiers of the Takasago-Giyutai Today* (1992); Choshyu Kadowaki's *The Takasago-Giyutai of Taiwan: The Spirit Never Dies* (1994); Kazunori Tsuchibashi's *Loyalty Unsurpassed: Soldiers of the Takasago-Giyutai of Taiwan* (1994); and Eidai Hayashi's *The Fifth Takasago-Giyutai of*

Taiwan: Name Rosters, Military Savings Accounts, and Testimonies by Japanese (1994) and his other book *Testimonies: Takasago Volunteers* (1998). All four authors collected their accounts directly from surviving Takasago-Giyutai members and their relatives.

Among the cited authors, only Hayashi is a journalist. Before he took up his research project, he had never heard of the Takasago-Giyutai, even though he was an authority on World War II history. While interviewing Korean "volunteers" sent to the South Pacific during the war, he learned of its existence and started to make inquiries. The other three authors were all first-time writers. Tsuchibashi had never been to the battlefield. Born and raised in Taiwan, he was the son of an official in charge of aboriginal affairs. When he revisited Taiwan after retirement, he was surprised by accounts of the Giyutai and began recording what he heard. Kadowaki was a war veteran who had served in Manchuria and was a member of a veterans' society of soldiers returned from Mainland China. Ishibashi must also have been in the battles on the mainland; he was detained in Siberia for 5 years after the war. Like Kadowaki, he met some Takasago-Giyutai members by chance while in the mountains of Taiwan. Moved by their stories, he began to write down their accounts.

In all, testimonies by twenty Japanese officers (from interviews conducted in Japan or manuscripts written by them) and thirty members of the Takasago-Giyutai interviewed in Taiwan are gathered in these five books. All of the interviewees were quite elderly when their accounts were collected, and many have passed away since the publication of the books. In their recollections, the Japanese officers were full of praise and gratitude for the Takasago-Giyutai. The following are typical examples.

Suzuki Masami (Major, medical officer of the 18th Army) said:

> December 8, 1943. Yamamoto's troops holding the Buna area on the north coast of New Guinea were all killed ("gyokusai" in Japanese) … . These troops were principally made up of units from maintenance and transportation divisions, and many of the men were members of the Takasago-Giyutai.
>
> Major Yamamoto's final communication to the headquarters was safely delivered by a member of the Takasago-Giyutai. Yamamoto praised the Takasago's expertise in jungle combat, their great spiritual strength, their fine-tuned senses of hearing and sight, their alertness in detecting enemy movements and airplanes, and their sharpshooting skills. In jungle combats in the South Seas, they demonstrated an ability several times greater than that of the Japanese soldiers … .
>
> In New Guinea, where the coasts are tropical while snow accumulates on the high mountains, Japanese soldiers had great difficulties, many succumbing to overexertion and passing out by the roadside. It is no exaggeration to say that only the Takasago soldiers maintained their fighting strength. Their spirit held the group together through combat,

re-supplies, and marches. Many units frequently requested Takasago men. They had become the eyes, hands, and legs of their respective units. As we were losing the war, the Takasago were decimated along with Japanese regulars. No one, officer or private, in the three divisions of our 18th Army ever expressed dissatisfaction with the Takasago soldiers.

(Kadowaki 1994: 167–73)

Naoto Yahaneda (First Lieutenant, 27th Commando Materiel Arsenal) also mentioned:

> They were very well-disciplined and obeyed their superiors. I trusted them very much. As volunteers, their morale was high. In comparison, the Han Taiwanese of the Agricultural Service Corps were ... untrustworthy. When they were assigned to my unit, I would request they be sent back at once
> ... .
> Some of the Takasago-Giyutai personnel had tattoos on their foreheads. Previously I would have thought this a sign of savagery, but I came to the discovery that they were braver than Japanese soldiers.

(Hayashi 1994: 290–1)

Tamotsu Ueno (Squad Leader, 5th Takasago-Giyutai) had this to say:

> It was only because of them that I survived in the foodless marshes. In order to pass through these areas, many soldiers had to abandon their guns. In the marshes one had to keep moving even while defecating. The marsh water we drank was contaminated by floating corpses and many of us consequently contracted dysentery ... . I ordered three Giyutai men in my squad to look after Second Lieutenant Yahaneda, who was suffering from dysentery and cholera. They obeyed my order readily and took turns carrying the sick. They accomplished their job under circumstances of extreme food shortage. Seeing such all-out and selfless efforts, I had to bow to them in respect, even though they were my subordinates.

(Hayashi 1994: 267)

Yozo Komata (Leader, Saito Squad and the 2nd Giyutai), in particular, continually expressed his inner thoughts through religious ritual after the war. In his own words:

> I was involved from the start in the planning and organization of guerrilla warfare by the Takasago in New Guinea. Up to this day, I have never for a single moment forgotten their *ongi* ("beneficence"). I am alive today only because they managed to obtain life-sustaining food when no supplies were forthcoming. Whenever I think of how we ate, slept, and talked together at the time, I always feel as if we had been very close in our previous lives. On every New Year's Day I would lead my family to make

bows in the direction of Taiwan. I light candles on the Buddhist altar at home to offer prayers to members of the Giyutai.

(Kadowaki 1994: 145)

In addition to the themes touched upon in these accounts, the issues of military marching routes and combat strategies are also the major preoccupations of the officers' reminiscences. But these have to be skipped over here because they are not the main concern of this chapter. In any case, when summing up their feelings about the Takasago-Giyutai, these officers almost unanimously mentioned the Austronesians' *Yamatodamashi* and asserted that "they have become Japanese." As Tatemichi Omori (a correspondent attached to the army) maintained: "Crew members of the Kaoru air battle unit were all Takasago youths. They were humble, honest, disciplined, and intelligent. They out-Japanesed the Japanese" (Tsuchibashi 1994: 240). And Nariai Masaharu (Leader, Odaka Scouting Squad) had this to say: "They had no fear for death. They had become completely Japanese" (Hayashi 1994: 331). Similarly, Keisuke Hori, a military physician, stated: "There was about a squadron of Takasago in the Solomon Islands. They were truly brave, and were even more loyal to the Emperor than the Japanese" (Tsuchibashi 1994: 188). Shin Moriyama (Instructor to the First Takasago-Giyutai) recalled the transformation in his feelings about the Takasago-Giyutai: "When I was first appointed to instruct the Takasago soldiers, I was a little apprehensive. But when I actually saw them, I found out their skin color was also fair, their features good-looking, and they didn't waste time on idle conversations. Their hearts were ablaze with the *Yamatodamashi* spirit of patriotism and loyalty to the Emperor. In this, they were much superior to new recruits from Japan itself" (Tsuchibashi 1944: 261).

After their contacts with the Takasago in the battlefields, the Japanese officers arrived at the judgment that they had not only metamorphosed into Japanese but had even surpassed the Japanese in certain characteristics. Such estimations are quite unusual; to have "become Japanese" was already such high praise by their standards that surpassing the Japanese must have been an extraordinary compliment.

The manner in which this praise was expressed must be examined in the context of the colony at the end of Japanese rule. Subsequent to the imperial government's proclamation of the "National Spirit Mobilization Act," attainment of the status of Emperor's subject was lauded as the highest value, both in Japan itself and in the colonies. Meanwhile, with the colonial policies prevailing in Taiwan, the Takasago were stigmatized as barbarians and simpletons, and their social status was extremely low. Consequently, "becoming the Emperor's subject" – in other words, to be Japanese – was a peerless achievement repeatedly propagandized by the colonizer. With regard to the question of whether the Takasago could actually be Japanese or "the Emperor's subjects," however, it appears that the colonial government's attitude at the time was ambiguous and unclear. In contrast, the testimonies of former Japanese military officers clearly assert that the Takasago could and did become Japanese, even more Japanese than the Japanese themselves.

The concept of *Yamatodamashi* was sometimes alternatively expressed by the terms *Nipponseishin* ("Japanese spirit") or *Nippondamashi* ("Japanese soul") in wartime documents; these phrases frequently appeared in government propaganda and the statements of officials, opinion leaders, and teachers. However, the term *Yamatodamashi* itself was not derived from the Emperor's sacred edicts. Nor was it an official creed contained in school textbooks or even administrative papers. Nevertheless, it was almost ceaselessly used and evoked. Its meaning is roughly "loyalty to the Emperor and the nation," as one of the cited officers puts it, and it implies the supreme greatness of Japanese people. As such, *Yamatodamashi* was a very important spiritual guidepost during the war, even though its interpretation could be stretched one way or another. As will be shown later in this chapter, the term is also of great significance to members of the Takasago-Giyutai, and it is repeatedly invoked in their testimonies.

In contrast to the Japanese officers' statements, the most salient themes in the Takasago volunteers' testimonies are the circumstances surrounding their departure from home and their encounters in the battlefield; the latter including the distress of Japanese soldiers and the revolting cases of Japanese cannibalism which the Takasago witnessed. Among the spiritual highs and lows expressed in the accounts, the Takasago unanimously recall excitement at the time when they volunteered their services, for after all that was a moment of supreme glory.

Attol Taukin (Akimoto Takeji in Japanese name, from the Tayal tribe, Army special volunteer) stated:

> When the war broke out, I was the only son in the family. My father and other villagers didn't want me to go to war. But I was fascinated by the bravery of the Giyutai. I cut my finger and with the blood wrote a letter volunteering for service. I vowed to His Majesty the Emperor that I would devote my humble self to Him as a national (*kokumin*). After writing this I felt an overwhelming sense of calm.
>
> (Kadowaki 1994: 270)

Buyan Nawi (a.k.a. Tokunaga Mitsuo, from the Tayal tribe, Fifth Takasago-Giyutai) also said:

> When my second elder brother volunteered for the Third Giyutai, my father did not shed a tear – he encouraged my brother to serve the country with all his heart. My mother's reaction was more complex; she seemed both joyous and sorrowful. Since ancient times, Tayal men have faced death in battle resolutely, and we would never feel sad about it. When I joined the Fifth Giyutai and was ready to go to war, the whole tribe threw a big farewell party for me and the dancing continued till daybreak. I

made my decision to do great deeds for Japan and the Emperor. We Tayal people have always been brave. We have never been fearful of going to war. We regard it as honorable."

(Hayashi 1998: 190–1)

In these two cases, it is evident that the Takasago young men's willingness to volunteer was strong, even if their families had different attitudes toward the matter. They were convinced that they were doing this "for Japan and the Emperor," and it was something a "national" was obliged to carry out. As a matter of fact, these ideas were new and foreign concepts to tribal societies, having been inculcated by the colonizer. Walis Piho (a.k.a. Yonegawa Nobuo, Second Takasago-Giyutai), a Tayal from a different settlement, made it very clear:

> We also organized a youth corps in our village of Kawanakajima. Our first task was to learn Japanese. Our mother tongue had been forbidden. The "Speak the National Language Movement" had been promoted in the countryside and police officers were keen on instilling the Japanese Spirit in us. Remarkably, when we began to speak only Japanese we felt quite at ease, as if we had been Japanese all along. We took up military exercises in the Youth Corps every day and night, and we had to recite silently to ourselves the Emperor's *Kyoikuchokugo* ("Edict on Education") and *Gunjinchokuyu* ("Edict on Military Personnel"). On the day of our departure, all of the tribe came to see us off. They stood along the roadsides waving the *Hinomaru* flag. I felt extremely proud to be a Japanese military man!

(Hayashi 1998: 129)

Walis Piho's reasons for volunteering are significant: "By volunteering for military service, I intended to erase the stain of treachery and regain our honor.[7] If we could become loyal citizens, then we would be able to be the equals of Japanese."

In other words, they were not yet "nationals" at the time; regardless of how the concept of *national* and *nation* were conceived by them, they were making great efforts to attain a status equal to the Japanese. Interestingly, these efforts were complemented by an indigenous respect for bravery in the battle mentioned by Buyan Nawi.

When they arrived in the fighting zones of the southwestern Pacific, members of the Takasago-Giyutai, unlike the Japanese officers cited earlier, were placed in a very low position in the military hierarchy. Therefore, they were not very knowledgeable about the strategies of the entire army, or the number of personnel, their location, and so forth. What they were certain about was their mission. In their reminiscences, they consistently dwell upon their perceptions of the Japanese in the battlefield.

Prin Suyan (Japanese name Yasuoka Tsugio, from the Tayal tribe, Third Takasago-Giyutai) emphasized:

The Japanese army was very strong. The Japanese and the Takasago-Giyutai were equal in spirit, and we were not outrun by the Japanese soldiers. When we moved into the jungles, the Japanese got mired down while we marched forward bravely, wielding our traditional knives. We were hailed with the chant "Taiwanese Army, Taiwanese Army." ... The military spirit of the Takasago-Giyutai was highly admirable, it was on a par with the Japanese spirit.

(Hayashi 1998: 164–5)

The aforementioned Buyan Nawi had this to say:

Whenever the Japanese officers drank unboiled water they would suffer diarrhea. I climbed up a coconut tree and brought down two or three coconuts for them to drink. Sometimes I would gather wild vines, cut them to drain water into a canteen. Eventually, the Japanese soldiers began to salute me, saying, "Taiwanese Army, please pick me a coconut!" This gave me quite a start.

When I was moving alone in the jungles, I witnessed many incidents in which Japanese soldiers killed their comrades and ate their flesh. Even though they were the Emperor's soldiers, they would still lose their senses when no food was available. Even the high-ranking officers partook of the corpses of their own comrades. Survival is the human instinct of first priority, and anything could be done for its sake. While consuming the flesh of your comrades, the human conscience was held at bay.

(Hayashi 1998: 199)

Pawan Taimo (Japanese name Sato Toshiaki, from the Tayal tribe, the Marine Corps, Fourth Takasago-Giyutai) recalled:

On the island, we were in charge of patrolling and pacifying the natives. We taught them agricultural skills and gave the children lessons in Japanese language. We also learned their language and became good friends with the chief, who accompanied us on patrols.

(Hayashi 1998: 176)

When referring to the Japanese officers, he reflected:

Graduates of the Japanese Navy Academy might know the strategies of warfare, but they certainly lacked elementary survival skills. Despite their intelligence, they were not fit for jungle combat. When they were searching for food, their behavior was ridiculous. Their idea of food was limited to rice and canned goods. It is quite difficult to tell if the plants in tropical jungles are edible or not, and one can die from madness as a result of accidentally eating poisonous grass. The plants on the island were very similar to those in the mountains of Taiwan. When we trapped

birds, we would always examine the food inside their stomachs. Plants
edible to birds are equally safe for humans.

(Hayashi 1998: 176–8)

These recollections clearly demonstrate the shock and even scorn which
the Takasago felt over the actions of their Japanese superiors. With respect
to status hierarchy, the former had to absolutely obey and serve the latter.
Hence the shock when the Japanese "salute me" and "lose their senses." The
Takasago's superiors might be experts in military strategies, but they were
embarrassingly incapable of coping with basic survival needs. On the other
hand, these narratives also indicate the Takasago's confidence in their own
culture, which proved superior to that of the Japanese in helping them to
adapt to battlefield environments and survive in the jungle.

Talpan Pukiringan (Japanese name Gakita Kaizo, from the Paiwan tribe,
squadron chief in the Fifth Takasago-Giyutai) observed some changes in
Japanese officers after the war:

When the armistice was declared, Japanese soldiers lost their status and
became ordinary civilians. One of our superiors, who had inflicted corporal
punishment upon us without justification, now began to treat us nicely,
softening his speech and flattering us. We were so happy to be able to
strike him back. In this hellish world people tend to show their weakest
points and do the worst things, especially when in a group. On our return
trip, platoon leader Ueno Tamotsu knelt down on the ship's deck to offer
us his apology. One of the Han soldiers from Taiwan told him to go jump
overboard.

(Hayashi 1998: 250–2)

Incidentally, the platoon leader mentioned in this account has also offered
his own testimony (cited earlier), although he did not say anything about his
kneeling down to apologize. There are other discrepancies: almost all
members of the Takasago-Giyutai talked about cannibalism as their most
distressing experience during the war, while none of the Japanese officers'
recollections mention the practice.

Arucu'ucu Rava (Japanese name Noguchi Yoshikichi, from the Paiwan
tribe, First Takasago-Giyutai) continued to suffer from this experience after
he returned from the war:

As a human being, this is the most shameful thing I have ever done. We
ate the flesh of an Australian soldier. On the brink of death from
starvation, people are driven to desperate measures. This is the regret
of my life … . After several months without normal food, the dead enemy
began to look appetizing. Many Japanese soldiers fell upon a corpse and
carved the flesh with knives and ate it raw. Later the corpse was cooked
until only white bones were left. In retrospect, it was extremely cruel,

but a man has no choice if he wants to guarantee his own survival. If I had been alone, perhaps I would not have done such a thing, but there was a sense of security committing such a crime in a group.

(Hayashi 1998: 91, 104)

Walis Piho makes a similar confession:

Driven by hunger, I didn't think of it as human flesh, but rather as the meat of a wild boar. If one had done it by oneself, there would have been revulsion of the conscience. But since all of the squad took part, nothing seemed out of the ordinary … . In our weakened state, a lick of salt could revive a man. With such pervasive starvation, a soldier with rice or salt was in danger of being robbed and killed by his comrades.

(Hayashi 1998: 135–8)

After returning to Taiwan, the Takasago were unable to share these painful experiences with others. Ruraden Ramakao (Japanese name Kawano Eiichi, from the Paiwan tribe, Second Takasago-Giyutai) recalls:

Forty of us disembarked at Kaohsiung and were treated to a welcome by representatives of the women's association, students, and many other citizens waving *Hinomaru* flags. The bereaved wanted to know how their sons and brothers had died. I could not bring myself to tell them about the hunger, disease, or cannibalism. I could only say they had died bravely in battle. I still have nightmares. In particular, I dream of a terrifying hunger which drives me in a state of stupefaction to seek food, until I am awakened by the image of eating an enemy's flesh.

(Hayashi 1998: 86–7)

In addition to being unable to share these unspeakable experiences, some Takasago were also filled with shame when faced with the bereaved relatives of their deceased fellow volunteers. Zakara (Japanese name Nakano Mitsuo, from the Amis tribe, Third Takasago-Giyutai) put it this way:

I would prefer to have died along with my comrades in New Guinea. I am the only survivor and this turn of events has put a heavy burden on my conscience. Nothing has been more excruciating than facing others in the tribe who have lost their beloved in the war. I have always felt guilty about my comrades who died in battle.

(Hayashi 1998: 160)

Returning home after the war, the Giyutai members found a society that had undergone tremendous changes. In the first place, they had to deal with yet another foreign political regime and learn another language. This was entirely unexpected. Iyon Habas (Japanese name Kato Naoichi, from the Bunun tribe, Seventh Takasago-Giyutai) recalled:

Of the 800 members of the Seventh Takasago-Giyutai, only a few more than 100 survived the war. On our return to Taiwan, Chiang Kai-shek's Kuomingtung army regarded us as Japanese soldiers – that is, the enemy. The volunteers were especially singled out and treated as Japanese collaborators and traitors to the nation. Even our families and relatives were afraid to mention the fact that we had been in the Japanese army. We were constantly fearful of being arrested and convicted of crimes. Such were the dangerous lives of the Takasago-Giyutai's surviving members.

(Hayashi 1998: 277–83)

Artul Rava, cited earlier, concurred:

Under the post-war Chiang Kai-shek regime, we couldn't mention the fact that we had volunteered for the Japanese Army. I removed my wartime picture from a photograph album and carried it on my person. We had to cover up our past. It was a hard, repressive time.

(Hayashi 1998: 89–92)

After the war, members of the Takasago-Giyutai found themselves trapped between old and new regimes. On one hand, they had to endure repression from their new rulers. But what made them most unhappy was that the successor to their former colonizer – the postwar Japanese government – abandoned them, and for more than 40 years delayed compensating them for their service by claiming that they were not of Japanese nationality. Walis Piho explained:

I couldn't believe it when I heard the Emperor's proclamation of surrender on August 15th. I fell on the ground, hitting it with my hands, and felt completely at a loss. We the Takasago-Giyutai did not lose the war; what happened was merely that the Emperor had put up his hands in surrender. I do not harbor hatred for Japan. I did what a volunteer Japanese soldier should do. It was an honor … . In New Guinea our monthly salary was 45 yen, and it is a matter of course to repay us. The Japanese government should deal with this sincerely. At the minimum it should offer us thanks.

(Hayashi 1998: 140–2)

At the time of the interviews, the Takasago-Giyutai members had complicated and contradictory feelings about their situation. Although they expressed sadness at their abandonment, they were proud of their *Yamatodamashi*. Talpan Pukiringan described his feelings in this way:

After we returned to Taiwan, the Japanese military did not pay any tribute (*aisatsu*) to the Takasago-Giyutai, a negligence beyond my comprehension. As a Japanese soldier returning from the New Guinea battles, certainly

I deserved at least some sort of appreciation or thanks. Is losing the war reason enough for such acts of irresponsibility? I was saddened by this. At that point I came to think of the war as a wasted effort. I could, though, sympathize with the viewpoint of the Japanese military. Because of the defeat, they were at a loss as to what was to be done. It means a great deal that the youths of Taiwan, inculcated with the Japanese spirit, went to the war for Japan and sacrificed their lives. As I think about what that war meant to us, an emptiness invades my heart. The Japanese government claims that Taiwanese are of a different nationality, but during the war we were true Japanese soldiers. I hope this is recognized.

(Hayashi 1998: 252–3)

According to Iyon Habao:

Three brothers in my family joined the Takasago-Giyutai (my two younger brothers both died in the war) and were willing to sacrifice our lives. At the time, I went to the war as a Japanese national, and was fighting alongside soldiers from Japan. We have sued the Japanese government not for the sake of money, but rather to redress the injustice done to us, who, being equally Japanese, have nevertheless been given the cold shoulder. It has been almost forty years since the war ended, and yet the matter [of compensation] has not been addressed. This is intolerable. I can only say – what a shame! In post-war Taiwan, especially among the Takasago, the Japanese spirit has been highly regarded ... . Loyalty to the country and safeguarding the security of the entire people – this is the *Yamatodamashi*, and perhaps the *Bushido* ("way of the samurai") too! The Takasago-Giyutai were truer Japanese than the Japanese. I am still Japanese in spirit; I have the *Yamatodamashi* in my soul. Among the Takasago people of Taiwan, the *Yamatodamashi* will never die.

(Hayashi 1998: 282–3)

Takasago-Giyutai volunteers' own assessments of the past often emphasize that they are genuine Japanese who possess *Yamatodamashi*. Artul Rava told Hayashi: "Please tell the Japanese people there are Japanese like us here in Taiwan. We members of the Takasago-Giyutai are perhaps more Japanese than the Japanese" (Hayashi 1998: 89–92). These claims to being 100 percent Japanese soldiers or possessing the *Yamatodamashi* appear repeatedly in the self-evaluations of Giyutai members from various tribal backgrounds. Confronted with these assertions, some of the Japanese writers reacted with puzzlement while others expressed appreciation.

History, texts, and authors

Although the experience of the war naturally varied from person to person, the foregoing narratives concerning the same war zone (the southwestern

Pacific) contain a number of significant common themes. The members of
Takasago-Giyutai, despite being drawn from different ethnic groups and
tribes, faced the same circumstances before, during, and after the war.
Moreover, all their narratives were presented in fluent Japanese.
Consequently, no significant ethnic or personal differences distinguish one
account from the other. Their common themes can be divided into two
categories: reminiscences about actual wartime conditions and postwar
retrospection. These focal narratives contain mutual images of "the Other"
held by the colonizer and the colonized, images that illuminate the
complicated interrelations between the two parties. Clearly, the Takasago's
repeated claims to be Japanese and possess *Yamatodamashi* complicate attempts
to define what being Japanese means.

It is significant that in the cited texts the authors all use the term
"testimonies" to refer to the narrative records. However, *shogen*, the Japanese
equivalent of testimonies, broadly speaking means true words. It is not limited
in its connotation to statements made in a court of law. Now, to whom are
these testimonies addressed? And what are their goals? The answers to these
questions depend on how we choose to look at these texts. Natalie Davis's
analysis of pardon texts from sixteenth-century French archives is a case in
point: here, the primary objective of the testimonies was the remission of
crimes, and as a consequence the testifying peasant women's story-telling
skill, their style, and how their testimonies got transcribed into documents
were all affected. Seen from this perspective, although the texts examined
in this chapter were addressed to the visiting writers (who were Japanese), it
can be maintained that they were appeals intended for the Japanese people
and former colonizers in general, to whom the writers only served as
convenient conduits. This is suggested by Artul Rava's request to Hayashi:
"Please tell the Japanese people there are Japanese like us here in Taiwan.
We members of the Takasago-Giyutai are perhaps more Japanese than the
Japanese" (Hayashi 1998: 89–92).

I would propose that these testimonies were made to serve three purposes.
First, the testimony givers wanted to preserve their own memories. In other
words, the texts are records of oral history. Second, they serve as appeals for
repayments and compensation, to which the Giyutai members felt entitled.
Third, and most significant, they are claims of identity made toward former
colonizers. This last, in my view, is a form of resistance in the postcolonial
situation. It is so because, as stated earlier, their records in the war have
been all but erased. Their commanders, graduates of the Nakano Army
Academy, were under strict orders of secrecy and they continued to keep
silent even after the war (Kadowaki 1994: 139; Hayashi 1998: 24–7). Besides,
members of the Takasago-Giyutai had to dodge prosecution as traitors
(collaborators) from the Taiwanese government. Furthermore, they were
illiterate people to begin with, although they had all gone through some
elementary schooling in Japanese reading and writing.[8] After the war, they
felt slighted by society in both Japan and Taiwan. This significant chapter in

their personal history, the result of the lacunae in written archives, could only be reconstructed by means of oral accounts.

A researcher on oral history has pointed out that "all history is selection and the basis of selection is our current concern" (Grele 1991: 251). In accordance with this view, we have to pay attention to the fact that many of the Takasago-Giyutai members expressed in their testimonies a concern for repayment of debts by the Japanese government. The wartime salary of some has yet to be paid. Others received their pay only in postal savings accounts, and these deposits have never been released. Furthermore, unlike native Japanese soldiers, neither they nor their families have received from the government any annuities for survivors of the war-dead (*Choyikin*) or soldiers' special bonuses (*Onkyu*).

In 1977, 30 years after the war's end, the widespread attention given to the return of Suniyon from Morotai prompted a group of former Japanese soldiers and relatives of war-dead from Taiwan to sue the Japanese government and demand that they be paid what was due to them. In the meantime, a support group in Japan itself was organized and led by Shigeki Miyazaki, a Meiji University professor whose father had been a lieutenant general in the Takasago-Giyutai during the war. However, the lawsuit was defeated at both the first- and second-level courts after 15 years of litigation, and in 1992 the Supreme Court decided to overturn the plaintiffs' case. In the view of the Japanese judicial system, the issues can only be resolved by legislation initiated by the administration and passed by the Diet.

As a matter of fact, some members of the Diet took up the task during the later phase of the litigation and legislation was finally passed in 1988, dividing the issues into two categories: compensation and debts. With regard to the former, each Taiwanese war-dead and war-injured was to be awarded 2,000,000 yen by the Japanese government as a token of "condolence." However, as we can see from the Takasago testimonies made in the 1990s, it would appear that no one was satisfied with this. In their statements, the following complaint is often heard, "This is tantamount to an obituary gift and not compensation at all. If any compensation is intended, it should be like the annuities received by relatives of the war-dead in Japan."[9] The Japanese government maintained that the Takasago were no longer Japanese nationals after the war, and therefore were not to be treated in the same manner as Japanese veterans. On the other hand, the new regime that took over Taiwan after World War II took the position that when these debts were incurred the Takasago were not its subjects, and consequently it did not have any responsibility for their repayment. The government in Taiwan did not make any effort to seek redress from the Japanese government for the Takasago volunteers.

By contrast, the unpaid wartime salaries were considered "confirmed debts." But with regard to this, no agreement has yet been reached, for the inflation of the cost of living since the war has been so enormous that the Japanese government and the Taiwanese debt-holders could not come to a mutually acceptable rate of conversion. The Japanese government insisted on repaying 200 times the amount of the original debts, whereas debt-holders in Taiwan calculated that the monetary value had increased between 5,000 and 10,000 times and were not satisfied with the Japanese government's offer. All of these debt holders are over 70 years of age now. They are still awaiting some sort of solution even as their number is dwindling.

In the early 1990s when the interviews were conducted, the issues of repayments and compensation were on the agenda, and perhaps this encouraged the Giyutai members to be more enthusiastic in talking about their past and presenting their claims.

In fact, when the Japanese government began in 1996 to offer repayments of 200 times the original debts, very few members of the Takasago-Giyutai were willing to take the offer. Therefore, I should think that this is not an issue to be resolved by money. Indeed, what they were most concerned with was not the amount of recompense, but rather with the question of their identity. They wanted to be recognized as (once) having been Japanese, Japanese nationals, and Japanese soldiers.

The writers of the texts cited in this chapter were the first people to hear these claims. These Japanese interviewers, who came to them purely by accident after the war, served as a bridge between former members of Takasago-Giyutai and the Japanese people. Consequently, the question of why Giyutai members wanted to make testimonies and the question of why Japanese authors wanted to collect the testimonies become two sides of the same coin.

Reading between the lines, we can see that the four Japanese authors have one thing in common: they were all deeply moved. They volunteered to record the history of the Takasago so that a neglected episode of history could be related to the Japanese people, and thus they acted as spokespersons for the Takasago, who were illiterate. In view of the authors' ages at the time of writing and the contents of their books, commercial or some other ulterior considerations were not factors in these undertakings. When his book was published, Kadowaki's greatest wish was to travel to Taiwan to present in person a copy to everyone interviewed in his book. He was 80 years old at the time (Kadowaki 1994: Preface).

Among the four authors, Ishibashi (born 1924) and Hayashi (born 1933) share another characteristic. Yoshikawa (of the Amis tribe) told Ishibashi: "You ask me why I went to the war, but of course it was for the Emperor and Japan. This is what the Japanese spirit means." Ishibashi retorted: "But don't you have any regret now? You are not really Japanese. You were referred to as Takasago and discriminated against. It would only make sense to sacrifice for Japan if you had been a Japanese." To this Yoshikawa replied with disbelief: "Hey, you don't seem to understand. We *were* Japanese at the time during the Great East Asia War! We volunteered for the war from our heart. The sufferings in battles, even death, were undertaken by us willingly!" Ishibashi was deeply moved by this, and he came to realize how much evil the war had done (Ishibashi 1992: 279–80). Similarly, Hayashi was told by Pirin Suyan: "I am a Japanese and will be even in my death. I feel ashamed to have come back alive from the war." Hayashi was dumbfounded by this statement. He wrote: "After listening to his words, my reaction was very complicated. I wanted to ask him if he felt used and betrayed. But it was impossible to ask such questions, for he was so innocent at heart" (Hayashi 1998: 164–5). Both of these writers were indignant at the Japanese government's procrastination in making repayments.

Tsuchibashi (born 1928), an amateur writer, spent 8 years on his book. He confesses that he wanted to complete his book so that he could let his late father and the Takasago soldiers who had died in the war rest in peace. His father had been a police officer in the colony. He held the Takasago in high esteem for their sense of honor and their innocent dispositions. He treated Takasago youths as his own children. In the early period of the war, he was often in tears when he had to send Giyutai volunteers in his precinct off to the war. In its later years, he was transferred to a post on the plains of Taiwan, and as a result he was unaware of the heavy casualties suffered by the Takasago.

His father's acts and words must have had a tremendous effect on Tsuchibashi, so that in his writings he would himself come to emphasize the Takasago's brave contributions. "In the history of war," he maintains, "there has been no case where one people have made so great a military contribution to another people. With gratitude in my heart, I hope this friendship [between the two sides] will survive forever." He later adds: "The great nation of Japan should not be an ungrateful [*bo-on*] people" (Tsuchibashi 1994: 346). As we read between the lines, however, Tsuchibashi tends to be evasive in his judgment of the war (or, there is no indication that he is negative about it). Kadowaki, who is the oldest of the group, is quite straightforward in his stance: he does not see the war in a negative way. On the contrary, he asks: "Do the words of the victors always stand for justice? My book takes as its point of departure a questioning of and displeasure with the victors" (Kadowaki 1994: 393). He also sees a deep affinity between the Takasago and the Japanese: "Today in the mountains of Taiwan I have discovered a source of the Japanese spirit." He emphasizes that, in his interview experiences, he found the Takasago had a healthy attitude toward the past, unlike Japanese soldiers whose recollections of New Guinea were full of regret and sorrow (in connection with starvation). When, 50 years after the war, he asked the Takasago how they had managed to overcome all their difficulties during the war, he was unanimously assured: "It was because of the Takasago's *Yamatodamashi!*" (Kadowaki 1994: 1) In particular, when he was told by the Takasago that "We were not defeated because we possessed *Yamatodamashi*," he was tremendously moved (Kadowaki 1994: 213). That statement, it seems to me, also reflects his own feelings, and although he did not praise the war he did not want to deny everything in his past.

As stated earlier, the Japanese authors' attitudes toward Giyutai members' identity claims were of two sorts: one skeptical, the other affirmative. Quite paradoxically, however, the skeptics were not doubtful because they felt the Takasago couldn't become Japanese; they were skeptical because they considered becoming Japanese to be something negative. On the other hand, those who praised Giyutai members possessing *Yamatodamashi* and being Japanese were affirming the supreme value of *Yamatodamashi* and becoming Japanese. These two attitudes are perhaps to some extent representative. Yet the question of why Giyutai members themselves would make such strong claims remains to be answered. I propose some possible explanations in the following section.

Battlefield trick: reversal and elevation in the hierarchy

In the texts under consideration, the colonizer–colonized hierarchy underwent significant, even dramatic, changes through three time periods: the prewar period, the wartime period, and the present postcolonial period. I believe that the Giyutai members' feelings about their identity claims and the rise of their status can be productively analyzed as a rite of passage.

In the prewar narratives, policemen who kept law and order among the Takasago tribes in the mountains represented the so-called colonizers and rulers. They were in charge of inculcating a sense of loyalty to the nation among the Takasago youths. As a result, they had to present themselves as strict disciplinarians. In fact, in all the colonized territories of the Japanese Empire, the police played a pivotal role. This was especially so in Taiwan, where the police system was first instituted and served as a model (Peattie 1996: 171–89). In the mountains of Taiwan, policemen also functioned as educators, transmitting in person the aura of the nation and the Emperor. As stated in Walis Piho's testimony cited earlier, policemen indoctrinated tribal youths with the so-called "Japanese spirit." To these young Takasago, possessing "Japanese spirit" was not an innate characteristic but a supreme and difficult goal to be striven for with great effort. Therefore, within the colonial system their status was naturally below that of the colonizer. On the battlefields, the hierarchy of military ranks was even more strict and clear-cut.

The Takasago volunteers often served as porters in the early period of the war, in charge of military supplies and communications. They did not participate directly in combat and occupied the lowest ranks of the military. As the Japanese suffered more and more defeats and as they realized that they did not have the necessary survival skills for jungle warfare, they became increasingly dependent on the Takasago. As mentioned in one of the texts, when their superiors begged them to get coconuts, the Takasago were dumbfounded. In other words, under the special circumstances of the battlefield, the difference in rank underwent a transformation. The original strict hierarchy was affected by a type of status reversal.

This type of change occurred in extreme situations and is similar to what Victor Turner (1985 [1969]: 96–7) observed in passage rites; it is a case of *communita* induced by *liminality*. In such situations, those individuals participating in the ritual are removed from the profane social structure and experience role ambiguity, equality, and even status reversal not encountered in daily life. Afterward, when they return to normal life, this status will transit to a new level. With regard to the cannibalistic episodes described in the texts, Turner's theory can be applied to the critical moments on the battlefield, when the hierarchical status structure was reversed and such an unlikely event as cannibalism could occur. In some sense, going to the war was an act carried out in the name of the nation and the Emperor, and, as defined by the Japanese state apparatus, the war was a "sacred war" (*seisen*), a condition far removed from ordinary life.

In this manner, the Takasago came to witness the embarrassments suffered by their superiors. Their testimonies indicate that what they saw was a lack of survival skills among the Japanese soldiers, who, driven by hunger, would do anything to survive, even to the extent of killing their own comrades in arms. They were surprised by the helplessness shown by Japanese officers at the end of the war, such as the officer who begged for forgiveness aboard the ship. They were also puzzled by the Japanese soldiers' "lostness" before they were sent home from Taiwan. In the eyes of these Takasago volunteers, the Japanese officers were absolute superiors and dominators, but in the war they came to see another side of the officers. In some way, the status difference between the two parties was closed or even reversed. The Takasago, by their survival skills, bravery, discipline, and loyalty to the Emperor, came to exemplify the *Yamatodamashi*, whereas Japanese officers failed to do so. In consequence, as if by a trick of the battlefield, the self-image of the Takasago was transformed from a stereotypic other, inferior and dominated, to one representing *Yamatodamashi*, a virtue that had been trumpeted by the dominators. In other words, the Takasago acquired the status of true Japanese nationals.

The liminality observed by Turner frequently occurs in rituals of status elevation. It is significant that, in the incidents described in the texts, once a person went through the liminal stage of the rite of passage and thus had his status elevated in the hierarchical structure, he would no longer suffer status demotion, even though the collective status of his group remained the same (Turner 1985 [1969]: 170–1). Following their war experiences, the Takasago-Giyutai members continued to believe that they, like the Japanese, had made great sacrifices during the war and had demonstrated their possession of *Yamatodamashi*. Therefore, they thought of themselves as true Japanese. It was the elevation in status, without regard to racial or ethnic identity, which made it possible for them to raise themselves up from the dominated position of the past. However, the collective status of the Takasago, to which they belonged, was not elevated in the same time. It was as though their special battlefield experiences had effected an elevation of their own individual status.

Postcolonial situation after dual colonialism:
forms of resistance

When they returned home to Taiwan with their extraordinary war experiences, the Takasago-Giyutai members faced a new international arrangement: the previous colonizers had departed, and a new foreign regime was in power. Since Japan had been forced to yield Taiwan, it was unclear how the Japanese would acknowledge what they had accomplished with so much suffering during the war. Moreover, the Takasago also had to deal with the Han regime coming over from the mainland. In doing so, their emotional reactions were quite distinct from those of the majority ethnic group of Taiwan, the Han; for the latter, the Chinese regime was part of the mother country, whereas for the Takasago it was a new and strange foreign power.

This government demanded that they speak Mandarin and arbitrarily changed their names into Chinese. It also relabeled what the Japanese had called "Takasago Tribes" as "Mountain Tribes." In its education policy, the greatness and supremacy of Chinese culture was emphasized, and other ethnic groups were required to assimilate. Meanwhile, and more seriously, this regime had been at war with Japan, and therefore wanted to abrogate the policies of the previous colonial government. Those educated in the Japanese school system were stigmatized as having been "enslaved," and the veterans who had served in the Japanese army were treated with great hostility. As Artul Rava and Iyon Habao testified, they suffered a great deal under Chiang Kai-Shek's postwar dictatorship.

Under such oppressive circumstances, why didn't the Takasago give up the previous colonizers' culture and adopt that of the new colonizers? Why have they continued to retain a Japanese way of life and persisted in their claim to be Japanese? When Hayashi interviewed Pirin Suyan, he described the latter's living conditions in the following words:

> On the wall of their living room hung a three-meters-square picture of the five lakes under the Fuji mountain. *Ranma* and *shoji* separated the rooms, and the bedrooms were furnished with *tatami* and *futon*, with both upper coverings and lower mattresses. The couple spoke Japanese with each other. All this made one almost forget that he was in the high mountains of Taiwan. Pirin Suyan told me: "I am a Japanese, and will be until I die." On hearing this, I had the feeling that he was more Japanese than I was. I really couldn't understand why an aborigine of the Tayal tribe could have such a near-genuine Japanese mind-set. Did he truly regard himself as a Japanese? Or was it only out of courtesy toward a visitor from afar? In any case, it wasn't likely that the house had been built for Japanese to look at!
>
> (Hayashi 1998: 164)

Hayashi goes on to add in amazement that it certainly was not arranged deliberately for the interview.

As I see it, when they made claims of being Japanese, they were experiencing complex emotional turmoil. Their attitude might be explained as a form of postcolonial resistance: identity claims serve as a resistance weapon against both the older colonialism and the one newly imposed upon them after the war. In the postcolonial period, the "former colonizers" who offered their testimonies, i.e. the former Japanese officers, were no longer colonizers, and, in the new relation, many of them expressed their gratitude to the Takasago volunteers for saving their lives during the war. The Giyutai members had been their benefactors. They were unreserved in their praises for the Takasago's exemplification of *Yamatodamashi*, and acknowledged their indebtedness to them in a *giri* relationship. For their part, the Giyutai members strongly emphasized the *Yamatodamashi* that they possessed, and wanted this to be recognized by their former colonizers. Such a recognition would not only give them a status equal to that of the Japanese but also point to the fact that Japanese officers had failed to live up to the spirit of *Yamatodamashi*. In short, only they had truthfully and fully carried out the demands of *Yamatodamashi*, and therefore they had "out-Japanesed the Japanese." To maintain that they have surpassed the Japanese was a way of negating all the discrimination and mistreatment that they had suffered under Japanese colonialism.

If such endeavors of decolonization had occurred during the colonial period, then they would seem to be akin to what Homi Bhabha refers to as "mimicry" and would act as a "camouflage" threatening the colonizer (Bhabha 1994: 85–101). In the case discussed in this chapter, however, this is not valid. The "Japanese spirit" of the Takasago was deliberately inculcated during the colonial period; it was not mimicry by the Takasago. Furthermore, the so-called "Japanese spirit" was an ideal to the Japanese themselves and was only promoted during the war; it was not something that Japanese were born with. Therefore, in the minds of the Takasago, with their dedication to, and sacrifice for, the nation and the Emperor, their claims of having "Japanese spirit" were testimonies to the battlefield weakness of the Japanese officers and proof of their own superiority.

In his study of colonialism in South America, Michael Taussig (1993) proposes that mimesis is one way of coming to know the Other. In the context of complex inter-reflections, he discerns the phenomena of mutual mimesis between colonizer and colonized. The case of the Takasago-Giyutai was different from what happened in South America, for the intensive interactions between it and Japan only occurred over a very brief time span as a result of military mobilization; they were not the consequences of long-term colonization. The study of all means of decolonization in the postcolonial period must, therefore, pay attention to the effects produced by local social contexts and historical circumstances (Barker *et al.* 1994).

What makes the postcolonial situation in Taiwan unique, I maintain, is the fact that when Taiwan was released from Japanese colonial rule after World War II it was immediately put under another foreign power and engulfed by a new alien culture. As a consequence, what we see in the postcolonial situation in Taiwan today has been the result of dual colonialism. So far as the colonized were concerned, it was not simply that they had been dominated or assimilated; rather, they were put in a position whereby they could compare the two sets of former colonizers, and then make their judgment and choice. As Artul Rava from the Tayal tribe and Iyon Habao from the Bunun both mentioned, because of the hostility from Chiang Kai-Shek's postwar regime, their past as volunteers in the Japanese army had to be kept a secret. During the martial law era in Taiwan, the mass media were forbidden to use Japanese or broadcast Japanese songs. It was only after 1987, when martial law was lifted, that Japanese programs were again received in households through satellites. The writers of the texts analyzed in this chapter were often surprised that members of the Takasago-Giyutai had been familiarizing themselves with contemporary Japan through satellite television (Tsuchibashi 1994: 346). In the case of Zakara, an Amis Giyutai volunteer, his house was furnished with a big Japanese-made television set, and his shelves were stocked with a set of videotapes with military songs and many other tapes by the popular singers Saburo Kitajima and Hibari Misora. As he explained to the visiting Hayashi:

> I am nostalgic for the Japanese era. I don't understand Chinese on the TV anyway. I studied in public school during my childhood; the teachers taught me a lot of things about Japan. Up to now I have always regarded myself as a Japanese. I wish Taiwan could revert to what it was before the war, so that we could be together with the Japanese again. I always think this way."
>
> (Hayashi 1998: 154)

On another occasion, Hayashi was told in a very serious manner that "compared to Chiang Kai-Shek's Kuomintang regime, the government of the Japanese era was a bit better." Hayashi was quite shocked by this (Hayashi 1998: 165).

What the cited testimonies indicate is that the Takasago compared the two foreign regimes that they had encountered and expressed a preference for the former regime. This may be due a nostalgic impulse, or the tendency for memories to acquire a positive glow in proportion to their distance from the present day. In any event, we have yet to consider the sufferings the Takasago endured after the war. Since these are not a major part of the text writers' concern, however, they are not presented in the texts. The important point is that, after the departure of their former oppressors, the Takasago did not retaliate against the Japanese, or choose to assert their own ethnic identities as a form of resistance against the new rulers who came after the Japanese. Instead, they elected to retain their previous Japanese identities, which they had attained through tremendous efforts, even though they had to keep their preferences to themselves until they were free to speak their minds some 40 years later.

Conclusion: the reality and illusion of the *Yamatodamashi*

In 1992 Tetsuo Watanabe, a former Japanese Marine Corps physician who was rescued by the Takasago-Giyutai on the battlefield, paid a visit to an Amis tribe to offer gratitude to his saviors. Unexpectedly, he was met by a grand reception party of about thirty people. The assembled tribesmen sang popular Japanese wartime tunes such as the "Patriotic marching song" and the "Rabaul serenade" and engaged in reminiscences about the past. These songs had long been obscure in postwar Japan. When they were saying good-bye to Watanabe at the airport, they told the former officer: "We have sacrificed our lives for Japan. Our children tell us the time has changed. But we still like Japan today, with *Yamatodamashi* burning in our hearts. Please don't ever forget us Takasago." On hearing this, Watanabe was speechless and could only respond with a deep bow. Speaking of the Amis village, he lamented that "the Japan which no longer exists in Japan is alive here" (Kadowaki 1994: 182–90). Such feelings, like Kadowaki's assertion that he found a source of Japanese soul in the mountains of Taiwan, were immersed in nostalgia for the colonial era. Because of Japan's defeat, the ideal of *Yamatodamashi* or "Japanese spirit" to which they had aspired during the war was regarded as an obsolete product of militarism. Thus the reencounter with their past among the Takasago was wholly unexpected.

Perhaps this is what makes the Japanese feel that the Takasago are "pro-Japan." After all, the latter are no less nostalgic for the past. As indicated in my analysis, however, the Takasago's pro-Japanese sentiment has been engendered by a complicated postwar process of decolonization and is not as simple or as naive as some Japanese believe.

In the accounts of the interactions among the Takasago-Giyutai members, the former Japanese officers, and the visiting writers from Japan, the term *Yamatodamashi* plays a key role. Its invocation opens a passage to the past, helping the Japanese officers and the Giyutai to find each other. *Yamatodamashi* is also something like a chain to link all parties concerned together. But there is a significant difference here: for the former Japanese officers *Yamatodamashi* has only been an illusion pursued but never attained in the war, while for the Giyutai members it has been something real that they have achieved through great personal effort.

This sense of reality may have been consonant with the youth or warrior culture of the Takasago, so that they would mingle the two together during the war. Among the Tayal, for instance, a youth who pretended not to know that his tribe was going to war would be ridiculed as not being a man (Ozawa 1942). In other tribal traditions, the emphases on obedience to authority, service to the public, tribal security, and self-sacrifice even to the point of giving up one's life were all compatible with the tenets of the *Yamatodamashi*. The spirit to persevere and survive under adverse circumstances, furthermore, was cultivated among the Takasago in their mountainous habitats, and in many tribes youths were required to pass an endurance test as an initiation rite. As a result, they could easily assimilate the *Yamatodamashi* and put it into practice.

On the other hand, the Japanese officers felt gratitude toward the Takasago, and indebted to them in a *giri* relationship. We may recall here Ruth Benedict's (1989 [1946]: 133) succinct statement that " '*giri*,' runs the Japanese saying, is 'hardest to bear.' " This sense of indebtedness drove Japanese officers to make almost religious confessions, and the authors of the books analyzed here all carried the albatross of collective debt, trying to make some kind of redress with the writing of their books. Even though Benedict's analysis has been criticized as deficient in many respects (Aoki 1990: 30–63), I would not agree with the criticism that her perspective is ahistorical, for Benedict is referring to a Japanese people swept up by the tide of militarism. Maurice Pinguet (1986: 286–302) has carried out an exhaustive analysis of these traditions of Bushido spirit and self-sacrifice. In his view, after the schools were mobilized, and people were required to recite *Gunjinchokuyu* and *Kyoikuchokugo* every day, cultural themes that in the Edo era had only prevailed among certain social elite were now inculcated in every citizen. The Takasago youths who volunteered in the Giyutai were trained in the same sort of schools and army and the impact was distinct and deep.

At the same time, because such inculcation of Japanese spirit was also carried out in Japan's other colonies, it is worth asking why the colonial subjects in those areas were not so driven to make sacrifices in Japan's war efforts. For instance, the Korean and Han Chinese soldiers in the South Pacific theater of war were quite lackluster in their performance compared with the Takasago. They demonstrated a passive and desultory resistance.[10]

Perhaps because the Takasago did not have a state organization and had no concept of the modern nation-state, when they first came into contact with the state apparatus under Japanese colonial rule they were quickly dragged into an international war. This also partly explains why the Takasago tended to confuse national warfare with traditional tribal conflict.

Participation in the war and change in postwar political conditions had a great impact on the Takasago's self-identity. Joining the military transformed their status from that of the ruled to that of equality with the ruler. Once this status was achieved, their self-identity would not suffer subsequent diminution. But after the war they had difficulty understanding why they had suddenly been deprived of their nationality and had to submit to the sovereignty of others. The rules of international politics were beyond their comprehension. More than that, they were disappointed with their treatment at the hands of the Japanese government. Those, such as T. Pukiringan or I. Habao, who attained high ranks in the military hierarchy were especially severe in their criticism of the Japanese government. They were not only unhappy with its total neglect of them after the war but were also especially disappointed when they were denied the annuities and compensation given to Japanese soldiers because they were not of "Japanese nationality." They were also indignant at the Japanese government's delay in repaying their wartime salaries. Therefore they felt abandoned, and were overcome by a sense of purposelessness and sorrow. They had devoted their lives to practicing *Yamatodamashi*, but their self-claimed "Japanese" identities, because of the postwar international political rearrangement, turned out to be as illusory as a mirage.

In discussions on Japanese cultural discourse, or *Nihonbunkaron*, the question of how to define "Japaneseness" has frequently been raised. It is apparent that the Japanese government's definition of *Japanese* has disappointed members of the Takasago-Giyutai. In his study of Japanese cultural discourse, Harumi Befu (1997 [1987]) examines the definition of the Japanese within the framework of the nation-state. According to the result of his questionnaire survey conducted in Japan, the largest percentage of the people (49 percent) maintain that the necessary condition for being Japanese is to possess "Japanese nationality." Following in importance are "speaking Japanese" (37 percent), "having a Japanese name" (26 percent), "having Japanese parents" (25 percent), and so on. Obviously, the first viewpoint, which is quite political in nature, is very akin to the position of the postwar Japanese government. But the Takasago fulfill some of the other criteria. It was only because of the failure to meet one condition in the framework of the nation-state that the Takasago were denied what they deserved.

Befu worried about the result of the survey. Political considerations put limits on what could be included in the cultural sense. He was also surprised by the fact that, to the question "Are the Japanese a unique people?" 49 percent of the Japanese respondents answered in the affirmative. Related to this is the fact that all researches on *Nihonbunkaron* tend to emphasize the uniqueness of Japan instead of the commonalties (Befu 1997 [1987]: 253–74), whereas empirical studies indicate that the supposed uniqueness is far from being confirmed (Sugimoto and Mouer 1992 [1982]: 83–103).

In conclusion, the case of the Takasago-Giyutai provides a different way of thinking about the issue of Japanese identity, one which troubles the simplistic binary of Japanese uniqueness and commonality. Properly contextualized with reference to history and geopolitics, the Takasago-Giyutai demonstrate how Japanese culture and the Japanese spirit could be shared, and even exemplified, by an Other.

Notes

1 Within the Austronesians, nine tribes are categorized by the Japanese colonial government. These are Amis, Tayal, Paiwan, Bunun, Tsou, Puyuma, Rukai, Saisyat, and Yami groups. Within the Han group, however, a distinction with regard to

the time of immigration must be made between the "mainlanders," who came after the war, and the "natives" – the majority of the Han population – who began to migrate to Taiwan about 400 years ago and thus lived for 50 years under Japanese colonial rule. The former were citizens of a nation at war with Japan and the latter were Japan's colonial subjects, and their respective attitudes toward Japan were consequently quite different.

2 Almost all Japanese anthropologists who have conducted fieldwork among the Austronesians of Taiwan have had the same impression, and I (using Japanese as my fieldwork language) can personally attest to this.

3 According to the statistics contained in "Takasago: Education" (published in 1944 by the Police Commission of the Taiwan Colonial Government), the average enrollment rates among the Takasago for the 5 years from 1938 through 1942 all exceed 80 percent; the rate of 1943 is even as high as 87.7 percent.

4 The numbers and dates of dispatch were military secrets at the time, and are still difficult to ascertain today. According to Kadowaki's (1994: 14) tabulations, the total number of volunteers comes to about 5,000. There are, however, some discrepancies between different sources. For example, Kadowaki puts the number of the second volunteer corps at 100, whereas Hayashi's (1998: 140) informants attested that the number was 1,000 – among these men only fifty-seven returned alive. Again, Kadowaki estimates the number of the Third Corps to be 618, whereas I myself have been told by a survivor that 1,200 men were dispatched in that group. Kadowaki adds that they were later sent to various locations, so that they returned to Taiwan at different times. Thus the number of those who returned alive is impossible to know. As for the Sixth Corps, Kadowaki doesn't have any data, but according to one member interviewed by Hayashi (1998: 256) it consisted of 800 men. From all this, I would estimate the total number of the Giyutai to be at least 8,000. With regard to the survivors, their number may be calculated in accordance with the survival rate of the whole Japanese army engaged in eastern New Guinea, in which only 11,000 out of a total of 160,000 survived the war.

5 Strangely, they were thus designated as Han, although in fact they were Austronesians.

6 First to appear was *The Life of Suniyon* by the novelist Sato Aiko, who reconstructed her subject's life through interviews with Suniyon's relatives and other residents in his village. Since this book does not include verbatim statements from Suniyon, it will not be used in my textual analysis.

7 He was referring to the aftermath of the Mushya incident of 1930, which was the largest Takasago insurrection during the colonial period. Walis Piho was a descendent of an executed rebel.

8 Two of them kept notes (Kadowaki 1994: 110–12) and some wrote diaries during the war, but these were confiscated at the postwar camps. They are now unable to remember the details (Ishibashi 1992: 278).

9 Said by Talpan Pukiringan, see Hayashi (1998: 229).

10 In his book, Hayashi mentions a Korean volunteer by the name of Kim. His testimony is relevant here:

> I was astonished by their discipline, for they would carry out their missions without taking any food themselves, and upon arriving at the destination they would collapse from exhaustion. If it had been us, we would have eaten the provisions ourselves. There was no need to practice *giri* to the Japanese Army; it would be such a stupid thing. But those Giyutai members were so upright in all circumstances. They gave up their lives for Japan. As for us Korean volunteers, we would take our own survival as the first priority.

They didn't hesitate in making sacrifices. In the battles of New Guinea, they were the only real winners.

(Hayashi 1994: 4)

Bibliography

Aoki, T. (1990) *Nihonbunkaron no Henyo (Transformation of the Discourse on Japanese Culture)*, Tokyo: Chyuokoronsha.

Barker, F., Hulme, P., and Iverson, M. (eds) (1994) *Colonial Discourse/Postcolonial Theory*, Manchester: Manchester University Press.

Befu, H. (1997 [1987]) *Ideorogi toshite no Nihonbunkaron (The Discourse on Japanese Culture as an Ideology)*, Tokyo: Shisonokagakusha.

Benedict, R. (1989 [1946]) *The Chrysanthemum and the Sword*, Boston: Houghton Mifflin.

Bhabha, K.H. (1994) *The Location of Culture*, London: Routledge.

Chen, C.-c. (1984) "Police and community control systems in the empire," in R. H. Myers and M. R. Peattie (eds) *The Japanese Colonial Empire, 1895–1945*, Princeton, NJ: Princeton University Press.

Daiyamondo Sha (1997) *Chikyu no Arukikata: Taiwan (Ways Around the World: Taiwan)*, Tokyo: Daiyamondosha.

Davis, Z.N. (1987) *Fiction in the Archives*, Stanford, CA: Stanford University Press.

Fanon, F. (1967 [1952]) *Black Skin, White Masks*, New York: Grove Press.

Gann, H.L. (1984) "Western and Japanese colonialism: some preliminary comparisons," in R. H. Myers and M. R. Peattie (eds) *The Japanese Colonial Empire, 1895–1945*, Princeton, NJ: Princeton University Press.

Goody, J. (1987) *The Interface Between the Written and the Oral*, Cambridge: Cambridge University Press.

Grele, J.R. (1991) *Envelopes of Sound: The Art of Oral History*, New York: Praeger.

Hall, S. (1995) "Negotiating Caribbean identities," *New Left Review* 209: 3–14.

Hallbwachs, M. (1992 [1952]) *On Collective Memory* (L. Coser, ed. and trans.), Chicago: University of Chicago Press.

Hayashi, E. (1994) *Taiwan Daigokai Takasago-Giyutai: Meibo, Gunjichokin, Nihonjinshogen (The Fifth Takasago-Giyutai of Taiwan: Name Rosters, Military Savings Accounts, and Testimonies by Japanese)*, Kitakyushu: Bunei Shuppansha.

—— (1998) *Shogen: Takasago-Giyutai (Testimonies: Takasago Volunteers)*, Tokyo: Sofukan.

Ishibashi, T. (1992) *Kyushokuminchi no Otoshiko: Taiwan "Takasago-Giyuhei" wa-ima (Illegitimate Sons of the Old Colony: Soldiers of the Takasago-Giyutai Today)*, Tokyo: Soshisha.

Jusdanis, G. (1995) "Beyond national culture?" *Boundary2* 22: 23–60.

Kadowaki, C. (ed.) (1994) *Taiwantakasago-Giyutai: Sonokokoroniwa Imamonao (The Takasago-Giyutai of Taiwan: The Spirit Never Dies)*, Tokyo: Akebonokai.

Kato, K. (1979) *Isshidonin no Hate: Taiwan moto Gunzoku no Kyogu (The Upshot of Equal Treatment: The Circumstances of Auxiliary Troops from Taiwan)*, Tokyo: Keisoshobo.

Komagome, T. (1996) *Shokuminchiteikoku Nippon no Bunkatogo (Cultural Consolidation in the Colonies of Japanese Empire)*, Tokyo: Iwanami Shoten.

Kondo, M. (1996) *Soryokusen to Taiwan: Nihonchokuminchi Hokai no Kenkyu (Total War and Taiwan: A Study of the Collapse of a Japanese Colony)*, Tokyo: Tousui Shobo.

Kozakai, T. (1996) *Ibunkajyuyou no Paradokusu (The Paradox of the Acquisition of Foreign Cultures)*, Tokyo: Asahi Shinbun.

Murakami, H. (1995) "Nihonjinwa Senso o Taiken Shinakatta" (The Japanese had no experience of the war), in Shinjinbutsuoraisha Senshishitsu (ed.) *Nihongun Haiboku no Honshitsu (The Crucial Factor in the Defeat of the Japanese Army)*, Tokyo: Shinjinbutsuoraisha.

Nandy, A. (1983) *The Intimate Enemy: Loss and Recovery of Self Under Colonialism*, Delhi: Oxford University Press.

Noda, M. (1998) *Senso to Zaiseki (War and Guilt)*, Tokyo: Iwanamishoten.

Ogbu, U.J. (1987) "Opportunity structure, cultural boundaries, and literacy," in J. A. Langer (ed.) *Language, Literacy, and Culture: Issues of Society and Schooling*, Norwood, NJ: Ablex.

Oguma, E. (1995) *The Myth of the Homogeneous Nation*, Tokyo: Shinyoshya.

Ozawa, T. (1942) "Danshi no Kokoro" (Man's heart), *Riban no Tomo* 125: 5.

Peattie, R.M. (1996) *Shokuminchi: Teikoku Gojunen no Kobo (The Colonies: The Rise and Fall of the Fifty-year Empire)*, Tokyo: Yomiurishibunsha.

Pinguet, M. (1986) *Jishi no Nihonshi* [Japanese translation of *La Mort Volontaire au Japan* (Paris: Gallimard, 1984)], Tokyo: Chikumashobo.

Sato, A. (1987) *Suniyon no Issho (The Life of Suniyon)*, Tokyo: Bungeishunjusha.

Shiba, R. (1994) *Taiwan Kiko (My Journey in Taiwan)*, Tokyo: Asahi Shinbun.

Sugimoto, Y., and Mouer, R. (1992 [1982]) *Nihonjinwa Nihontekika (Are Japanese People Japanese Enough?)*, Tokyo: Toyokeizaishinposhya.

Taussig, M. (1992) "Culture of terror – space of death: Roger Casement's Putumayo Report and the explanation of torture," in N. B. Dirks (ed.) *Colonialism and Culture*, Ann Arbor: University of Michigan Press.

—— (1993) *Mimesis and Alterity: A Particular History of the Senses*, New York: Routledge.

Tsuchibashi, K. (1994) *Chyuretsubatsugun Taiwan Takasago-Giyuhei no funsen (Loyalty Unsurpassed: Soldiers of the Takasago-Giyutai of Taiwan)*, Tokyo: Senshikankokai.

Tsurumi, E.P. (1984) "Colonial education in Korea and Taiwan," in R. H. Myers and M. R. Peattie (eds) *The Japanese Colonial Empire, 1895–1945*, Princeton, NJ: Princeton University Press.

Turner, V. (1985 [1969]) *The Ritual Process*, Ithaca, NY: Cornell University Press.

Index

aging society in Japan 177–8
Akiko, Wada 204
All Japan Judo Federation 84, 87
America, Japanese contemporary
  photography in *see* photography
anthropological perspective, Japan
  outside Japan 26–7
anthropological unwieldiness,
  multinational corporations 43
Appadurai, Arjun 3, 126–7, 167, 183
Arakawa, Rika 129
Araki, Nobuyoshi 143
Artforum 141
artistic interpretation, globalization
  and 131–3
artists, independence of 111–12
Asahi Shinbun 163
Asian Development Bank 44
Asian financial crisis 202
asymmetrical core–periphery
  relationship, Soka Gakkai in
  Germany 98
ATV, Hong Kong 159
Augé, Marc 38
Aum Shinrikyo 14
Austria, Judo cultures in *see* Judo
  cultures
Austrian (Amateur) Judo Federation
  [A(A)JF] 77, 82, 84, 85, 87
Austronesians of Taiwan 222–3, 224,
  236–40, 242–5
authenticity: protection of 219–220;
  Soka Gakkai in Germany 104–5
auxiliary positions of female workers 54

backlash against Japanese pop 124–5
Bälz, Erwin 88
band boom 122
battlefield status reversal 240–2

Bauer, Karl 72
Beijing perspective on Diaoyu/Senkaku
  Islands dispute 163–4
Benedict, Ruth 246
Beyer, Peter 3
bonsai 209
Bourdieu, Pierre 71–2
British disease 180
Buddhism 14
Budokan, Vienna 70–1
business expatriates, rotational
  communities 12
business strategies, supermarkets vs.
  department stores 54–5

Callahan, Harry 137
Candy, Candy 118
Canto-pop 123, 125, 128–9
capitalism 168–70, 171
categorical interrelationships in
  Japanese expatriate diffusion 18–19
center–periphery concept in Japanese
  expatriate diffusion 19–20
central nature of Hong Kong pop 122
Chage and Aska 125
Chan, David 155, 156, 161, 163
change and tradition in Judo cultures
  83–5
chanoyu (for tea ceremonial) 209, 211,
  214, 217–18
China/Tiawan, mutual antipathy 162
Chinese activism, Diaoyu/Senkaku
  Islands 160–2
Chinese University of Hong Kong 159
Chineseness and Diaoyu/Senkaku
  Islands dispute 156, 164–5
Chosun Ilbo 202
The Chrysanthemum and the Sword
  (Benedict, R.) 27

Chung wah ying hung (Chinese Heroes)
117
Cinémathèque, Paris 212
City Hunter 116
Clark, Rodney 184
clothes, the issue of dress 99
Comfort Women 202–3
*Comic Books, The Report on the Campaign
against Violence and Pornography of* 115
comics, Japanese in Hong Kong: artists,
independence of 111–12; comics in
Japan 111–13; competition 117–18;
content of 112–13; distribution/
marketing 119; harmful to children,
regarded as 115; implications for
globalization theories 120;
importation 116, 119; legal
constraints on 115–16; originality of
112; popularity of everything
Japanese 116; *shojo* comics 118;
social status 113–14, 119; translation
116–17; Wong, Yuk Long 113–15,
116–17; work-related comics 112–13
community support in Japanese welfare
179–81
compensation claims, Taiwanese
Takasago-Giyutai members 237
competition in comics, Japanese in
Hong Kong 117–18
concentrations of multinational
corporations 5
conflict and politics, Judo cultures 80
Confucianism 182, 195
consumer products, industrially
produced 13
conventional emigration 6
corporate circumstances, personal
orientation at Yaohan 52–3
corporate culture 46–7
corporate direction in personal matters
64–5
corporate reproduction, cycles of
activity and 47
cosmopolitanism in Hong Kong 166–7
Cotter, Holland 135
cover versions, popular music, Japanese
in Hong Kong 122, 124, 125
Crawcour, Sydney 184
cross-cultural work forms,
multinational corporations 47–8
cultural associations, bridging nature of
211–12
cultural brokerage: martial arts and 69;

Soka Gakkai in Germany 94–5, 104–
5
cultural calendars, information source
210
cultural capital, exploitation of 9–10
cultural definition, Soka Gakkai in
Germany 97–100
cultural diffusion, Japan outside Japan
13–15
cultural disjuncture, Korea and identity
201
cultural mishmash of Hong Kong pop
128–9
cultural model, Japanese female
workers 53–4
cultural representations, Judo cultures
70
cultural shaping 165–7

Daiei 55
Daimaru 55
decentralization aims, Soka Gakkai in
Germany 100–1
demographically negligible, Japanese in
France 31–2
department stores, business strategies
of 54–5
deregulation of Japanese pop culture
203
designation of Japanese cultural
properties 219–20
destabilization, factors tending towards
198–200
development, Judo in Austria 73–6, 81
Diaoyu/Senkaku Islands, protests in
Hong Kong regarding: Beijing
perspective on 163–4; capitalism
168–70, 171; China/Taiwan, mutual
antipathy 162; Chinese activism
160–2; Chineseness 156, 164–5;
cosmopolitanism 166–7; cultural
shaping 165–7; discourse 167–70;
guidebook contents 156; historical
conditioning 170–1; history of
dispute 153–6; Japan as scapegoat
164; Japanese nationalism 168–70;
Japanese residents in midst of 158–
60; Japanese tourists affected by
156–8; metacultural aspect 167;
miscomprehensions of disputants
167; motivational complexity 162–5;
nationalism as world discourse 168–
70; press coverage 154–5, 159, 160–

1, 163; social position and mutual
incomprehension 165; sovereignty
issue 153; World War II 154, 156,
163, 166, 171
discontent, emigration through 6–7
discourse in Diaoyu/Senkaku Islands
dispute 167–70
discrimination: in France 32, 33; in
multinational corporations 11
distribution of comics, Japanese in
Hong Kong 119
Diwischek, Josef 72–3
Domon, Ken 143
Doraemon 118
dormitory life, Yaohan workers 62–3
Dragon Publishing Company 116
Dschiu-Dschitsu-Film 74

East Asian welfare model 176–7, 186
ecological concerns and Soka Gakkai in
Germany 97
educational system 181–2
elsewhere and here, uncertain nature
of 28
emigration: conventional 6; discontent
and 6–7; policies and expatriate
religion 94
employment system, Japanese 183–5
engagement with Japanese
circumstances 143–4
Enyeart, James 138
ephemera, cultural production of *see*
French perspectives
epistemological preamble, Japanese
invisibility in France 25–6
equality: female workers seeking
outside Japan 58; in relationships
145
ethnic boundaries, Japanese invisibility
in France 36–8
ethnic composition of Taiwan 222–3
ethnic group, notion of 25
ethnocentrism 3–4
ethnographic basis of globalization
theory 4
European dimension in Judo cultures
81, 84–6
everyday life and comics in Hong Kong
115–16
evolution of modern societies 27–8
expansion by self-selection 96–7
expatriates: communities of 11–12;
diffusion, complex nature of 18–19;

Japanese, imaginings of Japan 15–
16; permanent 12; "un-returnees", 8

family welfare provision 185
Featherstone, Mike 132, 143, 144–5
Feik, Alois 75–6
Felsinger, Edith 72
female perspectives, Japanese
businesswomen of Yaohan: auxiliary
positions of female workers 54;
business strategies, supermarkets vs
department stores 54–5; corporate
circumstances, personal orientation
and 52–3; corporate direction in
personal matters 64–5; cultural
model, Japanese female workers 53–
4; dormitory life 62–3; equality,
seeking outside Japan 58; Hong
Kong, Yaohan's arrival in 56–7;
housing allowances 60; Japanese
communities abroad, orientation of
52; Japanese ethnoscape,
implications for 66–7; *kaigai
shukkosha* (overseas transferees) 58,
59–60; marginal nature of Yaohan
55–6; marginality, company and
worker 53; overseas transfers 58, 59–
60, 60–6; personal relationships,
conflict in 63–4; responses to
transfers overseas 60–6; risk
avoidance 61; society of industry,
corporate positioning within 53;
staff recruitment strategy at Yaohan
57–9; strategic maneuvers 61–6;
subordination, strategizing 66–7;
supermarkets, differences from
department stores 54–5; *tsukiai*
(obligatory socializing) 61; Yaohan
as regional supermarket 55–6
Ferguson, James 137
Festival of the Four Seasons 212–13
*The Fifth Takasago-Giyutai of Tiawan:
Military Savings Accounts, and
Testimonies by Japanese* (Hayashi, E.)
225–6
film, French perspectives on Japan 212
flower arrangement *see* ikebana
foreign communities, imaginings of
Japan 16–18
framework for studies of migrant
populations 25–6
France, image as migratory influence
30

France, Japanese invisibility in: anthropological perspective, Japan outside Japan 26–7; demographically negligible numbers 31–2; discrimination 32, 33; elsewhere and here, uncertain nature of 28; epistemological preamble 25–6; ethnic boundaries 36–8; ethnic group, notion of 25; evolution of modern societies 27–8; framework for studies of migrant populations 25–6; France as social model 29–30; French attitudes towards Japanese 32–3; French perceptions of Japanese 32; identity, multiple nature of 28; image of France, migratory influence 30; individual nature of Japanese migration to France 30–2; integration 26; Japanese identity, multiple nature of 28; Japanese migration in France, characteristics of 29–38; macrosocial conditions 29, 32–33; managerial migrants 35–6; microsocial dimension 34; migration, phenomenon of 26, 29–30; nipponity 25–6; objects of Japanese production, visibility of 34–5; otherness 36–7; participation 30–1; perspectives on Japan 25–8; temporary nature of Japanese migration to France 30–2; thema of Japanese in France, summary of 37–8; wandering and commitment 36–8

France, social model 29–30

Freeman Publishing Company Limited 117, 118

French attitudes towards Japanese 32–3

French perceptions of Japanese 32

French perspectives on Japan: bonsai 209; *chanoyu* (for tea ceremonial) 209, 211, 214, 217–18; cultural associations, bridging nature of 211–12; cultural calendars, information source 210; designation of Japanese cultural properties 219–20; ephemeral nature of introduced Japanese culture 216–20; Festival of the Four Seasons 212–13; film 212; *Haru-hime dôchû* 212; ikebana 209–10, 214; international relations 214–16; Japanese Days/Weeks 210–14; Japanese participation in events 212;

large-scale events 212–13; *Matsuri*, outside Japan 213–14, 219–20; non-Japanese participation in events 211–12; organized events 210–13; origami 209, 214; Paris as main field of study 210; protection of Japanese authenticity 219–20; Shinto 212–13; sister cities 214–16; traditional handicrafts representative of Japanese culture 209–10; White Books 219; Year of Japan in France 210–14

Friedlander, Lee 145

Fukase, Masahisa 136

G-7 nations 44

Gabriel, Edmund 73–4, 75

Geesink, Anton 84

generalization, globalization theory and 4

German: attitudes to foreign residents 102–3; culture, adaptation to 96, 105; perspectives on development of 95–7; religious communities 101

Germany, Soka Gakkai in *see* Soka Gakkai

global context *see* Japan outside Japan

global cultural flows, "scapes" of 48–9, 126–7

global culture, importation of pop music 126–7

global interactions of multinational corporations 43

globalization: freedom in defining 48–9; as governing ideology in Korea 198; inconsistencies, rhetoric and fact in 47–8; internationalization and 44–5, 49, 50; *see also* implications for globalization theories

Globalization of Japan: Cosmopolitanization or Spread of the Japanese Village? (Befu, H. and Stalker, N.) 52

Goffman, Erving 47

Gold Plans 178

Goldin, Ned 137

Gould, Arthur 183

grading in Judo cultures 78–9

Green Movement and Soka Gakkai in Germany 97

growth of Soka Gakkai in Germany 95–6

guidebook contents, Hong Kong 156

Gupta, Akhil 137

Han people of Taiwan 222
Hannerz, Ulf 37, 127, 167
harmful comics, Japanese in Hong
Kong 115
*For Harmony and Strength: Japanese White-
Collar Organization in Anthropological
Perspective* (Rohlen, T.P.) 54
Haru-hime dôchû 212
"health miracle" in Japan 178
Heavy Athletics 76
here and elsewhere, uncertain nature
of 28
Hiroshi, Izuki 204
historical conditioning, Diaoyu/
Senkaku Islands dispute 170–1
historical context, multinational
expansion 10
historical perspectives, Taiwanese
Takasago-Giyutai 236–8
history of: comics in Hong Kong 113–
15; Diaoyu/Senkaku Islands dispute
153–6; pop music in Hong Kong
121–5, 126
Hong Kong: globalization of pop history
126–9; Japanese comics coming to *see*
comics; Japanese pop music in *see*
popular music; Japanese residents
during Diaoyu/Senkaku Islands
dispute 158–60; Japanese tourists
during Diaoyu/Senkaku Islands
dispute 156–8; roots of pop in 121;
Yaohan in *see* female perspective
Hong Kong Post 158, 159, 162
Honkon/Macau 158
Hori Production 129
housing allowances, Yaohan workers 60
Howell, David 176
Hugo Boss Awards 142
Hui, Samuel 123
human dispersal 5–9
Huntington, Samuel 144
Hyashi, Eidai 225–6, 239, 242–3, 244
hybrid nature of Korean cultural
identity 200–1
hybridization: of Hong Kong pop 128–9;
of popular culture 13

Ibuka, Masaru 57
identity, multiple nature of 28
ideological understanding, Soka Gakkai
in Germany 98–9
ikebana 209–10, 214
Ikebana International 217
Ikeda, Daisaku 95, 104

*Illegitimate Sons of the Old Colony: Soldiers
of the Takasago-Giyutai Today*
(Ishibashi, T.) 225
Illich, Ivan 181
illusion of *Yamatodamashi* for Japanese
245–7
image construction through
globalization 128
imagining Japan, selective memory and
15–18
Imperial soldier, return of last 223–5
implications for globalization theories
120; art photography and 145–7;
comics, Japanese in Hong Kong 120;
female workers and the Japanese
ethnoscape 66–7; generalization 4;
multinational corporations 49–50;
popular music, Japanese in Hong
Kong 126–9
importation of comics, Japanese in
Hong Kong 116, 119
indeterminate emigration, Japan
outside Japan 8–9
indigenization, Soka Gakkai in
Germany 96
individual nature of Japanese migration
to France 30–2
individuality of photography, Japanese
contemporary in America 132–3
industrial system, Japanese 181–2, 183–
5
industry restructuring 117–18
innovations, predominant in Judo
cultures 82–3
*Inside/Out Contemporary Japanese
Photography* 132
integration, Japanese in France 26
International Judo Federation (IJF) 78–
80, 82–8
international marriage 7
International Monetary Fund 44
International Museum of Photography
138
International Olympic Committee
(IOC) 69, 87
international relations 214–16
International Relations, Council of
Local Authorities for (CLAIR) 215
internationalization (*kokusaika*) 58, 142,
163
Ishibashi, Takashi 225, 238–9
Ishihara, Etsuro 140
Ishimoto, Yasuhiro 137, 143
Ito-Yokado 55

Japan: French perspectives on 25–8; and Korea, reversely opening up 204; modernization model 195; object of hatred 195; relative wealth of 44–5; scapegoat, Diaoyu/Senkaku Islands dispute 164; United Kingdom interest in 176–7, 183, 185–6
Japan as Number One: Lessons for Industrial America (Vogel, E.) 181
Japan Judo Federation 81
Japan Local Government Data Book (CLAIR) 215
Japan outside Japan, global context of: business expatriates, rotational communities 12; categorical interrelationships, complexity of Japanese expatriate diffusion 18–19; center–periphery concept in Japanese expatriate diffusion 19–20; consumer products, industrially produced 13; conventional emigration 6; cultural capital, exploitation of 9–10; cultural diffusion 13–15; discontent, emigration through 6–7; ethnocentrism 3–4; ethnographic basis of globalization theory 4; expatriate communities 11–12; expatriate diffusion, complex nature of 18–19; expatriate Japanese, imagining Japan 15–16; expatriate "un-returnees", 8; foreign communities, imagining Japan 16–18; generalization, globalization theory and 4; historical context, multinational expansion 10; hybridization of popular culture 13; imagining Japan, selective memory and 15–18; indeterminate emigration 8–9; international marriage 7; Japanese Americans 12; Judo cultures 86–8; Korea, relationship with 16–17; local hires by multinationals 10–11; martial arts 14; multinational corporations 10–11; nonpermanent human dispersal 5–6; opportunities, searching abroad for 7; permanent expatriates 12; permanent human dispersal 6–9; popular culture 13; religion 14–15; tourists, "revolving door" expatriates 12; volunteer service 8

Japan Travel Bureau 157
Japan Youth Federation 154
Japanese: Americans 12; businesswomen *see* female perspectives; communities abroad, orientation of 52; community patterns 18–19; cultural properties, designation of 219–20; culture, negative images of 200; culture in Korea *see* Korea, cultural identity in; Days/Weeks in France 210–14; domination in Judo, interruption of 82; ethnoscape, implications for 66–7; expatriate diffusion, center–periphery concept in 19–20; expatriate diffusion, complexity of 18–19; female workers, cultural model 53–4; in France, thema of 37–8; in France, wandering and commitment 36–8; in Hong Kong during Diaoyu/Senkaku crisis *see* Diaoyu/Sankaku Islands; identity, multiple nature of 28; industrial commodities, consumption of 196; invisibility in France *see* France; language as cultural baggage 99; melodies, suited to Asian listeners 124; migration in France, characteristics of 29–38; migration to France, nature of 30–2; multinationals *see* multinational corporations; nationalism, Diaoyu/Senkaku Islands dispute 168–70; participation in French events 212; photography , beginnings 141–2; pop culture, deregulation of 203; pop culture, regulation in Korea 197–200; production, visibility of objects of 34–5; religion, diffusion of 14–15; studies, Judo as incentive 87–8; welfare state 176–87
Japanese Bosses, Chinese Workers: Power and Control in a Hong Kong Megastore (Wong, H.W.) 68
Japanese Language Education Center 196
Japanese-style: management 11, 45–8; welfare society 179–82
Japaneseness: Korea, cultural identity in 196–7; photography, Japanese contemporary in America 134–5, 138–40, 141, 142–3; Takasago-Giyutai 228–9, 235, 236, 239, 245–7; welfare state, images of Japan as 187

Japanization of British welfare system
183
Jirô, Sakamoto 180
Jodo Shinshu 14
Ju-jutsu as Practised in Japan, Textbook of
(Uenishi, S.) 72
Judo cultures: conflict and politics 80;
cultural representations 70; culture
brokers, martial arts as 69;
developments in Austria 73–6, 81;
grading 78–9; incentive to Japanese
studies 87–8; innovations,
predominant 82–3; Japan outside
Japan? 86–8; Japanese domination,
interruption of 82; jujitsu 72–3;
Kadokan 75, 76–7, 80, 81–2;
kadokan judo 75–6; martial arts,
proliferation of 69–70;
olympification 86–7; overseas
introduction of 72; power shift,
European dimension 81, 84–6; self-
colonization 76–81; subculture,
notion of 88; submissive attitudes
88; television, role of 82–3, 86–7;
territorialization 71–6; tournament
organization 79; tradition and
change 83–5; universalization 81–6;
Vienna Budokan 70–1
Judo (Jujutsu) (Kano, J.) 75
Jujitsu 72–3

Kadokan 75, 76–7, 80, 81–2
kadokan judo 69–70, 75–6, 78–9
Kadowaki, Choshyu 225, 239–40
kaigai shukkosha (overseas transferees)
58, 59–60
Kanazawa 214, 215–16
Kano, Jigoro 69–70, 72, 73–5, 76–7, 88
Kano, Risei 79, 88
Kano, Yukimitsu 84
Karaoke 13
Keiko, Matsuzaka 204
Kim Dae Jung, President-elect 202–3
Kim Young Sam, President 194, 198
Kinzley, Dean 184
Klimek, Otto 73–4
Köck, Hans 72, 76
Koizumi, Gunji 81
Kokufukuji, treasures of the 218
Kominka movement 224
Komuro, Tetsuya 129
Kondo, Masahiko 124
Korea, cultural identity in: Asian
financial crisis 202; Comfort Women

202–3; consumption of Japanese
industrial commodities 196; cultural
disjuncture 201; deregulation of
Japanese pop culture 203;
destabilization, factors tending
towards 198–200; globalization as
governing ideology 198; hybrid
nature of 200–1; import source
diversification policy 196; and Japan,
reversely opening up 204; Japan as
modernization model 195; Japan as
object of hatred 195; Japaneseness
196–7; Korean perceptions of Japan
195–7; Ministry of Culture and
Sports 194, 197, 198, 203; modernity
in Korea 201; negative images of
Japanese culture 200; policing (and
opening) national borders 194;
prevalence of Japanese culture 200–
1; regime shift 202; regulation of
Japanese pop culture 197–200; social
forces, resistant to spread of
Japanese culture 204; symbolic
boundaries 203; television imports
199–200; transnational dialogue
200–1
Korea, modernity in 201
Korea, relationship with 16–17
Korean Ministry of Culture and Sports
194, 197, 198, 203
Korean perceptions of Japan 195–7
Kowalsky, Heinz 72, 76
Kudara Kannon 218
Kuno Hako 146
Kuspit, Donald 141
Kyôchôkai (Harmonization Society) 184
Kyoto City University of Art 143

labor, traditional division of 99–100
Labour Party (UK) 185
large-scale complexity, multinational
corporations 43–4
large-scale events, French perspectives
on Japan 212–13
Lau, Ting-kin 117
Leach, Mark Richard 134–5
legal constraints on comics, Japanese in
Hong Kong 115–16
lifetime employees 184–5
local hires by multinationals 10–11
*Loyalty Unsurpassed: Soldiers of the
Takasago-Giyutai of Taiwan*
(Tsuchibashi, K.) 225

McCormack, Gavan 140
macroglobalization 45–6
macrosocial conditions, Japanese in France 29, 32–3
Maeda, Mitsuyo 72
major museums, photographic exhibitions in 132
managerial migrants, Japanese in France 35–6
managers, globalization of 45–9
manga 13
mapping of photography, Japanese contemporary in America 137
marginality, company and worker 53
marketing of comics, Japanese in Hong Kong 119
martial arts 14; *see also* Judo cultures
Matsumae, Shigeyoshi 70, 84–5, 87
Matsumae Budo Center (MBC) 70–1, 85
Matsuri, outside Japan 213–14, 219–20
media, negative attitudes of, Soka Gakkai in Germany 101–2
media, role in promotion of Japanese welfare 181
media-mixing 142–3
Meiji period 29, 144, 185, 218
metacultural aspect, Diaoyu/Senkaku Islands dispute 167
methodology, investigative structures 49, 50
Michael Shapiro Gallery 146
microglobalization 46–8
microsocial dimension, Japanese in France 34
migrant laborers (*gannen-mono*) 6
migration, phenomenon of 26, 29–30
Ming Pao 154, 155, 160–1
minority groups, German attitude towards 103
miscomprehensions, Diaoyu/Senkaku Islands dispute 167
missionaries 96
Mitsukoshi 55
Miyuki, Nakajima 125
modernity in Korea 201
modernization (*kindaika*) 58
Morimura, Yasumasa 132, 133, 141–4
Morita, Akio 57
Morotai, Island of 223–5, 237
motivational complexity, Diaoyu/Senkaku Islands dispute 162–5
Mulgan, Geoff 176
multinational corporations: anthropological unwieldiness of 43; concentrations of 5; coping with large-scale complexity 43–4; corporate culture 46–7; corporate reproduction, cycles of activity and 47; cross-cultural work forms 47–8; discrimination in 11; G-7 nations 44; global cultural flows, "scapes" of 48–9; global interactions of 43; globalization, freedom in defining 48–9; globalization vs internationalization 44–5, 49, 50; inconsistencies, rhetoric and fact in globalization 47–8; Japan, relative wealth of 44–5; Japan outside Japan, global context of 10–11; Japanese-style management 45–8; local hires by 10–11; macroglobalization 45–6; managers, globalization of 45–9; methodology, investigative structures 49, 50; microglobalization 46–8; organizational complexity of 43–4, 49–50; political economy of globalization 44–5; prejudice in 11
Munroe, Alexandra 144
Museum of Contemporary Art, Chicago 132, 141
Museum of Modern Art 132

Nakagawa, James Osamu 137
Nakamura, Akio 223–5
Nakamura, Yoshio 140
national borders, policing (and opening) 194
nationalism as world discourse 168–70
negative images of Japanese culture 200
Nemzeti Torna Egylet 76
New York Times 135
Nichiren Buddhism 95, 98, 104
Nihon Keizai Shinbun 55
Nihonbunkaron 247
Nihongata shakai fukushi 179–82
Nihonjinron (idealized Japan) 15–16, 18, 132, 137, 139, 140, 182, 186
Nikkei Ryutsu Shinbun 56
Nimführ, Franz 80
Nippon Hoso Kyokai (NHK) 195
nipponity 25–6
Nipponseishin (Japanese spirit) 222, 229
non-Japanese participation in French events 211–12
nonpermanent human dispersal 5–6

objects of Japanese production, visibility of 34–5
Occidentalism 182–3, 187
"The office: way station or blind alley?" (McLendon, J.) 54
Ohmae, Kenichi 168
Olympic Games, Tokyo 80
olympification of Judo 86–7
OPEC (Organization of Oil-Producing Countries) 44
opportunities, searching abroad for 7
organizational complexity of multinational corporations 43–4, 49–50
organizational transplant 10–12
organized events, French perspectives on Japan 210–13
Oriental Daily 155
Orientalism 132, 139, 140, 145, 186–7
origami 209, 214
originality of comics, Japanese in Hong Kong 112
Osamu, Tezuka 111, 119
oscillation between national and global 133–4, 135
otherness, Japanese in France 36–7
overseas introduction of Judo cultures 72
overseas subsidiaries, Japanese multinationals *see* multinational corporations
overseas transfers, female workers 58, 59–60

Paris as field of study, French perspectives on Japan 210
Park Chung Hee, President 197
participation, Japanese in France 30–1
Patten, Chris 176
perceptions of Japan among Hong Kong pop listeners 125–6
permanent expatriates 12
permanent human dispersal 6–9
personal relationships, conflict of 63–4
photography, Japanese (contemporary) in America: artistic interpretation, globalization and 131–3; commodities (or not) 131, 132–3; determination of 131; equality in relationships 145; individuality of 132–3; internationalization of Japanese photography 142; Japanese arrival of photography 141–2; Japanese circumstances,

engagement with 143–4; Japaneseness 134–5, 138–40, 141, 142–3; major museums, exhibitions in 132; mapping of 137; media-mixing 142–3; Morimura, Yasumasa 141–4; Nihonjinron 132, 137, 139, 140; oscillation between national and global 133–4, 135; postcolonial theory, Japanese demise overstated in 144–5; private galleries, exhibitions in 132; Shibata, Toshio 137–41; subnational role 136; success of 131–3, 137; Sugimoto, Hiroshi 133–7; Yamamoto, Masao 145–7
Pinguet, Maurice 246
policing (and opening) national borders 194
political economy of globalization 44–5
politics, social and legal constraints on comics 115–16
Pompidou Center, Paris 212
popular culture 13
popular music, Japanese in Hong Kong: backlash against 124–5; band boom 122; Canto-pop 123, 125, 128–9; central nature of Hong Kong pop 122; cover versions 122, 124, 125; cultural mishmash of Hong Kong pop 128–9; global cultural flows, "scapes" of 126–7; global culture, importation of 126–7; globalization in Hong Kong pop history 126–9; history of pop music in Hong Kong 121–5, 126; hybridization of Hong Kong pop 128–9; image construction through globalization 128; implications for globalization theories 126–9; Japanese melodies, suited to Asian listeners 124; Japanese pop prominence 123–4; local culture and global influences 127–8; perceptions of Japan among listeners 125–6; prominence of 123–4; roots of Hong Kong pop 121; television, role of 123; television dramas, theme songs of 123; Western music, copies of 122
popularity (of everything Japanese) 116
positive views on welfare, construction of 179–85
postcolonial theory, Japanese demise overstated in 144–5
postcolonial Taiwan 222, 242–5

preindustrial structures 184
prejudice in multinational corporations 11
press coverage, Diaoyu/Senkaku Islands dispute 154–5, 159, 160–1, 163
prevalence of Japanese culture in Korea 200–1
private galleries, exhibitions in 132
proliferation of martial arts 69–70
prominence of Japanese popular music in Hong Kong 123–4
protection of Japanese authenticity 219–20

Rautek, Franz 73
reality of *Yamatodamashi* for Takasago members 245–7
Redwood, John 176
regime shift in Korea 202
regulation of Japanese pop culture in Korea 197–200
Reich, Robert 168
relevance, Soka Gakkai in Germany 94, 104
religion 14–15
responses to transfers overseas 60–6
Rhi, Hanho 80
Riban no Tomo (Friends of Aborigine Administration) 225
risk avoidance 61
Robertson, Roland 3, 167
Ryu Jong Ha 202

Sager, Franz 72, 76
Said, Edward 186
Samaranch, Juan Antonio 87
Sartrian existentialism 30
Scandinavian welfare model 180
Seal Publishing Company 116
Seisenbacher, Peter 82
selective memory and images of Japan 15–18
self-colonization, Judo cultures 76–81
Shibata, Toshio 132, 133, 137–41
Shinto 212–13
Shôichi, Kurada 204
Shôichi, Rôyama 180
shojo comics 118
Si Doi Kuk 121, 122
Siskind, Aaron 137
sister cities, French/Japanese 214–16
Siu Lau Man (The Little Gangster) 113
Slamdunk 118

social forces, resistant to spread of Japanese culture 204
social position, mutual incomprehension during Diaoyu/Senkaku Islands dispute 165
social status of comics, Japanese in Hong Kong 113–14, 119
society of industry, corporate positioning within 53
Soka Gakkai in Germany: adaptation to German culture 96, 105; aims, purpose of 100–1; asymmetrical core–periphery relationship 98; authenticity 104–5; clothes, the issue of dress 99; cultural brokerage 94–5, 104–5; cultural definition 97–100; decentralization aims 100–1; ecological concerns and 97; emigration policies and expatriate religion 94; expansion by self-selection 96–7; German attitudes to foreign residents 102–3; German perspectives on development of 95–7; German religious communities 101; Green Movement and 97; growth of 95–6; ideological understanding 98–9; indigenization 96; Japanese language as cultural baggage 99; media, negative attitudes of 101–2; minority groups, attitude towards 103; missionaries 96; relevance of 94, 104; slow early growth 95–6; specificity, cultural 95, 104–5; time frames, significance of 103; traditional division of labor 99–100; universality 95, 104–5
Soseki, Natsume 142
South China Morning Post 154, 155, 157, 164
sovereignty issue, Diaoyu/Senkaku Islands dispute 153
strategic maneuvers, workers at Yaohan 61–6
subculture, notion of 88
submissive attitudes, Judo cultures 88
subnational role of photography 136
subordination, strategic 66–7
success of photography, Japanese contemporary in America 131–3, 137
Sugimoto, Hiroshi 133–7
Suniyon 223–5, 237
supermarkets, business strategies of 54–5

symbolic boundaries 203
Szarkowski, John 142–3
Taiwan: and China, mutual antipathy
162; ethnic composition of 222–3;
resistance to postcolonial situation
242–5; Takasago volunteers of *see*
Yamatodamashi
Takao, Saito 113–14
Takasago-Giyutai: battle honors 225;
battlefield elevation of 240–2;
compensation claims 237;
documentary deficit on 225; *giri*
relationship with Japanese officers
246; homecoming of 242–5;
Japaneseness 228–9, 235, 236, 239,
245–7; memories of volunteers 229–
36; records of volunteers 222–3;
source of Japanese spirit 239–40;
superiority as soldiers 228;
testimonies of Japanese officers
225–9
*The Takasago-Giyutai of Taiwan: The Spirit
Never Dies* (Kadowaki, C.) 225
Takasago *see* Austronesians of Taiwan
television: imports to Korea 199–200;
promoting Japanese pop in Hong
Kong 123; role in Judo cultures 82–
3, 86–7
temporary nature of Japanese
migration to France 30–2
territorialization 71–6
Testimonies: Takasago Volunteers (Hayashi,
E.) 226
Tok Islands (Takeshima) 197, 201
Tokugawa 29
Tomatsu, Shomei 132
tourists, "revolving door" expatriates
12
tournament organization, Judo cultures
79
tradition and change in Judo cultures
83–5
traditional: division of labor 99–100;
handicrafts representative of
Japanese culture 209–10; welfare
practices in Japan 179–80
translation of comics, Japanese in Hong
Kong 116–17
transnational dialogue, Korea/Japan
200–1
Travis, David 136, 138
Tsim Sha Tsui 157
Tsuchibashi, Kazunori 225, 239

tsukiai (obligatory socializing) 61
Tucker, Anne W. 138
Turner, Victor 241
U-Beat 161
Uenishi, Sadakuzu 72
Ueno, Shinnojo 141–2
"un-returnees", 8
United Kingdom, Japanese interest in
178–9
universality, Soka Gakkai in Germany
95, 104–5
universalization in Judo cultures 81–6
university students as comic readers
118
Utsunomiya 216

Vienna Budokan 70–1
Vienna Jiu Club 72
Vogel, Ezra 181
volunteer service 8

Wada, Kazuo 56–7
Wallerstein, Immanuel 3, 132, 145
wandering and commitment, Japanese
in France 36–8
Watanabe, Tetsuo 245
Waters, Malcolm 3
welfare laggards, East Asians as 177
welfare state, images of Japan as: aging
society 177–8; British disease 180;
Confucianism 182; East Asian
welfare model 176–7, 186;
educational system 181–2;
employment system 183–5; family
provision 185; Gold Plans 178;
health miracle in 178; industrial
system 181–2, 183–5; *Japan as Number
One*, Ezra Vogel on 181;
Japaneseness 187; Japanization of
British welfare system 183;
Kyôchôkai (Harmonization Society)
184; lifetime employees 184–5;
media role in promotion of 181;
mutual community support 179–81;
Nihonjinron 182, 186; Occidentalism
182–3, 187; Orientalism 186–7;
positive views, construction of 179–
85; preindustrial structures 184;
promotion of Japanese-style welfare
state 179–81; Scandinavian model,
attacks on 180; traditional practices
in Japan 179–80; United Kingdom,
Japanese interest in 178–9; United

Kingdom interest in Japan 176–7, 183, 185–6; welfare laggards, East Asians as 177; Western welfare model, repudiation of 180–1; women and welfare support 180
Western music, Hong Kong copies of 122
Western welfare model, repudiation of 180–1
Weston, Edward 141
White Books 219
Willetts, Dave 176
women and welfare support 180
Wong, Yuk Long 113–15, 116–17
work-related comics 112–13
World Bank 44
World War II 154, 156, 163, 166, 171; *see also Yamatodamashi*

Yamamoto, Masao 133, 145–7
Yamashita, Yoshiaki 72
Yamatodamashi in Taiwanese Takasago-Giyutai members: battlefield status reversal 240–2; compensation claims 237; debts, unpaid wartime salaries 237–8; ethnic composition of Tiawan 222–3; historical perspectives 236–8; Hyashi, Eidai 225–6, 239, 242–3, 244; illusion of *Yamatodamashi* for Japanese 245–7; Ishibashi, Takashi 225, 238–9; Kadowaki, Choshyu 225, 239–40; memories of Takasago volunteers 229–36; motivation of Japanese authors on 238; narrative records as 'testimonies,' 236; postcolonial Taiwan 222, 242–5; purposes of testimonies 236; reality of *Yamatodamashi* for Takasago members 245–7; records of volunteers 222–3; resistance to postcolonial situation 242–5; return of last Imperial soldier 223–5; testimonies of Japanese officers 225–9; Tsuchibashi, Kazunori 225, 239; unique nature of postcolonial Taiwan 244
Yancey Richardson Gallery 146
Yaohan: marginal nature of 55–6; regional supermarket 55–6; staff recruitment strategy at 57–9; *see also* female perspectives
Year of Japan in France 210–14
Yellow Cab: The Women Who Left Haneda (Ieda, S.) 9
Yo Na Nuki 124
Yususuke, Murakami 180

Zeit-Foto Salon, Tokyo 140
Zen 14
Zensanren (All-Japan Producers Union) 184